Canon Stanley Luff, who had a 'late vocation' to the priesthood, studied at the Beda Collage in Rome from 1962 to 1966, during which time he explored Rome in detail – both above and below ground. Those years were for him a crossroads in a lifelong interest in religion, history, architecture and archaeology. Initially he became a guide for his fellow students, then for groups from Stanford University, California, then for British pilgrim groups.

His experience of showing pilgrims and tourists round Rome, and his previous pursual of various branches of knowledge, enabled him to bring the compilation of a guide book a breadth of interest that makes it engaging while simple to use. When it was originally suggested to him that the write a guide book, it was put thus: would he write it just the way he spoke. This he has done, and has made a point of writing 'on location' as far as possible – describing things as he looked at them.

Numerous testimonials from users of this book since its first publication (see over page) confirm that Canon Luff has succeeded in what he set out to do: to offer each visitor his company and wit as they explored together the streets and squares of this city that gave the Christian faith so much of its shape and tradition, while preserving, sometimes tenuously, sometimes full-bloodedly, the civilization and culture of its past.

D1584525

People who have used the first edition of the book say:

"We noted your continuing command of accurate detail when sharing your knowledge of Rome . . . we relied upon your book for guidance, humanity and humour. It is most gratifying to be able to thank you on behalf of countless visitors who used our favourite book on Rome".
MS, Scotland.

"Although we have visited Rome almost every year since 1947, your book, by introducing us to many new sites, made that visit (1983) the most enjoyable we ever had. We cannot even begin to tell you how grateful we are to you for that excellent Guide. It is our sincere hope that a new edition will soon be published".
JMLP, France.

"Your Guide to Rome was my constant companion and has tremendously enriched my year here. The practical pieces of advice are so valuable. This is to record my great gratitude".
Sr. As, IBVM, Rome.

". . . How absolutely invaluable I find your Guide to Rome".
GS, England.

"I had your Guide with me all the time and found it absolutely invaluable. You never miss a point, do you? – and you never use a word too much".
KF, England

"I am sure other guides would find it difficult to reach your standard".
EJMcH, England.

"Four of us went round with copies of *The Christian's Guide to Rome*, which were in great demand. I found your book an invaluable help and recommend it to many other people. Though I have foot-slogged through Rome before, your book greatly enriched my seeking. I would dearly love to go again, book in hand once more".
MP, England

"The book has now become one of my most treasured possessions. . . I can honestly say scarce a day passes but I have cause to refer to it, or open it at random and find some fascinating piece of information about the Eternal City which is new to me. It is a mine of information, very clear, very concise. The sketch maps at the beginning of each chapter are excellent".
EMcE, Scotland.

"I am writing to let you know how much I enjoyed using *The Christian's Guide to Rome* recently. It really is a good guide and was appreciated very much by myself and others who were there last month".
WC, England.

"I think you must be the great Father Luff, author of the magnificent Guide Book to Rome".
Sr.P, England

"Your Guide Book is recommended to every visitor; it is the best ever published".
Sr.D, England.

THE CHRISTIAN'S GUIDE TO ROME
New Revised Edition

S.G.A. LUFF

BURNS & OATES

Burns & Oates
Wellwood, North Farm Road,
Tunbridge Wells, Kent TN2 3DR

First published 1967
This revised edition 1990
Reprinted 2000

ISBN 0 86012 178 X

Typeset by Scribe Design Ltd, Gillingham, Kent
Printed and bound in Great Britain by MPG Limited, Bodmin, Cornwall

Contents

Illustrations

Rome revisited

A new edition after more than twenty years clearly called for a visit to Rome. There was no possibility of returning to every single item mentioned, to check whether something had happened to it. Rome is called the Eternal city, and it is its job to conserve. I had however collected hints about some minor alterations and I knew where major ones were likely or possible. What concerned me most was the impression Rome would make on me.

I had considered — but not enough — how different it would be to come to Rome as a visitor; when I first wrote the Guide I had lived there four years as a student for the priesthood at the Beda College. I came back to find I had lost the sense of belonging, in spite of Rome being, in some ways, the centre of my faith. Superficial things account for this. So many clergy have abandoned the cassock or their religious habit, once conspicuous in almost any Roman street. I recall Pope Paul VI at an audience smiling wryly over this and complaining that he could not think *why*. I must mention that this time, in contrast, I saw a good many sisters in decent and even beautiful habits. Possibly when I was in Rome I saw too many soutanes, for they were the years of the Second Vatican Council. Maybe clerics were getting special treatment then. I would call at the Rome Tourist Office in the Via Parigi and have to summon a taxi to take away bundles of free books — very good ones too — published for visitors to Christian Rome. I was unwise to publicize this generosity which I am assured no longer applies. The Banco di Roma produced a magnificent book on the Baroque Altars of Rome. A bishop passed his presentation copy on to me. I sent a note to the bank on behalf of a friend who fancied a copy. Within hours a motor cyclist arrived to deliver it. Those were the days.

Then the cats seem to have disappeared. When I arrived in Rome in 1962 I had the day on my hands and began to explore. The first church I visited was Santa Francesca Romana by the Forum. I counted twenty-four cats sleeping on the steps. These Roman cats were very nicely behaved, supported by little old ladies who seemed to have keys to the enclosures around the ruins so that they could feed them. Later I heard of lady social workers from England who went to Rome to teach the cats birth control. They had been frustrated and moved on to Venice. I suspect it must be some municipal edict that has sent the cats flying. They are an endangered race but not extinct. I found them at Trefontane and in an untidy bit of enclosed ground by the Porta Asinaria, next to the Lateran.

Rome is more expensive than it used to be but I think in comparison with prices at home it remains good value. I had an excellent meal at a mere wayside kiosk at Trefontane and later, after visiting the shrine, idled away an hour at the café across the road. Overhead trailing greenery gave us shade, a litter of kittens provided entertainment and, humble though the establishment was, the tables were made up from fragments of antique sculpture. You may consider this the accidental Rome to which a Guide Book does not undertake to direct, although I do sometimes try.

I have written mainly for the average vistor coming as a pilgrim – that is, interested in Rome as the centre of Christianity after the Holy Places of Jerusalem, Bethlehem and Nazareth. Here the faith took root and grew, nourished on the blood of martyrs, enriched by what it assimilated of classical civilisation and culture. From our English-speaking world we look to Rome as the hearth from which we received the light and warmth of faith.

At the same time the interests of the ordinary tourist who wants to see whatever a place has to show have not been disregarded. That tourist needs to appreciate anyway that without the art inspired by religion Rome has not much left to show.

The chapters try to cover everything a Guide Book can well pay attention to, given pocket-sized limits. There is a way of doing this that I have, on the whole, tried to avoid. I have *not* provided a monochrome description of the contents of a building — a church, say — all the way round from left to right. No one can see and appreciate all these details and contents; it would be a killing job to identify them alone, and interest would wear thin in no time. So I have selected. I chose items of interest under three heads: what everyone ought to see; other items which in my experience can interest most people, and finally certain subjects which I think become interesting given a little explanation. You may recognise these last in, for example, cosmatesque work, mosiacs, and the sculpture and architecture of Bernini.

I risk giving some practical hints on life in Rome, a few woven into the text, the rest collected in chapters 1 and 32. In this respect, experience teaches one to be reticent. Things do not remain the same. Roman practical information is not always as reliable as it looks in print. Museum times of last year may disagree with this year's. The best advice is: check beforehand or risk it, and of course try to get a current tourist brochure which can hardly be all wrong. Acquire a good map, which I hope you will be able to use in conjunction with the plans for each chapter.

The cure to many traveller's pains is a little homework before you set out, or midway while you take a morning coffee somewhere. Much frustration will be saved if you bear in mind that churches close for the afternoon and their evening opening hours are erratic. Major basilicas and many monuments are open all day.

Chapter 31 represents a choice of trips outside Rome, to no small extent the fruit of my own experience. Much is omitted because it is beyond the scope of the 'average' traveller with average time. I have omitted some because I do not think they make reasonable one-day trips, although they can be done – Naples and Monte Cassino for example.

I must still record my thanks to Mgr J.J. Curtin, my Rector at the Beda College, for allowing to me devote so much time to this book when I should have been doing something else. He has since gone to his reward. Professor Iosi, of the Pontificial Institute of Archeology, just by signing a permit (perhaps he did not know he did it) enabled me to explore catacombs not accessible to the public, and the German Brothers of Mercy at Domitilla were particularly kind in allowing me to wander over their catacomb. I am very grateful to all users of this book who have written letters of appreciation. The nicest observation — found in several letters — was that using the Guide was like going round Rome in my company. I have tried to use any corrections or criticism in this revised edition.

I am grateful to Pippa Parsons, Richard Owen, and Emmanuel and Sabrina Micallef for help with proof correcting and index. I am deeply indebted to Archbishop Paul Marcinkus of Vatican City and to the Direction and staff of the Vatican Museums for courteous and detailed help with the revision of Chapter Three.

CHAPTER 1

Hints of all sorts

This chapter is simply a collection of small items of information that may prove handy. Some details are obviously liable to change.

Railway Travel

Organized groups nearly all arrive by air and your first point of reference will be your hotel. For you it is not only important to have a map in advance, but also to have studied it. For others the first place they will know in Rome will be the main terminal railway station – Stazione Termini. In my time in Rome I found its amenities efficient but I have had letters from travellers finding the queues long and the service unsatisfactory. The various offices however mostly have English-speaking attendants. You may be well advised to buy tickets in advance, either from CIT in the Piazza della Repubblica or from British Rail in the Via Torino nearby. You hardly need to bother yourself about other stations in Rome, except the 'Roma Nord' Station outside the Porta del Popolo, for a trip described in Chapter 31.

Country Bus Travel

Not far from Stazione Termini there is a bus station at Castro Pretorio for services to the countryside north and east of the city. Since a new Underground Line was constructed – Metropolitana A – the bus station formerly opposite the Lateran has been moved to that line's terminal station, Anagnina. The CIT office in the Piazza della Repubblica may help you with coach travel up to a point.

Buses in Rome

With Roman bus services a major problem is that bus map routes and the indications given at bus stops give *streets* and *squares* and not monuments and churches – hence the importance of having an up-to-date bus map and noting on paper the routes that will help you before you start out. No doubt the ticket system is always liable to change. At present you get your ticket – one for morning use, another for afternoon use, usually at a street tobacconist, or possibly from your hotel reception.

They enable you to travel the whole morning, or the whole afternoon and evening, and so can be very economical.

You enter the bus at the end and, for your first journey only, insert your ticket in a gadget, which maybe doesn't work. Exits are at the middle or the other end (or both), so keep moving up, even if it appears to be physically impossible. The helpful word is *'Permesso.'*

The Metro
The underground has two lines. Metropolitana Line A (the new line) runs from Via Ottaviano (near the Vatican Museum), via Stazione Termini to Anagnina, where you find the bus departures for Frascati and the Alban Hills. Line B is from Stazione Termini via Basilica di San Paola to EUR and Laurentina, change at Magliana for trains to Ostia Scavi.

Taxis and Car Hire
I hope no one lets me down, but I am going to say: Don't be nervous of Roman taxi drivers. I have found them reliable, courteous, helpful, and not expensive. Be friendly. If I have a companion I talk about places in Rome so that the driver realises they are familiar to me and is not tempted to choose the longest route. Accommodation is for four only.

To hire a car look up *'Autonoleggio* in the telephone directory, or look out for the sign, or enquire at your hotel reception.

Postal Services
The Roman postal service will drive you mad if you have too much to do with it. Post Offices are few and far between and smaller ones are open in the morning only. The Central Post Office is in the Piazza San Silvestro, and there is another useful one in the Park by St Paul's Gate. Don't forget you can use Vatican postal services. There is a mobile post office in the Piazza of St Peter's and another in Vatican City – enter by St Anne's Gate. Italian postage stamps are on sale at tobacconists and probably at your hotel reception. Public telephones are operated by a 'token' – I advise you to ask to use the phone at your hotel.

Banks and Exchange Offices
Banks have limited hours – morning and late afternoon, closed Saturdays and Sundays. An office marked *'Cambio'* – exchange – will deal with currency and traveller's cheques. One in Stazione Termini is open all day.

Restaurants and Cafés

Restaurants are not usually to be frequented at all hours for small dishes. If you want a snack, take it at the counter of a café or bar – this is the way to buy a light, and therefore cheaper, meal. See also Chapter 32 on pizzas. In a bar you usually decide what you want and then buy a ticket for the appropriate amount at the cash desk. You then present the ticket at the counter and say what you want. This can be difficult when you have no Italian but staff are usually helpful. Normally there is a higher charge if you take your drink or snack sitting down. Tipping is usually added to the bill – you show appreciation by giving more. I have had an agreeable meal at a wayside kiosk (at Trefontane) with no tickets, no tips, and a seat in the sun or the shade.

Public Toilets

Rome is short of public toilets. To ask the use of the toilet in a café is the done thing. One of the passwords is *'gabinetti'*.

Newspapers

British and American newspapers can be bought at most of the busier bookstalls – at a price.

Lost Property

Try not to lose anything or be taken ill. There is a municipal lost property office in the Via F Negri, 11 (off the Via Ostiense, beyond St Paul's Gate) and for loss on city transport there is an ATAC (name of the transport company) lost property office in Via Volturno 65, not far from Stazione Termini.

First Aid

For medical help, a chemist, when closed, should display the address of one that is open. *'Pronto Soccorso'* outside a hospital means that there is a First Aid department. There is a First Aid Post at Stazione Termini.

Tourist Brochures and Guides

Tourist brochures and information about accommodation are available from a counter at Stazione Termini. Try your luck at other tourist offices. Many churches have very well-written guides or histories on sale in the sacristy, either in Italian only or in several languages. Guides sold at monuments are also written with unusual expertise and usually available in several languages.

Climate

Rome has two seasons – a summer like a good old-fashioned English scorcher, and a winter like a bad English summer. March to June and October to November are best. Winter can be wet, and cold too, and midsummer is not merely hot, but humid and oppressive. Trust in this: the street fountains, large and small, that are so ubiquitous in old Rome, all offer pure, sweet, and refreshing water.

Accommodation

The Italian word for the smaller type of hotel is *'Pensione'* (pensioh-nay). There are many of these in Rome, usually one floor of a large building – you find them over shops of the Via Sistina and the Via Nazionale, near Santa Maria Maggiore, and in the Piazza della Repubblica. Tourist brochures include lists of these places.

Opera and Concert Halls

Rome's Opera House is in the Via del Viminale – very near Stazione Termini, and for a brief summer season, there is opera in the ruins of the Baths of Caracalla. Among Concert Halls note one in the Via della Conciliazione, a few doors from the end of the road on the left as you approach the Tiber coming from St Peter's. Concerts are also held in the ruins of the Basilica of Maxentius in the Forum, in the Hall of Castel Sant' Angelo, in the 'Aula Borrominiana' adjacent to the Chiesa Nuova. Notices outside churches may announce concerts in other churches – they do of course make beautiful settings.

Papal Audiences

There are various kinds of Papal Audience and ways of applying for admission to them. When the Holy Father is in Rome there are usually 'public' audiences on Wednesdays, either in the audience hall in Vatican City or in the open air in the Piazza, according to the weather and the number of people expected. It is prudent to come to Rome with a letter of recommendation from your parish priest (unless of course you are with a pilgrimage group, when the agency arranges it all for you). In any case make your enquiries early in the Office to the left of the Piazza of St Peter's as you approach the Gate of the Bells.

Vatican Gardens and 'Scavi'

This information Office will also give you a list of the current possibilities of visiting the Vatican City and its Gardens. Armed with a suitable letter of recommendation you may enter the City at the Gate of the Bells to apply for a permit to see the Excavations under St Peter's – guided tours only.

HOW TO USE YOUR TIME — JUST SUGGESTIONS...

I know readers are going to look for these suggestions and so I make them, hoping for the best. Of course Rome has its 'musts', but once you have covered them your choice should arise from your own tastes and interests, needs for relaxation, availability of transport, etc.

A Week (twelve half-days):

St Peter's and either the Vatican Gardens or the Vatican Museum; possibly also a visit to the excavations under St Peter's and to the roof and dome.	2 or 3 half-days
St Paul's, St Mary Major's, the Lateran and the Holy Stairs, the Passion Relics at Santa Croce.	2 half-days
Forum and Palatine, Colosseum, and the Capitol – the last is recommended floodlit by night; you should see the Capitoline museums if you miss the Vatican Museum.	2 half-days
A day out of Rome at choice – Alban Hills, Ostia Scavi, Subiaco, etc.	1 full day or 1 half-day
A catacomb, San Clemente with its excavations, and a choice of some other churches; a meal out at an interesting restaurant.	2 half-days
A stroll through side streets and markets, the Trevi fountain and Piazza Navona, over the Janiculum for the view *or* the Spanish Steps and the Pincian *or* the Quirinal and the Changing of the Guard.	1 half-day
Shopping.	1 half-day

To be worked in: Papal Audience or other function.

Other suggestions: Castel Sant'Angelo, Trefontane and EUR, Museo Nazionale in the Baths of Diocletian, fountains and piazzas by floodlight.

Seasonal: Passiontide – the altars of repose; Christmastide – the Piazza Navona market and the cribs; Ara Coeli for the shepherd pipers and children preaching.

THREE DAYS:

St Peter's and St Paul's.	1 half-day
The Lateran Basilica, Santa Croce and its Passion Relics, the Catacomb of St Callixtus or that of St Domitilla (in this order if you make your visit in the afternoon).	1 half-day
St Mary Major's, the excavations under San Clemente; an evening stroll through side streets and piazzas, including the Trevi Fountain and the Piazza Navona or the Spanish Steps.	1 half-day
Colosseum and Forum, the Capitol and its museums (omit the museums here if you visit the Vatican Museum or Castel Sant'Angelo).	1 half-day
Trip in the Alban Hills – with a picnic or restaurant meal out.	1 half-day
Shopping.	1 half-day

TOUCH DOWN – OR ONE DAY IN ROME:

Early visit to St Peter's; mid-morning visit to Capitoline Hill, from which you survey the ruins of the Forum; walk through the Colosseum. If you have time, you may now either visit the excavations under nearby San Clemente or return to the Piazza Venezia and stroll through side streets in the direction of St Peter's: lunch and relax. In mid-afternoon take bus or Metropolitana to St Paul's outside the walls, and from there taxi to the Catacomb of St Callixtus or that of Domitilla (unless San Clemente was enough underground work for you). Towards dusk take a view over Rome from the heights of the Pincian, Quirinal, or Janiculum – in the last case returning on foot through old Trastevere. Dine at a well-chosen restaurant or *trattoria* and to close the day visit fountains and piazzas – especially Trevi, Capitol, Farnese or Navona, by floodlight.

CHAPTER 2

St Peter's, the Scavi, and the Vatican Gardens

ST PETER'S

St Peter's, as architecture, is a masterpiece of the age of renaissance and discovery – discovery of the New World, of Science; a rebirth of the classical learning and art of Greece and Rome. As a church, it is a monument over one of the meanest things in Rome – a poor man's grave in a cemetery on the slopes of the Vatican Hill, but this poor man was the fisherman-apostle of Christ who established Christianity in the heart of the Empire. He was buried here because his execution took place close by in Nero's Circus.

The design of St Peter's

Nearly everyone associates Michelangelo's name with the great dome – quite rightly, but it was Bramante's idea first, nor did Michelangelo live to complete it. Domenico Fontana finished the dome in 1589. But Michelangelo's real genius is hidden from you. He planned St Peter's, which replaced a church that had stood here since the fourth century, as a Greek Cross, but it was transformed by Carlo Maderno into a Latin Cross.* That great master of the renaissance, Michelangelo, had conceived something very simple, a cruciform church, completely dominated by a great dome which was to lead your eye upwards, both externally, as you approached, and within as well, from the moment you entered the door. The popes had this plan changed partly because the Latin Cross was more traditional, but also because a longer nave really was necessary to provide accommodation for large congregations. The same problem was to arise later over the designing of St Paul's in London.

To help you appreciate what St Peter's was meant to be, I suggest you walk straight forward along the nave until you arrive at the last bay (arch) before the altar. Stand there and imagine you have just entered the basilica of Michelangelo's design. I think it is more impressive. Your eye is carried straight up into the interior of his dome, and each of the four great arms

---

*A Greek Cross is one of equal arms: +; in a Latin Cross the upright is longer: †. Nearly all great medieval churches are on the plan of a Latin Cross.

1. St Peter's from the Vatican Gardens

of the church is present to you. To get a similar idea of his design externally you must either visit the Vatican Gardens or get a view from one of the roads to the left of St Peter's, or better still from a window of the Vatican Galleries as you hurry on your way to the Sistine Chapel.

As you walk forward from the door you will notice let into the inlaid marble floor, in metal, the names of various great churches throughout the world – in Latin, but fairly easy to follow. They indicate the point where the doors of these churches would be if they were fitted into St Peter's; i.e. the first you encounter is the next longest.

Stand before the high altar. From here you should observe four features which express the place of Peter and the mission of his successor the pope in the life of the Church; the altar with its canopy (*baldachino*) over his tomb, the 'confession' or open crypt which admits you close to it, the dome which proclaims its presence to the world, and, in the far apse, the golden 'Gloria' of Bernini which enshrines the traditional 'Chair' of Peter, symbol of his authority to rule and teach.

The Confession

I think a 'confession' is rarely well understood. It has nothing to do with confessing sins. There is a saying of our Lord: 'Whoever shall confess (or acknowledge) me before men, the same I will confess before my Father in heaven'. No one so clearly 'confesses' Christ as does a martyr. Consequently altars were raised over the tombs of martyrs, or their bodies were brought in from the catacombs to be placed under the altars of the churches. St Peter was not buried in a catacomb but in an open cemetery and Constantine built the first church here with his grave as its focal point. Subsequently the top of his tomb was used as an altar, but in the sixteenth century the present altar was constructed high above the tomb. A second-century monument over the grave we know now, through excavation, to lie just behind a niche protected by the grille you see at the back of the 'confession'.

You will identify the 'Confession' easily. It is an open crypt at the foot of the great central altar. Along its balustrade many oil lamps are always alight. This is where bishops pray when they make their '*ad limina*' (to the threshold – of the apostles) visits to the Holy Father. Every pilgrim should pause here for prayer.

Behind the grille the pallium, a woollen vestment and token of an intimate share in the Pope's office as shepherd of Christ's flock, rests over the tomb of Peter and awaits the appointment of archbishops anywhere in the world, to whom it is then sent.

The High Altar
The altar is papal, and the Pope celebrates Mass from the far side, approaching from a throne set in the apse. The immense bronze baldachino is part of Gian Lorenzo Bernini's contribution to the enrichment of St Peter's. The dome apart, one is more conscious of his genius than of that of any other architect who controlled the work during a century and a half – 1505 to 1667 – when the colonnade was completed. His baldachino is not an entirely original conception, but perpetuates the surroundings of Peter's tomb in Constantine's church. The emperor arranged around the huge cube of marble that he raised over the apostle's grave a sort of pergola of beautiful twisted columns, Bernini followed their pattern in designing his new canopy, as you can easily check by glancing up at the niches in the piers supporting the dome, each flanked by two of the original columns.

The Altar of the Chair
Finally, look to the end of the basilica, to Bernini's 'gloria'. The gloria – a speciality of Bernini much favoured in the baroque period (at Rome see those at Sant' Andrea al Quirinale and Santa Maria in Campitelli) is a 'dramatization of light'. Light, admitted through a window of fine alabaster that already gilds it, appears to be transformed by sculpture into golden shafts and clouds, vitalized by a host of happy little angels. Among the clouds, below the window where the Holy Spirit is represented as a dove, is cradled a symbolic chair. The original, hidden within all this décor is certainly an antique Roman chair of carved wood representing the Labours of Hercules. Very likely it is not, as tradition claims, a chair authentically used by St Peter, but one made by pagan craftsmen later adapted for liturgical use. Statues right and left of the Chair represent two Western Doctors, Augustine and Ambrose, and two Eastern, Basil and Athanasius.

Statues below the Dome
At the base of the four great piers sustaining the dome are statues which allude to certain relics kept close to Peter's tomb; St Helen for part of the True Cross, Veronica for the Veil with which she wiped the face of Jesus, the Centurion Longinus for the lance with which he pierced Christ's side, and Andrew, brother of Peter, for the relic of his skull which was recently

returned to the Greek Church at Patras. One of these four statues is by Bernini. See if you have acquired some feeling for his skill by guessing which. The answer is at the end of this chapter.

The Statue of St Peter

Close to the statue of Longinus is an ancient and deeply venerated statue of St Peter, cast in bronze, with a silver foot kissed by pilgrims. There is something of a mystery about it. Some hold that it is an antique pagan statue adapted, others that it is an early Christian statue of St Peter made before the classical style had expired, others that it is by Arnolfo di Cambio – thirteenth century. This diversity of view can be explained by the fact that a mould could easily have been made from an ancient statue, and this one cast from it, with modifications of head and arms to represent St Peter.

Pilgrims who are wisely economizing their time – not to mention their capacity for appreciating – can well omit the right aisle beyond the High Altar unless, admirers of Canova, they want to see his huge monument to Pope Clement XIII, with its amiable lions.

Left aisle beyond the High Altar

The left aisle is interesting. The altar at the far end is to St Leo. In fact five Popes Leo are buried in this corner. The Leo buried beneath the altar is he who persuaded Atilla the Hun to spare Rome, buying him off, in 451, with pounds of precious pepper. He is also the pope named in the great fifth-century mosaic at St Paul's. The relief above the altar by Alessandro Algardi, a seventeenth-century sculptor, represents the Attila event. To the left of this altar is one enshrining a medieval Madonna painted on a column carefully preserved in the structure of the altar – notice the convex surface of the painting. As you return towards the south transept (St Peter's faces East, back to front compared with most European churches) there is the tomb of Pope Alexander VII by Bernini. A feature characteristic of his work is the massive marble drapery, and in the dramatic manner of his age, the bronze personification of Death. Access to the crypt is from the base of one of the four great piers supporting the dome, indicated by a temporary sign not always easy to see.

Sacristy and Treasury

As you leave the transept to return to the nave there is a passage to the right leading to the sacristy and treasury. A little way

along is a fifteenth-century polychrome statue of St Andrew –
a survival from old St Peter's. Close by this statue notice a tablet
listing the popes buried here – but don't look for all their tombs,
for some were interred in the open-air cemetery near St Peter's,
and many of the tombs from old St Peter's are lost.

Off the passage to the Sacristy is the entrance to the Treasury.
The first exhibit is one of those twisted columns that were
arranged by Constantine around the shrine of St Peter. They
provided the inspiration for the columns of Bernini's baldachino
to the High Altar. Although others remain in St Peter's, notably
high up in the piers supporting the dome, it is only here that
their magnificent design and craftsmanship can be appreciated.
The tradition that they came from Solomon's Temple at
Jerusalem is absurd, but do they perhaps come from Herod's?

In one room is a plaster copy of Michelangelo's Pietà, marking
the place where it stood when he made it. With the texture of
Michelangelo's Carrara marble lost, his design and skill seem to
lose all their quality.

2. *The Teaching Christ, on the fourth-century sarcophagus of Junius Bassus,*
Vatican Treasury.

Another exhibit is the gilded cock that formerly topped the campanile of old St Peter's from the ninth century, perhaps the father of all cocks on church towers.

The so-called dalmatic of Charlemagne, which is assessed as Byzantine work of a century or so later, will repay study.

The bronze tomb of Pope Sixtus V by Pollaiuolo, brilliant craftsmanship though it is, will impress by nothing so much as its size.

Just as you are about to leave – if you have not come to grief against the numerous glass walls of this labyrinth – you will find the most remarkable exhibit of this collection, of which at least a third could be thrown away without loss: the sarcophagus of Junius Bassus. The central sculpture is a youthful Christ flanked by Peter and Paul. You are left to identify the other panels of this fourth century masterpiece of emerging Christian art. The sacristy proper, to the left, is a fine domed building of the late eighteenth century. Its principal room has eight columns from Hadrian's Villa at Tivoli.

The Altar of the Lie

Back in St Peter's, close to the entrance to the sacristies is one of St Peter's best-known altars – the Altar of the Lie. Its mosaic represents an incident from the Acts of the Apostles. The primitive Christian community at Jerusalem had instituted a common fund, but a couple named Ananias and Saphira deceived the apostles about the price received from the sale of their land. At the reproof of St Peter, each in turn collapsed and died. Interesting is the background of colonnade and rotunda, between which the young men are carrying off the corpse of Ananias for burial.

Raphael's 'Transfiguration'

Round the corner (at the end of the left nave aisle) is a mosaic reproduction of Raphael's famous 'Transfiguration'. Only the upper part of the original picture – Christ with the Prophets and Apostles – was completed by the artist, the rest is the work of his disciples after his early death in 1520. There is a nice story that when news of the young artist's death reached the Pope he came down to his lodgings to kiss his hand. The painting from which this mosaic is copied is in the Vatican Art Gallery.

St Gregory's Altar

The altar in the corner of this bay is St Gregory's – the Pope who, while abbot of St Andrew's on the Coelian (now St Gregory's on the Coelian) admired and purchased young

English slaves on sale in the forum, of whom he commented with a famous pun: 'Not Angles but angels' (there is a lot more word play in this story as related by Bede in his seventh-century History of England). Under the altar, visible behind the grille, is the sarcophagus containing the saint's relics. The mosaic above represents St Gregory offering imperial messengers sand from the Colosseum, rich with the blood of martyrs.

The Choir Chapel

At this point you are about to leave that part of the basilica which follows Michelangelo's design and to enter the extension added by Domenico Fontana. The style of architecture evolves from classical renaissance to baroque. To identify this change, note that the dome by St Gregory's altar is a circle, but the three each side of the nave are ellipses. A large chapel opening off the aisle is the Choir Chapel, that is to say, one where the daily services of St Peter's are celebrated with some solemnity. It has fine carved wooden stalls and a richly moulded ceiling. Behind the altar is a painting of Our Lady with a crown added to it on the jubilee of the definition of the Immaculate Conception – 1904.

Left nave aisle

The next two chapels contain respectively the tomb of Pope St Pius X and the baptismal font. The latter is the beautiful porphyry cover of an ancient sarcophagus, said to have been used for centuries as the tomb of the Emperor Otto III.

Standing by the baptistery is a good point to notice the elliptical pattern of the inlaid marble floor, and to look up to the corresponding dome above, rich with mosaic. The Baptism of Christ represented above the font you will almost certainly take for a painting – approach more closely and you will see that it too is mosaic – with such a finely finished surface and so perfect a gradation of tone that – as in nearly all the altarpieces of St Peter's – the art of the mosaicist simulates the skill of the brush. The advantage is that mosaic is more durable. All these mosaics were made in the Vatican mosaic workshops. Close by is the memorial to the exiled house of Stuart. In the crypt below are buried the Old Pretender – 'James III', Bonnie Prince Charlie, and his brother the Cardinal Duke of York – 'Henry IX'.

Crossing the basilica to see Michelangelo's Pietà – at the façade end of the right aisle – you may well pause to look down the nave and re-assess your general appreciation of St Peter's in the light of the understanding you have acquired so far. Under your feet is a huge roundel of porphyry marble. This is a survival from old St Peter's, preserved as the traditional site of the coronations of Holy Roman Emperors from the time of Charlemagne.

Michelangelo's Pietà

The Pietà is something you should judge for yourself. Much of its beauty is to be discovered from close-up photographs of which a good variety is usually to be found in the shops. The subject represents the moment when the dead Christ, taken down from the cross, was laid by his friends – as we may suppose – to lie once more on his mother's knees and against her breast. It is difficult really to imagine that a grief-stricken woman could sustain so great a burden. Here, however, the difficult and the intolerable are smoothed over with the perfection of form with which the young sculptor – he was twenty-two when he began it – has graced his figures. This is said to be the only work of Michelangelo that he ever signed. His contract had stipulated 'that the said Michelangelo will do the said work within a year and it will be the finest work in marble that there is in Rome today and no master today would do it better.' None the less, he soon overheard guides attributing it to other sculptors, so, coming into the basilica one night and chiselling by the light of a candle, he wrote on the band that crosses Mary's breast: 'Michelangelo Buonarotti of Florence made this'. Here at Rome there are two copies – in Santa Maria dell' Anima and Sant' Andrea delle Valle. Since an attack was made on the Pietà it can only be seen from a distance, protected by bullet-proof glass. Personally, I think the more mystical effect produced by the dim lighting is an improvement. Beware of buying models of the Pietà – most of them are very bad.

Blessed Sacrament chapel

In the first large chapel after the Pietà is a rather grandiose bronze statue of Pope Pius XII, and the tomb of Innocent XI, a great reforming pope of the seventeenth century – his body is visible beneath the altar. After this the Blessed Sacrament Chapel, corresponding architecturally to the Choir Chapel on the other side, should be visited for a few moments of prayer; in fact, you should not 'sightsee' here. There is a very fine painting of the Trinity above the altar, by Pietro da Cortona – one of the few not replaced by a mosaic. To the right of this chapel are two more of the columns from the original arrangement of St Peter's tomb in the basilica of Constantine.

The right transept

The altars as you turn into the transept are particularly interesting, though they do not all need to be described here in detail. Enshrined in one is an eleventh-century painting of 'Our Lady of Good Help', and under the altar of St Basil is the body, clothed in the vestments of the Byzantine rite, of St Josaphat. Josaphat was martyred in 1623 after a considerable section of the Russian Church around Kiev had returned to Catholic unity. Catholics of his rite today are known as Ukrainians. It is sometimes possible to see a Mass celebrated in Byzantine rite at this altar.

The crypt – tomb of St Peter

Back under the dome you should now descend the staircase indicated to the crypt. A narrow passage leads round the apse, its walls lined with fragments of sculpture and mosaic from old St Peter's. Midway, chapels open to right and left. One contains the tomb of Pope Pius XII. Opposite is the Clementine Chapel (after Pope Clement VIII, d. 1605). Its importance here is that, beyond the grille, you can see something of the discovery made during the famous excavations under St Peter's in search of the Apostle's tomb, under Pope Pius XII, between 1940 and 1950. Beyond the altar appears a wall of grey marble, with a vertical band of purple porphyry. This is one side (the back) of the great cube of marble raised as a memorial or shrine over the tomb of Peter by the Emperor Constantine in the fourth century. Nothing else you see will bring you closer in time to the presence of St Peter in Rome, yet I have watched visitors trailing past the Clementine Chapel without giving it a glance.

Other chapels opening from the circular passage are dedicated to saints who have only recently made their way into the iconography of St Peter's. There is one dedicated to the missionary monk St Columbanus of Ireland (not St Columba), others to Our Lady of Czestochowa and to a Lithuanian Madonna.

You emerge into the main crypt. The right-hand chapel has a fifteenth-century relief of Our Lady over the altar and, against the wall, an interesting fourth-century sarcophagus (stone coffin). Its sculpture represents a subject very common to early Christian art – the Magi adoring Jesus in his Mother's arms, but with the addition, unusual at that time, of their camels.

Here too is the tomb of Pope John XXIII, despite his wish to be buried in the Lateran Basilica. Nearby lie Pope Paul VI and Pope John Paul I – this last, I am glad to say, by incorporating a little old material, has an elegance surpassing the others, which have a touch of the monumental mason's yard about them.

Flanking the corridor by which you leave is a large chapel to St Stephen and the saints of Hungary. It has interesting modern sculpture but the chapel is usually closed and you can only peer through a grille. Notice in the passage by which you leave the crypt massive fragments of Constantine's primitive basilica.

The bronze doors of old St Peter's

After visiting the crypt you emerge into a courtyard under the very wall of the Sistine Chapel – look up and see it towering above you. At the far end is the narthex (porch) of St Peter's. The great central bronze doors are an inheritance from the golden age of the Florentine renaissance. These, completed in 1445 by Antonio Filarete, commemorate Pope Eugenius IV's attempt – which for a brief while succeeded – to reunite the Churches of East and West. Its main panels represent: above, Christ and Our Lady; centre, Peter and Paul; below, the martyrdom of Peter and Paul. Remember that when Antonio Filarete drew his designs for these martyrdom scenes the study of antiquity was still young, yet his composition of a Roman background is brilliant and skilled. Between the panels are details of the Council of Florence – the Eastern Emperor greeting the Pope; the Coptic delegation entering Rome. Other decorative motifs are borrowed quite frankly from pagan mythology.

The 'Navicella'

A modern bronze door to the left represents saints and, at the base, a charming if inconsequential row of animals and birds – squirrel, hedgehog, owl, etc. Another to he right represents the Sacraments. If you stand with your back to Filarete's door and look up, shielding your eyes from the light, you will see a mosaic representing the Apostles on the Sea of Galilee, with Peter summoned across the water to meet Christ. This, representing the Church, is known as Giotto's *Navicella*, but it has been so often moved round and restored that not much can be left of the master's work.

Look down now onto Bernini's colonnade. A good deal has been written about a symbolism of embracing arms – even Browning did it: 'arms wide open to embrace the entry of the human race'. Old St Peter's, like other early basilicas, was approached through an atrium or courtyard, with garden and fountain, so that the church would be withdrawn from the noise and traffic of business. As a true artist of the baroque, Bernini planned his atrium of vast proportions and the sweeping arms of his colonnade describe the elliptical shape he loved so well.

The Obelisk

The fountains, splashing water from Lake Bracciano, are by Carlo Maderno. Between them the Egyptian obelisk, brought to Rome by Caligula, is claimed to be the only obelisk in Rome that has never been overthrown. The rest fell with the Empire and had to wait for the renaissance to upright them. St Peter's obelisk stood on a spot still marked in the Piazza of the Roman Protomartyrs in Vatican City, just outside the sacristies, and if tradition be accurate it had always been just there, even in the days of Nero's Circus, when it witnessed the crucifixion of St Peter. Sixtus V had it moved when the basilica was a-building but long before Bernini arranged his colonnade around it. Domenico Fontana came first in a contest of five hundred competitors with a scheme for its transfer – there is a fresco in the Vatican showing the operation in progress, and very complicated it appears to be. Fontana himself published an illustrated book about the transfer.

There is a well-known tale related in connection with its re-erection in the Piazza on the 10th September 1586. Nine hundred men and fifty horses operating windlasses were employed to raise the great monolith to its vertical position, and during those breathtaking moments the pope imposed silence under severe penalty. A sailor looking on observed that the strain was heating the cables to danger point and impulsively called out, 'Water on the ropes!' Instead of punishment he was offered as reward the choice of some privilege, and chose that of supplying palms from his own plantations for the papal ceremonies of Palm Sunday.

On the top of this obelisk is a reliquary containing a portion of the True Cross. The obelisk has no hieroglyphics to identify it, but there are holes by which a metal inscription was once affixed to the stone. Notice that the very cobbles around the obelisk are of serpentine and porphyry.

The Piazza of St Peter's

The two fountains play water from Lake Bracciano brought to Rome by Pope Paul V, and they achieve those lofty jets because of the force the water acquires travelling over the heights of the Vatican Hill, behind St Peter's. Only the one on the right, nearer the Vatican Palace, is original, designed by Maderno before the shape of the colonnades required a companion to balance it. They are similar, except for the coats of arms of the popes who commissioned them: those of Paul V for the older fountain, of about 1612, and those of Clement X for the later, added in 1675.

The two arms of the colonnade are perfect arcs. You

may check this for yourself, by locating the round stones set in the pavement on the outer sides of the two fountains and duly inscribed. If you stand on these stones, each of the rows of four columns composing the triple galleries of the colonnades falls perfectly into line. The centre gallery was a carriageway, and has been used for Corpus Christi processions.

From the Piazza at midday you can look up at the Pope's window, on the right side, and wait for the Holy Father to come, according to recent custom, to recite the Angelus with the crowds and bless them. Very high up a mosaic has been installed to Mary under the title Mother of the Church'.

3. In the Piazza of St Peter's

THE VATICAN 'SCAVI'

The *'Scavi'* (excavations) were undertaken below St Peter's from 1940 on – it would be a mistake to say they are even yet complete – in the hope of finding the Tomb of the Prince of the Apostles, or at least clear evidence that the great basilica was, as Catholic tradition has always held, built expressly as a monument over his grave. For centuries it has been understood that the high altar and its 'confession' marked the place of Peter's burial, and also that he had been executed nearby in Nero's Circus. The obelisk in the Piazza formerly stood to the left of St Peter's, and it was supposed that this was its position in the arena when it witnessed the shedding of martyrs' blood. This tradition was made more precise by a fine detail – that the south wall of Constantine's basilica actually rested on the foundations of the north wall of the destroyed circus.

Pope Pius XII had the courage to put these traditions to the test. He authorized – as an initial step – excavation below the nave. The results were remarkable. Two rows of mausolea were discovered in a wonderful state of preservation – a street of the dead. This cemetery path, climbing the Vatican Hill, had been developed between the first and third centuries. It was an open-air cemetery, not a catacomb, and not Christian. The elaborate mausolea were mostly the property of freed slaves, quite an affluent class.

Also discovered was the south wall of Constantine's basilica – but it did *not* rest on any earlier circus wall. However, the last mausoleum to be unearthed – but only as far as its door – has over its entrance an extract from the will of the deceased, in which the testator asks to be buried '*on the Vatican, near the Circus*'. So clearly one link in the chain of tradition was true, though, as handed down, a little inexact.

Several Christian tombs were found. One was a small mausoleum with a splendid third-century mosaic of Christ represented as a Sun God (Helios) – many early Christian hymns, some of them still used in the Divine Office, compare Christ to the sun. As Christian tombs in pagan burial grounds are rare, this seemed to point to a special Christian interest in this particular cemetery.

Accordingly, excavation was commenced anew from a crypt behind the high altar – the Clementine Chapel. To cut a long story short, this immediately provided access to a monument of grey marble built by Constantine as the focal point of his basilica – and this in turn enclosed an earlier one erected in the open air about the year 150. Peter, after his execution, had been buried in a poor man's grave in a plot some feet to one side of the cemetery path. As, in the course of a century, the mausolea encroached on this plot with the development of the cemetery, the Christian community build a wall round their land. The wall actually crossed the apostle's tomb, so they arranged a small memorial in the wall, and as the ground sloped, a drain was provided to keep the plot dry. A maker's stamp on a tile used in this drain enables the whole structure to be dated very close to the year 150. As this monument was referred to in a letter written by a Roman priest named Gaius about the year 200, it is now called the 'Trophy (or memorial) of Gaius'. Thus, over Peter's tomb, the following monuments have been raised: the Trophy of Gaius in the second century, the grey marble monument of Constantine in the fourth, Michelangelo's dome in the sixteenth, and last, the great baldachino of Bernini. Visits to the *Scavi*, conducted by expert guides, are arranged for groups of one language on application. It is best to ask first at the Information Office on the left of the Piazza.

THE VATICAN CITY AND GARDENS

The Gate of the Bells to the left of the façade of St Peter's is one of four entrances to the City. The Swiss Guard may let you pass if you wish to visit the Mosaic Studio only. The most commonly used entrance (which does not lead to the Gardens) is St Anne's Gate, along the street to the right of the colonnade. This is the business end of the Vatican. The guard – who usually wears the nearest the Swiss Guard gets to 'fatigues' – will almost certainly allow you to pass. The Basilica and the Piazza are themselves Vatican territory. There is a mobile First Aid post and a mobile Post Office to the right of the Piazza and a very useful Information Office to the left. At the end of the right colonnade are the Bronze Doors by which a pilgrim granted an audience in the Palace must enter. You may try presenting yourself any weekday morning if you want admission to an audience or a ticket to a special function but I would advise enquiring at the Information Office first.

It is by the Information Office that a regular Vatican bus service takes visitors to the Vatican Museum entrance via the Vatican City Gardens, a far more attractive approach than walking there by the road past St Anne's Gate. Note that normally the only access to the Sistine Chapel (although it is right up against St Peter's) is via the galleries of the Vatican Museum. Longer conducted visits to the Gardens are available at advertised times.

Piazza of the Protomartyrs of Rome

The visitor to the Gardens will have the impression of visiting a beautiful private estate, cleverly arranged on the steep slopes of the Vatican Hill. Through the Gate of the Bells is the Piazza of the Protomartyrs of Rome – St Peter and his fellow early Christians. Here stood the Circus of Nero (or Caligula) where they shed their blood. A plaque on the outside wall of the Teutonic Cemetery commemorates this. Over near the sacristy arch a paving stone, without inscription, marks the former site of the obelisk, now in the Piazza, that we may reasonably believe witnessed Peter's death.

The German Cemetery

The German Cemetery (*Campo Santo Teutonico*) is well worth a visit. There is a tradition that Constantine filled this plot with earth from Calvary. Around the walls is a Way of the Cross in ceramic. On one side there are modern bronze church doors with sculpture symbolizing resurrection – look down to the foot of the door to see the graves rendering up their dead. In the building on the far side is an interesting collection of Christian antiquities.

St Stephen of the Abyssinians
A bridge connecting St Peter's with its sacristies leads to the vast Piazza of St Martha, on the far side of which, near the apse of the basilica, is the picturesque little church of St Stephen of the Abyssinians, with a beautiful ninth-century door.

The Mosaic Studio
More or less behind San Stefano, to the left, is the Mosaic Studio. You should ask the assistant's permission before going round the three exhibition rooms, of which the innermost is the best. The customer may ask for the reproduction of a famous painting – I have seen some delightful Rembrandts here. Mosaic seems to be more true to itself when the texture of its fragments of stone and glass is not only obvious but really contributes to the effect. Still, the reproduction of paintings here is done with wonderful skill, partly due to the incredible stock of 28,000 tints, and they end up with a charm of their own and the merit of durability.

The origin of this studio is connected with the interior embellishment of St Peter's in the late sixteenth century. The mosaics of the dome and those above the altars were made here. The studio will accept orders for anywhere in the world, and some of the mosaics exhibited are for sale.

Before leaving the Mosaic Studio you should look up at the apse and dome of St Peter's – this is how Michelangelo meant his design to appear from all approaches. Photographers please note that no subsequent view will improve on this.

Railway Station
Behind the Studio is the Railway Station – used for goods only. Sculptures of Christ on the Sea of Galilee and Elias going up to heaven represent scriptural instances of transport! On the hill behind the station you will find the following:

> The ninth-century Leonine Walls (built by Pope Leo IV), with one tower adapted by Pope John as a summer retreat. It has a large commemorative inscription. I believe it has been very little used, except for the visit of the Orthodox Ecumenical Patriarch Athenagoras.

Behind the Walls, a reproduction of the Lourdes Grotto, with the original altar brought here from Lourdes in the Centenary Year, 1958.

The Ethiopian College, a modern building, with a chapel in Abyssinian style for the liturgy of that rite. You may ask to see the chapel.

The shrine of the Madonna della Guardia of Genoa – a sailor's madonna similar to Notre Dame de la Garde at Marseilles.

Opposite is a bench made of fragments of sculpture that was one of Pope John's favourite retreats.

The Eagle Fountain (*Fontana del Aquilone*), from which Acqua Paola flows down to the fountains in the Piazza.

In the course of your excursion – ride or walk – you will have enjoyed some grand views of St Peter's and of the Vatican Palace, especially the fifteenth-century part above which towers the Sistine Chapel. If you follow the drive down from the Eagle Fountain a narrow path on the left leads to the Casina of Pius IV, an enchanting example of sixteenth-century renaissance architecture. Pius was the uncle of St Charles Borromeo, who often met him here. The delicate reliefs, mosaics, shell work, statuary, and fountains are completely exquisite. The architect was Pietro Ligorio. It can be viewed very well from the Vatican Galleries.

There is a fountain visitors will not see, but deserving of mention – it lies over the far side of the museum. Flemish seventeenth-century work in lead, it represents a leaden three-masted galley, with cannon, yardarms, and everything spouting water.

ROOF AND DOME

The roof is a pleasant place on a fine day. If you have not planned to visit Vatican City, here is a chance to have a bird's-eye view of much of it. Notice too that even one of St Peter's smaller domes would look quite sizeable on a cathedral anywhere else. The ascent of the dome itself is very much to be recommended, partly for the novelty, partly for the interest of its construction, and also for the views. At one part, as the dome curves, the corridor curves with it, and so do you. To commemorate the third centenary of Michelangelo's death a bust was placed at the entrance to the dome in 1964. For access, look for notices posted near the entrance to St Peter's.

Note: The statue by Bernini is that of Longinus, the centurion.

CHAPTER 3

The Vatican Museums and Galleries – The Sistine Chapel

I should like to make two points. No one on a first visit to Rome can hope to see the Vatican Museums and Galleries thoroughly. Secondly, it is perhaps misleading to think primarily of a museum. To a large extent the galleries are apartments of the Papal Palace open to the public, though it is true that some have been constructed as exhibition halls. These two points suggest the following policy – that the visitor should make for the Sistine Chapel, which happens to be right at the end of the galleries, and on his way should use what leisure he has to appreciate what interests him most. An early start is recommended, and perhaps a sustaining breakfast as well.

It is a good long trail to the far corner of the Vatican City, to the right of St Peter's, to find the museum entrance. The nearest well-known traffic centre is Piazza del Risorgimento. If you are not too far from the Vatican a taxi is worthwhile. You may find the little Museum bus running from the Piazza of St Peter's; it takes you there through the Vatican Gardens.

The entrance is a recent addition built by Pope Pius XI. A monumental double spiral staircase – that is to say, one where the way up is distinct from the way down, though this could easily escape your notice – does not really take you 'upstairs', but to a higher level of the Vatican Hill, very steep on this side. You will doubtless prefer to go up by the lift, but it is worth while coming down this novel staircase on your way out. Since many visitors come primarily to see the Sistine Chapel a choice of signposted routes is indicated. An amenity useful for anyone wishing to spend the day here is the Vatican Museum restaurant.

Past the upper gate there is a small vestibule, often ignored by the visitor in haste to get on. Here are the first of the Vatican's magnificent collection of early mosaics from sites in and around Rome, many of them from Hadrian's Villa at Tivoli. Some of the favourite subjects of these mosaics are four seasons, or four winds, or displays of market produce, animal or vegetable. Noting this from the start saves repeating a lot of explanation. Many mosaics are easily missed because they have been re-used as floors – visitors are apt to look for 'exhibits' and

·forget those that have been made a part of the building. Some mosaics are black and white, but those employing red, brown and ochre – with occasional use of green and blue – are really admirable in their tone qualities. In this vestibule there is a 'cosmos' mosaic that certainly ought to recall to lovers of Fitzgerald's 'Rubáiyát of Omar Khayyám' that handsome metaphor: 'the bowl of night'.

The Bronze Pine Cone

You leave the vestibule to enter a courtyard from which, in the early morning, one of the best photographs of the Dome of St Peter's can be taken. Behind you, in a modern and rather tasteless building, is the Pinacoteca or Art Gallery. At the main entrance to the Museums, it is possible to turn left or right. Through the glass door ahead you can glimpse the famous Pine Cone of Bronze, which once stood in the Atrium of St Peters' and, before that, according to some, on the summit of Hadrian's Tomb, the Castel Sant' Angelo. It was formerly a fountain and has a little hole at the top of each 'leaf'.

Sculpture

The entrance to the left leads to the Sculpture Galleries (Pio-Clementine and Chiaromonti Museums). The sculpture concerned is Roman (first three centuries A.D) or Roman copies of older Greek work. The first Hall is the Greek Cross, easily recognized by the two immense porphyry sarcophagi for the mother and daughter of Constantine, St Helena and Constanza (fourth century). They stood originally in great round mausolea in Rome, not unlike the mausoleum Constantine constructed over Christ's tomb at Jerusalem, now the Church of the Holy Sepulchre. For some reason these magnificent sculptures are often passed by unnoticed – I have never even seen them illustrated in the lavish photographic souvenirs. The sculpture on the tomb of Constanza – to the left – represents the vine harvest; notice children treading the press. That of Helena has Roman cavalrymen, prisoners, and fallen warriors – yet the mood suggests a restrained and stately dance. I have heard the suggestion that it does in fact represent a sort of ritual military parade before Caesar, and also that the tomb was originally intended for Constantine himself. It is certainly not very matronly.

The coloured floor mosaic of a basket of flowers as you enter this room is a beautiful and much imitated composition – second century, from the Appian Way. The handsome sphinxes beside it are Roman copies of Egyptian art.

The Circular Hall has in the centre an immense porphyry basin, antique, and a mosaic floor made up of two ancient ones representing mythological figures. The statues and busts around the walls are of divinities and emperors. No. 543 is a bust of Hadrian from the Castel Sant' Angelo, his tomb.

At the centre of the 'Room of the Muses' is displayed a powerful sculpture, the Belvedere Torso, signed by an Athenian artist of the first century B.C.

The Animal Room

The Room of the Muses is unlikely to retain many visitors, but you may well be pleased to give a double share of your time to the Animal Room that follows. This collection was founded by Pope Pius VI. Most of the statues have been so extensively and freely restored by Francesco Antonio Franzoni (1734–1818) that they may be almost considered his own work. Regardless of an interest in art, any animal lover will be fascinated. The sculptor must have had amazing powers of observation. I should love to have a book illustrating these delightful animals. There are beautiful mosaics in the floor, mostly of foodstuffs, animal and vegetable – asparagus, ducks, a fisherman's creel, etc. Some delicate little mosaics on the walls, including an amusing one of a cat and a cock, are from Hadrian's Villa at Tivoli.

Statuary

The next room is the Gallery of Statues with, opening off it, the Mask Room. Interesting pieces here are the Sleeping Ariadne (at the left as you enter), a beautiful head of the Emperor Verus – on a body to which it did not belong, and also 'Apollo the Lizard Slayer', and a reposing Satyr, both Roman copies of work by the Greek Praxiteles – fourth century B.C. The little Mask Room, which has another of those revolting satyrs and a good view over Rome, is named after masks in its beautifully fine mosaic floor from Hadrian's Villa, except the border, which is an eighteenth-century frame showing the arms of Pius VI, a wind-blown lily and stars. It is worth noting these arms; they crop up in all sorts of places.

At the far end of the Gallery of Statues is a Gallery of Busts, including interesting heads such as Julius Caesar's and Augustus's – emperor at the time of Our Lord's birth.

The galleries just described are round an octagonal courtyard. Fountain and fresh air make such a pleasant break from trudging through galleries that one is capable of overlooking two famous exhibits – the Laocöon and the Apollo Belvedere. The Laocöon was found in Rome in 1506 on the Esquiline Hill. According to recent research this group is a Roman copy of the

Tiberian Age from a bronze original made at Pergamon towards the middle of the second century B.C. Laocöon was a Trojan priest who had understood the fraud of the wooden horse; the gods, favouring the destruction of Troy, sent the snakes to kill him and his sons.

On the same side of the courtyard is the Apollo, a Roman copy of a fourth-century B.C. Greek original of the young god who has just shot an arrow and studies its flight. To appreciate this you must replace the lost bow in the left hand.

You now reach a long gallery of sculpture, divided into thirty sections. This is called the Chiaromonti Gallery, after the family name of Pope Pius VII. There are wall paintings illustrating his various undertakings – first on the left shows a restoration of the Colosseum that you may recognize. Few visitors can give this gallery the attention it deserves, and it would be futile to list the hundreds of exhibits here. Your best plan is to glance right and left and linger over what appeals to you most. An interesting relief not far down on the right represents a blindfolded horse turning a millstone – in fact a horse and a half, for the rear quarters of another animal represent its colleague treading in the opposite direction. The horse is blindfolded to prevent it becoming giddy. Observe the millstone too, for you will see many like it when you visit the excavations at Ostia.

The New Wing

At the end of the gallery opens the New Wing (*Braccio Nuovo*) which has several exhibits of major importance. In the fourth niche on the right there is perhaps the most famous statue of any Roman Emperor, the Augustus of Prima Porta – Augustus ruled from 31 B.C. to 14 A.D., a period covering the childhood of Jesus; Prima Porta is the place where the statue was found. The appearance of the Emperor, in the act of addressing his troops, is regal and handsome. You will see Christ represented in a similar stance in early paintings and mosaics. Notice the Emperor's rod of authority – in early Christian art only Christ, Moses, and Peter are shown with this rod.

In the centre of the Wing is a river god – the Nile – that repays careful study from all sides. For instance, the sixteen children playing over the figure are said to stand for the sixteen cubits full height of the periodical Nile flood, according to Pliny the Elder. Behind this statue is a mosaic representing Artemis, the 'Diana' of Ephesus, goddess of fertility. Perhaps you will recall the passage in the Acts of the Apostles when the preaching of St Paul at Ephesus thoroughly upset the silversmiths who sold statuettes of the popular Artemis.

You will now have arrived near where you started – without by any means having seen everything, nor being guided by this account into every possible gallery, but at least you will have made an intelligible tour of what is more characteristically Roman. Your route is left towards the Sistine Chapel. Not a little of the interest here lies in the painting and furniture of the galleries, dating from the sixteenth to the eighteenth centuries, and in glimpses of the Vatican Gardens through the windows – look out especially for the delightful renaissance 'Casina' or summer house of Pius IV.

The Sistine Hall

Soon the Sistine Hall opens to your left, a magnificent sixteenth-century apartment named after Sixtus V – the more famous Chapel is named after Sixtus IV. This Sixtus V was a tremendous builder, and much of his work in Rome four centuries ago can be studied here in progress because it was painted on the walls of this hall. Here are some subjects you may easily recognize and appreciate:

(all in left aisle)

Over first window:	A section of the 'Sistine' or Blessed Sacrament Chapel at St Mary Major's.
Over third window:	The Ponte Sisto, near Casa Pallotti – built by Sixtus IV to facilitate Holy Year traffic.
At the end:	The coronation of Pope Sixtus V on the steps of St Peter's in 1585 – an interesting picture of the unfinished basilica.

Many valuable gifts to popes are to be seen in this hall, as well as treasures of the Vatican library, such as the famous biblical manuscript known as the Codex Vaticanus, beautiful illuminated manuscripts, a collection of autographs including those of Michelangelo and Henry VIII, and also a coin collection.

In the vestibule of the Sistine Hall there is a case with gifts from Eastern Patriarchs and from King Hussein of Jordan on the occasion of Pope Paul VI's visit to the Holy Land – they include a lamp dating from the time of Abraham. On the second room as you continue along the gallery are paintings of St Peter's as it would have been had Michelangelo's design been faithfully followed, and also (but you must look back to see it) one showing the removal of the obelisk now in the Piazza of St Peter's from its original site in 1586. Notice – to the left – that Michelangelo's dome had not advanced beyond the drum. Behind the scaffolding (centre) is the nave of old St Peter's, and to the right the obelisk, which has just been lowered to the ground. Quite a document!

'Gold Glasses'

Further on are nautical instruments of the renaissance and several cabinets devoted to Christian art, including ivories, Limoges enamels, metal work, and – most important – lamps and 'gold glasses' from the catacombs. These are glass plates into which has been fired a picture in gold leaf. There is the usual repertoire of profane and early Christian art – the Good Shepherd for forgiveness, Noah for baptism, Jonas for Baptism and Resurrection and so on. Most beautiful, however, are several pictures of the departed of a very high standard of portraiture. These 'gold glasses' were fixed into the mortar around the slab closing the sepulchre at the time of burial and were useful for identifying tombs in the long, dimly lighted underground galleries.

The Room of the Aldobrandini Wedding

Towards the end of these galleries a room to the right has a small but very interesting collection of early Roman paintings – removed intact from walls at Ostia and Rome. The room itself is named after a large Augustan Age fresco representing wedding preparations, known as the 'Aldobrandini Wedding' because its first owner was Cardinal Pietro Aldobrandini. To the right of the door is a painting of a third-century grain vessel. The small mosaics on the right wall are exceptionally rich in colour.

Returning to the Gallery, the cases here exhibit chalices, enamels, ivories and other treasures of Christian art.

The Borgia Apartment

The Borgia Apartment was built by the pope of that family, Alexander VI, whose name seems to have become a by-word for what popes ought not to be, but its decorations were carried out mostly under Leo X, the pope who contended with Luther. Much of the work is by the warm and colourful Pinturicchio.

The Sistine Chapel

The Sistine Chapel, named after Pope Sixtus IV for whom it was built between 1473 and 1477 by, most probably, Giovanni dei Dolci, is not only the most impressive and colourful room of the Vatican Palace, but it is older than many – antedating the building of St Peter's – and has the most significant function in the public rôle of the papacy, for here takes place the Conclave to elect a new Pope, on the result of which, in our own day, the entire world waits in expectation.

A useful bit of advice here, unless you manage to visit Rome at a particularly quiet time, is – to quote Kipling:

*. . . keep your head when all about you
are losing theirs . . .*

Take stock. Under your feet is yet another of those marvellous floors in cosmatesque style, made at the time of Pope Nicholas V. The beautiful marble screen is a bloom of the renaissance, for its shallow, restrained relief was one of the earliest forms in which the art of antiquity was restored to life. This screen, along with the Gallery for the Sistine Choir, is by three renaissance sculptors: Mino da Fiesole, Giovanni Dalmata, and Andrea Bregno. Notice, carved on the screen, the oak tree arms of Pope Sixtus, whose family name was Della Rovere (of the Oak). With regard to the paintings of walls and vault, they are distinguished into three sets. Lives of Moses and Christ on the side

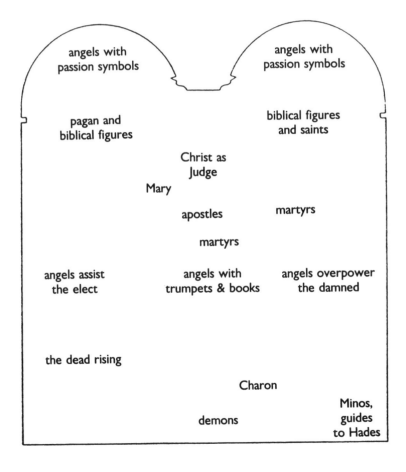

walls, by several artists, the Creation by Michelangelo on the vault, and his great Judgment behind the altar.

To take the Judgment first (though ideally the Creation precedes it) – this is dominated by Michelangelo's most splendid concept, the Christ whom art must depict as perfect man while faith accepts him as God. This muscular Hero is indeed a Christ of the renaissance. The Judgment scene is easily followed by studying its composition in a clockwise direction, beginning at the left-hand corner. A diagram is given opposite to guide you. Perhaps the part more easily repaying close study is the mythical Charon transporting the damned. This Judgment was painted between 1536 and 1541.

Dominating the vault is that other grand concept: the Father creating Man – see that subtle approach of fingertips by which God communicates to his creature some spark of himself! The central panels, beginning above the altar, represent the following:

> The separation of light from darkness.
> The creation of sun, moon, and planets.
> The separation of land from water.
> Creation of Man.
> Creation of Woman.
> The Fall.
> The Sacrifice of Noah.
> The Deluge.
> The Drunkenness of Noah.

The drunkenness of Noah is a reminder that our present lot remains burdened with moral and physical ills. The vault was completed in 1512.

The wall paintings to the left depict the life of Moses, to the right the life of Christ. This parallel arises from a profound Christian sense of 'theological drama' which saw in Moses, leader of God's first chosen people, wonderful parallels to the life and mission of the Father's Incarnate and Redeeming Son. (Compare the reliefs at the Lateran which point out parallels between Old and New Testaments). The first two paintings – the finding of the infant Moses on the Nile bank, and the Nativity of Christ – have been blotted out by the Judgment. The rest follow in this order:

Left.	*Right.*
Moses returning to Egypt with wife and child (Perugino).	The Baptism of Jesus (Perugino).

Moses killing the harsh Egyptian (in Egypt) and driving away the shepherds who bothered his future sisters-in-law (in Arabia) – this picture is out of sequence (Botticelli).

The Temptation of Jesus (Botticelli).

The Crossing of the Red Sea (Cosimo Rosselli)

The Call of Peter and Andrew (Ghirlandaio).

Moses receiving the Law on Sinai (Cosimo Rosselli).

The Sermon on the Mount (Cosimo Rosselli and Piero di Cosimo).

The punishment of the presumptuous Levites (Botticelli).

The Delivery of the Keys to Peter (Perugino).

The Testament and the Death of Moses (Signorelli).

The Last Supper – notice the dog and cat in the foreground (Cosimo Rosselli)

Entrance wall:
The disputation over the body of Moses (Matteo da Lecce)

The Resurrection (Arrigo Paludano (van den Broeck))

At the time of revising this book for a new edition the restoration of these paintings has been in hand for over twenty years. The final phase – Michelangelo's 'Last Judgment' – has not begun. There has of course been criticism, mostly to the effect that neither Michelangelo nor the other artists intended their works to be as colourful and bright as they now appear; in other words, that they used techniques to tone down the colour applied. They seem to expect what a modern artist might do to impart an 'antique' effect.

The fact is however that the frescoes have been covered with dust and soot and at some time 'fixed' with glue. This last has itself contracted and pulled the pigments about. My own expectation is that the critics – and, more important, the public – will settle down and acknowledge the restoration an overall success. It is worth noting that each century has seen one attempt at least to clean the frescoes, even, in 1625, rubbing them with damp bread. A problem for the future will be the prevention of future discolouration, etc. This will be done by what is called a 'controlled microclimate'.

The Raphael Rooms

The 'Raphael Rooms' – *Stanze di Raphael* – are on no account to be missed. Here you are in the Palace built by Nicholas V in the

fifteenth century. First painted by great artists of the renaissance
– Baldassare Peruzzi, Perugino, Sodoma and others – Julius II
had their work obliterated in favour of his favourite artist, the
gentle, short-lived Raphael.

To reach the four Raphael Rooms you pass through the
Sobieski Room and the Hall of the Immaculate Conception. The
first, painted from the master's cartoon by his disciples Giulio
Romano and Penni, is known as 'The Room of the Fire in the
Borgo' after the most appealing of its four subjects. The Fire
occurred in the ninth century, in the Saxon quarter around the
Church of Santo Spirito in Sassia, and was belived to have been
extinguished by the blessing of Pope Leo IV. Note in this
painting the figures escaping from a burning house, the façade
of old St Peter's, and, to the right, the famous water carrier. The
figure of a youth carrying his aged father on his back inspired
the sculpture of Bernini in the Villa Borghese, entitled 'Aeneas
and Anchises fleeing from burning Troy'. There is a tapestry
copy of this painting in the Farnese Palace.

Also from the time of Leo IV is a Battle at Ostia, a victory over
Saracens sailing up the Tiber. The artillery fortress of Ostia is
represented in this painting — an anachronism.

The two other walls are painted with subjects from the life of
Leo III – the Pope clearing himself by oath of false charges, and
the coronation of Charlemagne in St Peter's at the Midnight
Mass of Christmas 799. This painting had a political significance,
for Charlemagne was given the features of Francis I of France
and Leo III those of Leo X, to commemorate the concordat
between France and the Holy See concluded in 1515.

The ceiling of this room retains paintings by Perugino,
deliberately preserved by Raphael out of respect for his old
master.

Next is the Room of the Segnatura, named after an ecclesiastical court which used to hold its sessions here. A painting known
as 'The School of Athens' represents philosophers of ancient
Greece, but many wear the faces of Raphael's contemporary
architects and artists. For example, of the central figures, Plato
and Aristotle, that to the left is Leonardo da Vinci. Archimedes,
stooping to measure on a slate laid on the ground, is Bramante,
and behind him, holding a star-spangled sphere, is Raphael
himself.

The beautiful cosmatesque style floor of this room must not
escape your notice. It is one of the latest in this style, not
counting a modern revival.

The third Raphael Room is also known after one of its
paintings – 'Expulsions of Heliodorus'. This depicts the dramatic incident told in the third chapter of the second Book of the

Machabees, in the Old Testament, when Heliodorus, sent to plunder the Temple at Jerusalem, was thrown to the ground by angelic warriors, but restored by the merciful sacrifice of Onias the priest. The architectural rendering of the Temple shows the mastery of perspective characteristic of the renaissance. The Angel on horseback is superb.

Opposite is Leo I repelling Attila the Hun from Rome, a subject also rendered in Alessandro Algardi's sculpture over the altar of St Leo in the Basilica of St. Peter's. The meeting took place far from Rome, but artistic licence permits Raphael to represent it at the gates. The broken aqueduct in the landscape is an allusion to something that happened often enough when Rome was besieged; Peter and Paul overhead assist the Pope. This painting too is reproduced in tapestry in the Farnese Palace.

A third wall is dedicated to the Mass at Bolsena, when the Corporal now at Orvieto is believed to have become miraculously bloodstained. The fourth subject is the Liberation of St Peter from Prison, with some dramatically painted mailed figures

Note biblical subjects in the ceiling, and a fine second-century mosaic floor.

The 'Hall of Constantine' depicts the first Christian Emperor's vision of the Cross, his subsequent victory over his rival Maxentius at the Milvian Bridge (in Rome's northern suburbs), his Baptism which, in the circumstances given, is unhistorical, and his donation of Rome to the Popes. There is another second-century mosaic floor.

The Chapel painted by Fra Angelico

To reach the Loggia of Raphael – a cloistered gallery of which he painted the vault – you pass through the 'Room of the Chiaroscuri' in which his work was later obliterated in favour of monochrome decorations. It makes an effective transition both to the Loggia and to the delightful little chapel in the corner, painted by the great fifteenth-century Florentine Dominican, Beato Angelico. His subjects are the deacons St Stephen, of whose martyrdom by stoning you read in the Acts of the Apostles, and Lawrence, Roman martyr of the third century. It is almost a waste of time to enter this chapel if it is crowded. It is recorded that for nearly two centuries the key was lost, and the paintings almost forgotten – an indication of poor housekeeping in the Vatican.

The Loggia of Raphael

In the Loggia there are four paintings to each of thirteen compartments; the last set of four is of the Life of Christ, all the others are Old Testament. It has been named 'Raphael's Bible'. Looking up at paintings can be very tedious – a mirror-topped trolley would be useful here – and I suggest you study up to half a dozen that you find yourself able to identify and appreciate, and forsake the rest.

Tapestries

Of the many interesting rooms through which you will pass, probably exhausted, on your way out, it would be a pity if you had no attention left for the splendid tapestries. The oldest here is one made at Tournai in the fifteenth century – characteristically medieval and as colourful as a pageant – representing the Apostles' Creed article by article. Notice the flowers and animals. The rest are of the sixteenth century and are mainly from cartoons by students of Raphael. There are some fine expressions, notably in the overthrow of the wicked Athalia (Old Testament), of shepherds in the Nativity scene, of almost everyone including the elephant in the Adoration of the Magi, and of bereaved mothers in the Massacre of the Innocents.

The Gallery of Maps

The Gallery of Maps will be a joy to those who find maps fascinating. They are maps painted on the walls in the late sixteenth century, of Italy and Italian islands, and also of papal possessions at Avignon. Places are represented pictorially, and there are also interesting pictures of naval battles and fortifications. If you are too absorbed by the maps you will miss other paintings of a variety of subjects on the ceiling.

The Room of the 'Biga'

I shall omit details of the Gallery of Candelabra. Apart from the candlesticks that name it the contents are mostly smaller pagan sculpture. In a room just off the gallery at the exit end is the handsome 'Biga' (first century A.D.) – chariot and horses – completed from original fragments by Franzoni in the eighteenth-century.

The Egyptian and Etruscan collections represent special interests which I think this pilgrim's guide-book should not be expected to meet.

The Art Gallery

As you leave the museum, and before you take the lift or staircase to street level, you may find time for the Pinacoteca, or Vatican Art Gallery. It is relatively small, but covers a wide range, including early Italian painting (from the eleventh century) and late Byzantine ones. Most famous is room eight devoted to Raphael's Transfiguration as well as his Madonna di Foligno and Tapestries of the Acts of the Apostles. Of other works, I should like to mention especially Bellini's 'Pietà'.

Other Collections

Other collections are:

Modern Religious Art, inaugurated in 1973 by Pope Paul VI, in the so-called Borgia Apartments, some of which are under the Sistine Chapel.

The Carriage Museum, also set up by Paul VI in 1973. It includes the carriage said to have been used by Pius IX when he fled from Rome to Gaeta in 1849.

The Missionary Ethnological Museum, transferred from the Lateran Palace. Two itineraries are provided, one for the general public and another for specialists. The collections include not only objects of pagan and cultural interest but also Christian exhibits, some from early missionary periods.

The Pio-Christian Museum, founded by Pius IX in 1854 and transferred here from the Lateran in 1963. This includes early Christian sarcophagi with their fascinating repertoire of iconography, inscriptions from the catacombs, and the famous statue of Christ as a Shepherd Boy – a theme frequent in early Christian art and low relief but rare as a free-standing statue.

The Gregorian Profane Museum, a collection of classical antiquities formerly in the Lateran Museum, brought here by John XXIII and opened in 1970. It is perhaps a little unkind that this 'profane' collection should house inscribed stones from one of Rome's few Jewish catacombs.

The 'Itineraries'

Visitors are now offered a choice of four itineraries or routes through the galleries, guided by colours, and ranging from an estimated hour and a half to five hours. It brings home to you the fact that one visit will never cover so extensive a collection of museums. Very informative brochures are available to help your choice. Visiting times at present are from 8.45 am to 1 pm on winter weekdays and till 4 pm in the summer. On Sundays and some Church holydays the Museums are closed but on the last Sunday of each month they are open and admission is free.

CHAPTER 4

Around St Peter's

Via della Conciliazione – Santo Spirito in Sassia – Santa Maria in Traspontina – Castel Sant' Angelo – San Gregorio Settimo – Santa Maria Mediatrice – Christ the King

'Around St Peter's' is a rather vague description, I know. I propose to describe a number of places that might interest you within a short walk or bus ride of the Vatican, on the right bank

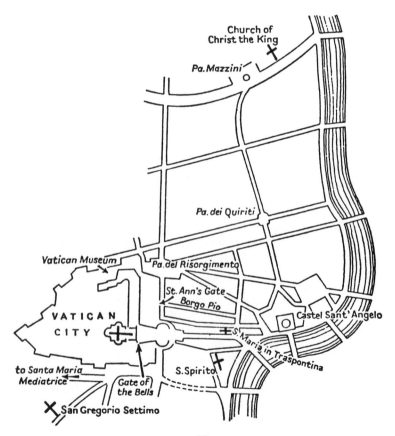

of the Tiber, but not including the Janiculum Hill or Trastevere. There is only one visit I would strongly recommend for almost everyone, and this is to the Castel Sant' Angelo.

Via della Conciliazione

The Via della Conciliazione can hardly be missed. It was the Italian Government's gift to the Holy See to commemorate the signing of the Lateran Treaty of 1929 that restored to the popes that token – but quite real – temporal sovereignty judged necessary for the free exercise of their office. The advantage, if it is one, is that St Peter's is seen in the perspective of a sort of grand boulevard – but the merits of the 1930 fascist-style architecture are another thing. In the old days St Peter's used to 'spring on you' from the network of streets known as the *'borghi'* – and you can still experience this effect by taking one of the turnings to the left and approaching the Colonnade by the Borgo Santo Spirito. This word *'borgo'* by the way is a German suffix of many English towns, not to mention Edinburgh. It means a settlement, and it was given to the various colonies of northern peoples who settled around St Peter's. The full title of the church – and the hospital attached – in the Borgo just mentioned is 'Santo Spirito in Sassia' – 'in Saxony', but the Saxony in question is West Saxony, Hardy's Wessex, for the founder of this hospice for pilgrims from our island was King Ine of Wessex, in the year 717.

Santo Spirito in Sassia

The hospital was refounded by Innocent III in 1198, and rebuilt to the design of an early renaissance architect, Baccio Pontelli, between 1471 and 1494, under Pope Sixtus IV. His work – and there is not much fifteenth-century architecture in Rome – is that attractive façade and octagon which you could easily take for a church, just as you cross the Ponte Vittorio Emmanuele on your way to St Peter's. Although characteristically renaissance there is a touch of gothic about it. In the later hospital buildings behind there is a handsome courtyard, with fountain, frescoes, and arcades, well worth a glance as you pass along the Borgo.

The Church of Santo Spirito itself lacks major interest. The architect is uncertain, but Baldassare Peruzzi, sixteenth century, is favoured. In the apse is a vast sixteenth-century painting of Pentecost by the Zucchi brothers of Florence. The sacristy has a series of seventeenth-century paintings, now in poor condition, of the history of the hospital – they include a 'Madonna of King Ine' (of Mercia).

Across the road from Santo Spirito is the Generalate of the Society of Jesus.

To slip back to the Via della Conciliazione; two of its *palazzi* (in Italian, any large residence is a 'palace') are both old and interesting. On the right, midway, is the Palazzo Torlonia, fifteenth century, and under our Henry VII and Henry VIII (part of his reign anyway) the residence of English ambassadors to the Holy See. On the left is the picturesque fifteenth-century palazzo of the Knights of the Holy Sepulchre, now the Hotel Columbus. Some of its apartments are splendid renaissance halls.

Santa Maria in Traspontina

Santa Maria in Traspontina is the one church in the Via della Conciliazione. It is served by the Calced Carmelites and its altars and shrines would interest tertiaries. The high altar, 1734, by Carlo Fontana, has one of the more elegant baroque baldachinos of Rome; I would pair it with that at Santa Croce. The tabernacle is original – a globe. Above the altar is yet another of Rome's many ancient Greek icons of Our Lady. Santa Maria was built in 1566 by Sallustio Peruzzi, son of the architect to whom Santo Spirito is attributed.

If you should hear bells ringing from its picturesque campanile as you pass, listen to a sound that, though modified, rang out over English meadows six hundred years ago, for it is an old English bell recast.

Castel Sant' Angelo

There are three modern churches within reach of St Peter's that I want to mention, but as only architectural enthusiasts are likely to wander off to find them I shall describe at this point the Castel Sant' Angelo – one of the most enjoyable places to visit in Rome. You will have seen the Castle when crossing the Tiber on your way to St Peter's. Maybe at first it makes little impression as a fortress – too low-lying, for instance – yet from many an angle, especially from the park behind it, and in certain lights, it makes a most striking picture.

Three things go to make Sant' Angelo: Roman tomb, artillery fortress, papal palace. Though not so clear from outside, they divide your visit very obviously into distinct parts. The great round tower at the heart of the fortress was built by the Hadrian who made that wall separating Britons from Picts, as a sepulchre for himself and his family. You can see where the coarse fabric of the tomb – once beautifully faced with marble – gives way to the fortification begun by Pope Nicholas V towards the end of the fifteenth century. Under subsequent sixteenth-century popes the fortress was crowned with handsome papal apartments of which you can see the terrace, facing the river.

From the great gate of the castle you pass into the sinister galleries of the eighteen-centuries-old tomb house, then into the courtyards, guard-rooms, and other offices of the castle. Here are instruments of medieval warfare, catapults and cannons – the first cannon fired from here was in 1378 – dungeons and store rooms. The oil storage room is interesting because the system used is exactly the same as in second-century Ostia – great earthenware jars sunk in the floor. There are 84 of them, capable of holding about ten thousand gallons of oil. Nearby are silos for grain. If children are with you, they should be kept carefully in hand in this part of the castle.

High up in the tower we reach the splendid papal halls, with views towards St Peter's and over the Tiber. Notice in the Pauline Hall the sombre, formalized, yet strangely attractive painting of Hadrian. Neighbouring apartments – bedroom, library, etc. – with their wealth of decoration, authentic furniture, and early Italian paintings, are especially attractive for their intimacy.

You emerge finally on the roof, overshadowed by the Archangel Michael after whom the castle is named. When Hadrian was buried here the summit of the mausoleum was a conical garden planted with trees and terminating, in the opinion of some archaeologists, in the bronze pine cone fountain now preserved in a Vatican courtyard. Within little over a century it had become an outer defence of the new fortifications built for Rome by the Emperor Aurelian. In 590, a year of plague, Pope St Gregory was leading the people in a procession of penance when he saw on the summit of 'Hadrian's Mole' the vision of an angel sheathing his sword. A chapel was raised here, subsequently replaced by a statue of St Michael. The present figure dates from the eighteenth century.

Here is a good spot for photography – you can take the whole extent of Vatican City. Lovers of opera may reflect while they are here that these battlements are the scene of Act III of Puccini's *Tosca* – here Tosca, desperate at the death of her lover, throws herself into the courtyard below.

In connection with the castle the *corridoio* must be mentioned. This is a fortified wall in which is an escape gallery for the popes from the Vatican to Sant' Angelo, first built by Nicholas III in 1277. On 6th May 1527, Swiss Guards defending Clement VII as he fled down the *corridoio* were massacred by the mercenaries of the Emperor Charles V; the anniversary each year is the occasion for swearing-in new recruits.

The *Memoirs* of Benvenuto Cellini, which should be found on the shelves of any well-stocked library, give you an exciting picture of life in the Castel Sant' Angelo in the sixteenth century.

Parallel with the *corridoio* are two *borghi* where you will find small reasonably-priced restaurants and also shops where religious articles can be bought in gross at trade rates – but check that this is so.

In the new suburbs behind St Peter's to the left are two of the more important modern churches of Rome, both of the Franciscan Friars Minor; San Gregorio Settimo (St Gregory VII, Pope of the eleventh century, known as Hildebrand) and Santa Maria Mediatrice. St Gregory's is only about ten minutes' walk from the Piazza of St Peter's: a left fork and two railway bridges, one being the Vatican goods line entering the City.

San Gregorio Settimo

The importance of this church, by the oddly-named architects Paniconi and Pediconi, is due to its ingenious construction and the beauty of its internal decoration. Built of brick and concrete, walls and roof are structurally independent. This may sound like a riddle, but you will easily understand what I mean when you see it. Ten immense concrete piers – they look like girders – support the roof. The walls end before they meet this roof and the intervening space is glass. Functionally, the walls are a mere screen against sound and weather. The decoration of the church maintains a beautiful system of tones, red, brown, and buff. There are inlaid marble floors representing scriptural subjects (in front of the sanctuary), magnificent frescoes around the sanctuary, and in the crypt brilliant ceramics and an unusual technique of stone inlay representing the life of St Francis.

I list the subjects of the paintings left and right of the sanctuary:

left: Baptism of Christ, Pentecost, Last Supper.
right: The Wedding Feast at Cana, the Mission of the Apostles, the Healing of Peter's Mother-in-Law.

The idea is to represent sacraments of the Church as suggested by incidents in the Gospels.

The extraordinary sculpture overhanging the altar may be baffling at a glance; if you study it you will find it represents the Crucifixion, Our Lady, St Francis and Angels.

Santa Maria Mediatrice

Santa Maria Mediatrice is the church of the new Generalate of the Friars Minor on the Monte Gelsomino (a pretty name; it means Jasmine Hill), not far behind and above San Gregorio. Built between 1945 and 1950 by Giovanni Muzio, who has since designed the new Basilica of the Annunciation at Nazareth, you will be struck first of all by its unusual form – an octagon preceding the long friars' choir. Don't mistake this for a modern plan; it has very ancient roots in history. The attraction of this church is its wealth of marble, mosaic, and sculpture – the architect was assisted by twenty-seven artists. It could be overwhelming, but in fact it is warm and harmonious. The mosaics of the dome represent the Church Militant, Suffering, and Triumphant. Other themes you may look for in the church are the Life of Our Lady and St Francis's Canticle of the Sun.

Away to the north of St Peter's (right of the Via della Conciliazione as you approach the Vatican) is a quarter of Rome developed largely at the end of the last century. I am going to mention one modern church, Christ the King on the Viale Giuseppe Mazzini, not in order to drag you all that way on an unnecessary excursion, but in case you are staying in that neighbourhood, and also because you could cross the Tiber by a nearby bridge and arrive in the interesting neighbourhood around the Piazza del Popolo.

Church of Christ the King

From the Castel Sant' Angelo it is possible to see right down the Via Virgilio to the fountain in the Piazza dei Quiriti. This fountain is not a masterpiece of art, but the garden round it is a pleasant place to take a rest. Water reflects the sunlight on to the underside of the huge basin with a very tranquillizing effect on the observer. If you continue straight ahead you soon reach the Piazza Mazzini, with another pleasant garden. A stone's throw across the splendid Viale Giuseppe Mazzini, an ambitious boulevard with gardens and clipped trees down the centre, are the brick belfries of Christ the King. I am not going to say that this is a very fine modern church; with a foundation stone laid in 1920 it is hardly modern, and it has features unhappily reminiscent of big chain cinemas. But I am sure it was thought a very fine church when it was built. The great painted Christ of the apse, and the monochrome evangelists under the cupola, are still impressive. There is some pleasant work in bronze too – Stations of the Cross, and a delicate Baptism of Christ over the font.

CHAPTER 5

The Other Major Basilicas

St John Lateran – St Mary Major's – St Paul's outside the Walls

ST JOHN LATERAN (SAN GIOVANNI LATERANO)

History

The Lateran is frankly the Cinderella of major basilicas. This must be because its baroque eighteenth-century reconstruction by Borromini is in many respects poor, and both the fervent life of St Mary Major's and the profoundly religious atmosphere of St Paul's are lacking. Yet the Lateran has its pride; the inscriptions on its façade proclaim its title: 'Most Holy Lateran Church, Mother and Mistress of all churches of the City and the World'. It holds this title as the first cathedral of Rome, where Constantine after 312 allowed the popes to set up their episcopal chair in a church built on the confiscated property of the Laterani family. As first cathedral of the Empire it was rightly dedicated to Christ himself as Saviour – *Basilica Salvatoris*. The later change of name is due to the importance of its baptistery. In early times baptism was administered for the most part annually, by the bishop, during the great Easter Vigil, in the baptistery of his cathedral, which carried a dedication to John the Baptist. Here at the Lateran John has taken over in popular usage, and it has come to apply to both the Baptist and the Evangelist.

Visitors very often arrive at the entrance to the basilica in the Piazza di San Giovanni Laterano – the one with the great obelisk, but I very much wish you to avoid entering there. Entering a place of importance by its front door is far more helpful. The main façade of St John Lateran opens on to a meeting of roads where traffic converges to leave the city by the Porta San Giovanni – a sixteenth-century gate replacing the ancient and beautiful Porta Asinaria (deep in a hollow to your right as you stand with your back to the church). Totila the Goth entered Rome by this gate in 546. Here were once the gardens and courtyards of the old Lateran Palace swept away by Sixtus V (sixteenth century) in favour of the vast block formerly the home of the Pontifical Museum of Christian Art and noted for being extraordinarily cold. It is now used as administrative offices for the diocese of Rome.

The group of St Francis

Stand on the terrace and look down the vista towards the distant façade of Santa Croce in Gerusalemme. Just beyond the traffic is an impressive bronze group of St Francis with his disciples. He stands with his arms extended towards the Lateran. This commemorates an event in the history of St Francis which sums up his vocation. The Poor Man from Assisi was in Rome seeking approval of his new religious family and its rule; Pope Innocent III was sleeping in the Lateran Palace beside the great cathedral which, as several times before, was on the verge of collapse. It was a token of the Church in general in an age when wealth and power had sapped its spirituality. In a dream the Pope saw a man support the tottering building, and the following day recognized in St Francis the saint sent by God to restore, not the mere fabric of the Lateran, but the Church generally from the funds of his poverty and simplicity.

The mosaic of Pope Leo III

Of that Palace all that remains is incorporated in a group of buildings to your left as you look down towards St Francis: the famous Holy Stairs alleged to have been brought by Helena from the Holy Land, a medieval papal chapel and – visible on the outside from where you stand – a restored mosaic from the apse of the papal dining hall, dating from 800. To the right of Christ with his apostolic college are represented Christ again, with Constantine and Pope Sylvester; to the left St Peter with Pope Leo III and Charlemagne. Leo III will be recognized by the square nimbus behind his head – a sign that the person depicted was living; his name too appears at the crown of the apse.

The façade

To appreciate the façade you must step down among the lawns of the Piazza and look back at the austere concept of the Florentine Alessandro Galilei (1736), a composition of light and shade as five lofty arches open onto the shadow of its narthex. Contrastingly dramatic figures of Christ, St John Baptist and St John Evangelist with apostles and saints crown the parapet.

4. St John Lateran

The narthex

Enter the narthex. The great central door of bronze comes from the Senate House in the Forum where its place has been taken by a copy. The doorway here was too large and the border is a seventeenth-century addition. At one end of this narthex is a restored fourth-century statue of Constantine excavated from the Baths of Diocletian. To the right, the last of the five doors is the 'Holy Door' – walled up and opened only for the Years of Jubilee proclaimed at intervals by the popes in order to celebrate the Mystery of our Redemption in a specially solemn way.

Once in the basilica, it is a good idea to station yourself for a moment at the head of the nave and note the elements that make up the vista before you – the cosmatesque floor, the coffered ceiling, statues of apostles dynamic with all the energy of baroque in its final decades, above them panels in high relief, the distant baldachino of the papal altar and, beyond that, a great apse mosaic.

The nave

The cosmatesque floor is late – fourteenth-century – and less interesting than usual; note the column for the Colonna family of Pope Martin V who laid it. The coffered ceiling is pleasing. It contains the arms of Pope Pius VI, of the eighteenth century; but wait till you reach the transept to appreciate a better and earlier example of this type of work. It is a mystery to me why the apostles and evangelists whose great baroque figures are so completely characteristic of the Lateran receive such mediocre attention in many guide-books. It is interesting to identify their symbols – Bartholomew with his flayed skin, rather alarming; Matthew the tax collector with a bag of coins. My favourite is St James in pilgrim's costume – because of the great pilgrimage to his shrine at Compostela in Spain. The panels in high relief above these statues represent, to the left, Old Testament 'type' incidents faced, on the right, by their realization in the New: for instance, near the altar the Ark of Noah, salvation by water, typifies Baptism, across the nave; and near the door the incident of Jonas emerging after three days from the sea serpent is fulfilled in the Resurrection of Christ. The sculptor of these interesting and vigorous panels is Alessandro Algardi.

The nave of the Lateran has five aisles – as did the nave of St Peter's and as St Paul's still has. I suspect that the primitive columns exist within the pilasters. The side aisles here are a little tatty in appearance and I select only a few points of interest. Behind the first pilaster to the right is a fresco attributed to Giotto. It represents Boniface VIII proclaiming the first Holy Year in 1300. Notice that his tiara has only one crown, and how delicately the artist has drawn the head of the cleric holding the scroll. Across the nave is the famous Corsini Chapel, built by Clement XII to the designs of Alessandro Galilei (who also designed the façade) as a mausoleum for himself and his family. The decoration of its dome, and the corresponding pattern in the floor which gives it unity, is very rich but harmonious. You will probably have to peer into the chapel through a grille. Deep below is a vault containing a very dramatic (but at present poorly lit) Pietà, of similar proportions to Michelangelo's at St Peter's, by Antonio Montauto (eighteenth century). If you are keen to see this you may ask for the key at the sacristy. Next after the Corsini Chapel is one with, over the altar, a fourteenth-century painting on wood of the 'Falling Asleep' of Our Lady, surviving from the earlier basilica.

The tomb of Pope Martin V

Before the papal altar is a Confession. It is not original, but a modification of Pius IX. The tomb down there is that of Pope Martin V, beautiful bronze work by the Florentine Simone Ghini, a disciple of Donatello and a collaborator with Antonio

Filarete who made St Peter's bronze doors. Martin V (d. 1431) was elected by the Council of Constance to bring to an end the 'Great Schism' which had divided the Church with its rival popes. Following some strange primitive instinct, people insist on throwing coins down to this tomb, as they do down other holes, dry or wet. The inscription at the foot of the tomb describes Martin as *temporum suorum felicitas*, 'the joy of his times'.

The high altar

The baldachino over the altar, by the Sienese Giovanni di Stefano (about 1370), is, like others in Rome, gothic and somewhat out of proportion but it is less satisfactory and top-heavy on account of the great relic chamber where the heads of Peter and Paul, or parts thereof, have been traditionally preserved.

The apse mosaic

The great choir beyond the altar is a nineteenth-century rebuilding, but its apse mosaic was completely restored and reconstructed. The artists were two Franciscan friars who also worked on the apse of St Mary Major's, Jacopo da Torriti and Jacopo da Camerino, who by way of signature left their kneeling figures among the apostles – to the right and left of the pointed windows. Franciscan interest occurs again in the smaller figures to left and right of Our Lady and St John Baptist, representing St Francis and St Anthony. Kneeling close to Our Lady is Nicholas IV, whose work at the Lateran was praised by Dante in his *Paradiso*. Above the gemmed crucifix is the Holy Spirit as a dove, from whose beak water flows down the sides of the Cross dividing into four streams – the fourfold gospel by which we receive the life-giving word of Christ – to enter finally the broad flowing Jordan, all along the base of the mosaic, rich with abundant life. From the Gospel sources stags and sheep drink living water. The symbolism of all this is, of course, 'baptism with water and the Holy Ghost'. Notice between the divided streams the Heavenly Jerusalem with golden walls, within which the phoenix bird of immortality is perched on the Tree of Life.

The upper part of this mosaic represents the head of Christ amid seraphim. Although this is common to many mosaics, here it is associated with a tradition that Christ appeared during the original consecration of the Lateran. The theme is repeated on the coffered ceiling of the transept, and where it occurs on buildings – even on farms out in the country – it indicates that they are or were Lateran property.

The transept

The transept of the Lateran, designed at the end of the sixteenth century by Jacopo Della Porta, is unusually rich, because the Blessed Sacrament altar enshrines a table traditionally accepted as that used by Christ at the Last Supper. The altar incorporates marble and bronze columns said to have been taken from the Temple of Jupiter on the Capitol, the latter having been recast from the bronze prows of Cleopatra's ships taken in battle. In the papal altar, incidentally, is part of another wooden table believed to be from the home of Pudens, with whom Peter stayed. He is credited with having used it when offering the Holy Sacrifice. To the right of the Blessed Sacrament altar is a monument to Leo XIII, author of the pioneering social encyclical *Rerum novarum*, and in a corresponding position on the far side of the church one to the thirteenth-century Pope Innocent III, erected by Leo XIII when he had his great predecessor's remains transferred here from Perugia. Anyone keen on woodcarving should look into the choir chapel with its richly worked seventeenth-century stalls by Rainaldi.

The cloister and treasury

At the transept end of the left aisle is the entrance to a cloister in cosmatesque style by the Vassalletti – responsible also for the cloister of St Paul's. The Lateran cloister is smaller, has lost much of its mosaic, and is cluttered with fragments of sculpture, some of which have rather apocryphal identifications as relics; for instance, a porphyry slab 'on which the soldiers diced for Christ's robes'. The sculptured well-head is ninth century. The sad state of this cloister must be due to the years of neglect at the Lateran when the Popes had gone to live at Avignon. There is a fee to enter the cloister which seems hardly worth paying, but it does include a small nicely arranged exhibition with some old English church needlework.

The Lateran Chapter has arranged a 'Treasury' accessible through a shop off the north transept (right of the altar). The exhibits are mostly late renaissance vestments. Two other items are of unusual interest. The first as you enter is a 'Golden Rose', a papal gift associated with Laetare Sunday. The other is a fine crucifix with biblical scenes, in appearance romanesque but officially attributed to the early fourteenth century.

The Lateran obelisk

You may leave the Lateran by the door at the end of the transept – noticing over it a collection of sculptured musical instruments representing King David's genius at psalmody. Through a portico by Domenico Fontana – in which a statue of Henry IV of France reminds you that each major basilica was under the protection of a sovereign – enter the Piazza di San Giovanni Laterano with its great Egyptian obelisk. About 1500 B.C. it stood before the Temple of the Sun at Heliopolis, where I suppose Moses saw it. Constantius, son of Constantine, set it up in the Circo Massimo, the great sports stadium. Sixtus V found it in fragments in a swamp and transferred it here in 1588. The inscription on the base recording the baptism of Constantine in the baptistery across the way is historically inaccurate.

The baptistery

Bear to the left to see the ancient baptistery and its adjoining chapels. An octagon in shape – as are many early baptisteries in Europe – it covers a great bath into which, when Constantine arranged a baptistery here in the fourth century, candidates went down into the water up to their knees; water was poured three times over their head. This practice, known as partial immersion, was common in the West. Sixtus III restored the baptistery in the fifth century, and its general appearance, with the great porphyry columns and mosaics in its adjacent chapels, dates from then. The fifth-century mosaic in the Chapel of St Rufina, a pattern of twining acanthus, may well have inspired the apse of San Clemente nearby – six hundred years later. The central feature of the vault in the Chapel of St John the Evangelist is a simple Lamb of God surrounded by a wreath woven of seasonal fruits – an early Christian mosaic in truly classical style. The ancient doors of the chapel of St John Baptist, said to be an alloy of bronze, silver and gold, give a beautiful note as they move on their hinges. It is well worth 'arranging' for an attendant to do this for you.

The Scala Santa

Associated with your visit to the Lateran will be one to the Scala Santa – 'Holy stairs' – which may have borne the footprints of Christ, believed to have been brought here from Pilate's headquarters in Jerusalem. Although the Holy Stairs cannot be proved authentic, there is nothing intrinsically impossible about them. These twenty-eight marble steps are cased with wood, and the devotion is to climb them on your knees meditating simply on the Passion of Christ – if you like you may repeat an ejaculation or short prayer on each. There is an account which makes out that Luther was the only person ever to give up and walk down. There are four other staircases by which you may walk up, and of these the two inner ones may be used for the devotion in passiontide.

There are several chapels served by a Passionist community, but the principal one, at the top of the Scala Santa, is probably eighth-century at latest, decorated by the Cosmati in the twelfth. It was the relic treasury of the papal palace. Far too obscure for you to make much of it, you will see through the grille the twelfth-century silver shrine of an ancient icon of Christ known as the Acheiropoeta: 'picture not made with hands' – on what authority you will never find out. A postcard of what passes for the 'Face' makes you feel that most human hands would not have fabricated such a silly picture. The original painting has virtually disappeared but, with the thirteenth century silver panel that covers it and its fifteenth century silver doors, there is still something mystic and solemn about the 'Acheiropoeta'.

It is a pity that more cannot be seen of this interesting chapel – surviving from the old Lateran Palace – because it has, out of sight, a fine ninth-century mosaic roundel of Christ supported by angels.

A devotional area behind the chapel contains a very effective sixteenth-century wooden crucifix as its focus for meditation.

Regrettably the frescoes of the Scala Santa are faded and not particularly attractive, not even Paul Brill's, but the statues by Giacometti – 'Behold the Man' and the 'Kiss of Betrayal' are good and simple.

ST MARY MAJOR'S (SANTA MARIA MAGGIORE)

To many who know Rome well, St Mary Major's is the most loved of the four patriarchal basilicas. To appreciate why, you need only sit there for half an hour early morning or late afternoon. Worship and prayer – and penance – are the business of the day here more than at any other great Roman church. The tourist instinctively moves more reverently.

History

The 'Mother and Mistress of all the Churches' is dedicated to Christ himself (though we call the Lateran St John's, it is really St Saviour's), the other two archbasilicas are dedicated to Rome's apostles Peter and Paul, so we should expect another to be dedicated to the Mother of God. The special way in which it

5. St Mary Major

is connected with Mary's great title we shall see shortly. St 'Mary Major' simply means that it is Rome's 'major' or principal church in honour of Our Lady.

This basilica was built about 350, after St Peter's and the Lateran but probably before the first St Paul's, by Pope Liberius, on the summit of the Esquiline Hill, a part of Rome that was largely gardens in ancient times. It was either rebuilt, but more probably just restored, by Pope Sixtus III, to commemorate the declaration of Mary's Divine Motherhood by the Council of Ephesus in 432. In many respects this venerable church remains unaltered, but as you approach through busy streets its antiquity is concealed behind façades, chapels, and residences added between the sixteenth and eighteenth centuries. A bird's-eye view, however, would reveal this truly ancient church nestling among them.

The façade
Exploring Rome, you are likely to come upon St Mary Major's where its apse dominates a vast piazza. It can be entered at this end, but it is better to enter by the main doors, even in fact to walk some distance down the Via Merulana first, the better to appreciate its façade, an essay in *chiaroscuro*, that is to say, contrasts in light and shade. You will recognize the same effect at other churches, but here there is a subtle and very beautiful

difference, for behind the deep arched openings of the architect Ferdinando Fuga (1743) gleams, at least in certain lights, the noble Christ of fourteenth-century mosaics signed by Filippo Rusuti. The upper part of this mosaic, in spite of its late date, is still in the Byzantine tradition, representing Christ the Ruler (Pantokrator) and Teacher, with symbols of the evangelists. The lower part tells the legendary history of the foundation of St Mary Major's in the fourth century, when a miraculous August snowfall is said to have outlined its plan. Rather amusingly, Christ and his Mother are shaking out snow from heaven. This tale, pretty as it is, is too late to be taken seriously. Although these mosaics are not normally accessible to the public, the leader of a small pilgrimage might well apply to the chief sacristan for permission to view them.

The nave

You enter the basilica. The columns of Athenian marble that flank its nave are almost certainly of the first church of 350. So are the mosaics of Old Testament history above them, perhaps the oldest Christian mosaics *in a church* in Rome. The light is usually too poor for them to be recognized, let alone appreciated. If you stand to the right-hand side of the high altar, in the afternoon, you may be able to make out the beginning of the series, as you look across the nave: (1) Abraham visited by three angels (taken to symbolize the Trinity); (2) The sacrifice of Melchizedech; (3) The separation of Abraham and Lot.

As you make your way up the church, observe the floor beneath your feet, the ceiling overhead. The floor is cosmatesque inlaid marble, but too much restored. The coffered ceiling, designed by Sangallo, is said to be gilded with the first gold from the New World, gift of Ferdinand and Isabella of Spain.

Fifth-century mosaics

Behind the altar are three distinct mosaics, two on the arches and a third in the apse. The two arches were enriched with mosaic by Pope Sixtus III (fifth century). The Council at Ephesus, to express in the clearest possible way the perfect union of divinity and humanity in Christ, defined that Mary was the Mother of *one person*, and that as he was God, as well as man, she was rightly to be called Mother of God. The subject of the mosaics on the first arch behind the altar is the childhood of Christ, but he is always escorted by angels to express his divinity. These subjects are not all easy to identify, but the top left band can be easily recognized as the Annunciation, with angels around Mary because she has just conceived Christ in her womb. Some of the details in this mosaic are not from the

Gospel, but from early legends about Christ's childhood. In the centre of the arch Sixtus signs and dedicates his work with simplicity: SIXTUS EPISCOPUS PLEBI DEI – 'Sixtus the bishop to the people of God'.

The apse mosaic

The mosaic in the apse is late thirteenth century, by the Franciscan friar Jacopo Torriti, who also did the mosaic in the apse of the Lateran. It departs from the great Roman (and Eastern) tradition of showing Christ alone as Ruler and Teacher. Here he is with Mary his Mother, crowning her and sharing his throne with her. They are surrounded by a great blue orb, representing the universe, filled with stars and sun and moon. This orb is supported by beautifully grouped and coloured angels and flanked by saints. The other elements of this mosaic are traditional: the beautiful fan-like ornament at the crown of the apse, foliage among which nestle peacocks and other birds, and at the base a River Jordan (regarded as the 'birthplace' of the Church) with fascinating details – if you have the patience to examine them. The mosaic continues between the four pointed windows with episodes from the life of Our Lady – similar to those in Santa Maria in Trastevere and equally lovely.

The arch above the apse is fifth-century work. The subjects of the mosaic are from the Apocalypse – notice, for instance, the beautiful Lamb of God, and the seven candlesticks for the seven churches to whom John sent his book of visions.

Altar and confession

The high altar – as at other major basilicas – is a papal altar, reserved to the Holy Father's use, though the privilege for others to use it is now more readily granted. The great canopy, by Ferdinando Fuga – who made a better job of the façade – has the fault of hiding the great mosaics from view. Before the altar is a crypt known as a 'confession' (see ch. 2). The martyr buried here is St Matthias, the thirteenth apostle, elected to fill the vacancy left by Judas. In addition, however, a closed reliquary above the confession altar enshrines five pieces of wood held to be the manger of the cave at Bethlehem – the Santa Culla. There is sound evidence that from the seventh century the crypt beneath the Blessed Sacrament altar was arranged as a reproduction of the cave at Bethlehem. In fact, the remains of St Jerome, who had lived as a monk beside the Cave of the Nativity at Bethlehem and been buried there, were transferred to this 'Bethlehem in Rome'. It is impossible to prove the authenticity of the Santa Culla, and it may be nothing more than the manger originally used in this first of all Christmas cribs. It is worth mentioning that the great fifth-century mosaic of the Divine Motherhood – described above – does not include the Nativity, probably because even then the Santa Culla had its shrine in St Mary Major's. The relics of the manger are exposed at Christmas, on the 25th of each month, and to large pilgrimage groups on request at the sacristy.

Blessed Sacrament Chapel

The Blessed Sacrament Chapel is a large domed chapel to the right of the high altar. It has its own 'confession' – the crib chapel I have just explained. When the gate to this confession is locked it is possible to look over the balustrade and see the cosmatesque altar with, above it, a charming fifteenth-century sculpture of the Nativity, at which St Ignatius Loyola offered his first Mass. Facing it is Bernini's statue of St Cajetan with the Infant Jesus in his arms. St Cajetan, writing to a nun at Brescia, told her that the Divine Child had in fact clambered into his arms when he was lost in prayer on this spot.

The tabernacle above the main altar of this chapel is a lofty domed structure made in 1599 – now used only for Holy Thursday. Pope Sixtus V is buried in a tomb to the right, and after him the chapel is called 'Sistine' like that in the Vatican named after Sixtus IV. The tomb on the far side is that of the Dominican Pope St Pius V, whose body is exposed here for veneration. Make a point before you leave here of looking up into the dome – the insides of domes are usually wasted on travellers, who forget to look at them.

The corresponding chapel across the nave was built in 1611 by Paul V (and so it is called Pauline), a little later than the Sistine Chapel. It enshrines an ancient icon of Our Lady – sometimes thoughtlessly attributed to St Luke, but at any rate at least a thousand years old. Its title is 'Salus Populi Romani' – the health, or well-being, of the Roman people. Above the altar is a representation in sculpture of the legendary foundation of this basilica in a wonderful snowfall. Even though we cannot admit the historicity of this, the gracious compliment it pays Mary's purity is commemorated each 15th August by a snowfall of rose petals from the dome during the festal Mass.

The baptistery of this basilica, entered from the right aisle, near the entrance, is impressive. You may ask the sacristan to admit you to several adjacent rooms with seventeenth-century frescoes and fifteenth-century sculpture. There is also an important relic of St Thomas of Canterbury which, if convenient, might be exposed for veneration by a group pilgrimage.

There is of course a Chapter of Canons who officiate at functions in St Mary Major's, but in addition Redemptorists assist here as sacristans, and a special 'college' of Dominicans hear confessions, at almost every hour of the day and in many languages.

If you should leave St Mary Major's by the door at the sanctuary end of the right aisle, notice on your right a fine tomb to a thirteenth-century Spanish cardinal, signed by its craftsman – Giovanni de Cosma, of the family after which cosmatesque work is named. This mosaic has inscriptions telling us that St Matthias is buried under the high altar and St Jerome in the Crib Chapel. Close by in the pavement is an inscription recording the resting place of the Bernini family, including the great sculptor and architect Gian Lorenzo.

ST PAUL'S OUTSIDE THE WALLS
(SAN PAOLO FUORI LE MURA)

History

St Paul's outside the Walls is in some ways a sister church to St Peter's. Peter and Paul were both apostles of Rome, both martyred here; liturgically they are always commemorated together. When Constantine raised the first St Peter's it is almost certain that he also built a church – though a very small one – over Paul's tomb in a cemetery beside the road to Ostia. About fifty years later however the Emperor Valentinian replaced this by a vast basilica which, at least basically, is the one you see today. Here is the great difference. Whereas the old St Peter's has given way to the great baroque church of the sixteenth century, St Paul's remains in appearance the same. Contemplating its vast columned nave, you can faithfully picture to yourself the first St Peter's.

Having said so much to recommend the antiquity of St Paul's, it must be admitted that the atrium (forecourt) and all the nave are a complete rebuilding after a disastrous fire of 1823. In those days the walls really did contain the city, and as this neighbourhood was malarial, most of the monks spent the hot months elsewhere. The roof was under repair, and a labourer must have left something burning, for a cowherd on the Via Ostiene gave the alarm in the small hours of the morning. More than half of the nave was gutted, and the technique of the day was not up to saving what had been spared. Rebuilding lasted over a century, but the basilica has emerged even more complete than before the catastrophe, for it has a magnificent new atrium – the original had disappeared by the fourteenth century.

Augustus Hare in his chatty *Walks in Rome* calls St Paul's 'a huge railway station'. This would not be inappropriate for so tireless a traveller as Paul. I think, however, that Hare must have approached the basilica from only one direction. If you come over the Ponte Marconi (from Trastevere) towards sun-down, the façade is afire as its gold mosaics reflect the sun. Seen from across the Piazza as you leave St Paul's Underground Station there is the impressive, half-fortified pile of the medieval abbey which serves St Paul's. In any case the pilgrim is advised to walk round to the atrium and enter by the west doors. If these, and the north doors facing the park and bus terminus, are closed, the door by the sacristy on the Viale Ostiense will very likely still be open.

The view – I nearly wrote vision – of St Paul's façade floodlit at night is one of the unforgettable memories I shall take from Rome. It always reminds me of a great ship about to be launched – another thought that might please Paul the Seafarer.

Bronze doors

The great doors of bronze and silver, completed as late as 1931, depict the careers, Roman apostolate, and martyrdoms of Peter and Paul. The doors that were here before the fire, also of bronze inlaid with silver, were the gift of Pope Gregory VII, known to history books as Hildebrand, and set up here in 1070. It was one of Pope John XXIII's last wishes that they should be restored. They are now set up on the inside of the Holy Door.

Within the nave you have, in my estimation, the most *religious* interior in Rome, architecturally. At St Mary Major's it is devotion that makes the atmosphere so impressive; here it is the sheer power of architecture. The thin light filtering through windows of fine alabaster, the forest of columns, create an atmosphere most apt for meditative prayer.

The nave

The nave is the rebuilt part of St Paul's, but much of the marble used is ancient. Around the walls are roundels representing the succession of popes (beginning to the right of the apse, and concluding at the end of the right aisle) of which only recent ones are authentic likenesses. The paintings high up, by a number of artists, depict the missionary career of St Paul.

The fifth-century mosaic

By the time you have paused and tried to appreciate the atmosphere your eyes will have become used to the half light. Note ahead the high altar with a mosaic on the great arch above, and another mosaic gleaming in the apse beyond. You should now advance up the nave, but not beyond a point where you can conveniently study the first mosaic. There is a head of Christ in a roundel, severe and wielding the staff of authority. To right and left are symbols of the evangelists, ancients of the Apocalypse, and angels with thuribles of incense. Around the edge is an inscription in white letters against dark blue – the blues and greens of this fifth-century mosaic are superb. The text mentions first the Emperor Theodosius, and then Galla Placidia, the dowager empress who completed this arch, and finally Pope Leo I – who saved Rome from Attila the Hun. Although this arch and its mosaic were saved, the immense granite columns supporting it are new – monoliths which, for size, created a modern record at the time they were quarried.

The high altar

The baldachino (canopy) of the high altar may strike you as out of keeping with the rest of the church both in proportion and in style. It is gothic – rare in Rome – and the work of one of Italy's greatest medieval architects, Arnolfo di Cambio (1285). The porphyry columns had to be renewed after the fire, but the white marble with its inlay of mosaic and elegant sculpture is intact. At the base of the little pinnacles Arnolfo has recorded his name and that of his colleague, Peter of Rome. About the same time a Roman craftsman in cosmatesque – also named Peter – worked on a new shrine for St Edward the Confessor in Westminster Abbey – the style less successful because he had to use dull English Purbeck marble. Very likely it was the same man.

This altar is over the tomb of St Paul. Bishops who come to Rome, as the Church requires them to at regular intervals, to visit the 'threshold of the apostles', kneel here in prayer. If you go down into the confession you should be within a few feet of the apostle's grave. I know of no reason to doubt this tradition. Excavation would, I think, certainly find the tomb – the relics are another matter. If you glance back down the nave you will see four fine columns of alabaster, apparently supporting nothing. They are supporting nothing. Gift of the Khedive of Egypt, they were part of an enormous baldachino which covered even Arnolfo's, but after a short time better taste prevailed and this was taken down. When these columns were erected, the excavation revealed a first- or second-century tomb of St Paul, which the architect, Vespignani, saw and sketched in his notebook. If the basilica is not crowded you may persuade an attendant to open the grille and let you put your head under the altar and look down on a huge slab crudely inscribed PAULO APOSTOLO MART. There are openings in this slab by which incense, and cloths to be taken away as relics, were passed to be closer to the apostle's body. Many authorities accept this stone as fourth century. If you are not able to see the stone itself, there is a cast in the abbey museum.

The apse mosaic
The mosaic in the apse is by thirteenth-century Venetian artists. The figure of Christ is glorious. Rather whimsically, between his feet is represented one acanthus leaf, weed of the Mediterranean World which, in the corinthian capital, has been perhaps the most common decorative motif in architecture. Peter and Paul, accompanied by Andrew and Luke, flank their Master. The odd tortoise-like figure close to Christ's foot turns out to be Pope Honorius III, whose monogram you will also find in the crown of the arch. The apostles in the lower zone carry scrolls with the text of the *Gloria in excelsis*, but the version is not quite the same as in the Mass. Beneath the figure of Christ is a throne bearing the instruments of the Passion and a gemmed Cross – an enlarged photograph reveals that in the centre of this Cross is a 'cameo' with yet another representation of the Teaching Christ.

If you stand close to the rails cutting off the apse and turn round to look up at the inside of the arch over the high altar you will see more thirteenth-century mosaics – these were brought here from the outside of the façade, after the fire, and replaced by new ones executed at the Vatican workshops.

It is an experience to assist at a Papal Mass in St Paul's. During the Liturgy of the Word the Pope sits on his throne beneath the great mosaic of Christ as Ruler and Teacher, whom he represents. After the Offertory he approaches the Papal Altar (over a sea of carpet which transforms all this area into a vast sanctuary) to represent Christ as Priest and Victim over the tomb of his apostle. This early liturgical arrangement is more easily understood here than in any other basilica.

Chapels
Only two chapels opening on to the transept need detain you. Left of the apse is the Blessed Sacrament Chapel. It contains a crucifix which St Bridget of Sweden claimed spoke to her, and a twelfth-century mosaic of Our Lady before which St Ignatius and his companions made their first vows of religion. This puzzles people who know the story of St Ignatius, but the vows he made at Montmartre, Paris, before he came to Rome, were simply a private act of dedication. To the right of the apse is the monastic choir where the Office and Mass are sung on ordinary days.

The paschal candlestick
Against the wall of the right transept is an enormous twelfth-century paschal candlestick, work of Nichola dell'Angelo and Vassalletto – the base and top may be more ancient. Its sculpture

represents Christ's Passion, Death, and Resurrection. The soldiers are curiously reminiscent of Norman Knights in the Bayeux tapestry. The transept altars are enriched with green malachite given by Tsar Nicholas II of Russia.

The cloister

Beyond is the cloister where the genius of thirteenth-century cosmatesque marble and mosaic inlay is best represented – work of the Vassalletti family. From the garden you will notice lettering in mosaic on three sides – a poem describing the place of the cloister in the life of a monk, as the scene of his meditation and study. The interesting fragments of tombs pagan and Christian were found under the floor of the destroyed basilica.

The Garter Arms

Some books tell you that the Garter Arms are to be seen in this cloister as witness to the tradition that Abbots of St Paul's were prelates of that English Order of Chivalry (and English kings in turn canons of St Paul's). You won't find them – but they are to be seen, dating from the seventeenth century and later, in a gallery upstairs, not accessible to visitors.

The relic chapel

Off the cloister is a hall with some interesting exhibits and a shop. Adjacent is a chapel where you may see, among other relics, what are believed to be the prison chains of St Paul. On his feasts they are exposed in the church for veneration. The baptistery is an interesting modern arrangement of a very ancient room. Anyone interested in Benedictine history will wish to know that Dom Guéranger, founder of the French Congregation of Solesmes and author of the famous *Liturgical Year*, made his monastic profession in the sacristy when it was in use as a temporary church after the fire.

As you leave St Paul's there are three points of interest. In the north porch (facing towards the City) the second column from the right of the inner row has around the top the dedication inscription of Pope Siricius of 386: *Siricius Episcopus tota mente devotus* – 'The Bishop Siricius (to Christ) with all his heart'. The bell tower, an odd addition of the rebuilders, reproduces a Roman tomb in the south of France. Under the covered building in the middle of the road, and also against the base of the cliff, are tombs of the very cemetery in which Paul was buried.

CHAPTER 6

The Capitol

The Cordonata – The Piazza del Campidoglio – The Statue of Marcus Aurelius – The Capitoline Fountain – Marforio – The Capitoline Museums – The Church of Ara Coeli – The Tabularium – The Church of St Joseph the Carpenter and Chapel of the Crucifix – The Mamertine Prison

THE CAPITOL – CAMPIDOGLIO

The *Campidoglio* is one of Rome's seven hills – indeed it is a crag more than a hill. It is Rome's ancient seat of government. When

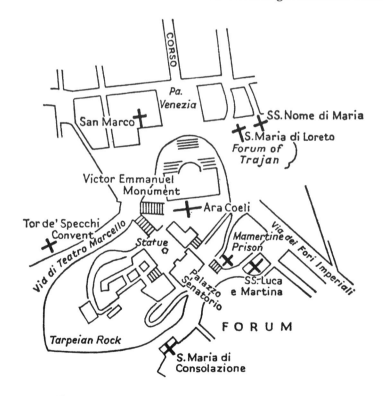

THE CAPITOLINE HILL

71

the city began in the days of Romulus, seven centuries before
Christ, it was a walled settlement on the neighbouring Palatine
Hill, but it soon estabished its principal temples, its civic centre
and its fortress on the easily defended capitol. It has not lost
this character – formal civic functions still take place at the
Palace of the Senators, Santa Maria in Ara Coeli is still Rome's
City Church, and United Italy has raised that shining white
monument that tries to outdo the past, the memorial to King
Victor Emmanuel II. The principal glory of the Capitol today is
the beautiful Piazza designed by Michelangelo for a visit of the
Emperor Charles V.

The best approach is to start from the Gesù and walk up the
Via di Ara Coeli. Tall houses that line this narrow street frame
an elegant composition of palaces, statuary, and stairs –
illuminated at night it surpasses description.

The Cordonata

The broad *Cordonata* – Italian word for a road mounting in
shallow steps, so easy to ascend – is your obvious approach to
the Piazza, which lies in a saddle between the two 'peaks' of the
hill. There are other approaches – you could take the adjacent
steps to Santa Maria di Ara Coeli and walk through the church,
and in April, when the wisteria is in bloom, I prefer the little
path under the pergola, between the two staircases.

At the foot of the Cordonata are two antique basalt lions, that
in their day have spouted wine and water. Some guide-books
tell you they are only copies, the Egyptian originals having been
put away in a museum, but these apparently are the originals,
restored in 1955. They are drinking-water fountains.

The statue to your left, after the first few steps, is to Cola di
Rienzo, a popular and handsome demagogue of the fourteenth
century, who fell from power, lost his good looks, became
paunchy and red-eyed, and was finally slaughtered at the foot
of the steps to Ara Coeli and his body hanged upside down
outside the church of San Marcello in the Corso. His statue is
here as tribute to a Roman with a sense of national pride, but I
am not sure I care to be reminded of his unpleasant career. A
little farther is the cage where two pacing, or sleeping, wolf dogs
are kept in memory of the she-wolf that forged history by
suckling the founders of Rome.

The Piazza

As you approach the top, two huge figures of the 'Heavenly
Twins', Castor and Pollux, dominate the scene and advertise
their lack of proportion. You may read the story of these popular

divinities in Chapter 7. These figures, found at the Tiber-side near the island, are by no means as handsome as their fellows on the Quirinal. They are flanked by sculptured suits of armour known as the Trophies of Marius, which formerly adorned a huge aqueduct terminal fountain of which the ugly core remains in the gardens of the Piazza Vittorio Emmanuele. This is the only terminal fountain of antiquity to survive, and it may deserve a glance if you happen to be staying at the Napoleon Hotel in that Piazza. Farther along the terrace are statues of the Emperor Constantine and his son Constantine II, and beyond them, in the form of short columns, are milestones from the Appian Way. The grouping of these relics of antiquity is part of Michelangelo's decorative scheme for the Palatine.

The statue of Marcus Aurelius

Now you can step back and take in the beauty of this unique instance of thoughtful town planning. At the end is the Palace of the Senators. The façade is Michelangelo's – sixteenth century – but the building behind is mostly fifteenth century (as you can see from the sides) and the basement is the *Tabularium*, or Records Office, of the Republican period – B.C. Before you walk forward to admire its fountain, pause at the famous equestrian statue of the philosopher emperor, Marcus Aurelius.

There is a good deal of folklore about this statue. One tale has it that the gilt, which is of course wearing away, is in fact returning – a point you may check for yourself if you return at frequent intervals, and when it is once more gilded all over the world will end. If you stand in the right position you will notice that the horse's forelock resembles an owl, and this is supposed to hoot.

This is the only equestrian bronze that has survived from ancient Rome, and the reason is that it was long taken to be a statue of the first Christian Emperor, Constantine. It stood throughout the Middle Ages before the Basilica of the Lateran, till it was brought here in 1538. Although Marcus Aurelius was a man of fine principles (read his *Meditations*), Christians were persecuted in his reign because he considered them dangerous to the security of the State – one of his victims, St Polycarp, is buried not far away in the church of St Ambrose in the Ghetto.

Note: At the time of revision this statue has been removed for restoration. In places the hollow bronze figures of horse and emperor were perforated. It is likely that Marcus Aurelius will have to find a new home under cover, and be replaced in the Piazza by a replica.

The Capitoline fountain
Below the steps of the Senatorial Palace is a fountain representing two river divinities, personifications of Nile and Tiber, and
the goddess Minerva. The last reminds me of Britannia on the
back of the old English penny. The figure to the right,
representing the Nile, was once the Tigris, and rested on a tiger,
but when it was made part of this group the tiger was turned
into Romulus and Remus being suckled by the she-wolf.

Marforio
There is another fountain up here, very famous too, the
'Marforio', a river god in the cortile of the palace on the left.
You can see it through the gate when it is open. By floodlight
at night it expresses the peculiar appeal of mingled water and
light in a very powerful and impressive way. This barbaric old
gentleman used to be in the 'Forum Martis', of which his name
is a corruption.

Return to the top of the stairs, and take the road to the left.
It leads in a few yards to a terrace with charming views over
renaissance Rome – in the foreground the medieval convent of
St Frances of Rome and the Theatre of Marcellus, beyond the
square-domed synagogue, the statue of Garibaldi clear on the
skyline of the Janiculum, and to the right a lovely cluster of
domes with St Peter's in the distance. Follow the road round,
past the remains of the Temple of Jove (in an excavation at the
left of the roadside), and an arch leads to a flight of steps by
which you descend once more to the Piazza.

I think it is a good idea to make your visit to the Capitoline
museums separately, but I shall give you now an idea of what
they contain.

The Capitoline Museums
Both *palazzi* either side the Piazza constitute the Capitoline
Museums – that on the right as you stand with your back to the
steps is far more extensive and takes longer to see.

To take first the Palazzo Nuovo, to the left. Note, as you enter
its courtyard, that you look up on the mouldering walls of Ara
Coeli. The more interesting rooms are upstairs. The sarcophagus at the top of the staircase (second century A.D.) represents
Amazons in battle – they were a legendary race of warlike
women.

Off the main corridor is a room in which the famous
Capitoline Venus, found near the Via Nazionale, is exhibited all
on her own. She is a Roman copy of a Greek original.

Opening off the end of the corridor is the room with busts of Roman Emperors, which will probably interest everyone. On the right, with their garments sculptured in alabaster and red marble, are Septimius Severus – whose great arch you see nearby in the Forum – and Caracalla, builder of the famous Baths where you may be going to see the opera. In the centre Helena appears to be reclining on a *chaise longue*, though she is really sitting on a straight stone seat. This is St Helena who recovered the Holy Cross, and whose palace you are in when you visit Santa Croce. Opposite her on a column is the bust of the finely featured Augustus, and last on the left the friendly bearded head of Verus.

In other rooms the most important exhibits are the Dying Gaul – not really a gladiator but a victim of Greek warfare – and the famous but ugly faun; he is meant to be ugly. A room near the stairs is called the Sala delle Colombe from a mosaic of doves found at Hadrian's Villa. As you descend the staircase you are faced by a magnificent statue of Mars in armour.

Across the Piazza you enter first the Cortile (courtyard) of the Palazzo dei Conservatori. On the far side a seated figure represents Rome, flanked by dark grey marble figures of trousered and dejected captive barbarian kings. These date from the third century A.D.

The first part of your visit to this museum will be through the rooms of the palace; then you will go through galleries of more recent construction. In the palace itself I would recommend you to glance at floors, doors, and ceilings – in several cases they are interesting, but they are so easily missed.

On the staircase are some splendid sculptures representing the Emperor Marcus Aurelius – whose bronze figure you saw outside – offering sacrifice before the Temple of Jupiter (Jove) on this hill. Note the temple, because later you will see what little remains of it.

Paintings in the first few rooms represent legends and history of Rome. In further rooms are two famous statues. The Boy with a Thorn is Greek, of the first century B.C. You can revolve this statue on its base. The Capitoline Wolf is an Etruscan sculpture in bronze of about the fifth century B.C.; the twins Romulus and Remus were added in 1509, by Antonio Pollaiuolo, to transform it into a symbol of Rome. In the former chapel you will find a pleasant renaissance Madonna between angels by Antonio da Viterbo, late fifteenth century. This room has an ancient mosaic from the site of the present Via Nazionale. The next room has an antique dog very nicely sculptured in a rare green marble. Here too is a portrait bust of Michelangelo.

The recent galleries contain sculpture of pagan antiquity and also some good Christian sarcophagi (stone coffins). Eventually you reach rooms where you meet the rough tufa walls of the great temple of Jove on the Capitol, religious centre of ancient Rome. They date from 509 B.C. You will be able to come out from ground level into a garden, sometimes locked, and from the first floor onto a terrace with excellent views over renaissance Rome. If the garden is locked, you will still be able to see from the terrace, in the middle of the shrubbery, a sculptured lion tearing the vitals out of a horse. This was found, perhaps

6. The Victor Emmanuel Monument and the Church of Ara Coeli seen from the Capitol

as early as Charlemagne's time (eighth century), lying in the bed of the Almo stream near Rome, and in the Middle Ages was used as a sort of pillory in the market at the foot of the Capitol – if public officials offended they had to sit astride it with hands tied behind their back. Michelangelo had it brought up the hill, but it reached its present position only in 1903.

There are also collections of porcelain in this museum, and an art gallery in which I would point out especially Caravaggio's John the Baptist – I am sure his faun-like appearance will shock you – and a Baptism of Christ by Titian. The burial and glory of St Petronilla is one of the original canvases from St Peter's, now replaced there by a copy in mosaic.

The Palace of the Senators – the one at the back of the Piazza with the Fountain of Rome and the Rivers against its façade – can be visited on application, at the museum in the 'Palazzo Nuovo'.

Another place that I think can well be the object of a separate visit is the church of St Mary of Ara Coeli, but I shall describe it now, because it can be entered by a flight of steps from the Piazza.

If you are following this chapter you will enter the church by a side door, but I recommend you to walk straight down the nave to the main doors. There is, by the way, a thirteenth-century mosaic of the Madonna over that side entrance, on the outside.

Ara Coeli

Ara Coeli is the City church of Rome. 'Ara' means altar, and the title originates from a tradition that an oracle, before the Nativity, foretold to the emperor the birth of a Son of God, to whose honour he raised an altar here on the Capitol – *Ara coeli*, altar of heaven. It is fairly certain that the site was occupied by an altar to Juno, Jupiter's female counterpart. One of her favours was to warn Romans in time of danger – for instance, her sacred geese are supposed to have cackled when the Gauls tried to attack the citadel by night – so to her name was added the title 'Moneta' – 'Juno who warns'. As in due course Roman currency was minted in the precincts of her temple it came to be called 'moneta', from which comes our word 'money'.

Leaving legend aside, there were Greek monks here in the sixth century, later replaced by Benedictines, and in 1250 Franciscans were installed. They rebuilt the church – from the Piazza del Campidoglio you will notice it has gothic windows – but retained the ancient columns. They differ in size and type of marble, as is so common, but here even the bases differ

considerably, and some are without bases, to accommodate
their varied length. Inscribed on the third column on the left
side is 'A CUBICULO AUGUSTORUM', which points to a
tradition that this, and maybe others, came from the palace of
the Caesars.

I am afraid I always register the Ara Coeli as an untidy church,
which understandably comes into its own when it is filled with
Roman crowds, as at Christmas time. They flock here to
venerate the crib and to preen themselves while their children
– little girls as well as boys – preach 'sermons'.

The pavement is not interesting, except for medieval tombs
that interrupt it, but the ceiling is richly coffered, with a
Madonna in the centre, and commemorates the victory of
Lepanto in 1571, credited with having saved Christendom from
Turkish domination – perhaps you remember Belloc's poem
about Don John of Austria. The first chapel on the right, closed
with plate glass, is painted with the life of St Bernardine of Siena
by Pinturicchio, and also has a good cosmatesque floor. The
fourth chapel, very recently restored, has a venerated crucifix
and another cosmatesque floor, but this one of unusual design.
In this chapel the crowds of Rome witnessed an ecstasy of their
beloved St Frances, raised off the floor while praying by the
body of her sister-in-law.

Most of the interest lies in the transepts. To the left a little
octagonal temple, eighteenth century, enshrines in an urn the
relics of St Helena. If you peer through a grille at the foot of this
monument you will see some early Christian sculpture believed
to cover the original 'ara coeli'. The thirteenth-century tomb
near this shrine, of Cardinal Acquasparta, has a Madonna in
mosaic attributed to Pietro Cavallini. The corresponding transept across the church has more cosmatesque work – there are
handsome pulpits in this style too – and also the resting place
of St Francis's companion, Fra Juniper, known to everyone who
reads the *Fioretti*.

At Christmas the venerated Santissimo Bambino – most holy
Infant Jesus – is placed in the crib – and the municipality
provides him with a uniformed guard, but at other times you
must ask to see this curious little statue, beloved of Romans, in
the sacristy. It has never struck me as beautiful. The tradition is
that any sick person may ask for it to be brought to his bedside.
The princely Torlonia family used to provide a coach and
attendants for these journeys.

If you leave the church by the main doors you will enjoy a
splendid view, especially of the Gesù and San Marco to the
right. At Christmas the city is blessed with the Bambino from

these steps, and shepherds from the hills play their pipes while they collect alms from an endless stream of pilgrims.

The Tabularium

Supposing you did not go to Ara Coeli, you could now take the road to the left of the Palace of the Senators. Stand back – towards those steps that climb up to Ara Coeli – and you will see easily that Michelangelo only added a façade to a building clearly medieval. The tower on this side was probably built by Pope Martin V (1417–1431). Note the small reproduction of the famous 'Capitoline Wolf'. A few steps down there is a gate on the right by which you may enter the basement of the Palace of the Senators – to find yourself high above the Forum below. This is a very good spot from which to view the Forum, because there are on the wall numbered pictures of the Forum as it is now, and as it was in the early fourth century. The gallery in which you stand is the Tabularium, or Records Office of ancient Rome. Like most Republican buildings it is of rough tufa rock quarried in huge blocks. Some of these appear very worn. This is because the Tabularium was used as a salt store in the Middle Ages; salt corrodes the stone.

Church of St Joseph the Carpenter and Chapel of the Crucifix

As you leave, you may take a flight of steps beside the Church of San Giuseppe il Falegname – St Joseph the Carpenter, which is over the Chapel of the Crucifix – also known as San Pietro in Carcere, St Peter in prison, and beneath them both is the famous Mamertine Prison. The top church, baroque in style and by Jacopo della Porta (early sixteenth century), is open on Sundays and deserves a visit if you are passing. It has a beautiful gilt coffered ceiling and a carving of the Nativity. Opening off the church to the right is the Carpenters' guild chapel, rich with frescoes of the life of St Joseph. They need restoring. There is a charming baroque altar, a gay little lectern, and two quaint gilded groups of statuary representing the Espousals of Mary and Joseph and the Flight into Egypt. In the middle church is venerated one of those late medieval crucifixes so numerous in Rome. The Mamertine Prison will be part of your pilgrimage in the steps of St Peter and Paul.

The Mamertine Prison

Since the seventh century B.C. this has been the State prison for condemned criminals, the upper dungeon, made of great blocks of tufa, said to date from 640 B.C., the lower, excavated in the rock, was made about sixty years later. The stairs by which you enter are not one of the original amenities – there is a hole in the vault by which the prisoners were lowered. There are other galleries in the rock hereabouts, probably quarries originally, later adapted as cells.

The tradition of the imprisonment of the apostles here cannot be called improbable, but neither can it be shown to be older than the fifth century, at most. The 'Acts' of martyrs also assign it as the prison of SS. Hippolytus, Eusebius, and Marcellus. Down there you will see a long, perhaps ambitious, list of all its famous guests, including Vercingetorix, who defied Julius Caesar in Gaul, and Simon Bar Jioras, defender of Jerusalem when Titus captured the city and destroyed the Temple – fulfilling the prophecy of Christ – in A.D. 70.

CHAPTER 7

The Forum and Palatine and their Churches

*The Forum – Arch of Titus – The Basilica of Maxentius –
The Memorial to Romulus – Temple of Antoninus and
Faustina – The Aemilian Basilica – The Senate House – The
'Niger Lapis' – Arch of Septimius Severus – Temple of
Saturn – The Julian Basilica – The Column of Phocas –
Temple of Julius Caesar – Temple of Castor and Pollux –
The Well of Juturna – Santa Maria Antiqua – Temple of
Vesta – The Palace of Domitian – 'House of Livia' – Sixth-
century-B.C. Village – Palace of the Caesars – Stadium –
The Circo Massimo – Museum – Churches nearby –San'
Luca e Martina – San' Cosma e Damiano – The Neapolitan
Crib – San Lorenzo in Miranda – Santa Maria Nuova, also
known as Santa Francesca Romana – Temples of Venus and
Rome – St Sebastian's – San Bonaventura – (for other
churches of the Forum and Palatine see Chapter 9).*

I think the pilgrim in a hurry might well content himself with
the general panorama of the Forum from the terraces of the
Capitol. On the other hand, even if you are not really keen on
ruins and archaeology, the Palatine is a most pleasant place to
relax, and perhaps picnic, on a fine day; a visit would make an
agreeable break in your exhausting holiday.

The Forum
The Forum is ancient Rome's civic and religious centre, a
triumphal way to the even more important temples of the
Capitol. The Palatine is the adjacent hill on which are the scanty
remains of imperial palaces. Tickets to the Forum admit to the
Palatine as well, in fact they are in the same enclosure, but some
visitors fail to realize this or to locate the paths leading up there,
and so miss half their money's worth. One path or other may
at times be closed for construction work.

There are two public entrances usually open, one between the
Victor Emmanuel Monument and the Colosseum, but nearer the
former, and the other between the Colosseum and the Circo
Massimo Metropolitana (Underground) station. The latter
admits direct to the Palatine. This account will suppose that you

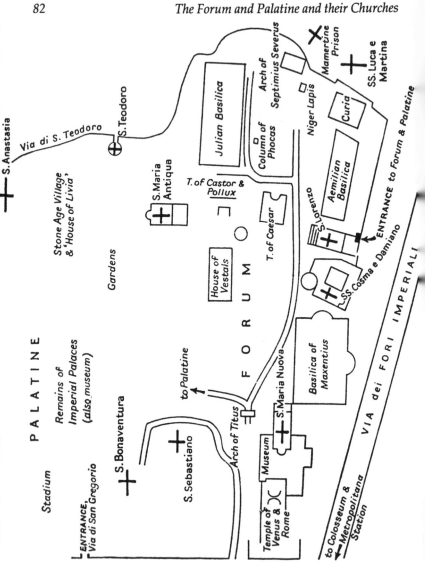

enter by the former, which is more convenient for most people. I suggest that, as soon as you reach the main path, the ancient Via Sacra, a few steps down from the ticket office, you turn left and follow it as far as the Arch of Titus at the Colosseum end. Standing under the Arch and looking back towards the Capitol, you have before you the entire vista of this proud centre of ancient Rome with, as its climax, the hill that was the seat of its gods. Through this arch and along the Via Sacra emperors returned in triumph from the campaigns by which they subdued a barbarian world.

The Arch of Titus

The Arch of Titus and the Colosseum are closely related, for that great sports drome was built for the young emperor by Jewish captives whom he brought back from the destruction of Jerusalem in A.D. 70 – a destruction fulfilling Our Lord's prophecy that the Temple would be laid waste till not a stone remained upon a stone. On the inside of the arch is depicted the victory procession carrying the last treasures of the Temple, notably – and this is easy to recognize – the great Seven Branched Candlestick, the most popular Jewish token, as much today as then, of God's presence among the chosen people.

The Basilica of Maxentius

To the left, as you stand with your back to the Arch of Titus, is a path climbing to the Farnese Gardens and the heights of the Palatine. For the moment retrace your steps along the Via Sacra. The immense arches and vaulting on your right are all that remains of the last great edifice to grace the civic centre of ancient Rome, the Basilica of Maxentius. This emperor was the rival overthrown by Constantine – the victory that led to the Peace of the Church. In this case the word 'basilica' has no ecclesiastical significance at all – it has its original meaning, a royal hall. The importance of the great building – for what remains is only a part – is the success in carrying an arched vault over a span of about seventy-five feet.

The Memorial to Romulus

Next you will notice a small round building which is in fact part of the church of Saints Cosmas and Damian. This too was built by Maxentius as a memorial to his son Romulus, and it has the distinction not only of retaining one of the few ancient bronze doors to survive in Rome, but a lock in which the key still turns. Many people enter this building without knowing it when they visit the famous Neapolitan crib – approached through the cloisters of the church.

Temple of Antoninus and Faustina

As you arrive back at the point where you entered the Via Sacra the great façade of the Temple of Antoninus and Faustina soars above you – you will see it better when you are farther away. It

helps you to appreciate the function of pagan temples. They
were far more monumental than useful – that is, they were not
intended to accommodate a crowd of worshippers. The actual
room or *cella* of the temple, with the statues of its gods, was
quite small. Sacrifice was offered either inside or on the steps,
and if it were a public occasion the people would look on from
a distance. Climb the steps and you will find *graffiti* –
inscriptions or drawings scratched in stone – on the columns.
Antoninus Pius was a second-century emperor. The temple was
built to his 'divinized' wife – that is, she was raised to the rank
of a goddess by the Roman senate, and as her husband
happened to die before it was completed he was divinized too
and the temple dedicated to them both. Notice the rough stone
exposed along the side of the building – the original marble
covering is now a part of St Peter's. The temple itself is now the
church of the Apothecaries' Guild of Rome, and is called San
Lorenzo in Miranda. The entrance is outside the Forum, but it
is not usually open to the public.

The Aemilian Basilica

To the right after the temple appears to be an area of barren
ruins, stumps of columns and broken walls. This is the Aemilian
Basilica, a money exchange dating, in its present form, from the
early first century. It was damaged by fire in the sack of Rome
by Alaric in 410, and of the coins thrown on the floor as
merchants escaped many can be seen fused into the marble
pavement.

The Senate House

Beyond the Aemilian Basilica rises the great Senate House
(Curia), so well preserved largely because in the sixth century
it was turned into the church of St Adrian. The present bronze
doors are only copies of the originals, which are now at the
Lateran. This was the Parliament House, or Council Hall, of
Rome, first built by Julius Caesar but brought to its present form
by a restoration under Diocletian – end of the third century.
Don't throw a knowledgeable guess and suppose that Caesar
was murdered here, because apparently at that time another
building, near the present Largo Argentina, was being used for
meetings of the Senate. Of course the exterior was once much
richer than it is now. The most perfectly preserved feature is the
inlaid marble floor – it was from remains such as these that the
Cosmati inherited their craft. The two stone balustrades exhibited inside do not really belong here. The sculptures of the one
on the left represent a cancellation of debts – you can see the

tablets on which debts were registered being brought to the emperor for destruction, that on the right the institution of new child welfare laws – a mother with her children is represented thanking the emperor, but it is not easy to see this.

The 'Niger Lapis' (Black Stone)

Directly in front of the Senate House you will notice some stairs leading underground. The stone covering the area is called the Niger Lapis, or Black Stone – although it may not strike you as particularly black – it would be if polished. Down there you will see a conical stone with an inscription written vertically that no one has been able to read. So the real significance of this monument remains a mystery, but two guesses made by scholars of Roman history are that it is either the tomb of Romulus, the city's founder, or of the shepherd Faustulus who found the abandoned twins being suckled by the she-wolf.

If you now stand facing the great arch of Septimius Severus, you will notice on the left a small carved and inscribed monument. On one side is an interesting sculpture representing animals being led to sacrifice – all dressed up for the occasion. This dates from about 303 A.D.

The Arch of Septimius Severus

The Arch of Septimius Severus dates from 203 A.D. and commemorates a victorious campaign in the East, and as you pass through you will be able to recognize that much of its sculpture represents prisoners in chains. What appear to be angels over the arch are conventional Roman figures of victory.

Temple of Saturn

When you have passed through the arch I suggest you turn left towards the Temple of Saturn; you can hardly miss it. At this point you can survey the remains of the Tabularium – Record Office – on the Capitol, from which, conversely, you can enjoy the best view of the Forum. This temple of Saturn is believed to be the oldest in the Forum, but the great columns are part of a fourth-century A.D. restoration. Here, in the middle of December, was held a popular festival called the Saturnalia, at which everyone exchanged gifts – maybe the origin of Christmas presents!

The Julian Basilica

You should now stand with your back to the Capitol. On your right are extensive remains of another vast basilica first built by Julius Caesar, and so called the Julian basilica. It was a law court for civil cases, and while waiting to be called the public idled away their time playing games on the pavement. As you walk along you will be able to find several of these 'gaming boards' cut in the stone for games of dice – usually in the form of circles divided into eight segments.

The Column of Phocas

Now if you pause and look back towards the Arch of Septimius Severus, the Senate House, and the church of San' Luca e Martina, you will notice the bases of several 'honorary columns' – that is, columns that served a purpose similar to our Nelson's Column. One complete column still standing was raised here in Christian times – although it was almost certainly just pinched from some abandoned monument – to the Emperor Phocas, as a mark of appreciation for, among other things, his having handed over the Pantheon for Christian worship.

Temple of Julius Caesar

Before you draw level once more with the Temple of Antoninus and Faustina you will – with a bit of luck – find yourself standing before all that remains of the Temple of Julius Caesar. There is hardly anything to see, but the rough core of the altar is believed to mark the spot where his body was burned – after that impassioned speech by Mark Antony familiar to us in Shakespeare's famous version.

Temple of Castor and Pollux

If you have lost yourself at this point, look around for three noble corinthian columns standing together; they can hardly be missed. These are the surviving fragments of the Temple to Castor and Pollux, the heavenly twins whose figures still adorn the Capitol and the Quirinal. Immediately opposite is a little pool at the corner of which there was, till very recently, an altar to these young gods. Here, however, is the story that accounts for their popularity.

The Well of Juturna

In 499 B.C., when the dynasty of the tyrannous Tarquin kings had been overthrown, the news of the battle was brought to Rome by two young horsemen who appeared in the Forum, watering their horses at this spring. Then they disappeared. Taken to be the sons of Jupiter, the site was consecrated to them and a great temple raised. Behind the sacred pool is the Waterworks Office, with boats and fishes in mosaic, and an inscription 'to the genius of the water administration', and a few paces beyond it a well sacred to Juturna, goddess of springs.

Santa Maria Antiqua

If you continue along this path you will find the wonderful basilica of Santa Maria Antiqua, constructed in what is thought to have been a monumental approach to the imperial palaces on the hill above. Were it fully restored, it would look much the same as other ancient Roman churches, though exceptionally rich in early paintings. Although its foundation as a church can be placed about the end of the fifth century, these paintings, which you will find its most interesting feature, date from the seventh and eighth centuries. The most impressive are those at the end of the left aisle – a beautiful Crucifixion, of which I think one may fairly say that it is a very rare type. The figure of Christ is powerful, peaceful, serene, robed in a long blue garment – with the Roman bands of rank; either side are Mary and John, and the smaller figure of the centurion who pierced Christ's side. The other paintings are so damaged that you may find them a little tedious to study in detail.

In the left aisle is a very fine Christian sarcophagus sculptured with the story of Jonas – because Jesus himself had quoted that old Testament chronicle as symbolic of resurrection.

Temple of Vesta

You should now walk back past the Temple of Castor and Pollux and you will easily recognize the fragment of the round Temple of Vesta. As you approach you will see that a great deal of it is reconstruction, necessary in order to unite sufficient of its fragmentary remains so that you can have an idea of its original appearance. Later, on the Palatine, you will see traces of the round huts in which the early Romans lived – huts where, as in primitive civilizations still, the fire in the central hearth was never allowed to go out. The cult of Vesta was precisely the cult of the home,

7. Fishpond in the house of the Vestals with a view towards the Capitol

represented by a temple that evoked the pattern of the primitive log hut, and where the foremost duty of the Vestal Virgins was to tend the sacred fire – literally, to keep the home fires burning. Between the temple and the foot of the Palatine Hill is the convent of the Virgins built around a courtyard. The only residents today are goldfish. When you see such a large house, you will be surprised to hear the virgins numbered only six. Statues around the court are memorials to the Chief Vestals, dating from the third century and later.

The Palace of Domitian
From the courtyard of the Vestals there was an ancient road that passed through the basement of the imperial residence begun by Domitian, 81-96 A.D. It may be reopened. Above ground the palace has disappeared. Its place is taken by the delightful Farnese Gardens, and if antiquity has begun to bore you a little I hope you will make the most of them. On a warm day this is one of the coolest retreats in Rome.

'House of Livia'
You will probably have had to return to the Arch of Titus to take the uphill path through the gardens to the so-called Casa di Livia, and the stone age village of Romulus and Remus – also for good measure vestiges of a Temple of Cybele, the Earth Mother. The 'House of Livia' is named after the wife of Caesar Augustus, but this is little more than a guess. It has interesting painted rooms. You may only visit accompanied by an attendant, who is usually somewhere about. Very near the house is a cistern providing a water supply for the primitive settlement. It dates from the sixth century B.C., if not earlier. Note the little well head beside it – the water filtered into this well from the cistern through porous materials, so even that primitive age enjoyed its domestic refinements. Under the temporary roofing nearby are remains of the village which can be dated archaeologically to the seventh or eight century B.C., the same that legend assigns for the foundation of Rome. The excavations are not easy to follow, but you can make out small holes in the rock, roughly in circular patterns: these took the upright timbers of the small round dwellings.

Palace of the Caesars
Walking across the summit of the Palatine to the farther end you will pass across large fragmentary floors with here and there well preserved patterns of inlaid marble. You will find little

more than this to indicate the sites of the imperial palace, although with a detailed plan it is possible to distinguish audience chambers, great courtyard, banqueting hall and so forth. The best viewpoint giving you the impression of a palatial building is from the far side of the Circo Massimo, on the slopes of the Aventine Hill – and that especially at night, when it is floodlit.

Below these ruins a second-century-B.C. residence known as the 'House of the Griffins' has been excavated, as well as some other buildings. There is a wealth of rich decoration buried underground here, but it has not been accessible to the public for several years.

Stadium

From these ruins of the imperial palace you look across to the picturesque little monastery of San Bonaventura, which might be miles away in the countryside, instead of in the very heart of Rome. If you walk in that direction you will suddenly find yourself looking down into a large stadium, the exact use of which is uncertain – it was probably for races and games reserved to the imperial household. Views over the Coelian hill and its churches of St Gregory and SS. John and Paul are splendid – morning photography indicated.

The Circo Massimo

It is possible to descend the hill by steps and paths at this point (and also to leave by the exit giving on to the Via di San Gregorio, and visit either the Colosseum or the churches on the Coelian) or, having reached the foot of the hill, you may turn right to encircle the Palatine on the side of the Circo Massimo, over which you will have a good view. This was Rome's largest sports stadium, founded by the Tarquin kings over five centuries before Christ. Obelisks now in the Piazza del Popolo and before St John Lateran formerly stood here. Today it is no more than an open space serving little other purpose than to offset the ruins of the Palatine, which look grand when floodlit and viewed after dark from the far side of the Circus.

This part of the Palatine is seldom visited and makes a very pleasant retreat. You will find a few fairly well preserved rooms here, with fragments of mosaic floor. The original purpose of these rooms is uncertain, but a variety of *graffiti* were found scratched on the walls, among them a crucified figure with a donkey's head, believed to be a parody of someone's confession of Christian faith.

Museum

There is a Forum museum in part of the buildings dependent on the Church of Santa Francesca Romana – worth a visit if you find it open.

Churches nearby

There are a surprising number of churches actually in the area of the Forum and Palatine, though not – with the exception of Santa Maria Antiqua, which is no longer used for worship – within the enclosure you pay to enter. Some are described in another chapter simply because they are more easily approached from the routes described there, but I shall list them all now:

In the Forum:	Santa Maria Antiqua.
Near the entrance to the Forum:	San' Luca e Martina.
	San Lorenzo in Miranda (not open to public).
	San' Cosma e Damiano.
Near the Colosseum:	Santa Maria Nuova, also known as Santa Francesca Romana.
	San Bonaventura.
	San Sebastiano.
At the foot of the Palatine:	Sant' Anastasia.
(described in Chapter 9)	San Teodoro.

San' Luca e Martina

San' Luca e Martina is just beyond the Senate House and right opposite the Mamertine Prison, in fact you must have been aware of it frequently whilst walking about the Forum – it is best seen from there and makes a good architectural photograph. It is open only on Sunday mornings. The architect, Pietro da Cortona, has designed a domed cruciform church with gentle curves – but without that freedom of line that really characterized baroque. There is the church itself dedicated to St Luke the Evangelist, but in his traditional quality of artist, for it was built for the Accademia di San Luca. Over the high altar there is a painting of St Luke at his easel. The altar to the right is dedicated to another artist saint, the Eastern monk Lazarus, an eighth-century victim of the Iconoclast persecution (directed against the veneration of sacred pictures) – his right hand was burned with hot irons. The predominant colour of this church is white, rare in a city of renaissance frescoes and baroque decoration.

You will need to ask the sacristan if you wish to visit the crypt – I find it even more interesting than the church. You enter a long corridor, in which you will find an Entombment of Christ sculptured by Alessandro Algardi, and a monument to the architect, Pietro da Cortona. In the main chapel is an altar over the relics of St Martina, third-century Roman martyr and deaconess of a church on this site. This too is by Pietro da Cortona and assistants. The bronze work alone is beautiful, but the delicate tones of marble raise it to a very high degree of excellence. In sculptured alabaster and lapis lazuli is represented St Martina praying before the Madonna. A throne is preserved in this crypt in which the pope sat to distribute the candles at the beginning of the Purification procession, in the early days of the Church.

Church of SS. Cosmas and Damian

The most important of all these churches – and I do urge every pilgrim not to miss it – is SS. Cosmas and Damian, only a stone's throw from the turnstile to the Forum in the Via dei Fori Imperiali, the one most commonly used. If I list this church as a 'must' it is for the sake of its great sixth-century mosaic.

Go in and sit down, wait for its details to emerge from the gloom of the apse, and meditate on it meanwhile. Here is something so truly *religious* art that you cannot just look at it and say that you have seen it. It is meant to lift up your heart, and if you give it a chance it will.

Unlike most earlier mosaics, and many later ones, it does not represent Christ enthroned, but Christ of the Second Coming – in all his glory, on the clouds of heaven. Here is no Byzantine figure frozen into courtly immobility in garments stiff with gems, but a truly Roman figure in robes of gold, advancing towards you on radiant clouds. When the floor of this church was lower this 'Coming' of Christ was even more impressive. Later we shall see some eighth-century attempts at reproducing this theme; they succeed in being naively charming, but completely lack this splendour. Either side are the patrons of this church, the physicians and martyrs Cosmas and Damian, whose relics are in the crypt. Peter and Paul stand beside them, arms round their shoulders.

The high altar is a very harmonious example of baroque art (1638), enshrining yet another of Rome's many ancient Byzantine Madonnas. These paintings are not always superficially pleasing – very seldom are the faces pretty, but there is often a wonderful tenderness of gesture. Here you will see it in the delicately clasped hands of Mary and Jesus. To appreciate the

Madonna properly you should buy a reproduction – costing a few pence – from the ticket office to the permanent crib, at the corner of the cloister where you enter the church.

The church of SS. Cosmas and Damian and its circular narthex (now the exhibition hall for the Neapolitan crib) are adapted buildings of the Forum – the origin of the church itself is uncertain, though you will notice, on your way in, massive blocks of very ancient masonry; the rotunda is a fourth-century monument to Romulus, son of the Emperor Maxentius. You will have seen its more interesting exterior from the Forum.

The Neapolitan Crib

The seventeenth-century Neapolitan crib installed here from a private collection in 1950 is completely fascinating. It excels any other crib in size and comprehensiveness and, if you are not going to be here at Christmas, gives you a first-class idea of all the ingredients that can go into an Italian crib – the Nativity there for sure, but all the details showing you every possible facet of Italian life: hill towns and country farms, market stalls and taverns with dancing girls – equally interesting interiors if you think to look through the windows. The figures are of carved wood or terracotta, the buildings of real brick or stone and mortar. At the time of revising this text the Crib has been closed as a consequence of the theft of some of its figures.

This church is served by Friars of the Regular Third Order of St Francis.

San Lorenzo in Miranda

The church even nearer the entrance to the Forum, San Lorenzo in Miranda, is not open to the public. It was – and is – the church

8. *San Lorenzo in Miranda*

of the Apothecaries' Guild, and its special interest, historically, is that it is the adapted and rebuilt *cella* of the Temple of Antoninus and Faustina – an emperor and his wife exalted to divine rank – with its original approach in the Forum.

To visit the church of Santa Maria Nuova, also known as Santa Francesca Romana, you walk towards the Colosseum and take either steps to the right or, further on, a road. As you climb that road the massive ruins ahead are the Basilica of Maxentius.

Santa Maria Nuova, also known as Santa Francesca Romana

The correct title, Santa Maria Nuova – New St Mary's – explains the origin. It was built in the tenth century when St Mary's in the Forum, now rediscovered and named Santa Maria Antiqua, had fallen into disuse. Since the fourteenth century it has been an abbey of the Olivetan Benedictines who, like the Prinknash community in England, wear white.

Some years later a married Roman lady devoted herself to a life of prayer and charity as an oblate (similar to a tertiary) of this monastery, and established a community of ladies in a property near the Palatine known as Tor de' Specchi (Tower of Mirrors). Her relics, discovered in 1638, lie here in a crypt which, however, dates in its present form from 1858. Not everyone will like the Italian custom of exposing the skeleton, vested in the habit of her Oblate Sisters. Notice that she holds in her hands a prayer book open at the seventy-second psalm. One day the lady, Frances, was saying the Office of Our Lady when her husband sent for her four times in succession, so that she never managed to complete this one verse. Finally, when she got back to her prayers, she found inscribed in letters of gold:

> *Thou hast taken me by my right hand*
> *and by thy will thou hast conducted me*
> *and with glory thou hast received me.*

I shall never forget that anecdote, because the first time I visited Santa Maria Nuova I was in the crypt when a service commenced in the sanctuary through which I would have to pass to leave the church. I stayed put for half an hour with nothing to do but read all the leaflets and inscriptions. To visit the crypt you ascend the steps to the sanctuary and take a staircase at the extreme right.

In the sanctuary you should look up to study at close quarters its most beautiful twelfth-century mosaic of Our Lady with the Divine Child between Saints James, John, Peter and Andrew.

Its most delicate features are the fanlike ornament above the richly enthroned Madonna and the underside of the arch. To the right is a monument to Pope Gregory XI, representing one of the most significant events in the history of the Church. Throughout the greater part of the fourteenth century the popes – who of course rule the Church by virtue of their office as bishops of Rome and so successors of Peter – had deserted their charge to live at Avignon in France. In 1377, about two centuries before this sculpture was made by Paolo Olivieri, St Catherine of Siena persuaded Gregory to end the scandal and return to Rome. You can make her out, close by the Pope, as he is welcomed back to this eternal city.

Over the high altar is the historic icon of Our Lady dating from the sixth or seventh century. It had been overpainted and what was visible was rightly judged to be medieval, till the ancient icon was discovered preserved beneath a later coat of paint. This offers an explanation of the venerable traditions that so often accompany paintings of Our Lady that are known to be, stylistically, unreliable. There is probably almost always some truth in the tradition, but the ancient painting will have been overpainted, or perhaps even replaced. On the left of the sanctuary is a beautiful holy oil aumbry in the renaissance style of the fifteenth century. When you have returned to the nave, standing by the Confession, you can look up to a painting, on the right, of St Andrew welcoming his cross of martyrdom. Then you may look overhead at the beautiful seventeenth-century coffered ceiling painted in gold, red, green, and two tones of blue. Late evening instrumental concerts are sometimes given in this church.

Temples of Venus and Rome

If you walk round to the back of Santa Maria Nuova you will find yourself among the colonnades of the double temples of Venus and Rome, designed by the Emperor Hadrian himself, although he made some mistakes and had to be corrected by a professional architect. If you are (or have become by now) fairly knowledgeable about architecture you will note that the two temples were designed 'end on', and you can recognize where their apses, which survive, just touch. There are excellent views of the Colosseum from these ruins.

There is a flight of steps leading from the level of the temple down to a gate giving on to the Forum near the Arch of Titus (an entrance seldom in use). If you miss these steps you can go round the long way. When you reach the Forum gates a lane appears on the left that will lead you uphill to the churches of St Sebastian and St Bonaventure.

St Sebastian's

St Sebastian's is approached through a gate on the left. It is believed to mark the site of martyrdom of this soldier saint so beloved of both medieval and renaissance artists. The church was rebuilt in 1624, but the apse was preserved with impressive tenth-century paintings of Christ between Saints Lawrence and Stephen, the Deacons, and Sebastian and Zoticus; below them Our Lady flanked by angels.

San Bonaventura

By now you will be feeling you have left Rome to enjoy a change of air in the country. The lane turns a corner and a Way of the Cross, instituted here by that eighteenth-century Franciscan apostle of Rome, St Leonard of Port Maurice, leads up to a picturesque little friary founded in 1625.

It would be foolish to present this church as one of great interest, but you may also visit some rooms in the monastery, and I think you will find it a half-hour well spent away from hectic crowds. The friars here are men engaged in preaching missions and retreats; between times they are able to rest and study in what is virtually a hermitage in the heart of a city. The founder of the friary, Blessed Bonaventura of Barcelona, a Spanish brother, rests under an altar to the left (the church is named after St Bonaventura, doctor of the Church – not this brother), and under the high altar lies St Leonard of Port Maurice. It was he who began the custom of making the Stations of the Cross in the Colosseum, maintained by the Holy Father on Good Friday evening. To the right of the sanctuary is preserved a painted Madonna, and to the left a crucifix, both of which he used on his missions. He died here in 1751, and you may visit the room in which he lay during his final illness – the visit is well worth the opportunity of seeing something of what remains today an authentic Italian friary.

CHAPTER 8

The Colosseum, and a Walk over the Coelian Hill

The Colosseum – The Arch of Constantine – Nero's 'Golden House' – Trajan's Baths – San Clemente – Santi Quattro Coronati – The Irish College and The Navicella Fountain – Santa Maria in Domnica – San Stefano Rotondo – The Arch of Dolabella – The Gate of San Tommaso in Formis – Church of SS. John and Paul – The Villa Celimontana Park – St Gregory's on the Coelian.

The Colosseum

I should like to say straightway of the Colosseum that nearly everyone makes a mistake by heading inside. To appreciate a monument of this size you should look for a point of vantage where you can best see it as a whole. Try the ruins of the Temple of Venus and Rome (steps just across the road from the Underground Station) or from the terraced road approached by stairs a few yards beyond the Underground *'Colosseo'* Station. Afternoon sun is generally better for photography. Try to imagine the walls coated with fine marble and statues lodged within the arches. A series of corbels going round the outside wall near the top supported masts by means of which a team of sailors could, at short notice, raise awnings over given sectors of the theatre to shelter the audience from rain or sun.

The reason why I excluded the other side is that for roughly half its circumference the great stadium has been cannibalized by builders, and its outer walls are lacking.

The longer axis of the Colosseum is 607 feet – longer than any English cathedral. A reasonable estimate of its accommodation has been put at 50,000. Before it was built, there was a great pool here with Nero's 'Golden House' grouped around it on the flanks of the Palatine, Oppian, and Coelian hills. Vespasian destroyed most of this and began – to give it its proper name – the Flavian Amphitheatre, named after the imperial family. At this point it enters Christian history. Vespasian's son Titus brought it to completion with the labour of Jewish slaves from Jerusalem, captured in A.D. 70. Thereafter it was to be the stage, according to tradition, of many martyrdoms. In the sixth

century Gregory the Great, asked for relics, presented a bag of Colosseum sand. Imperial messengers thought this a mark of scant respect, but the Pope squeezed the bag and it shed drops of blood.

In its heyday the Colosseum was used for blood sports between man and man and man and beast, for mock battles and even naval spectacles – the arena could be flooded. Animals, kept in a menagerie thought to have been on the Coelian, came down through subterranean ramps and were hoisted to the arena in lifts. Statistics of a celebration in A.D. 240 record the slaughter of thirty elephants, ten elks, ten tigers, seventy lions, thirty leopards, ten hyenas, nineteen giraffes, twenty wild

asses, forty wild horses, one hippopotamus, one rhinoceros –
not to mention two thousand gladiators. This kind of thing went
on to some extent by public demand, even after the edict of
prohibition by a Christian emperor. In 404 an Eastern monk
named Telemachus threw himself into the arena to halt the
butchery and was stoned to death – he is St Telemachus,
commemorated on the first of January.

Throughout the Middle Ages the Colosseum was used for any
and every purpose. Churches were built there, rival families
claimed it for a fortress. When in 1806 Pius VI built a buttress
to support the crumbling wall they are said to have dug up the
Frangipani treasure. In the later Middle Ages it had been a
hospital and in the renaissance it became a quarry. Eventually
botanists were able to catalogue four hundred and twenty
species of weeds among the ruins. The last type of wild life to
survive here is the Roman cat, who values the seclusion of its
vaults and galleries for bed, and the charity of visitors for board.

Devotion returned to the Colosseum in the Holy Year of 1750,
with the sermons of St Leonard of Port Maurice, Franciscan of
nearby St Bonaventure's on the Palatine. Stations of the Cross
were built here. Today, by the site of the former imperial box,
there is just a Cross, but on Good Friday night Romans flock to
the Colosseum to follow the Way of the Cross preached by the
Holy Father himself.

The official name of the Colosseum is the Flavian
Amphitheatre. English historian St Bede the Venerable in the
eighth century is believed to be the first to write of it as the
'*Colisaeus*', probably after a huge bronze statue (*colossus*) of Nero
that stood nearby.

A visit to the upper storeys is recommended, if only for the
view. It is also worth while coming a second time after dark,
when the great vaulted corridors are illuminated with orange
lighting.

The Arch of Constantine

Just beyond the Colosseum is the Arch of Constantine, raised
about 318 to commemorate Constantine's victory over his rival.
Although there is nothing Christian about it, it does in effect
mark the conversion of the Empire. The arch is patchwork,
much of the sculpture probably taken from monuments raised
elsewhere to Hadrian, Trajan, and Marcus Aurelius. It is easy
to appreciate that Marble Arch and the Arc de Triomphe found
their inspiration in Roman examples such as this Arch of
Constantine.

Nero's 'Golden House' and Trajan's Baths

On the opposite side of the Colosseum in a park on the flank of the Colle Oppio, Oppian Hill – part of the Esquiline – are remains of Nero's Golden House, *Domus Aurea*, in part underlying the later Baths of Trajan. The latter can be seen in the park – great hulks of masonry that Romans insist on preserving so jealously. The vault-like apartments of Nero's Palace have not been open for some time and there seems to be no prospect of their becoming accessible to visitors in the visible future.

Instead of taking the Via di San Giovanni from beside the Colosseum to visit San Clemente, it would be possible to take the broad road beyond the Arch of Constantine and visit San Gregorio which soon appears on the left, before you reach a major cross-roads. You could carry on to visit SS. John and Paul, and, in fact, do the rest of this chapter in reverse, or part of it.

San Clemente

The church and excavations of San Clemente make one of the most interesting visits in Rome. Well, I have enjoyed guiding people there more than anywhere else. Usually there is no service of guides available, and as for using a guide-book – it took me several visits to master that. I think it is helpful to leave out some points of lesser interest in order to make the rest simpler to follow.

San Clemente is a church of about 1100, with later features, and it would rank high among the churches of Rome without its excavations. But then they are unique! Other churches have excavations, but none so informative and interesting as these.

Before you enter the church, take stock of your position. To one side, streets run up the slope of the Coelian Hill, to the other the Park of Nero's Golden House is on the slopes of the Esquiline. San Clemente lies in a valley between the two. The level of this valley, like others in Rome, has risen in the course of time. One of the reasons is that, when Romans raised new buildings, they generally took off the upper floors of the old house, threw the material into the ground floor rooms and courtyard, and so made a firm foundation for the new house – or church. San Clemente of 1100 is the second *church* here, but the house below these two churches was probably one in which a room was used for worship till the fourth century. In the excavations you may visit the fourth-century church below the present one, the first-century, or older, house below that, and – for good measure – the house next door!

So in we go and, if you choose to follow my route, do not

heed the church at all as you pass across the nave to the sacristy, where you take tickets to visit the excavations. At the foot of the steps is the long narthex (broad porch) of the first church. Look carefully and you will see columns bedded in the walls on both sides; those to the right opened into the nave, those to the left into the courtyard (atrium) by which the church was approached. These open colonnades were walled up in the ninth century as a result of an earthquake, and a local family had two interesting paintings executed on the emergency walling, which tell us something of the legend of St Clement, the titular saint of the church.

The tradition about Clement is that he was the third pope after St Peter, and had in fact actually been known to him. Some doubt that the Clement of this church ought to be identified with this early pope. Then the house below the churches is believed to have been his. He is said to have been exiled to the Crimea and finally martyred by being thrown into the Black Sea with an anchor round his neck. The legend goes on – now remember that there is often a foundation of truth to legends – that every year there was an exceptionally low tide when Christians visited the site of his martyrdom, to find a little chapel emerging there from the waters. One year a child was left behind and mourned by his parents as dead, but on the occasion of the following annual pilgrimage there he still was, safe and sound. This is the story told in the first painting to the right in the narthex.

Notice the delightful convention by which the sea, with a nice display of fishes, folds round the chapel, to which is attached the anchor of martyrdom. The happy mother appears twice – in many medieval paintings we have a sort of compressed strip cartoon: several incidents in the same picture – finding her boy, and embracing him. Out from the city comes the bishop, followed by a crowd of deacons. Below this picture is represented the family that had it painted for the church – the son was named, after the patron saint, *'Puerulus Clemens'* – Little Boy Clement.

A few yards farther is a second painting contributed by the same family which represents the return of the relics of St Clement to Rome. This introduces us to the interesting history of St Cyril, apostle of Russia – as it then was, the territory around Kiev. It is to this saint the Russians owe their 'Cyrillic' alphabet. The fact that Cyril managed to find relics of Clement and bring them back to Rome suggests that he, at any rate, when he arrived in the Crimea, managed to make sense out of the legends. This painting is interesting for what it shows us of church fashions and furnishings in the eleventh century. Notice that the pope's headgear is not the three-crowned tiara of the late Middle Ages, but a simple pointed soft cap held on by a firm band of material. As this band became more heavily ornamented, it developed into the first of the three crowns. The knot tied in this fillet at the back is the origin of the 'lappets' or ornamental bands hanging over a bishop's shoulders from the back of his mitre – which ought to have made you wonder before now.

Below this picture is the dedication inscription of the donor: 'I, Maria Macellaria, through reverence for God and for the salvation of my soul, had this painted'. This lady's name in English style might be translated: 'Mrs Mary Butcher'.

Opposite is a hinged marble slab. It has been used twice for different purposes. The inscription in poor lettering is Christian. If that is uppermost, revolve the slab. The earlier pagan epitaph, finely incised, is a parent's memorial of the kind of child we all know:

> 'Marcus Aurelius Sabinus, also known as 'the little rover',
> a most beloved child. He had no equal among the young
> men of his own rank and time.'

Now enter the nave – from between the two paintings of the life of Clement. The colonnade between nave and aisles has been walled up as a consequence of that ninth-century earthquake, but you will find the columns if you look for them bedded in the walls. Round the corner to the left is an interesting ninth-century painting either of the Assumption of Our Lady or of the Ascension of Our Lord. The date is easy to fix because Pope Leo IV (847–855) is represented on it with the square halo that means he was alive at the time. Those who favour the Assumption think that Mary is shown being raised into heaven, where her Son awaits her, and they have in their favour the fact that this Pope Leo decreed the keeping of an octave to the feast of the Assumption in Rome. On the other hand Our Lady could be raised above the apostles simply as a matter of convenience, because, as you can see, something was preserved in the wall here, and it could well have been an oval fragment of rock from the Mount of Olives, the place of Our Lord's Ascension.

Along the nave to the left are two more paintings we must describe. The first tells the story of St Alexius, whose church on the Aventine Hill is over the traditional site of his home. The tale goes thus. Alexius (probably in the fourth century) was persuaded by his parents to marry, but his ambition was really the hermit life. He soon abandoned his wife and became a solitary in the East. There, however, he found his reputation for holiness just as distasteful, so in due course he wandered back to Rome and begged his way up to the old familiar Aventine. There we see him (left) stretching out his hand for alms. His father, on horseback, fails to recognize his son but he gives him an alms and offers him a job about the house and a bed under the staircase. When Alexius died the Pope came and took from his hand a document which turned out to be an admission of his identity (centre). To the right of the picture you see father and mother tearing their hair, and his wife, whom the family had supported all that time, snatching in death the kiss refused her in life.

The next picture is a confusing and not very edifying story of St Clement. It represents the saint at Mass. Notice that at the time of the painting (eleventh century) the maniple was still a sweat-rag worn over the hand, and not a merely formal ornament on the arm. The book is open at *Dominus Vobiscum* and the priest extends his hands in the ancient gesture so often represented in the catacombs, and still used at Mass today. Sisinnius, the husband of a Christian lady, came to scoff and was struck blind. At the right you see his servant leading him away. He recovers his sight at the prayer of the saint, but spitefully orders his men to arrest him. Hallucinated, they lay hold instead of a column lying on the ground as building material. Now the great interest here is the writing in the lower part of this picture, which represents Sisinnius ordering his servants to drag away the column. Some of it is rather rude, but I will quote a part that is inoffensive: '*Falite dereto colo palo*' – 'raise it up from the back with a lever'. The importance of this is that it is one of the earliest known instances of a written Italian language, as distinct from the earlier use of Latin. Since I first saw these paintings the lettering seems to have become less legible, and now railings have been installed so that distance alone makes it harder to read.

Between these paintings a door leads into the aisle, and in the corner there are two staircases, one locked. Look down the locked staircase, the narrower of the two, and you will see the alley between the house of Clement and the house next door. You are looking into the first century A.D. The altar close at hand, by the way, is in honour of St Cyril, and is probably over the remains of his shrine.

Now you descend into 'the house next door', and if you turn right at the bottom of the stairs you will find yourself in a small room that betrays it was once lived in only by the richly moulded decoration of the vault. The great buttresses that plunge into it support the apse of the basilica above. There are arches that once opened into a garden courtyard, but in the third century A.D., when Christians doubtless already assembled in the house of Clement, worshippers of the mysterious Persian cult of Mithras built a temple there.

Enter the temple. Either side are stone couches, but the design was intended to give the impression of a cavern. There are openings overhead, in the centre a Mithraic altar, and at the far end a statue of the birth of Mithras.

Our knowledge of this 'mystery cult' is limited almost to what can be deduced from the art and furniture of its temples. Its following was all-male, especially military, and Mithraic temples have been found as far distant as our Hadrian's Wall. It was cosmic in the sense that earth, sun, and planets play an important part in its symbolism; for instance the openings in the vault, four rectangular and seven circular, are believed to stand for seasons and constellations; the cave-like milieu is to give the impression that you are in the womb of the earth, and either side the altar figures holding lowered and raised torches stand for the days of the year as they grow shorter or lengthen.

The sculpture of the altar represents the sun god Apollo (top left corner, with rays round his head like the Christ in the Vatican Scavi), who sends Mithras into the world. For this mission Mithras must be somehow identified with earth, so he is represented, in the statuette at the end of the cave, as born from the rocks. Apollo commissions him to slay a bull whose blood will be life-giving, but scorpion, snake and hound join in the killing and their share introduces evil. An inscription tells you that 'Father Claudianus' erected this altar.

As you leave the temple a narrow gallery to the left leads to a room with vestiges of decoration. Pause at the end and listen to the sound of water rushing into the Cloaca Maxima, main sewer of ancient Rome. Till the conduit was made, water from natural subterranean springs rendered further excavation and the access of visitors impossible.

Passages lead through the ground floor rooms of the house of Clement till you return by an iron staircase to the narthex of the fourth-century basilica. As you arrive, notice an interesting Roman sarcophagus, finely carved but with unfinished busts of a couple tenderly embracing. This was how masons prepared stone coffins for sale; when customers had made their choice they were expected to sit while their likeness was taken for the busts. Somehow or other sarcophagi were often sold with the faces left unfinished.

In my description of the underground church I have omitted mention of some paintings in favour of those I thought more worthy of your attention.

Now, if not exhausted, you should spare some time for the upper church. Its great mosaic has few rivals anywhere. Though twelfth century, in much detail and in its dominant motif – a pattern of twining foliage – it belongs to Rome's older tradition. The foliage represents the Church, with its roots in a Garden of Paradise (all acanthus leaves) from which springs the Cross of Christ, true Tree of Life, while the serpent is expelled, and the baptismal waters flow. The life that fills this symbolic Church is fascinating, not only the obvious saints, but ordinary folk about everyday business, such as the farm girl feeding poultry, and the shepherd who pets his dog, not to mention birds and peacocks. On the cross is the dying Christ with Mary and John, as on any medieval rood, but above is the Hand of the Father awarding the victor's crown. The rest of the imagery here is what you will see in other Roman mosaics, but I should like to draw your attention to a figure at the top left corner, St Lawrence in a woven vestment patterned with flames to symbolize his martyrdom on a grid-iron. You will be able to appreciate the details of this mosaic better by studying the postcards sold in the shop.

The choir enclosure is interesting sixth-century work brought up from the church below, but enriched by the Cosmati in the twelfth century – theirs too is the fine inlaid marble floor. In several places you will find the monogram of JOHANNES, Pope John II, 533-35, said to be the first pope to take a new name. On the columns of the baldachino he erected here, now incorporated in a tomb at the end of the left aisle, is his name Mercurius, which he changed to John.

Beneath the high altar are enshrined St Clement, St Flavius Clement, a Roman consul and martyr, and St Ignatius of Alexandria, believed to have been thrown to the beasts in the nearby Colosseum. Behind is an ancient throne of which the back is part of a martyr's tomb – you can see the word MARTYR inscribed on it.

There is much else of interest; the coffered ceilng, some beautiful renaissance tombs, a chapel of SS. Cyril and Methodius, apostles of the Slavs, with nineteenth-century paintings, a chapel of St John the Baptist with a sixteenth-century statue and a modern altar, and the famous chapel of St Catherine of Alexandria. It is gothic, rare enough in Rome, painted by the famous early renaissance artist Masolino. There is too much to go into detail, but I mention a delicate Annunciation, a knight in armour in the left corner of the Crucifixion, and the refusal of Catherine to sacrifice to the idol.

Lastly, if the main door is open, look into the atrium, through which, ideally, one should approach the basilica. Here St Servulus begged for alms in the sixth century, and here he died. Gregory the Great knew him and preached a sermon about him. Servulus is buried under the Blessed Sacrament altar at the end of the left aisle.

San Clemente is served by Irish Dominicans.

When you leave the porch of St Clement's, turn a few steps left, then cross and take the road, Via dei Querceti, that climbs the slopes of the Coelian Hill. After a few steps you will see towering above you the church of Santi Quattro Coronati – the 'Four Holy Crowned Ones'.

Santi Quattro Coronati

For some odd reason this is a church rather neglected by visitors, but you will be rewarded, for it has an atmosphere of its own. Its fortress-like character, as it towers above the narrow streets and market stalls of the quarter, is part of the charm; the rest you will find out in the course of your visit.

The 'Four Holy Crowned Ones' are rather elusive saints. To begin with, there were more than four – apparently three groups totalling thirteen. The first were sculptors who refused to make a statue of Aesculapius, god of medicine, the second soldiers who refused to adore an idol, and finally there was another group of soldiers who also won the crown of martyrdom.

Traditionally, the church was built in the fourth century, in the ninth century certainly rebuilt by Pope Leo IV, who brought here many relics of martyrs, and finally reconstructed with the buildings that now surround it by Pope Paschal II in the twelfth.

This church is unique in that you approach it through two courtyards – this gives you some picturesque vistas. Inside, you will notice embedded in the walls columns that, before the last rebuilding, opened into side aisles. Since the twelfth century the church has had side galleries. There is a cosmatesque floor and a coffered ceiling, but the most striking feature is the great apse frescoed by Giovanni di San Giovanni (early seventeenth century) representing the glory of the saints. This artist has earned for his work the nickname 'Choir of Angelesses', on account of his rather decided opinion that all angels are female.

You will notice an entrance to the crypt in which the martyrs' relics are enshrined in ancient sarcophagi, but, although recently restored, it lacks interest, and it is hardly worth your bothering the sister to unlock it.

You must, however, ask her to admit you to the tiny but beautiful thirteenth-century cloister. The charm is compounded of its delicate arcades, the upper storey, foliage, flowers and fountain — the latter believed to date from between the ninth and twelfth centuries, venerable among the fountains of Rome. Opening off the cloister is a chapel belonging to the earlier church, with beautifully sculptured corbels of the fourth or fifth century and vestiges of ninth-century painting.

On your way out you should enter a door on the left side of the inner courtyard where you will find a convent 'turn', a grille, and a bell. Ring the bell, and when a sister answers at the grille ask for the key to the chapel of St Sylvester (*Capella di San Silvestro*), which will be passed to you through the turn. This key unlocks a door on the left of the outer courtyard, and admits you to a chapel rich with thirteenth-century paintings of the story of St Sylvester, whom the Emperor Constantine is said to have invited from his hermitage on Monte Soratte to be pope. If you stand with your back to the altar, you will recognize in the far right corner Constantine's messengers setting off on horseback, and then prostrating themselves before the mountain hermit. In the centre of that far wall is a fine figure of Christ, with emblems of the Passion. This was formerly the Chapel of the Marble-workers' confraternity.

Tradition has it that Pope Honorius received St Francis at Santi Quattro Coronati.

The Irish College and The 'Navicella' Fountain

Farther up the lane from which you entered Santi Quattro Coronati is the Irish College. If you retrace your steps and climb up to the Coelian you will soon recognize the Navicella at the roadside, a fountain made of an ancient stone galley that was probably some Roman's gift to a temple on his safe return from a journey by sea – much as you see silver ship models in fishermen's shrines. This was set up here as a fountain by Leo X – the Pope with whom Luther quarrelled. The water is Acqua Felice.

Santa Maria in Domnica

The Navicella stands before the Church of Santa Maria in Domnica, believed, like so many, to have originated as a meeting place for Christians in the home of a well-to-do Roman. In this case the owner was a lady called Cyriaca, whose family cemetery was where the basilica of San Lorenzo fuori le Mura now stands – it was she who gave burial to the deacon-martyr Lawrence. Tradition tells us that he gave alms to the poor at the door of her house.

The present church is ninth century, with alterations made by Pope Leo X with the great Raphael as his architect. Most important here are the apse mosaics, commissioned in the ninth century by Pope Paschal I, also responsible for mosaics at Santa Prassede and Santa Caecilia. You will see his monogram, and himself too – the square halo means the person depicted was living – kneeling at Mary's feet; in fact, clasping her shoe. This is one of the earliest instances of a Madonna replacing the traditional figure of Christ, either ruling from his throne or coming on the clouds of heaven. Well, he is here too, first on his Mother's knee, and again, ruling and teaching, in the mosaic above the arch. Two points about this mosaic are the flowery fields in which stand the apostles above and the angels below, and the convention of representing legions of angels by dense blue haloes. The angels in the foreground have gold haloes.

There is a great deal of neatness about the church – perhaps a little too much. The confession (crypt) is interesting, but with so many fragments of sculpture that it has the atmosphere of a museum. There is a figure of Christ in Gethsemane, touching, if not quite in keeping with its surrounds.

In the church, notice the sixteenth-century coffered ceiling and modern paintings in the baptistery.

San Stefano Rotondo

Across the road from Santa Maria in Domnica you can see the round church known as San Stefano Rotondo; its entrance is a few steps along the lane by the aqueduct. Ring for the custodian who is usually willing to admit visitors. Over the porch by which you enter an inscription records a general restoration by Pope Nicholas V in 1453. San Stefano at present is the property of the German College.

That the church is round is obvious. When it was consecrated in 460 it consisted of three concentric aisles. The outermost has been suppressed and its colonnades blocked by the walls which now carry frescoes, not particularly good ones either, representing the agonies of martyrs, by Pomarancio and Tempesta. Formerly transepts extended beyond the colonnades in the pattern of a Greek cross. The columns marking these extensions are taller than the others – you can easily note this in respect of the transept on your left as you enter. A lofty colonnade over the central altar was added in the eighth century.

Such a unique building remains a puzzle to archaeologists. Had it been raised outside the walls I think there would have been a common conclusion that it was a mausoleum. Some authorities have believed it to be a meat market built by Nero and reconstructed as a church in the fifth century.

On the left side is a tablet recording the burial here of an Irish king, Donough O'Brien of Cashel and Thomond, son of Brian Boru. He died in Rome in 1064. Notice, as you leave, an antique chair with an inscription recording that Pope Gregory the Great sat there to deliver one of his famous homilies.

The hospital next door belongs to the English Blue Nuns – Little Company of Mary.

If you return to Santa Maria in Domnica and face the church, you now have the choice of entering the Villa Celimontana Gardens to the left (perhaps to eat your picnic lunch), or turning right to pass under the Arch of Dolabella and Silanus and walk downhill to San Giovanni e Paolo and San Gregorio. This description will suppose you do the latter; the gardens will be mentioned again.

The Arch of Dolabella

In the middle of the road is an isolated aqueduct pier. The remains of the aqueduct approach alongside the lane by San Stefano Rotonda and continue by crossing the Arch of Dola-bella, built for this purpose, and then into the gardens of the monastery of Saints John and Paul. The arch was built in the reign of Caesar Augustus (A.D. 10) to carry a water supply to a reservoir on the Coelian.

The Gate of San Tommaso in Formis

On the left is the gateway of the former Trinitarian monastery of San Tommaso in Formis with a mosaic signed by Jacobus Cosmati (thirteenth century) of Christ with two slaves, one black, the other white, whose hands he clasps. The Order of the Holy Trinity was founded for the redemption of captives – that is, its members were prepared to exchange themselves for Christians taken into slavery. The founder, St John of Matha, lived in a room over the Arch of Dolabella. The name 'in Formis' refers to the adjacent aqueduct.

The walk through the Arch of Dolabella to the church of SS. John and Paul is one to which you should return after dark. The charm of this floodlit setting – remains of the Claudianum, the arched street known as the Clivus Scauri, church, bell tower, and monastery – is unique.

Church of SS. John and Paul

The story of this church – and so the course of your visit – is not unlike that of San Clemente. There is a medieval church with later furnishing, but it incorporates some of the fourth-century fabric, whereas at San Clemente the earlier church was at a lower level. Below the church are second- and third-century houses in which Christian worship was certainly established.

Before you enter the church, glance down the hill. The road is arched by medieval buttresses supporting what appears to be the side of the church, but is in fact the third-century street-front of shops. The façade of the church as you see it now is to some extent the result – happy result – of Cardinal Spellman's restorations. Below it is a fine fourth-century arcade concealed for centuries. The narthex with solemn antique columns is attributed to Nicholas Breakspear, the only Englishman to become pope, as Adrian IV (1154-1159). There are several windows in the monastery wall at the level of the bell tower; locate a pair at third-floor level – they mark the room of St Paul of the Cross, eighteenth-century founder of the Passionist Congregation. A later resident in this monastery was the Blessed Dominic Barberi, apostle in England, who received Newman into the Church.

The bell tower is superb. Its base is the Claudianum – Temple to the Emperor Claudius. The rest is thirteenth century. You will notice a feature common to many Roman bell towers – roundels, that appear to be marble or glazed terracotta, let into the fabric, sometimes with no attempt at pattern or regularity. One might almost take them for plates. Some indeed are serpentine or porphyry, such as the cosmatesque workers used for their pavements, but others quite literally are *plates*. Those in the tower at present are substitutes; the originals have been removed and can be examined in a museum annexed to the excavations. They are glazed Moorish ceramic plates, some inscribed with arabic lettering, from Malaga in Spain.

The interior of the venerable church, now clearly proved to be fourth century, was transformed about 1718. Surviving from the thirteenth century are the fine cosmatesque pavement and, behind the chapel left of the high altar, one of Rome's most handsome thirteenth-century frescoes of Christ, in a strongly Byzantine style, flanked by apostles. You will need to ask the sacristan to unlock a door if you wish to see this. The coffered ceiling dates from 1598 but is dull compared with others of that period. In the apse are paintings by Pomarancio. Beneath the altar note the ancient porphyry urn in which the relics of SS. John and Paul were placed in 1726.

Opening off the right aisle is a great domed chapel, begun as late as 1862, to enshrine the relics of St Paul of the Cross. The smaller paintings overhead, depicting incidents in the life of the saint, are quite pleasing. Most noteworthy here is the lavish use of marble, especially alabaster.

Just after this chapel is the entrance to the excavations, begun by a Father Germano in 1887 and brought to their present very fine condition by the generosity of Cardinal Spellman and Joseph P. Kennedy, between 1956 and 1958.

To appreciate these remarkable finds something must be known of the story of SS. John and Paul. It used to be fashionable to debunk them entirely, but the existence of a basilica in their honour, raised in a special way over their very home on the Coelian within a few years of their death, seems once again to vindicate the merits of Christian tradition.

The sixth-century 'Acts' of John and Paul make them court officials of Constantine who, soon after his death, acquired a property here on the Coelian Hill. Later, the Emperor Julian reverted to paganism, and during his persecution John and Paul were executed and buried secretly in their own home, on the night of the 26th/27th January 361. To this must be added a detail from a later narrative, the beheading of Crispin, Crispinianus, and Benedicta while praying at their tomb.

The excavations are so complex that I indicate just a few main features and leave you to make your way round and about, as well as up and down. At the lower level you will come across a sort of well, at the bottom of which the martyrs are presumed to have been buried. A staircase leads to an upper level of this shaft, in which you will find paintings of martyrdom – though nothing specifically of the martyrdom of John and Paul themselves. These paintings can be confidently dated late fourth century, so a shrine must have been adapted in the apartments of the martyrs' home within a brief interval after their death. At the back of the cavity is an *orante*, a figure certainly Christian and representing the posture of prayer; it cannot be fairly identified more closely. Panels to the left represent, above, three persons being led to judgment by two soldiers (notice the dog in the corner), and below, two unidentified male persons. To the right is the execution of the same three persons, by beheading – they kneel blindfolded – and, below, two female figures. These paintings seem to lend substance to the story – from a purely documentary point of view too late to inspire confidence – of Crispin, Crispinianus, and Benedicta.

When you return to the church, notice on the right side of the nave a railed enclosure indicating the spot venerated as the original shrine – and in this case the place of martyrdom as well as that of burial. A glass disc in the pavement looking down straight into the shaft where you have seen the paintings of martyrdom proves this traditional site to have been just a little out of true.

In the rooms of the second/third-century houses are a number of very well preserved paintings, both pagan and Christian. They include another *orante* figure, and, over what was once an indoor water garden (nymphaeum), a beautifully executed mythological scene. Up a staircase in the wall, seeming to lead nowhere, you will find a ninth-century Crucifixion closely similar to that in Santa Maria Antiqua in the Forum.

The sacristan will open for you a very well appointed museum of articles discovered here. It may also be possible to leave the sacristy by a passage from which you can see extensive remains of the Claudianum.

The Villa Celimontana Park

Opposite San Giovanni e Paolo is an entrance to the Celimontana Gardens where, when you find it convenient, you can enjoy the fresh air of the Coelian Hill, a rest in the shade, a picnic lunch, or maybe a fine flower display. Municipal nurseries on the lower slope of the hill, and the Roman gardening technique of putting everything out in barely concealed pots, enable displays to be arranged with more artistic effect than if the flowers had to do all the work themselves. I recall a particularly lovely chrysanthemum display here. You will find an obelisk from the Capitol – and from Heliopolis in Egypt before that, brought here in 1582. When it was raised into position, a workman's hand was caught underneath, and is presumably still there.

St Gregory's on the Coelian

Down the hill, past SS. John and Paul, the façade of San Gregorio al Celio rises impressively to your left, at the top of a flight of steps. Here lived St Gregory the Great when, as abbot of a monastery established in his own home, he purchased English slave boys in the Roman market and, according to tradition, raised them as monks to form the band of apostles he later, as pope, sent to convert the English in 596. When Gregory was a monk here he suffered from a weak stomach, and his mother St Silvia daily sent a silver dish of specially prepared vegetables from her home on the nearby Aventine.

There can be little doubt that much of St Gregory's home remains below the present church and monastery, waiting to be excavated. Today, church and monastery are characteristically eighteenth century, to the designs of Francesco Ferrari, though the façade at the top of the steps is about fifty years earlier, by Giovanni Battista Soria. If the spirit of St Gregory can be recalled here it is because of the few but precious relics of his time that you will see, and perhaps too because of the white habited Camaldolese monks. Elsewhere they usually live the hermit life, but San Gregorio is a monastery on normal Benedictine lines.

In the atrium are paintings you may find interesting. To the left there is a naval battle, and to the right you will find a picture of the Castel Sant' Angelo, and also a dragon trying to get into someone's bed – presumably a last hour temptation.

Certain lights emphasize the austerity and elegance of the sanctuary of San Gregorio. It has been adapted for daily concelebration with a new altar and a pulpit for singing the gospel – the latter flanked by two medieval statues of St Gregory and St Andrew. In Gregory's day his monastery was dedicated to the apostle Andrew. This is probably the reason why his missionaries to Kent made Rochester Cathedral St Andrew's.

At the end of the right aisle is a beautiful little Chapel of St Gregory and, opening off it, a room believed to incorporate in its fabric whatever remains of Gregory's cell. Behind a grille to the right is the place of his bed, and to the left an ancient Roman chair in which he sat. Note the sculpture on the back of this chair.

At the back of the altar in St Gregory's Chapel is a painted panel of the fifteenth-century Umbrian school, representing St Michael and saints; the marble frontal of this altar, sculptured with St Gregory at Mass, is fourteenth century.

Cross the church, noting on the way the cosmatesque floor of inlaid marble and the vault, painted by Costanzi in 1727 with the 'Glory of St Gregory'. In the chapel corresponding to St Gregory's is a modern painting in renaissance style of Our Lady with saints; underneath is written its title: 'England, Dowry of Mary'. A door near this chapel leads to one incorporating a wall of the earlier church with a fresco of the Madonna, before which traditionally St Gregory prayed, but perhaps it has been repainted at a later date. There is a fifteenth-century retable to an altar by Andrea Bregno with, at the top, a representation of Hadrian's tomb and the apparition of an angel at its summit during a procession led by St Gregory at a time of plague. This incident is the origin of the name 'Castel Sant' Angelo'. The Castle appears again in a fresco on the wall behind this altar.

You may ask one of the monks – if necessary ring the bell at the door in the atrium – to show you the chapels in the garden, dating in their present form from the seventeenth century. Their frescoes are in poor condition, but fine coffered ceilings have been handsomely restored. In the chapel to the left is a venerable stone table at which St Gregory is believed to have entertained the poor, among them, one day, an angel unawares – as a painting shows you on the wall beyond.

CHAPTER 9

Between the Capitol and the Tiber

The Theatre of Marcellus – San Nicolo in Carcere – Santa Maria di Consolazione – San Giovanni Decollato – The Piazza Bocca della Verità; its temples – Santa Maria in Cosmedin – The Bocca della Verità – San Giorgio in Velabro – Arch of Janus, Arch of the Money-changers – Sant' Anastasia – The Circo Massimo – San Teodoro.

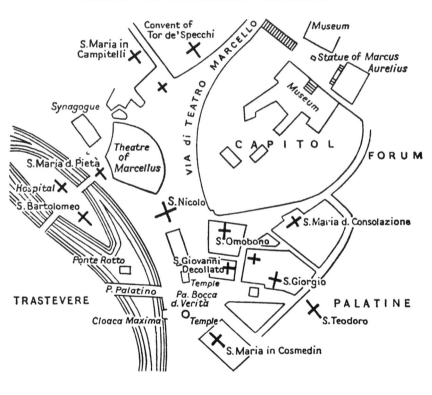

The best time to follow these pages, which describe a very compact little area, is Sunday morning, when its churches should be open for Mass, though some of them are likely to be closed. They could be combined with a visit to the Capitoline Museums.

The Theatre of Marcellus

If you leave the steps to the Capitol at the Piazza di Ara Coeli and turn towards the Tiber you will soon have a good view – from the Capitol side of the road – of the medieval convent building of Tor de'Specchi, the convent of St Frances of Rome. Then you pass the picturesque ruins of the Theatre of Marcellus, older than the Colosseum but smaller and only a half circle. Marcellus, nephew to Caesar Augustus, was dead when it was dedicated in his memory in 13 B.C. At the function the Emperor's ivory throne collapsed beneath him, but with an urbane smile (which you can easily picture once you have seen one of his portrait statues) he signalled for the show to go on. Part of the theatre is now a residence. A hundred yards or so after passing the Theatre look back and be rewarded by one of the best 'ruin views' in Rome.

San Nicolo in Carcere

Over the road is the Church of San Nicolo in Carcere, St Nicholas in the Prison, built, probably in the sixth century, among the ruins of two temples of which you see a great deal incorporated in its fabric. Part way down its length the nave narrows, doubtless due to adaptation to these ruined temples. Nicholas of Bari, or of Myra, is no less than Father Christmas – 'Santa Claus' – and patron saint of sailors. '*In carcere*' alludes to a tradition that there was a prison here. It is a pleasant little church, its ancient columns of beautiful marble and with rich capitals; the blue and gold coffered ceiling must just be called pretty. Notice beneath the altar an antique basalt bath containing the relics of martyrs, one being a St Beatrice, in case you know anyone with that name. On a fluted column near the door is a crudely cut tenth-century inscription.

Devotion to two Madonnas is fostered here, the Italian shrine of Our Lady of Pompeii, and the Mexican one of Guadalupe. The altar to the latter, opening off the left aisle, has a delicate reproduction of the miraculous painting done on silk. It was sent here from Mexico in 1773. In the right aisle is a most beautiful fresco of Our Lady by Antoniazzo Romano. The feast of Our Lady of Pompeii is kept here on 8th May.

Santa Maria di Consolazione

Now set your back to San Nicolo and look forward; you will see at the foot of the Capitol the façade of the former hospital church of Santa Maria di Consolazione, Our Lady of Consolation. Approaching it you pass the Tailors' Guild Church of St

Omobono, open for an eleven o'clock Mass on the first Sunday of the month. Our Lady of Consolation deserves a visit from anyone with a devotion to Our Lady, for it has four shrines to her under different titles, at the high altar and the chapels flanking it, and on the outside wall of the apse. The Madonna over the high altar – 'of Consolation' – is the least pleasing. I am put off by the enormous knees. That to the right is a delicate thirteenth-century icon of Our Lady of Grace, Mary without the Divine Child, from a church now destroyed. The dedication of the chapel to the left is to Our Lady 'in Portico', the Madonna of Santa Maria in Campitelli, but the ancient icon is only reproduced in a window; there is a pleasing modern statuette over the altar.

The origin of this hospital and church is interesting. In 1385 a nobleman imprisoned in the Capitol left two gold florins for a painting of Our Lady to be made nearby. Devotion increased and in 1506 the hospital was founded, to become the scene of the charitable ministry of several well-known saints: Ignatius Loyola, Camillus de Lellis, Philip Neri, and Aloysius Gonzaga, who contracted a fatal illness carrying a plague victim to its wards. An inscription on the wall – walk past the side of the church – records this heroic sacrifice. Close by, on the outside of the apse, another Madonna commemorates a plague of 1658. The hospital is now Fire Brigade Headquarters.

San Giovanni Decollato

If you return the way you have come you will find on your left the Via San Giovanni Decollato, with two churches. A flight of steps leads to San Giovanni Decollato, St John Beheaded, seat of a Florentine Guild for ministering to condemned criminals. It now uses its funds for the benefit of prisoners' dependants. As befits anything to do with Florence, the church is very beautiful in a simple renaissance way; it dates from 1580. Opening off the cloister is the Confraternity Oratory which deserves to be called a miniature Sistine Chapel, warm and rich with beautiful paintings of the life of St John the Baptist by several artists, including Salviati, Vasari, and del Conte – of the last there is a fine 'Preaching of St John'. This church is not readily shown to the public, but if you are really interested you should call between 11 and 12 on a weekday and ask permission to visit at the office of the Confraternity. And should you not do that, you will at any rate know why the buildings of this block have representations of a head on a dish – the martyrdom of the Baptist.

The Piazza Bocca della Verità – its temples

Return to San Nicolo in Carcere and turn left to the Piazza Bocca della Verità. You are well below the embankment of the Tiber, and it is easy to realize that there was an inlet here which was a handly place for unloading small vessels, so that a market developed, a number of the traders being Greeks. The two little temples in a garden were dedicated to what we might call trading divinities, for instance, the round one sometimes wrongly called 'Vestal', because it resembles the Temple of Vesta in the Forum, is thought to have been to Portunus, god of harbours. Both date from before Christ, but the rectangular temple is older. When Father Chandlery wrote his *Pilgrim Walks in Rome* (1903) they were in use as churches.

The fountain with tritons was provided by Pope Clement XI in 1717.

Santa Maria in Cosmedin

The church facing you, with a slender campanile, is Santa Maria in Cosmedin. The name comes from a Greek word meaning 'beauty', also the root of our 'cosmetic'. It had another name, Santa Maria in Schola Graeca, meaning 'for the Greek community', the Greek merchants already mentioned, and at one time Greek monks served it. This tradition has just been renewed. Santa Maria in Cosmedin is now open for the use of the Melkite community in Rome – mostly Lebanese Catholics of Byzantine rite using both Arabic and Greek as their liturgical languages.

Probably first built in the sixth century, rebuilding in the ninth and twelfth has brought about its present appearance. There is something gentle, almost feminine about the interior, due in part to the slight, delicate arcades. Glance back towards the door, and look into the left aisle, to see immense antique columns used in striking contrast.

Pavement, choir enclosure, pulpit, paschal candlestick, and the delicate screen dividing nave from sanctuary, are all work of the Cosmati in the twelfth and thirteenth centuries. So is the canopy over the altar, signed 'Deodatus, son of Cosmas'. The paintings of the three apses have an air of antiquity but they are fairly recent. There is a crypt.

The 'Bocca della Verità'

If the church should be closed, you can glance through the railings to see, at the left end of the narthex, the famous Bocca della Verità, or 'Mouth of Truth', after which the piazza is named. This is an ancient well-head or drain, fashioned like a mask. Its name is due to a popular superstition that a liar or perjurer placing his hand in the mouth would have it bitten.

San Giorgio in Velabro

Just round the corner, to the left, beyond the Arch of Janus, is San Giorgio in Velabro, similar in appearance to Santa Maria in Cosmedin, and perhaps it is because this was a Greek quarter that it was dedicated to one of the most popular saints of the East, George, the 'Great Martyr', devotion to whom was picked up by Crusaders and carried home so that he became patron of England. A relic believed to be his skull is preserved under the altar. The description '*in Velabro*' refers to that inlet of the Tiber already mentioned. In the history of Rome – which I am not going to call 'just legend' – the infants Romulus and Remus were washed ashore here, suckled by the wolf in her den on the slopes of the Palatine – which from this viewpoint is a wooded crag to this day – until they were found by the shepherd Faustulus.

If the doors are open, I suggest that you first stand in the narthex and look inside without entering. Perhaps more than anywhere else you are struck by the atmosphere of antiquity. Inside there is not so much to see, but it is a good place to rest and pray. Notice that the walls are not parallel – you check this by glancing up at the wooden ceiling, which is five compartments wide at the door end and only four at the altar. This church is known to be older than the seventh century, but since then it has been restored several times. The columns were of course taken from pagan buildings. Paintings in the apse are rather poor.

Cardinal Newman was titular of San Giorgio in Velabro, and Cardinal Pole of Santa Maria in Cosmedin.

Arch of Janus and Arch of the Moneychangers

The Arch of Janus, with four entrances, is one of the most dejected of Rome's ancient arches. Apparently there was never anything 'triumphal' about it. Probably it served as a covered meeting place for those who did business in the market already mentioned. It dates from about the fourth century. A small arch next to San Giorgio was built by the local moneychangers in honour of the Emperor Septimius Severus, about 204 A.D. If you should study its sculpture you will find it is all concerned with pagan sacrifice.

Walk past San Giorgio and in the road at the end of this street, following the base of the Palatine Hill, there is the round church of San Teodoro to the left, and to the right Sant' Anastasia.

These really belong to Chapter 7 on the Forum and Palatine, but there I give them just a mention; they are far more easily visited on this route.

Sant' Anastasia

Sant' Anastasia presents a seventeenth-century façade, but its history is far greater. It was even one of the original twenty-five parish 'churches' of third-century Rome, probably in one of the buildings annexed to the imperial palace on the nearby Palatine. Much of the fabric of the present building is of the fourth and sixth centuries.

The feast of St Anastasia, fourth-century virgin martyr in what is now Hungary, is commemorated on 25th December, and that is why this is the 'station' church for the Mass at Dawn of Christmas Day. Students from several colleges come to Sant' Anastasia early on Christmas morning to ensure that this is a truly festal occasion. Beneath the high altar is a reclining figure of the saint in the style of Bernini.

On the right side of the church is an altar to St Turibius whom, at a guess, you might suppose to be a Roman martyr. But he wasn't. He was a Spanish late vocation – ordained at forty – who became Bishop of Lima, Peru, and baptized those popular saints of the New World, St Rose of Lima and St Martin de Porres. On the first Sunday of May the Peruvian Ambassador assists at Mass here.

In the left aisle is an ancient altar, surmounted by an outer baldachino in the style of the Cosmati, at which, according to tradition, St Jerome offered Mass and where St Gregory distributed ashes on Ash Wednesday.

The Circo Massimo

Under the church are excavations of part of the Circo Massimo (Great Circus – or Stadium) which have revealed walls so thick that it has been estimated that the highest tiers of seats would have been at least as high as the walls of the Colosseum.

San Teodoro

Left along the foot of the Palatine you will find, set back from the road among the ruins of the Granaries of Agrippa, the round church of San Teodoro, exasperatingly closed, but I have known the caretaker to oblige. It may owe its round shape to being built in the remains of a temple. Theodore was a Greek soldier martyr of the fourth century.

The little courtyard before the church has hardly any architectural pretensions, but it is a real atrium – it separates you from the world over the wall. An ancient pagan altar in the centre formerly supported the altar of the church. At the back (the road end) there is an ossuary – peep through the grille if you want to see neatly stacked skulls and bones.

The only interest in the church is the mosaic, but that is no slight interest. At a glance its size, and the poor lighting, may prompt you to turn away disappointed, but if possible have the light put on and study it carefully. It is sixth century, and has something in common with the much bigger mosaic in SS. Cosmas and Damian. Christ is flanked by Peter and Paul and by two martyr saints – one Theodore, the other perhaps a companion in martyrdom. Christ, however, is not advancing on the clouds, as in Cosmas and Damian, but seated on an orb representing the heavens (as in an earlier mosaic recently discovered in the catacomb of Domitilla) with great elegance and a gentle face. His garments seem surprisingly to be black, with gold *lati clavi* (Roman stripes indicating rank).

The famous Etruscan Wolf used to be kept here, before Pollaiuolo added Romulus and Remus and it was sent to the Palatine.

If you continue past the church you will enjoy a very fine view of the Capitol with the Temple of Saturn in the foreground.

CHAPTER 10

Between the Capitol and the Largo Argentina

*The Largo di Torre Argentina – The Gesù – The Rooms of
St Ignatius Loyola – The Basilica of St Mark – The Palazzo
di San Marco – Convent of Tor de' Specchi – Santa Maria
della Pietà – Santa Maria in Campitelli – The Tartarughe
Fountain – Sant' Ambrogio – Santa Maria del Pianto – The
Palazzo Mattei*

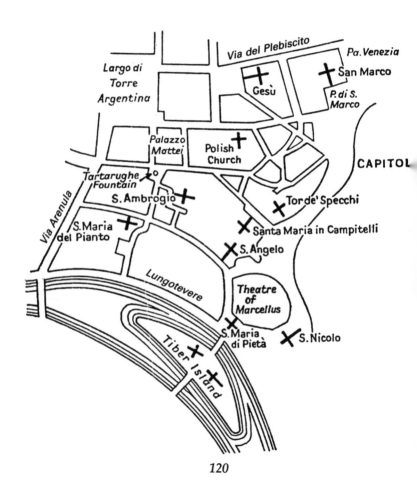

This chapter is about a fairly small area. There are at least three churches in it worth recommending, a maze of attractive old streets – some of it, since the fifteenth century, the Jewish Ghetto – and, if you can find it, Rome's most elegant of fountains, the Tartarughe – 'Tortoises'.

The bounds are the Tiber near the Island, the foot of the Capitol Hill from the Island to the Piazza Venezia, the Via del Plebiscito to the Largo di Torre Argentina, and from there to the Lungotevere (Embankment) by the Via Arenula. If it sounds complex, study the map and you will see how simple it is.

The Largo di Torre Argentina

The Largo di Torre Argentina is a well-known traffic centre (*Largo* is roughly equivalent to our 'Broad', as used at Oxford) around a tangle of ruins. The 'tangle' of ruins becomes intelligible if viewed from the side of the enclosure on which there is a small colonnade of arches; four distinct flights of steps lead to as many temples of the Republican era – B.C. The dilapidated-looking theatre saw Rossini's *Barber of Seville* cried off the stage at its first performance in 1816. Close by the viewpoint I have suggested is a shrine of Our Lady in the wall of the corner building, with an inscription recording that it was one of the twenty-four Madonnas of Rome believed to have become animated, before many witnesses, in 1797.

The name Argentina is derived from the Latin for Strasbourg (*Argentoratum*) – a sixteenth-century bishop of that city had a residence here.

The Gesù

Just beyond the Largo, down the Via del Plebiscito in the direction of the Capitol, is the Church of the Gesù and the Generalate of the Jesuits, where St Ignatius Loyola lived and died and established his Society. The dedication of the church is to the Holy Name of Jesus. When it is illuminated – inside – for a solemn function the impression is unforgettable; at other times I think it lacks any great quality (I accept blame for opinions like this) save for the magnificent eighteenth-century baroque altar of St Ignatius by the Jesuit brother Andrea Pozzo. This is in the left transept, but you view it first from the transept on the right, then approach to study the detail. The harmony of its marbles, bronze work, and groups of statuary – by different artists – makes it a masterpiece. Underneath the altar is the gilded bronze urn containing the saint's relics, by Alessandro Algardi (1637), above it the silver statue originally by Pierre Legros (1697); unfortunately it was despoiled during the French occupation of Rome in 1797 and had to be partly reconstructed by Canova. The globe in the hand of God the Father, in the Trinity that crowns the monument, is one enormous piece of lapis lazuli.

Next to St Ignatius's altar is the tiny shrine chapel of the Madonna della Strada (of the Road), a painting linked with the early history of the Jesuits and popular with motorists.

The altar of St Francis Xavier, opposite that of St Ignatius, by Pietro da Cortona, is overshadowed by the splendour of its rival. It enshrines, in a reliquary, the arm with which St Ignatius's companion baptized so many thousands in his apostolate to India and Japan. The painting represents the death of St Francis Xavier on the Island of Sancian near Macao.

The Gesù was begun in 1568, its architects Vignola and Jacopo della Porta. Should you be in Rome about New Year, you will find one of the finest Christmas Cribs here. On 31st July the feast of St Ignatius is kept with solemnity.

The rooms of St Ignatius Loyola

Your visit will not be complete without seeing the rooms of St Ignatius, the first little 'Generalate' that he had built, now incorporated in the vast block next to the church. Ask at the main door and you will be sent down a long corridor until notices direct you upstairs. There is a great deal worth seeing in these rooms, connected not only with Ignatius but other Jesuit saints and with the early history of the Society, but they are so poorly lit that it is hard to make much of it out. Note, however, the painting of the young soldier Ignatius in armour. There are two altars. The one with a painting of the Holy Family is that at which the saint offered Mass the day he died, before that very picture.

The Basilica of St Mark

If, leaving the house, you follow the Via di Ara Coeli leading straight to the Capitol, you may turn left at the end to find the Basilica of St Mark. Many visitors never discover this beautiful and historic church, partly because when they pass this way they are preoccupied with the Capitol, and also because the façade is screened by trees. St Mark's was reconstructed by Pope Paul II in the early fifteenth century when he built the adjacent Palazzo Venezia. Paul was himself a Venetian, and after he had used the Palace as a papal residence it became the Embassy of the Venetian republic – of which the patron saint is St Mark the Evangelist. His symbol, the lion, was also the badge of the Republic.

The basilica, first founded by another St Mark, the fourth-century Pope of that name, may be entered either from the Piazza di Ara Coeli or by a side door through the entrance to the Palazzo Venezia. Reconstructed in the ninth and fifteenth centuries, it was transformed again in 1744 in a delicate baroque style. The twenty beautiful columns are of Sicilian jasper. The interior reminds me of one of those small theatres you sometimes find in German castles.

The principal interest is the great apse mosaic. It is one of several set up in Rome in the ninth century in a style which I find charming while I admit that it is technically poor. Instead of the emperor-like enthroned Christ of both earlier and later mosaics, in these he is usually represented standing – coming on the clouds of heaven. He is flanked by saints, who in this case are identified as, to the left, Felicissimus, Mark the Evangelist, and Pope Gregory V who set up the mosaic; to the right, Pope St Mark, who founded this church and is buried under the altar, Pope Agapitus, and St Agnes. In a crypt below the sanctuary are relics of the Persian martyrs Abdon and Sennen. You may ask permission to see excavations of the earlier churches.

There is also a fine coffered ceiling by the architect of the Sistine Chapel in the Vatican, Giovanni dei Dolci. The porch is fifteenth century. Round the corner in the Piazza Venezia a door near the end of the Palace admits to a shrine chapel, the 'Madonnina di San Marco', ruined by electric votive lights, and to a further chapel where the Blessed Sacrament is frequently exposed, but which has been marred by very crude modernization.

The Palazzo di San Marco

The Palazzo di San Marco itself is now a museum. You may see Paul II's apartment that Mussolini used as a study. He harangued the Romans from the balcony opening on to the Piazza. The exhibits here are mostly medieval and renaissance sculpture, paintings, weapons, porcelain, majolica, tapestries, etc. Sometimes special exhibitions are displayed here.

Convent of Tor de' Specchi

At this point I want to describe a short walk through this quarter – not in order to drag you in my footsteps, but to be sure of giving clear directions. From San Marco follow the main road – Via di Teatro di Marcello – towards the Tiber. As you come level with the eagles' cage at the foot of the Capitol the shops on the right are in the ground floor of the Convent of Tor de' Specchi

– the home of the Oblate Sisters founded by St Frances of Rome – whose story is briefly told in the account of Santa Maria Nuova. During the week following her feast on 9th March several rooms in the house are open to visitors. Otherwise, you will have little idea you are passing a convent, let alone one so historic, unless you climb the Capitol and enjoy that beautiful view over the rooftops and into the very courtyards of Tor de' Specchi (Tower of Mirrors).

Church of Santa Maria della Pietà

Ahead of you is the Theatre of Marcellus – described in Chapter 6. If you pass to the right of the ruins you will come out beside the Synagogue, with its ungainly square cupola. There is a little church facing it, close by the bridge to the Tiber Island – Ponte Quattro Capi – the 'Bridge of Four Heads', or the Ponte Fabricio – known as the Madonna della Pietà. On its façade, facing the Jewish Quarter, there is a painting of the Crucifixion and this text from Isaias (65. 2) in both Latin and Hebrew: 'All day long I have stretched out my hands to a disobedient and faithless nation'. It is far from the spirit of the Church today to reproach good-living Jews for the failings of their ancestors, but I think if we set this reproach in its historical background, and especially in its Roman and papal background of relative kindness and forbearance towards Jews, there is something touching in the thought of the pious Catholics who built this little church with a perpetual sermon on its walls.

Retrace your steps. As you do so you will notice a most picturesque group of ruined columns around the entrance to the church of Sant' Angelo in Pescheria (Holy Angel in the Fishmarket). It will probably be closed, but the interior is dull. According to Augustus Hare these are the remains of a colonnade of 270 columns of the Porticus Liviae et Octaviae, built by the handsome Caesar Augustus, Emperor at the time of Christ's birth, to the memory of his wife and sister.

Santa Maria in Campitelli

When you have returned to the Via di Teatro di Marcello, turn left into the Piazza di Campitelli. It is hardly a piazza – just a wide road with a fountain and the church of Santa Maria in Campitelli. The fountain dates from 1589 and is by Jacopo della Porta. There are three things to know about the church – that it is, architecturally, an impressive composition in the Corinthian order, by Carlo Rinaldi (1659), that it has a most glorious shrine of Our Lady, designed by a Maltese named Melchior Cafà, in 1667, and that this church since the time of the Old Pretender and the Cardinal Duke of York, known to Stuart adherents as Henry IX, has been a centre of devotion for the conversion of England.

The Corinthian capital was one of the three types of capital used in ancient Greek and Roman art, and it is distinguished by the decorative use of the acanthus leaf. As a boy, I imagined this acanthus to be a rare sort of plant cultivated exclusively in the gardens of the botanically minded. At Rome I soon realized it was a Mediterranean weed – you cannot explore the Palatine without treading it underfoot, though I believe it was deliberately introduced there in the nineteenth century. It seems to me that the clustering effect of the Corinthian columns towards the sanctuary in Santa Maria in Campitelli is deliberate and very brilliant; I have seen it approached elsewhere, but never attained so well.

The shrine by Melchior Cafà is what is known as a 'Gloria', an architectural dramatization of light. The classic instance at Rome is the 'gloria' around the Chair in St Peter's (see ch. 2); this must be an imitation, for it was designed within a year of that masterpiece of Gian Lorenzo Bernini. Here it is all the more effective, since so grand an effect enshrines so tiny a Madonna – an enamel about ten inches by eight. The tradition is that it appeared miraculously in the year 524 at the table where a Roman lady named Galla was dispensing hospitality to the poor. You can take it that this venerable antiquity is not easily accepted by art critics. If you are very interested you may ask in the sacristy for permission to climb a staircase behind the 'gloria' and examine it closely.

The Tartarughe Fountain

Now if you carry on past Santa Maria in Campitelli you will come in a few steps to the Piazza Mattei, with one of the loveliest things in Rome, the Tartarughe (Tortoises) Fountain. Why do so many people place this fountain, splashing the Acqua Vergine but far less spectacularly than the Trevi, first on their list? I have never found the answer, but I do know that every time I look at it, it seems more perfect. The sculptor of the bronze youths was Taddeo Landini, in 1584. It used to be said that the fountain was designed by the great Raphael, which is not true, but Mrs Charles MacVeagh, who published in 1915 an excellent book on *The Fountains of Papal Rome*, comments very nicely that 'had Raphael designed a fountain, this is the fountain he would have designed'. The composition of various marbles is the work of Jacopo della Porta.

Sant' Ambrogio

Without leaving the fountain you can see a doorway with an inscription to tell you that there is the 'paternal home' of St Ambrose. Ambrose was archbishop of Milan in the fifth century, among whose important contributions to Christian life was the introduction of rhythmic hymns into our worship. There are no archaeological remains to be seen here, but the probability is that excavation would reveal something of Ambrose's family home. According to tradition, his sister, after his death, turned it into a convent. Benedictine nuns were here till the last century, when it became the Roman office for Benedictine monks of the Congregation of Subiaco.

The church has been restored. Although almost unknown, even to Romans, it is of great dignity and beauty. It has this special quality, that walls, vault, and dome are left cream coloured, harmonizing with a plain new marble floor, and against this background its baroque altars and paintings stand out with rare grace of proportion and form. The altar in the left transept, for instance, is rococo (a development of baroque mostly found in Germany, Austria, and Switzerland) in its airy elegance. There is a frieze of paintings above the nave side altars of which the two panels farthest from the high altar are very fine – a Nativity, and the Last Meeting of Saints Benedict and Scholastica. Beneath the high altar lies the body of St Polycarp, second-century bishop and martyr of Smyrna, who had known St John. The story of his martyrdom, one of the earliest in Christian literature whose authenticity has never been denied, gives us the portrait of a simple and lovable old bishop, the beauty and poetry of whose character transfigured the sordid circumstance of his execution.

Sant' Ambrogio is not really open to the public, but if you are interested in seeing the church or venerating the tomb of Polycarp you should ask at the door.

Santa Maria del Pianto

From the Piazza Mattei take the Via Reginella and, as you leave the street, you will glimpse above the housetops the dome of the Church of Santa Maria del Pianto, Our Lady of Grief. This is a beautiful baroque church, open daily for a few brief hours. Visit it early in the morning to venerate its Madonna, said to have wept at the sight of a murder in the streets of Rome.

Palazzo Mattei

If you made that last excursion you should return to the Tartarughe fountain, peep into two courtyards in the piazza, then turn right for a few steps along the Via dei Funari. When you notice a great arch on the left, giving you a glimpse of a lovely courtyard, turn in – no one will object. This is the Palazzo Mattei. The courtyard (early seventeenth century) is not merely picturesque, but a museum in itself, decorated with antique sculptures and tombs.

The Via dei Funari will lead you into a small piazza with a restaurant that might suit you for lunch. If you are economizing, however, choose somewhere more modest. Notice the shrine of Our Lady of Campitelli on the wall of the house opposite. It reproduces the ancient enamel which you cannot see properly in the church itself.

CHAPTER 11

The Tiber Island

*The Ponte Fabricio – Ponte Rotto and the Great Sewer –
Church of St Bartholomew – Hospital of the Brothers of St
John of God – The Madonna of the Lamp*

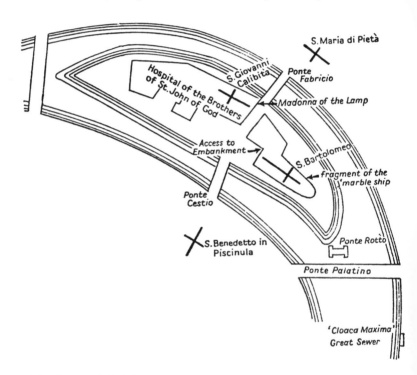

The Ponte Fabricio

Almost everyone likes an island, yet, while almost every visitor
to Rome must become aware the Tiber Island exists, few take
the trouble to visit it. Two bridges connect it with the
embankments, but I shall suppose that you are approaching
from the foot of the Capitol. Head for the Theatre of Marcellus.
Just beyond it is the Ponte Fabricio, also known as the Bridge
of Four Heads, from the effigies of Janus looking in all

directions. Janus was the god of gates and entrances, and this is why our first month takes his name – January. This bridge, which still carries traffic, was built in 62 B.C., and still bears the inscription of the Officer of Roads, after whom it is named 'Fabricio'.

History

A thread of history links everything on the Tiber Island. This thread is the art of medicine. The island is said to have been formed by a bank created in this bend of the river when republican Romans, having overthrown the dynasty of the Tarquins, hurled the royal crops into the river. Then, in 292 B.C., after a plague, envoys were sent to Greece to bring home a statue of Aesculapius, god of health and medicine. As the successful expedition returned up the Tiber a serpent concealed aboard slipped ashore at the island. Snakes are the symbol of Aesculapius, probably on account of their instinctive awareness of edible and poisonous herbs. As a consequence, a temple was built here to Aesculapius and the island was embanked to represent the shape of a ship, with an obelisk for mast.

The Church on your left is that of St Bartholomew. In the corner of the piazza a door admits you to a terrace with steps at the end leading down to the modern embankment. Close to the bottom of the steps is a sizeable fragment of the ancient vessel sculptured in travertine, including the serpent of Aesculapius.

Ponte Rotto and the Great Sewer

This promenade is a point of vantage to study – and, by morning light, to photograph – three historic bridges. From here you can read the inscription on the Ponte Fabricio. Its design is interesting too, for it has been copied in modern times, both at Rome and in Paris. From the tip of the island you see a single arch in midstream, Ponte Rotto, the Broken Bridge, a fifteenth-century rebuilding of one constructed in 180 B.C. It was destroyed by the swollen Tiber in the lifetime of Michelangelo, who commented on its instability a few days before the disaster. Just beyond this picturesque fragment can be glimpsed the exit of Rome's Great Sewer, dating from the days of the kings (fifth century B.C.). If you round the tip you can view the bridge leading to Trastevere, a structure of A.D. 370 rebuilt.

Church of St Bartholomew

Return to the piazza and visit the church of St Bartholomew, whose relics lie in an ancient bath beneath the high altar.

9. The Church of St Bartholomew on the Tiber Island

Bartholomew is believed to be that Nathanael whom Jesus so kindly called 'an Israelite in whom there is no guile'. The church dates from the year 1000 and was built to receive these relics; the leaden vessel in which they were sent from Benevento is preserved.

In the chapel to the left of the sanctuary is a monument on which is incised what appears to be a Noah's Ark. It is in fact a floating flour mill, and this was the chapel of the millers' fraternity. In the eighth century barbarians cut the aqueducts that provided water power for the mills of Rome, and thereafter they were moored to this island to take advantage of the rapid current where the river divides. These mills seem to have survived down to the nineteenth century.

In the eleventh century Rahere, a courtier of William Rufus, contracted malaria at Rome and was nursed to health by Canons of St Augustine who at that time served St Bartholomew's (today there are Franciscans). In gratitude Rahere became an Augustinian and founded in London the magnificent Priory Church of St Bartholomew that still stands by Smithfield Market and the famous hospital known familiarly to Londoners as 'Barts'.

Hospital of the Brothers of St John of God

The monument before the basilica was set up to commemorate the First Vatican Council, in 1870, and represents St Bartholomew, St Paulinus of Nola, St Francis, and St John of God. The charitable foundation of John of God occupies the other half of the island – upstream. Nursing brothers of this Order, founded in Spain in the sixteenth century, settled at Naples on their return from the famous victory of Lepanto, credited with saving Christendom from Turkish domination. After a time they made a foundation in Rome which soon transferred to the Tiber Island, around the ancient church of St John Calybites. This church is near the Ponte Fabricio, but should it be closed you may well ask at the hospital for permission to visit it, and you will enjoy the advantage of walking through the handsome hospital cloisters. The appearance of this church today is completely baroque.

The Madonna of the Lamp

Perhaps when you first crossed to the island you noticed a simple shrine of the Madonna against the wall. The original is venerated in the hospital church, under the title 'Madonna of the Lamp'. Formerly it was an open-air shrine known as the Madonna of the Mills – those mills already explained. In 1557 a flood submerged the painting, but the waters subsided to reveal the lamp still burning. Eventually it was transferred to the chapel where it is now venerated. In 1797 two crucifixes and twenty-four Madonnas of Rome were alleged, on the attested evidence of witnesses, to become animated – among them this Madonna of the Tiber Island. The phenomenon was followed by many miracles.

CHAPTER 12

Between the Corso Vittorio Emmanuele and the Tiber

San Giovanni dei Fiorentini – Santa Maria di Monserrato – The Venerable English College – San Girolamo della Carità – The Piazza Farnese and the Farnese Palace – St Bridget's Room – Santa Maria dell' Orazione e della Morte – Palazzo Spada – Santa Maria della Quercia – The Ponte Sisto – San Salvatore in Onda – Santissima Trinità dei Pellegrini – San Paolo alla Regola – San Carlo ai Catinari – The Campo dei Fiori – San Lorenzo in Damaso – The Palazzo della Cancelleria – Sant' Andrea delle Valle

This is an area shaped like a triangle (very roughly), with as its apex the Ponte Vittorio Emmanuele (by which you cross to St Peter's), the Corso Vittorio Emmanuele (not to be confused with *the* Corso) to the right, Tiber to the left, and the Largo di Torre Argentina and Via Arenula at the base. It would be very helpful to check this on a map before exploring the neighbourhood.

This is a charming sector of renaissance Rome. Among its narrow roads and alleys are attractive courtyards, palaces, piazzas, byways festooned with laundry, dark entries, fountains, markets, and churches. It is Rome *par excellence*. At its heart are the famous Piazza Farnese and the Campo de' Fiori, which should each be visited both by day and again after dark to see the Piazza illuminated and the Campo de' Fiori alive with its tumbling and colourful market (Saturday nights for the market). I shall give in detail a few walks which make a good introduction to this quarter but you will learn to get the best out of it by exploring at your leisure.

San Giovanni dei Fiorentini

Take the apex of the triangle. Here, by the Ponte Vittorio Emmanuele, is San Giovanni dei Fiorentini – St John of the Florentines, a handsome renaissance church, though it looks a bit mean seen from the river. Florence was the home of the greater minds of the renaissance, so it is not surprising that four famous fifteenth-century architects contested to design this church – Sansovino was the winner – and five others continued the building down to its completion by Borromini in 1734.

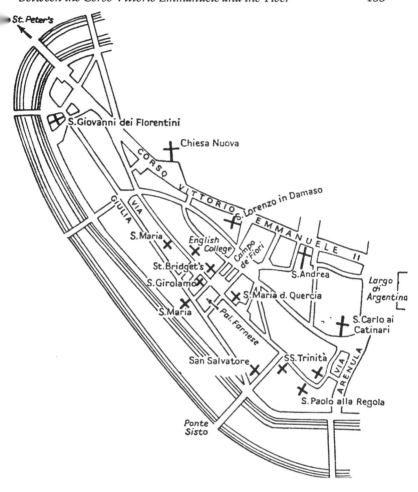

Borromini – responsible for the present appearance of St John Lateran – is buried near the third left column of the nave, where a commemorative tablet has been put up.

The interior is stately and dignified with plenty of interest if it suits your taste. It has a treasure that might escape your eye. The third bay on the right is not a chapel like the others, but the sacristy door. Over it is a delicate young John the Baptist, in the charming Florentine style of the fifteenth century, not unreasonably attributed to Donatello, who particularly favoured John the Baptist as a subject for sculpture. The last chapel to the right, before the transept, is St Philip Neri's, because he was parish priest here.

Turn right and walk up the Via Giulia as far as the Piazza della Moretta, where you may find a lively market in progress, and bear left to continue along Via Monserrato, as far as the Piazza Farnese. Many of the houses in Via Giulia deserve a second glance, but bear in mind that in a narrow street it is difficult to appreciate a tall building unless you take note of it and stand back to study it deliberately. Note Number 93, and 66, with the delicately rendered arms of Pope Paul III, built by the architect Antonio di Sangallo for himself.

Santa Maria di Monserrato

As you reach the Via Monserrato, on the left is a street notice from the days of papal government forbidding the Romans to distribute garbage, as they do nowadays! You may have wondered whether the name has anything to do with the Spanish shrine of Our Lady of Montserrat – it has; her church is along on the right. It was at the shrine at Montserrat that the young soldier Ignatius of Loyola hung up his sword, so it is not surprising that when he had come to Rome to found his Society of Jesus he used to preach and catechize in this church. 'Montserrat' means the jagged or sawn mountain – as anyone who has seen a photograph of the famous Spanish shrine will easily appreciate. Above the door of this Roman church is a shrine of the Madonna seated among rocky crags while the Divine Child cuts away at them with a hacksaw. The same quaint notion appears in a painting in the ornate chapel – with a reproduction of the Madonna, second on the left in the church.

A few doors from here, opposite No. 146, is an interesting courtyard. With ox-blood walls, graceful arches, and vista of greenery and water beyond, it would make a pretty stage set. On the walls is a fine collection of fragments of sculpture, mostly pagan, but including a Eucharistic Meal – a subject very frequently found in catacomb paintings of the second and third centuries but rare in sculpture.

As Via Monserrato narrows at the next piazza (Pa. Santa Caterina) you pass the Venerable English College on your left, the Church of Saint Catherine at the back of the piazza, and on the corner ahead San Girolamo della Carità.

The Venerable English College

The English College is styled 'venerable' and it has indeed a long history. Seminaries usually date only from after the Council of Trent in the mid-sixteenth century, and the early beginnings of this English foundation at Rome were as a pilgrim hostel shortly after the crowded Holy Year of 1350. During the reign of Queen Elizabeth it became a college for training priests – potential martyrs – for the English Mission, and St Philip Neri, who lived across the road, used to kiss the footprints of these courageous young men when they passed him. If you visit Shrewsbury Catholic Cathedral you can look for a window representing St Philip saluting the English boys in these narrow Roman streets. The first English College boy to suffer was Saint Ralph Sherwin, martyred at Tyburn in 1581. Although the chapel of the College was rebuilt between 1866 and 1888 its altarpiece is a magnificent painting of the Trinity, represented according to a beautiful medieval tradition. It dates from about 1580, and is by Durante Alberti. This picture was familiar to the martyrs of the English College. Anyone interested in epitaphs should read that on the memorial to Mary Swinburne, who apparently died at Rome in 1767 aged ten, having mastered all the virtues and more than three languages. You must ask permission at the door to visit the College chapel.

San Girolamo della Carità

Across the piazza is San Girolamo della Carità. 'Girolamo' is Jerome, the great fourth-century Doctor of the Church. According to tradition this church is on the site of the home of Paula, a Roman lady with whom Jerome stayed when he was summoned to Rome to help Pope Damasus, and who subsequently followed him back to the Holy Land and became abbess of a convent at Bethlehem, while Jerome lived there in a cave next to that of the Nativity. In 1524 the church passed to a Brotherhood of Charity, which gave us the rest of its title. In its present form it is seventeenth century, by several architects. There is something unusually attractive about the warmth of colour and decoration, the cluster of Corinthian pilasters towards the sanctuary, the semi-circular balconies supported by sturdy Ionic columns.

Two chapels here are very famous – the Spada and the Antamoro, both named after families. The Spada Chapel, first on the right, shows a unique use of inlaid marble in tones of chestnut and amber, by Francesco Borromini, 1660. It enshrines a fifteenth-century Madonna and, in the little urns right and left, relics of martyrs. Note the communion rail of marble transformed into drapery. The Antamoro Chapel by Filippo Juvarra, dedicated to St Philip Neri, is to the left of the sanctuary. Built in 1710, this is a gem of Roman baroque, and demonstrates to a remarkable degree in such a small space its use of varied marbles, dynamic sculpture, sweeping curves, and a 'dramatization of light' – look up into the vault.

It was here that St Philip (to Romans Pippo Buono – Good Pip) founded in 1551 his Congregation of the Oratory, established in England today at Edgbaston and Kensington. Even after the great Chiesa Nuova had been built for him he stayed on till he was made to go in 1583. His cat remained still longer, and Philip sent one of his priests daily to buy catmeat and see that pussy found it satisfactory. The fifteenth-century crucifix in a chapel to the right is said to have spoken to the saint. Upstairs – through the sacristy – you may visit his rooms and chapel.

St Oliver Plunket, martyred archbishop of Armagh, resided at San Girolamo in 1645.

This church, and the saint's rooms, are normally open only till 11 a.m. At other hours you may ask to be admitted to the church by ringing at the convent door in the piazza, but the rooms are not usually shown after 11. The annual pilgrimage in honour of St Philip is on 26th May.

The Piazza Farnese and the Farnese Palace

Just beyond San Girolamo della Carità the Via Monserrato leads into the Piazza Farnese. Apart from being packed with parked vehicles, this remains one of the quieter and more dignified of Roman piazzas. To appreciate the Farnese Palace you should stand back beyond the fountains. After dark, when palace and fountains are floodlit, it is transfigured into a new splendour the architect never imagined.

The solid façades of Roman palaces sometimes seem dull to the Englishman, who expects a grander setting. But you can do more than just admire the Farnese from a distance; return across the square and explore its courtyard; go through the arch beyond and enjoy its little garden. 'Farnese' was the family name of Pope Paul III, for whom the design – of this side of the palace – was begun by Antonio da Sangallo the Younger. It was completed by Michelangelo in 1580. The sarcophagus to the right side of the courtyard was brought here from that huge mausoleum of Caecilia Metella, turned fortress, on the Via Appia. The palace is now the French Embassy. Some of its apartments are usually open for an hour late on Sunday mornings. Especially interesting are tapestries, old and modern. The former reproduce paintings in the Raphael Rooms in the Vatican.

The fountains in the piazza were discovered in the Baths of Caracalla in 1466 and set up first in the Piazza Venezia – Paul II was building the Palazzo Venezia at the time. Paul III transferred them here to improve the piazza before *his* palace.

The Bridgettine Convent – St Bridget's room

On one side of the piazza Farnese is the façade, with a quaint little bell tower beyond, of Santa Brigida, a convent of Bridgettine Sisters where you may see the room and relics of their fourteenth-century foundress, a Queen of Sweden, and of their first abbess, her daughter Catherine. The Bridgettine Order has a convent in England, at South Brent, Devon, with an unbroken history since its foundation by Henry V to pray for the souls of those who fell at Agincourt. Before it went into exile the convent was at Isleworth, where Syon House now stands, over the Thames from Kew Gardens. Here in the Roman convent you will be shown the room where the saint died in 1373. It is a pleasant experience to arrive for sung Vespers in the late afternoon.

By way of a diversion, I will mention S. Maria dell' Orazione e delle Morte, behind the Farnese Palace. Belonging to a Confraternity for burying the dead, it is a beautiful baroque ellipse with blue grey – or is it purple grey? – and gold for dominant tones. You will probably find it open only on Sundays.

Palazzo Spada

You may care to leave the route I am describing, setting your back to the Farnese Palace and walking forward to the Campo de' Fiori. The route, however, goes on, past the palace, and into the next piazza with the picturesque Spada Palace to the right. This was built about the same time as the Farnese Palace, but the interesting stucco work in renaissance style on the façade and also in the cortile add charm. You may visit a small art gallery in the palace, but I am not encouraging anyone to do so – there are better collections to which to give your time.

Santa Maria della Quercia

As you leave the Spada Palace, there is, in the far corner of the Piazza, a little church with a garden on the roof. This is S. Maria della Quercia, Our Lady of the Oak, church of the Butchers' confraternity. You may find it open on Sundays. Above the altar there is an icon of Our Lady framed in foliage.

The Ponte Sisto

If you continue away from the Piazza Farnese a right turn leads to a bridge over the Tiber, the Ponte Sisto named after Sixtus IV who built it in 1473 to ease the flow of pilgrim traffic. An interesting event in the life of St Ignatius took place on this bridge. On his way to celebrate Mass at San Pietro in Montorio for one of his priests, a Father Codurius, who was sick, Ignatius stopped and said, 'We will go back; Codurius has just died!'

San Salvatore in Onda

The little church of San Salvatore in Onda was given to St Vincent Pallotti when he was establishing his missionary society. His remains lie under the high altar. Almost everything visible in this church is nineteenth century, except its ancient columns which, as usual, are a mixed assortment from pagan temples. The dedication 'Holy Saviour on the Wave' must allude to the days before the river was embanked. The Tiber in flood would have lapped the walls of the houses.

Santissima Trinità dei Pellegrini

If, instead of turning right to the Ponte Sisto, you had carried straight on past the rather dull church of Santissima Trinità dei Pellegrini – dull except for the façade viewed from a distance on a sunny day – you would have reached, in a few steps, San Paolo alla Regola. I do not encourage you to visit Santissima Trinità, but it is worth knowing that it was the scene of St Philip Neri's charity towards pilgrims, and Cardinal Wiseman, describing the Jubilee of 1825, saw pope and cardinals waiting on the poor.

San Paolo alla Regola

The streets round here, though picturesque, are so dark and narrow that you may be inclined to hurry on towards sunny piazzas. But spare a moment for San Paolo. It represents an interesting tradition in the story of St Paul at Rome. The Acts tell you that Paul, in his first period of captivity whilst awaiting trial before Caesar to whom he had appealed, was allowed to rent his own lodging and support his military guard, but he was free to hold assemblies there 'in great numbers' while he instructed the infant Church at Rome. Here is preserved the room in which he is believed to have given this instruction, and the dedication may be translated 'St Paul's at the place of his teaching'. I can present two facts in favour of this tradition. There is some evidence that tanners plied their trade along this bank of the Tiber, which makes it a suitable place for a tentmaker to set up business, and we do know that to have been Paul's trade and normal livelihood. Further, a life of St Paul that is probably second century describes him as having hired a granary for his meetings – more probably part of one. Excavations behind the church, when the Ministry of Justice was built, were described in an official report as very likely those of a granary. The room venerated as the school of Paul is to the right of the sanctuary. In the apse of the church are paintings by Luigi Garzi of the Conversion, Preaching and Martyrdom of St Paul.

San Carlo ai Catinari

You will come out from this maze of streets on the busy Via Arenula, not far from the Piazza Cairoli. This piazza has a rather sad little fountain, a barrow where flowers are sold, and a number of benches where elderly people sit and watch the traffic. On the far side is the rather massive façade of San Carlo ai Catinari. The saint is Charles Borromeo, sixteenth-century Archbishop of Milan and a great reformer; the *catinari*, according to Augustus Hare, were makers of wooden dishes who traded in the streets round the church.

Several architects have contributed to its design – the façade is by John Baptist Soria, built between 1636 and 1638. The dome is by Rosato Rosati, and its beautiful coffered interior is a lovely sight. The painting behind the high altar is by Pietro da Cortona and represents St Charles Borromeo carrying a Holy Nail (relic of Christ's Passion) in a procession to avert plague at Milan. To the right of the sanctuary is the tiny chapel of the Madonna of Providence, but the picture is only a copy of the original sixteenth-century canvas venerated in the house chapel of the Barnabite Fathers who serve this church. As you stand before this little sanctuary, dim and hung with lamps, look up at the contrast of light that floods in through the dome designed by Gherardi. Dramatic – but so very effective. This is the chapel of St Cecilia, patroness of music, and on her feast day, 22nd November, the Accademia di Santa Caecilia renders sacred music during the festal Mass.

The Campo de' Fiori

This Piazza Cairoli is a good starting place for a new walk, for which I recommend either the early morning or the evening after nightfall. Walk past the church, and the Via Giubbonari will lead you into the busy Campo de' Fiori – the Field of Flowers, with a market at its best on Saturday nights. In the middle of this piazza, maybe almost hidden by the market stalls, is a statue of Giordano Bruno, victim of misguided Catholic zeal for discipline, as I trust we can admit these days with all frankness. He was burnt here by the Inquisition in 1600.

I am now going to describe two churches on the right side of our triangle, that is, on the Corso Vittorio Emmanuele. Suppose you walk down the Corso from the river; the road soon broadens into the Piazza della Chiesa Nuova, described in Chapter 16, though you may find it convenient to make your visit now. The Church of San Lorenzo in Damaso is one you will never see if you look for it; it is built into the great Palazzo della Cancellaria. It is just before you reach the next piazza after that of the Chiesa Nuova, and you enter by a door in the wall of the palace skirting the Corso Vittorio Emmanuele.

San Lorenzo in Damaso

San Lorenzo in Damaso (St Lawrence in the house of Damasus) is one of Rome's most historic churches; as the translation I have given of its title suggests, it is believed to have been founded in the residence of the fourth-century Pope Damasus, famous for, among other things, transforming the tombs of martyrs in the catacombs into beautiful shrines. It was rebuilt by Bramante at the same time as the palace, but has been restored pretty drastically since and now has very little to commend it.

You will notice that you enter by a deep vaulted narthex – this is due to apartments of the palace overhead. Paintings above the colonnades represent St Lawrence as a young deacon, reproaching Sixtus II, going off to martyrdom, that he had left his faithful deacon behind, and also Lawrence's own martyrdom on the gridiron. His encounter with Sixtus is supposed to have occurred where the church of San Sisto now stands, near the Baths of Caracalla. There is a dark and ancient icon of Our Lady at the end of the left aisle. The relics of St Damasus are beneath the high altar.

The Palazzo della Cancelleria

The Palace of the 'Cancelleria', that is, the old Papal Chancery, is nearly a century earlier than the Palazzo Farnese – it was completed in 1494. Much of the design is by Bramante. Its travertine blocks were taken from the Colósseum, and – like the Palazzo Farnese – is another apt subject for the observation that, if the ruins of ancient Rome were restored overnight, half the palaces and churches of the renaissance would have dis-appeared in the operation. The forty-four pillars of the colonna-des in its courtyard are said to have come from the nearby Theatre of Pompey. You may step into the courtyard of this Palace.

Sant' Andrea delle Valle you will find by continuing along the Corso Vittorio Emmanuele, in which case the great church is obvious well before you reach it, or you could go through

narrow back streets parallel with the Corso and enter Sant'
Andrea by a side door. In the Piazza leading away from the
Cancelleria is one of Rome's 'district fountains', put up only in
1927. This is made up of a cardinal's hat, and alludes to Cardinal
Raffaelle Riario, who built the Cancelleria.

Sant' Andrea delle Valle

There is a superb sense of space about this church of Sant'
Andrea, which at first you might mistake for coldness. Look up
into the dome, which really will let you see its vast proportions,
although from outside it is hard to credit that in Rome it ranks
next to St Peter's for size. The architects were Olivieri and Carlo
Maderno, who completed the church by 1650, though Rainaldi
added the façade in 1655. The paintings on the vault of the nave
are nineteenth century and not good, but on the walls and half-
dome of the sanctuary are excellent paintings. The three large
ones on the walls by Calabrese represent the martyrdom of the
saint, but the smaller paintings in the compartments of the apse
above, by Domenichino, are far more attractive; they represent
John the Baptist proclaiming Christ as Messiah, and the call of
Peter and Andrew by the Sea of Galilee, as well as the
martyrdom of the saint. If you stand to the right and look at
two figures painted above the letters PERD you can quite easily,
in certain lights, imagine them to be sculptured in full relief.
Stand below the dome looking towards the nave, and you will
notice that the first two bays of the nave, instead of being open
arches, have been filled with twin renaissance tombs of Popes
Pius II and Pius III, who died in 1464 and 1503 respectively; they
were brought here from old St Peter's.

A chapel to the left of the sanctuary has a shrine to Our Lady
of Purity – a chapel with a beautiful little dome. Here too is a
popular and venerated Santo Bambino, statue of the Infant
Jesus, similar to that at the Ara Coeli.

Of the other side chapels, all interesting, I draw your
attention specially to the first two on the right of the nave,
counting from the door. The first is distinguished for rich
baroque sculpture, the second shows you how restrained the
same style can be; in its austere setting is a reproduction in
bronze of Michelangelo's Pietà at St Peter's, and also of the
figure of Leah and Rachel from his monument to Julius II, the
one famous for its Moses statue, at San Pietro in Vincoli.

There is a tradition that the body of St Sebastian was thrown
into a sewer here, though later recovered and taken to the
catacomb on the Via Appia now known as St Sebastian's.

The first Act of Puccini's opera *Tosca* is set in the church of
Sant' Andrea.

CHAPTER 13

The Aventine and its Churches

Santa Sabina – Sant' Alessio – Santa Maria del Prioratu –Sant' Anselmo – Santa Prisca – San Saba – Porta San Paolo – Monte Testaccio – Santa Balbina

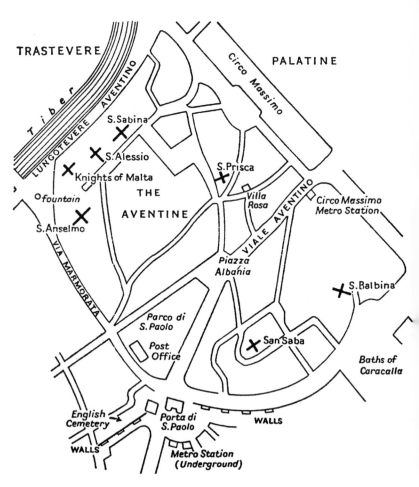

The Aventine is one of Rome's seven hills, and a fairly conspicuous one, because it ends in an abrupt cliff along the Tiber. The contour of the hill is triangular, with the Circo Massimo as the base, the river and the Via Marmorata as one side and the Viale Aventino as the other; St Paul's Gate is at the apex. It would be useful to check this on the map before beginning your visit to the Aventine.

Along the cliff over the Tiber are four churches with their adjacent monasteries. Approaching from the Circo Massimo end (because from near Santa Maria in Cosmedin you may climb to the Aventine by pleasant roads) they are Santa Sabina, Sant' Alessio, Santa Maria del Prioratu, and Sant' Anselmo. On the side of the hill above the Circo Massimo are the Camaldolese Convent and Santa Prisca.

Santa Sabina

Santa Sabina is perhaps the most important – the most 'visit-worthy'. It is a church outstanding architecturally; the adjacent monastery was the home of St Dominic and other saints. There are splendid views of it from the garden known as the Park of the Orange Trees, which also has a grand panorama towards St Peter's. Looking at Santa Sabina from this angle, you see an early fifth-century church barely altered in appearance. The size of the windows may surprise you (they are incidentally of silenite, not glass, set in pierced stone) but this church was built by an Illyrian, and is not characteristically Roman.

Instead of entering by the side porch facing the road, you should pass through the arcade in front of the monastery and find your way to the original main door of Santa Sabina. Few doors are more famous, for this one, of cypress wood, dates from between 420 and 430. Some of the panels are missing, and the survivors are thought to have been rearranged; they vary in quality, and the light is so poor it is hard to see anything clearly. I will explain a few of the panels, and anyone interested can learn all about the rest by buying postcard photographs of them at the shop in the monastery.

The first large panel to the left represents Moses as a shepherd, then God, through the mediation of an angel, speaking from the burning bush, while Moses reverently takes off his shoes; finally Moses receiving the Law from the hand of God – here he is shown twice: once in prayer, then actually accepting the scroll of the law. A hand extended from a cloud is the earliest way of representing God the Father known to Christian art.

Third from the left is the crossing of the Red Sea and the journey through the desert of Sinai. Notice the horses striving against the flood. The opinion has been advanced – and supported by very good authority – that Pharaoh's head is Napoleon Bonaparte's – a satirical substitution during the French occupation of Rome. The right-hand panel of Elias ascending to heaven, letting fall his mantle to his disciple Eliseus, is one of the most elegant of the series. The top left-hand panel is often quoted as one of the earliest representations of the crucifixion in Western Christian art.

A hole in the wall opposite the cypress doors gives you a glimpse of an orange tree, descended from one planted by St Dominic. Near the door, below a grating in the floor, is a room of a Roman house excavated here, which may be the original Christian meeting place, or 'house-church', known as the 'Title of Sabina'.

The interior of St Sabina's lacks the note of antiquity one expects – partly because of the flood of light admitted by its large windows, and also because of the absence of a great apse mosaic. There is a mosaic, however, over the cypress doors, not very attractive but of considerable doctrinal importance. The figures left and right represent 'The Church from the Circumcision' and 'The Church from the Nations'. Perhaps they do not simply stand for Old and New Testaments, but distinguish between Christians of Jewish origin and Christians converted from paganism. The text between them records the building of the church by Peter the Illyrian – its first line contains an assertion of the Pope's supreme and universal authority: a theological document in mosaic!

The nave is distinguished by its rows of twenty-four columns. The patterns of inlaid marble above them have long puzzled archaeologists. An expert of the Pontifical Institute of Archaeology satisfied himself that they represent in fact the standards of the Roman legions in Illyria in the fifth century. I do not swallow this.

Also of interest are the ninth-century choir enclosure, with sculptures in low relief of Persian inspiration; the shrine of the martyr Sabina and others, below the high altar; the fine mosaic of a Master General of the Dominicans in the middle of the nave floor, of 1300; a delicate cosmatesque aumbry at the end of the right aisle and, nearby, a handsome fifteenth-century renaissance tomb; finally, in the chapel half way down the nave on the left, Sassoferrato's famous painting of Our Lady of the Rosary with St Dominic and St Catherine of Siena.

Since John XXIII's time the custom has been revived of the pope assisting in person at the afternoon 'Station' at Santa Sabina's on Ash Wednesday.

Anyone may apply at the monastery to visit the rooms of St

Pius V, sixteenth-century Pope of the Counter-Reformation, and of St Dominic, who was visited here by St Francis, and men may ask to visit the beautifully simple romanesque cloister and the chapter house where SS. Celsus and Hyacinth, subsequently apostles of Hungary and Bohemia, gave their vows as Friar Preachers into the hands of St Dominic. St Thomas Aquinas too was a friar here.

There is an excellent shop in the monastery which should be particularly useful to tertiaries and anyone interested in Dominican spirituality.

Sant' Alessio

A few steps beyond Santa Sabina is Sant' Alessio, a fine church of extreme antiquity – fourth century – but as you see it now dressed up in a restrained eighteenth-century décor reminiscent of Wedgwood china. From earlier times it has one of the best cosmatesque floors in Rome, and also, in the choir behind the altar, two handsome cosmatesque columns. The right-hand one is signed by 'Laurentius' who states that it is one of nineteen – where are the seventeen missing columns? The fathers here say they were carried off by Napoleon.

In the Blessed Sacrament chapel, right of the high altar, there is a beautiful Greek icon of Our Lady of about the tenth century.

Alessio in English is Alexis, but this saint is often spoken of in the Latin form, Alexius. His story is very well illustrated in a ninth-century painting at San Clemente. He ended his days as a domestic in his own home, unrecognized by his parents after years as a hermit in Eastern deserts. Near the door, above an altar, is his recumbent figure, in pilgrim's dress, and clasping in death the letter that was to reveal his identity. Above him is the staircase under which he is said to have slept. The date of this composition is late eighteenth century and the sculptor Andrea Bergondi.

There is a crypt, of about tenth-century date, under the sanctuary, which is not usually open, except at Christmas time when one of Rome's most popular 'polyscenic' cribs is set up there.

Just before you leave the atrium, or forecourt, of the church, there is a porter's lodge where a small selection of postcards is sold. The community living around this courtyard are 'Somaschi', a religious congregation of priests devoted primarily to the care of youth. Their cloister has been taken over by the State as a 'Centre for Roman Studies'. A renaissance cloister, with antique columns, you will be allowed to visit it if you ring the bell at the first door – a very small door easily missed – past the monastery.

Santa Maria del Prioatu – the Keyhole

Immediately after Sant' Alessio is one of the most charming squares of Rome, the Piazza dei Cavalieri di Malta, so called because through the gate with the famous keyhole lies the Priory and garden of the Knights of Malta. House and garden and piazza were all designed by Piranesi towards the end of the eighteenth century – the keyhole too, in which St Peter's is perfectly framed, is quite deliberate. Piranesi is better known to collectors of prints, and once you have seen his etchings you will see that he was working in the same mood when he designed the sculpture of the piazza. Admission to the Priory is by special application only, but a glimpse of the church can be had from the atrium of Sant' Anselmo.

International Benedictine College of Sant' Anselmo

The campanile that dominates the Aventine beyond Piranesi's rather fantastic little piazza is that of the International Benedictine College of Sant' Anselmo, which is also the seat of the Abbot Primate of the Federation of 'Black Monks' – that is to say, of nearly all monks under the Rule of St Benedict except Cistercians and Trappists. The design of church and monastery can be attributed to the combined inspirations of Abbots Hildebrand de Hemptinne and Fidelis von Stotzingen, and it is, I think, just a little more Roman than it is German. For a church built at the dawn of our own century it is certainly fine, and the fact that it follows the plan of an ancient basilica is in keeping with both the Roman and Benedictine spirit of worship. Sant' Anselmo is very much frequented by people who appreciate dignity in worship.

A bronze figure of St Anselm – Norman Archbishop of Canterbury – has recently been placed in the tranquil little atrium. From here too you may have a glimpse of Piranesi's façade to the church of the Knights of Malta, Santa Maria del Prioratu. The church of Sant' Anselmo you may take in more or less at a glance. The mosaics are unusual in that the figures alone are in mosaic, without any background – I think this gives a weak effect. The paschal candlestick is a modern reproduction of cosmatesque. A door by the Blessed Sacrament altar will take you down to the crypt – an impressive vista of arches with, behind the altar, a statue of St Benedict with his hands raised in the ancient gesture of prayer – which happens also to be the posture in which he died. This is best seen in the afternoon.

In the entrance to the monastery – from the atrium – is a remarkable Roman mosaic of Orpheus charming some very quaint beasts. This is a discovery made here during the building of the college. Men interested in Benedictine life may ask for an English-speaking student to show them round.

After visiting Sant' Anselmo you could go down the hill to visit St Paul's Gate, the English Cemetery, and the Monte Testaccio, but these will be described at the end of this chapter.

Santa Prisca

Instead, retrace your steps till you have passed Santa Sabina and then bear right to the Largo Aventino, on the far side of which you will find the modest little church of Santa Prisca. Behind that modesty there is an impressive history, if tradition be true. You may read in the Acts of the Apostles how, when St Paul came to Corinth, he stayed with Jewish Christians exiled from Rome, named Aquila and Priscilla. Later they moved to Ephesus and Paul stayed with them again, and still later — we gather from greetings Paul sends in a letter — they were able to return to Rome. If Prisca is to be identified with Priscilla, and the tradition that her home was here be true, then this is a very venerable Christian site indeed. But of course that is challenged, and it cannot be proved. Excavations have been made, but far from revealing a primitive Christian home they have found another Mithraic temple. Some recent finds, however, of terracotta lamps with the Chi-Rho (☧) monogram for the name of Christ, suggest at least that Christian worship has been established here from a very early date.

The church itself need not detain you. Just notice the ancient columns, almost buried in later piers. To the right in a little baptistery is an ancient corinthian capital traditionally 'used by St Peter' as a font, but our knowledge of the early practice of baptism makes this very improbable.Near the baptistery a door leads to a terrace with steps down into a playground. From the yard you enter the excavations – you have to find the sacristan to admit you. These were initially made between 1935 and 1940. You pass through interesting substructures to the crypt shrine of St Prisca. Beyond that you enter the Mithraic temple. In some ways it is more important than the one under San Clemente – for instance, it has vestiges of wall paintings – but I think it is less impressive and less easy to understand.

Round the corner from Santa Prisca is the Villa Rosa, a pensione run by English-speaking Dominican sisters.

San Saba

As you continue straight downhill to the Viale Aventino you will notice on the crest of the hill beyond – known as the 'Little Aventine' – the picturesque church of St Saba. Old guide-books describe it as standing 'alone and isolated' among vineyards, and within its little courtyard you still appreciate the faded echo of that seclusion and charm. As it stands today the church is mostly tenth and thirteenth century and, frankly, a little disappointing, but it is full of history.

First, here was the home of St Silvia, mother of St Gregory the Great who admired those English slave boys in the Roman market, and later sent Augustine to convert England. When Gregory was a monk on the Coelian Hill he suffered from stomach disorders, and Silvia used to walk over with a silver dish of vegetables specially prepared – just what her boy needed. You may ask to see the remains of her chapel, below the church. They were brought to light in 1909.

If you should ever go to the Holy Land, I recommend a visit to the monastery of Mar Sabas out in the desert beyond Bethlehem – women never admitted, however. There in the sixth century St Sabas became for the monks of Palestine what Benedict was for monasticism in the West. Eventually the monks of St Sabas were driven away from their homes by invading Saracens, and were given shelter in Rome, here on the 'Little Aventine'. The memory of St Sabas is far from dead, and when the Greek Orthodox superior of the monastery came to Italy – towards the end of Vatican Council II – to take home from Venice the body of their holy founder, he called at St Sabas to venerate a relic still preserved here.

In the left aisle (find the light switch) there is a good medieval fresco of Our Lady flanked by St Sabas and St Andrew.

The former mosaics of the apse were replaced in 1575 by frescoes, not very good, though the painted Crucifixion below them is older and better. The church is served by the Society of Jesus.

Porta San Paolo; the Pyramid of Caius Cestius

The Viale Aventino, which you crossed to reach St Sabas, continues to the Porta San Paolo, St Paul's Gate. On your way you will notice, to right and

10. The sentry's walk of the sixth-century Porta San Paolo

left, massive sections of the Republican Wall of the city – B.C. The Wall of which St Paul's Gate is a part dates from the third century A.D. So St Paul, on his way to execution, did not pass through this gate, although he did follow the Via Ostiense and certainly saw that great pyramid just beyond the gate, the Mausoleum of Caius Cestius. Note its inscriptions.

The gate itself was altered in the fifth century. It is double, and the courtyard between is worth a glance. A little door on the city side of the gate admits you to a small Museo della Via Ostiense – Museum of the Road to Ostia.

Monte Testaccio

To the right of the gate, inside the walls, is the English Protestant cemetery, celebrated as the resting place of the poets Keats and Shelley. Further towards the Tiber is Monte Testaccio, literally a hill of broken pots. The wharves where wine, oil and grain were delivered were nearby, and it was apparently cheaper to dispose of the empties than to return them. If it is ancient Roman pottery you want, you can fill sacks here, mostly first to third century A.D. A cross on the summit reminds us that a medieval street pageant of the Passion used the Testaccio for its Calvary.

The small restaurants near the Porta San Paolo should be cheap and reliable.

Santa Balbina

There is one more church on the little Aventine, just beyond St Sabas, that ought perhaps to be mentioned. It is closed to the public, but the sisters who occupy the monastery buildings adjacent may let you in if you call at a reasonable hour. This is Santa Balbina, named after the second-century virgin martyr who is believed to have been the daughter of the Mamertine gaoler, and to have secured the chains of St Peter, now venerated at San Pietro in Vincoli, for Christian veneration. It is a fine basilica, structurally of the sixth century, in a quiet site overlooking the Baths of Caracalla. If you are able to get in, you will find a good cosmatesque tomb, an episcopal chair by the same craftsmen, and an altar from old St Peter's.

CHAPTER 14

The Quirinal and thereabouts

*The Piazza del Quirinale – The Quirinal Palace – Sant'
Andrea al Quirinale – San Silvestro al Quirinale – Santa
Caterina – San' Domenico e Sisto – Trajan's Market – San
Vitale*

In the piazza before the Quirinal you really do feel that you are
on one of the seven hills. The view over the rooftops and domes

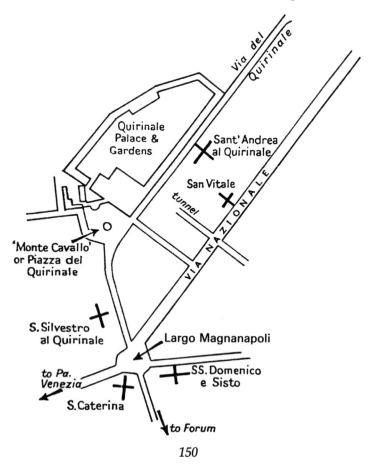

of renaissance Rome towards the heights of the Janiculum and the dome of St Peter's is splendid. Architecturally, each side of this piazza is distinguished, and the obelisk, fountain, and statues in the centre are one of the happiest combinations in Rome of relics of antiquity.

The Piazza del Quirinale

The Palace, now Presidential, was begun by Pope Gregory XIII in the sixteenth century when the heights of the Quirinal were still fairly secluded. The first Pope to live here was that tireless builder, the Franciscan Sixtus V. Apparently the Dioscuri – the heavenly twins, Castor and Pollux – those muscular young men with suits of body-armour and prancing horses, had already stood here for centuries; that is why it is called Monte Cavallo, Horse Hill. They were among the few monuments of antiquity to be left in peace. So Sixtus had them arranged with a fountain that played the water he had newly brought into Rome, carried over ancient arches, and called after his own name (Felix) 'Acqua Felice'. Two hundred years later the Egyptian obelisk was added; it had once stood near the Mausoleum of Augustus. The great granite basin at the foot was the last addition, in 1818. That was formerly in the Forum, where Marforio, now on the Capitol, had reclined above it.

The names of the Greek sculptors Praxiteles and Phidias carved on the pedestals are said to arise from a medieval legend, and not to represent the true authorship of these splendid statues.

The Quirinal Palace

In the Quirinal Palace Pope Pius VII was arrested at night by Napoleon's General Radet in 1809; he paused on this piazza to bless the sleeping city before he was hustled away to France. In the rising of 1848 Pius IX, carrying the Blessed Sacrament on his person, fled from the Quirinal to refuge in the Kingdom of Naples. Finally, in 1871, King Victor Emmanuel II, acting – as we can now recognize – under Providence, relieved the popes of the burden of temporal government, and also of their palace on the Quirinal.

A number of architects contributed to the design of this palace. The portal surmounted by a Madonna is by Flaminio Ponzio. Like other Roman palaces, it is rich with paintings and mosaic floors brought from the ruins of ancient Rome, and has extensive geometrically-planned gardens cooled by the play of fountains. One should enquire about the possibility of the Quirinal – and its gardens – being open to visitors on application. It is very pleasant on a Roman afternoon to stroll up here and watch the changing of the guard. This is a rather protracted function, but it pays to wait to the end, when the guard marches off escorted by motor bikes at foot pace, even when they swerve steeply downhill to their barracks. I have found the timing a little irregular, but if you arrive before four and exercise patience you should not be disappointed.

Sant' Andrea al Quirinale

The road along the right side of the Quirinal Palace – Via del Quirinale – leads in a few minutes to the church of Sant' Andrea al Quirinale, St Andrew's at the Quirinal, architecturally one of the most perfect in Rome. It is a creation of Bernini's genius, a jewel of the baroque age. Bernini seems to have realized he had surpassed himself when, along with his assistant Giovanni Mattia de Rossi, he refused to accept a fee for his work.

Sant' Andrea was begun in 1658 as the church of the Jesuit novitiate in Rome, cradle of many famous Jesuits and Saints of the Society – to name a few, St Stanislaus Kostka, St Aloysius, St Robert Bellarmine. It took its dedication from a dilapidated parish church of Sant' Andrea in Monte Cavallo, given to the Jesuits a century earlier. It differs from other churches on the elliptical or oval plan in that entrance and altar are set on the shorter axis. This may sound too geometrical, but when you are there you will recognize what I mean. Bernini devoted his genius to training the eye upwards to the source of light, which in its turn pours down in golden shafts and clouds among choirs of romping cherubs. Notice in particular the festooned angels above the windows right and left of the four beautiful columns of the sanctuary.

I think it is the harmony between the choice of marbles, sculpture, and the flow of light which makes this church, so full of architectural movement, one of the quietest and most peaceful in Rome. It certainly introduces you to another side of Bernini than the one he shows in his self-portrait as David the stone slinger (Borghese Gallery). In his old age he returned frequently to sit in Sant' Andrea, the devout Bernini who went to Mass daily, was to be found nightly in the Gesù, and who made the spiritual exercises of St Ignatius.

Enshrined here is St Stanislaus Kostka, a Polish novice who died in 1568 at the age of eighteen. His relics repose in the third chapel on the left, in an urn of bronze and lapis lazuli made in 1716. In the next chapel – one with a lárge crucifix – is a monument to King Carlo Emmanuele IV of Sardinia and

Piedmont, who abdicated to enter the Society and died here in 1818.

Note the Adoration of Kings and Shepherds in the first chapel on the left, on the side walls, and, in the first chapel on the right, paintings representing the death of St Francis Xavier, and his preaching and baptizing, by Gian Battista Gaulli. The chapel of the Passion has three excellent canvases by Giacinto Brandi, completed in 1682. You may ask to visit the room of St Stanislaus, reconstructed from a part of the house now destroyed. It contains a sculpture in polychrome marble of the dying saint, by the French artist Pierre Legros. The frescoed vault of the sacristy is by Jean de la Borde – note the draperies.

From Sant' Andrea you could walk on to the Quattro Fontane – four fountains at a cross-roads, and the church of San Carlino. These are described in Chapter 24. For the purpose of this chapter, however, take your stand with your back to the Quirinal and follow the Via Ventiquattro Maggio, downhill, towards the Piazza Magnanapoli. From the left pavement you will soon see the church of San Silvestro al Quirinale – if you follow the right side of the road or walk uphill it is very easily missed.

San Silvestro al Quirinale

You climb a staircase to reach the level of the church – little known because not easily detected, but with a very charming and colourful renaissance interior. The long vaulted and painted choir behind the altar and the great domed chapel to the left suggest space and unexpected vistas. Though first mentioned in 1039, the present church dates from the early sixteenth century, when it was taken over by the newly founded Theatine Order. Athough this order was never established in England, the last Catholic bishop of Queen Mary Tudor's reign, Thomas Goldwell of St Asaph's in North Wales, was a Theatine. Under Elizabeth he retired to Rome and in 1584 consecrated the high altar of this church. When conclaves to elect new popes took place at the Quirinal Palace, the inaugural procession of cardinals began from San Silvestro al Quirinale.

Almost every inch here is painted but the work is not all of the same merit. There are two pleasing paintings of St Francis and St John the Baptist in the pilasters of the nave. In the second chapel on the right is a thirteenth-century icon of Our Lady and, on the side wall, a Nativity of Mary by Nebbia – sixteenth century.

To the left of the sanctuary is a large domed chapel of the Assumption for which Domenichino painted four attractive roundels representing David dancing before the Ark of the Covenant, and Old Testament types of Our Lady.

Santa Caterina

A few steps farther you reach the Piazza Magnanapoli, with the church of St Catherine against the leaning Torre delle Milizie, Tower of the Militia, and, up a double flight of steps, San' Domenico e Sisto, church of the Dominican University called the Angelicum.

Santa Caterina is a bleakly grand baroque church of the seventeenth century, dominated by gold, white, and russet-coloured marble. Founded by Dominican nuns, it has been made the church of the Military Ordinariate, that is, of the adjacent headquarters of the bishop of Italian armed forces. The crypt, entered from the street, has been adapted as a memorial chapel.

San' Domenico e Sisto

San' Domenico e Sisto is similar but more colourful. What appears to be an icon of Our Lady enshrined over the altar is in fact an eighteenth-century terracotta plaque in low relief, but over an altar on the left is a large painting of the Madonna attributed to Benozzo Gozzoli, a pupil of Fra Angelico. Just to the right as you enter is a sculpture of Mary Magdalene meeting the risen Christ in Gethsemane, designed by Bernini but executed by a pupil. The group is ruined by a third-rate painted background which was not part of Bernini's design.

Trajan's Market

You could at this point visit the Market of Trajan, entered by a gate a few steps to the right of Santa Caterina. This consists of semi-circular terraces of shops overlooking the remains of Trajan's noble forum, all built in the early years of the second century. Here were fishponds supplied with both fresh and salt water – for the sale of fish; along with fruit, flowers, oil, wine, and Eastern spices. It is worth exploring, not only because it is so remarkably well preserved, but for the unusual views it gives you over the Capitol and Forum. There is also access to the thirteenth-century leaning Tower of the Militia, which you may climb to the top.

Before closing this chapter I suggest you follow the road down the left side of Santa Caterina – between the two churches. It leads round the back of the great forums of Augustus, Caesar, and Nerva, and you will be able to observe how they were adapted for use in medieval and renaissance times. For instance, the upper part of the Forum of Augustus was used as the Roman headquarters of the Knights of Malta. A more comprehensive view of both the Market of Trajan and the Forum will be gained from the Via dei Fori Imperiali.

San Vitale

A few words about San Vitale. This is beside the Via Nazionale, a busy modern shopping street which is hardly a pilgrims' way. Even from a bus you will notice this church, for it lies thirty-five steps below modern street level. Once within the portico, its most ancient feature, time recedes. First built about 400, it is dedicated to the martyr Vitalis, and also to his sons and fellow martyrs, Gervase and Protase.

The interior, which has no columns, is interesting for its walls painted with landscapes in which, as an inscription to each one tells you, a martyrdom is represented, but so discreetly that the landscape quality of the picture as a whole is not disturbed. The last on the right is of St Ignatius of Antioch, who was so impatient for martyrdom, calmly meeting his lions in a meadow with a *ruined* Colosseum in the background!

Cardinal St John Fisher was titular of San Vitale, although, as you may recall, Henry VIII saw to it he had no head to wear the hat on.

San Vitale can be reached by walking up the Via Nazionale for a few minutes from Santa Caterina.

CHAPTER 15

The Trevi Fountain and thereabouts

The Trevi Fountain – Church of SS. Vincent and Anastasius – Santa Maria in Trivio – Santa Maria in Via – San Claudio – San Silvestro in Capite (English Church) – San Marcello al Corso – Santi Apostoli – The Oratory of the Cross – Santa Maria di Loreto – Santissimo Nome di Maria – Trajan's Column – Victor Emmanuel Monument

The Trevi fountain is not so easy to find, but I gather everyone does find it, so it makes a fair point of reference for several walks in Rome's busiest quarter.

The Trevi Fountain

Let me tell you what the Trevi is. It is not just a fountain, it is a *'mostra'*. This means a fountain whose special function is to display one of Rome's principal water supplies. Trevi was built to show the water known as Acqua Vergine, to the source of which Agrippa's soldiers were shown by a young girl – hence the name. If you look up above the fountain you will notice two sculptures, one showing the discovery of the source (right) and the other the building of the aqueduct (left).

There seem to be several opinions about how properly to throw coins in the fountain. You should take up your position at the supply of drinking water at the extreme right, drink with your left hand, and with your right throw the coin over your shoulder into the Trevi. I accept no blame if this rite is criticized – nor if you fall in.

Trevi fountain dates from the eighteenth century, designed by Niccolo Salvi. It represents the sea god Neptune escorted by Tritons with wild sea horses in a setting of tumbling waterfalls. No noble piazza surrounds it, but a tangle of narrow streets full of shops, sightseers, the idle, the busy, souvenir vendors, carriages with demure horses waiting for custom. A little extra dignity is added by the façade of SS. Vincent and Anastasius, with a flight of steps useful for sitting on.

Church of SS. Vincent and Anastasius

This is a pleasant little church. You need not be put off by the gruesome information that it contains the entrails of popes who

11. Neptune and Sea Horses at the Trevi Fountain

died in the nearby Quirinal Palace. Corinthian columns and rather beautifully painted ornamentation in monochrome, mostly of acanthus leaves (a technique called grisaille), create its architectural mood. The third chapel on the left has an old fresco of Our Lady, the third on the right attractive paintings of the life of St Camillus de Lellis, founder of the Priests Ministers of the Sick.

Santa Maria in Trivio

In a little piazza to the left of the fountain is Santa Maria in Trivio. *Trivio* is thought to mean a meeting of three roads and to explain the name of the fountain. This was the first *small* baroque church I entered in Rome. It overwhelmed me and I have never forgotten it. Over the high altar is a venerated fifteenth-century painting of Our Lady surrounded by a 'gloria'. A pleasant effect of distance is created by the organ beyond the

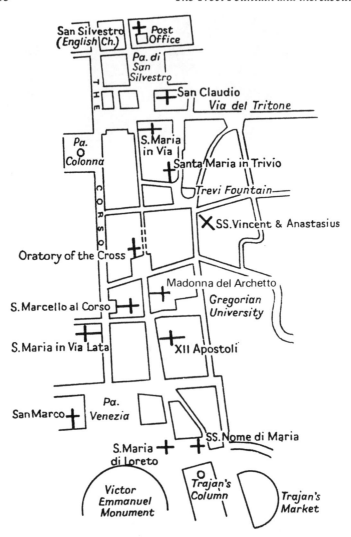

altar – an eighteenth-century instrument in a beautiful gilded case. Under an altar to the left is the tomb of St Gaspar del Bufalo (died 1837), founder of the Priests of the Precious Blood who serve this church.

The most interesting feature is the vault painted by Antonio Gherardi in 1670. There is often a fantastic touch about his work, and here it is his extravagant use of perspective. You will see what I mean. The subjects are the Presentation, the Assumption, and the Circumcision. In the first you have literally a worm's-eye view of one of Bernini's twisted columns in St Peter's.

To hint at a longer history, round the corner on the outside wall is an eleventh-century inscription recording the building of this church by Belisarius in the sixth century, in reparation for having exiled a pope!

Santa Maria in Via

Follow down the right side of the church and bear left round the block. You will arrive at the church of Santa Maria in Via, Our Lady on the Way. If you were told to find a holy well in Rome you would hardly look for one in this busy commercial square. Yet here it is, in the chapel immediately to the right on entering. This is the story. Seven centuries ago – to be precise, on 26th September 1256 – a Cardinal Capocci had a house here, with a well in his stable yard. That night the well overflowed. Frightened horses whinnied, and domestics rushed out to find an icon of Our Lady painted on stone (or slate?) floating on the brimming water. The well is still in the chapel, and so is the icon. People are always praying before it. A Servite friar waits by the well to serve you with glasses of its fresh water. There is a feast in honour of this Madonna on 8th September and a night vigil on 26th September.

The church itself is of the sixteenth century with much later restoration. The chapel of the well is unusual for Rome in having modern stained-glass windows of its history. To the left of the main door is another medieval painting of the Madonna called Our Lady of the Fire – a coincidence to have Madonnas of fire and water in one church! Over the high altar is a third Madonna, a statue of Our Lady of Sorrows – emotionally overdone, as this subject usually is in Latin countries.

Central Post Office

Beyond Santa Maria in Via is the busy little Piazza di San Silvestro with a central Post Office, where you can even consult English telephone directories, a bus terminus and, in its immediate vicinity, branches of several of the best Roman chain stores. Three churches verge on the piazza: Santa Maria in Via, San Claudio, and San Silvestro in Capite – St Sylvester at the Head of St John Baptist.

San Claudio

San Claudio is little more than a dome perched on a box-shaped church. St Claude was a monk in the Vosges mountains of Burgundy in the sixth century – and this was built in 1662 to be the national church in Rome for Burgundians.

San Silvestro in Capite

San Silvestro distinguishes itself from the other churches at a glance. It has a medieval campanile and a cortile – atrium, to give it its proper name – which, perhaps more than any other instance in Rome, fulfils its true function of separating you from the noise and bustle of the city as you approach the presence of God. It lacks a fountain, but to the left a jet of good drinking water pours itself into a little trough.

If you have already visited a number of ancient churches the fragments of sculpture around this courtyard may suggest to you that here is another to which the relics of martyrs were brought from the catacombs for greater security in the centuries when Rome was intermittently besieged by barbarians from all quarters and by pirates from the sea. The case here is a little different; San Silvestro was built in the eighth century by Pope Stephen II and Pope Paul I – they were brothers – on their family property, specially to receive bones from the catacombs. At that time it was served by Greek monks. In the thirteenth century Pope Honorius IV gave church and cloister to Poor Clares who built the present church between 1591 and 1601. Francesco da Volterra was the architect. For the consecration the relics of Popes Sylvester, Stephen I, and Dionysius were exhumed and re-enshrined beneath the altar. The nuns remained until 1876 – grilles either side of the altar formerly opened onto their choir. The convent buildings are in part used by the Post Office.

When you enter San Silvestro – a church rich with every baroque exuberance – notice first the high altar. It is older than the present church and there is good reason to believe that Michelangelo had much to do with designing it. The elegant little canopy with sweeping concave lines was added in 1667 by Carlo Rainaldi. Paintings either side are difficult to see well. Attributed to Orazio Borgianni, that on the left represents messengers from Constantine seeking St Sylvester on his mountain retreat of Monte Soratte, that on the right the martyrdom of Pope Stephen. Both these saints are enshrined here.

Above is the Baptism of Constantine by Pope St Sylvester, an event now recognized to be quite unhistorical. It is by Ludovico Gimignani, about 1688.

Move toward the transept altar left of the high altar and look up and then straight across the church. You will notice that the transepts are so narrow that their vault is elliptical and the dome at the centre is oval in shape. The altar to the right is best appreciated from the left, and *vice versa*.

The 'confession' is quite recent – 1906. Down there you are in the proximity of all those early Christians gathered from the catacombs. Near the door of the church there is a contemporary, eighth century, list of the saints among them. Down in the crypt you will notice huge blocks of masonry of republican date, that is to say, B.C., that doubtless had something to do with the ancestral property of the pope builders of this church. To the right, on the wall, is a delightful little coloured mosaic of birds at a bath.

Coming up from the confession, look up at the vault of the nave, a vivacious Assumption with Saints by the seventeenth-century artist Giacinto Brandi. The cupola too can be seen best from here, with Pomarancio's 'Glory of the Father'. The undersides of the arches supporting the cupola are enriched with the most delicate gilded sculpture of angels and foliage.

The chapels are worth visiting for their paintings. The right transept altar has a Madonna with Saints by Baccio Ciarpi – seventeenth century. The Baptist is very well drawn and the head to the extreme right is clearly a portrait of St Philip Neri. Notice in the second chapel on the right Gentileschi's Stigmata of St Francis, of 1610, and in the first chapel on the left paintings of the Passion (the Crucifixion is the least satisfying) by the Venetian Francesco Trevisani (1695).

On the beautifully carved pulpit, as well as elsewhere in the church, you will notice the head of the Baptist on a dish and the face of Christ on a veil. The latter alludes to an alleged portrait of Christ, traditionally believed to have been made for a King of Edessa, once preserved here. The head of the Baptist is the relic after which this church is named '*in Capite*'. You will find it in a dark little chapel to the extreme left as you enter. Parts of the reliquary date from the thirteenth and fourteenth centuries. You can see for yourself there is a head in it, but as it happens not to be the only head venerated as the Baptist's, it would be rash to make any unguarded statement about its authenticity.

San Silvestro is served by English Pallottine Fathers for the benefit of the English community and visitors in Rome.

San Marcello al Corso

From the Piazza di San Silvestro it is a step to the Corso. You meet it at the Piazza Colonna, described in Chapter 17. Beware of tea shops hereabouts; they can be very expensive. If you walk towards the Victor Emmanuel monument you reach, shortly before the Piazza Venezia, the church of San Marcello al Corso, set back in a little piazza of its own. Its concave façade is characteristic of the baroque period. So thoroughly baroque is this church, inside and out, that you ought to be surprised to learn that it is one of the oldest in the city.

Pope St Marcellus suffered under the last pagan emperor

before the conversion of Constantine – that Maxentius who built the great basilica named after him in the Forum and who was thrown into the Tiber from the Milvian Bridge. According to tradition the pope lived here in a house belonging to a Roman lady named Lucina, where he established a church, but the emperor turned the property into municipal stables and made the pope a stable hand. Marcellus died of privation in 309.

Subsequently a church was built on the site of Lucina's home, and in due course the relics of St Marcellus were carried there from the catacomb of Priscilla. Servite friars were established at San Marcello in 1369 and they still serve the church.

Today San Marcello is famous above all for the venerated crucifix, recovered unharmed from the ashes of the earlier church destroyed by fire on the night of 22nd May 1519 – an anniversary still celebrated. The great crucifix is carried through the streets of Rome at times of special intercession, such as the inauguration of Vatican II. The present church is built to designs of Sansovino and Sangallo, but that characteristically baroque façade was added in 1683 by Carlo Fontana.

The coffered ceiling, gift of its sculptor Vitelli (d.1600), represents Our Lady's titles from her Litany of Loreto. The chapel of the miraculous Crucifix is the last but one to the right, though it is sometimes taken out and set up near the sanctuary. In the chapel to the right is buried the English Cardinal Weld (d.1830) – married man and father before he became a priest. In this chapel there is a beautiful thirteenth-century painting of Our Lady of Grace, set in a sculptured surround of delicate renaissance relief. Across the nave from the Crucifix chapel is one in which are enshrined relics of St Felicitas and her sons, Roman martyrs. Opposite the Weld chapel is one dedicated to the Sorrows of Our Lady, a devotion specially fostered by the Servite friars (Order of Servants of Mary).

While you are at this end of the church you should look back towards the door to see a great fresco of the Crucifixion by Giovanni Battista Ricci, painted in 1613. The apse is also his work.

Important, if not beautiful to look at, is the baptistery of the primitive church. This is an almost unique relic of ancient Christian Rome, for tradition over many centuries allowed baptism only at cathedrals – in Rome, at St John Lateran. However, as the demand for baptism increased – to the point that every parish church now has its own font – other churches were given the right to confer baptism. This fourth- or fifth-century font at San Marcello is large enough for partial immersion, that is, the candidate if a grown person stepped into water up to about the knees and had the water poured over his head by the minister of the sacrament. Although this baptistery is, with keys, accessible from the church, it is in fact under the adjacent offices of the Banco di Roma. A light shaft has been constructed above the baptistery, which can be viewed by anyone during the hours of business.

Santi Apostoli

Santi Apostoli is in the street behind San Marcello or it can be approached from the Piazza Venezia. It is difficult to view the façade of this church. You enter by a broad narthex, designed by Baccio Pontelli in the fifteenth century. Notice the old lions, relics of cosmatesque doorways. They support nothing now, but the bases of columns still saddle their backs. At the far end is a carved eagle from the Forum of Trajan.

The interior is spacious and dignified rather than beautiful. Move into the dark aisle and look back, at an angle, across the nave. There is so much gloom in these aisles that there seems little point in having paintings there.

In 1873 a 'confession' was constructed before the sanctuary, in the course of which the bodies of the apostles Philip and James were discovered. If the gates are open you may go down, though you will be able to distinguish very little – unless a friar is at hand to switch on the lights – except elegantly grouped columns. In the chapels of the crypt are reproductions of catacomb paintings of the second to the fourth centuries. Here were reburied, in the ninth century, when the catacombs were emptied of the dead to preserve them from the sacrilegious hands of invaders, relics of many martyrs and early Christians. An inscription records that Pope Stephen VI, in 886, barefoot, helped to carry them here on his shoulders.

From the steps of the confession, look up at the painting overhead – angels appear to tumble out of the vault. I remember a tourist once asking me in which church 'the arms came out of the ceiling'. I suppose this was the answer to a rather odd question. A query of the same type that you encounter in St Paul's, where there is a series of medallions representing the popes, is 'Which is the one whose eyes glare at you?'

As you leave, note on a pier of the nave to the right a memorial marking the burial place of the heart of Clementina Sobieski, wife of 'James III', the old Pretender, son of Stuart James II and father of Bonnie Prince Charlie. A traveller in Rome, during his lifetime, wrote: 'The king of England is too devout! He spends his mornings in prayer in Santi Apostoli, beside the tomb of his wife.' In 1766 the exiled king lay in state here, before he was buried in St Peter's.

The first record of a church here dates from 565, but it was rebuilt several times and as you see it now it is eighteenth-century work. Conventual Franciscans serve the church. In their handsome cloister is a monument to Michelangelo, who was buried here temporarily before his body was taken home to Florence. A famous preacher at Santi Apostoli in the sixteenth century was a Father Felix, who later became the great builder Pope Sixtus V, whose work you see at the Quirinal, and in the Moses Fountain which terminates his new aqueduct, the Acqua Felice – from his name Felix.

As you leave the church, an entrance facing you on the right is that of the former Muti Palace (not all Roman palaces live up to the name, at least externally), where the Stuarts lodged in the eighteenth century.

Behind the church of the Apostles, in the Piazza delle Pilotta, is Rome's best known Catholic University, the Gregorian, and also nearby the Biblical Institute, under Jesuit direction.

The Madonna del Archetto and the Oratory of the Cross

If you follow the narrow street, a continuation of the Piazza Santi Apostoli, you pass on your right the entrance to a little shrine, the Madonna del Archetto, built in 1690 and enclosed with grilles in 1796 to protect it from vandals. James III arranged for a night guard so that it might be accessible for devotion. At the end of the street, across the tiny Piazza, is the Oratory of the Cross, a chapel in the form of a painted hall of the renaissance. Its walls have been painted by many of the finest artists of the sixteenth century, including Pomarancio and Baldassare Croce, with the story of the miraculous Crucifix of nearby San Marcello, and also the history of the True Cross.

To visit two more churches that must be described you will need to about turn and retrace your steps through the Piazza Santi Apostoli, over the road and down the Via dei Fornari. Ahead you will see the dome of Santa Maria di Loreto. This is one of two churches – they seem to be just domes without any extensions – and at a glance to be near-identical twins. They make a charming feature of many views, from the Forum, the Torre delle Milizie, the Colosseum, the Capitol. They are, however, far from being twins. There are more than two centuries between them, and the older church, Santa Maria di Loreto, is an octagon, while Santissimo Nome di Maria (Holy Name of Mary) is an ellipse, and just to add one more difference, while the former is the church of the bakers' guild, the latter is that of the Confraternity of St Bernard, the members of which are nearly all Vatican employees.

Santa Maria di Loreto

Santa Maria di Loreto was built by the architect Giuliano di Sangallo. Notice the picturesque little lantern with which he has crowned its dome. Characteristic of the renaissance period is the light relief of its delicate sculpture. On either side are very pretty organ cases covered with swags of fruit and flowers, trumpets, cymbals, lutes and pipes, and Mary riding her Holy House. To the right of the entrance there is a sixteenth-century mosaic – unusual in Rome – and left of the nave a crucifix enshrined in a reliquary. Just inside the sanctuary, to the left, is an amusing shrine to St Expeditus, with a statue of this saint whose devotion, apparently, is very close to his name, for he is represented holding a cross inscribed '*Hodie*' (today), while he tramples on '*Cras*' (tomorrow). If you are given to procrastination, here is your new protector!

Santissimo Nome di Maria

The neighbouring church of Santissimo Nome di Maria was built under Pope Clement XII to commemorate victory over the

Turks at Vienna, by John Sobieski, king of Poland, in 1683. There is a great sense of height in this church, which is just perceptibly oval. Above the high altar in a gloria is a beautiful icon of Our Lady painted on cedar wood, granted to the brethren of a 'Confraternity of St Bernard at the Column of Trajan' from the treasures of the Lateran '*Sancta Sanctorum*' about 1430 and transferred to this church when it was completed in 1741.

Trajan's Column

From near the church you may look down at the base of the great column to Rome's good emperor Trajan, who died in A.D. 107. The column was raised in

12. Trajan's Column and the Chuch of Santissimo Nome di Maria

113. The bands of sculpture, representing Trajan's wars beyond the Danube, have this peculiarity, that they increase in size so that they are not diminished by perspective. It is said that, unwound, the sculpture would be 200 yards long. Windows illuminating the staircase inside are almost concealed among the figures. Formerly the ashes of Trajan rested in an urn in the base, rare exception to the Roman law that all dead must be interred outside the walls, and on the top was a statue of Trajan that Pope Sixtus V replaced by St Peter. Some guide-books tell you that its height marked the level of ground – a sort of isthmus linking Quirinal and Capitol hills – excavated away by Trajan to create his forum, but I think it is a better interpretation that the column simply surveys the monuments with which the emperor had adorned this part of Rome. See his market over to your left.

Walking forward, past Trajan's Market, you pass remains of the Forum of Augustus, built to expiate the assassination of Caesar and inaugurated in 2 B.C., and the Forum of Nerva, completed in 98 A.D.

The Victor Emmanuel Monument

In the course of this walk you will see a great deal of the great white Victor Emmanuel monument, irreverently nicknamed 'the Wedding Cake'. It is fashionable to sneer at it as the basest imitation of antique art, but I dare say there will soon be a volte-face on this position and it will come to be admired – in my opinion, not without some merit. Once, standing under the colonnades of the Campidoglio (Capitol) and admiring this monument as it soared against black storm clouds above the bleak brick gothic Ara Coeli church, I thought that, if this was a wedding cake, sugar icing had never before attained such an apotheosis.

A Count Sacconi designed the monument, said to be based on the Temple of Fortune at Palestrina. It was completed in 1911 and commemorates Victor Emmanuel as first king of United Italy – it is his tomb you see in the Pantheon. The monument enshrines, on a platform part way up the steps and below the statue of Victor Emmanuel on horseback, an 'Altar of the Fatherland' and the tomb of Italy's Unknown Warrior; guards are mounted here daily.

Chapter 16

The Piazza Navona and thereabouts

Piazza Navona – Sant' Agnese – Santa Maria dell' Anima – Santa Maria della Pace – San Salvatore in Lauro – Ponte Sant' Angelo – Chiesa Nuova – The French Church of St Louis – Sant' Agostino – The Portuguese Church of Sant' Antonio

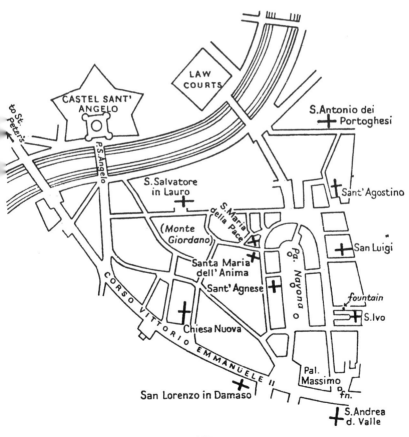

The Piazza Navona

The Piazza Navona is deservedly a favourite among the piazzas of Rome. It is a true piazza, not just a hilltop like the Quirinal, or a meeting of roads like the Barberini. Its wonderful shape is precisely that of the great Stadium built by Domitian between A.D. 81 and 96 to accommodate 30,000 spectators – even the odd ends, one straight, the other rounded, reproduce its plan. The houses are built on the lower structure of this stadium; you may see remains below the church of St Agnes, and on the outside of the rounded end, in the Piazza di Tor Sanguigna, a complete arch is preserved, visible from the street.

13. The Piazza Navona during the Christmas Crib Fair

A special feature of this piazza is its Christmas market; it begins over a week before Christmas for the sale of cribs, toys and sweets, and carries on to Epiphany-tide for the visit of the old witch Befana – the name is just a corruption of Epiphany, Italy's substitute for Santa Claus, though in recent years the piazza has had to extend hospitality to Santa and the Christmas tree as well. I was once asked which stall sold 'illiterate angels'. It appears that some hill-town making Christmas cribs has for centuries blundered over spelling '*Gloria in excelsis*'. I did not succeed in finding out whether this happy fault has been cunningly perpetuated as a sales gimmick.

The Fountain of Four Rivers

The central fountain is the 'Four Rivers'. We owe it to Bernini. Granite and travertine sculptured to represent natural rocks and vegetation support an obelisk from the Circus of Maxentius on the Via Appia – reminiscent of the spires of Newcastle and Edinburgh churches held up by flying buttresses. The figures stand for four continents: Europe, Asia, Africa and America, with four great rivers: Danube, Ganges, Nile, and Plate. The features I like best are the animals wandering about in this statuesque zoo, especially the horse prancing out on one side, and the lion coming stealthily to drink on the other.

A good story is told of the inauguration of this fountain by Pope Innocent X in 1651. Bernini had been appointed architect for this assignment in opposition to his rival Borromini – who did design the façade of St Agnes' church overlooking the fountain. Borromini spitefully told the Pope that the hydraulics were so defective that water would not flow, and when Bernini came to hear of this he deliberately kept the water cocks closed. At the function Innocent spoke kind words praising the architecture, but commented that since there was no water it could hardly be called a fountain. As the procession was making its way out of the piazza Bernini signalled for the cocks to be turned on, and Innocent, turning his head delightedly at the music of water, remarked, 'With this unexpected laughter you have added ten years to our life'. That anecdote comes from *The Life of the Cavalier Gian Bernini* by his son Domenico.

In those days the piazza was flooded during the summer heat for a sort of water fair, the aristocracy driving through in their carriages, the boys of Rome following them. This custom continued down to 1870.

Sant' Agnese

Dominating the piazza is Sant' Agnese in Agone, from a name given to this Stadium, the *Circus Agonalis*. It was here the child martyr was delivered to a brothel under the arches of the stadium, although, according to the ancient record, her purity preserved her from violation. The prison of Agnes is shown beneath the church, entered from a door to the right of her altar. If it is locked you have to find the sacristan.

There was a church here in the eighth century, but the present rotunda imposed on a cruciform plan wider than it is long (that is, the distance between the side altars is greater than that between door and high altar) was designed by Borromini and Rainaldi and completed in 1672. You can judge from the piazza how lofty is that dome, and from within it is even more impressive. I often urge you to look up into cupolas; perhaps this time I should warn you not to topple over backwards. I have seen its glory of angels, by Ciro Ferri, almost dissolve in a flood of light.

Each of its seven altars merits attention. Beginning on the left, the first is of St Eustace, represented exposed to lions. It is hard to decide who is more attractively sculptured, the handsome Eustace or the pussy-like lions. From the next altar, in the transept, I suggest you look across the church to the corresponding altar to St Agnes, and so appreciate the clever perspective in green marble, work of the architect Rainaldi. The statue of Agnes amid flames (more probably the fire of temptation than that of execution) is by Ercole Ferrata, but that of St Sebastian is an antique Roman statue modified.

14. Looking up into the cupola of Sant' Agnese

After St Sebastian's altar comes that of St Cecilia, then the high altar with a sculpture of the Holy Family amid saints. The next is dedicated to the milk-sister of St Agnes, Emerentiana, stoned while praying at her tomb, also by Ercole Ferrata. Finally there is a fine group by Francesco Rossi of the death of St Alexis (for his story see Chapter 8). The figure to the left, in armour, is remarkable.

A door to the right of St Sebastian's altar leads to a chapel where you may venerate the head of the thirteen-year-old Agnes, and through one to its left you will find the font in which Santa Francesca Romana was baptized.

Fountains in Piazza Navona

The two other fountains in the piazza tend to be neglected in favour of the 'Four Rivers'. That to your right (as you leave Sant' Agnese) is called the Fountain of the Moor, after the ugly naked fellow in the centre, supposedly Bernini's idea of Neptune. Italians used to call all gauche and ugly types 'Moors'. There is another Neptune fountain at the far end of the piazza, work of a nineteenth-century sculptor. Here the sea god is in the toils of an octopus, infant tritons cope with sea horses, and there are mermaids equipped with two tails, their natural fishy ones and an extra curly satyr's tail.

Santa Maria dell' Anima

Off the piazza near this fountain, on the same side as Sant' Agnese, you will find two churches, among the most deserving of your attention, although they are nearly always closed, but something can be done about that. They are in fact joined together by buttresses bridging an alley. On the left is Santa Maria dell' Anima, German National Church, and to the right Santa Maria della Pace, Our Lady of Peace. Pass through the alley – unless the doors of Santa Maria dell' Anima should be open – and ask permission to visit at the entrance to the college behind the church. You enter through a delightful courtyard full of interesting fragments of sculpture and with a useful little drinking fountain.

This is a most unusual church in Rome. Perhaps you noticed its minaret-like spire capped with coloured tiles, like the patterned slate roofs of German-speaking lands. The dedication refers to Mary as patroness of the departed in purgatory. Its founders were a Dutch couple in the fourteenth century – in those days of course 'Germany' meant the various German-speaking states of the old Holy Roman Empire. The church belongs to a type common in northern Europe – the *Hallenkirche* or hall church. This, instead of having a lofty nave with aisles under a lower roof, covered as broad a space as possible with one lofty roof, held up by rows of columns. Churches on this plan could be conveniently used for municipal assemblies. An unusual feature here is that each side of the church, which appears to be square but is in fact an irregular shape, has four lofty apses, containing altars. There is so little light, and that filtered through stained glass, that you will need to concentrate your attention on what you are able to see.

The sanctuary is like a rich gilded frame to Giulio Romano's canvas of the Nativity above the high altar. Of the tombs on either side, that to the left is Pope Adrian VI's, by Baldassare Peruzzi. Pope Adrian was a Dutchman who used to be tutor to the Emperor Charles V.

Important among the chapels is the last on the right. It contains a copy – though by no means an exact one – of Michelangelo's Pietà at St Peter's. The setting is austere, but it is puzzling that the sculpture should be so placed that you are more aware of the mother's knees than anything else, and they were always over-prominent, even in the original. The principal modification of Michelangelo's design is that Lorenzetti has brought Christ's head forward onto his chest – in my estimation, entirely disturbing the balance of the composition. This 'copy' was made in 1530. The next chapel, in which the Blessed Sacrament is reserved, has a fine sixteenth-century crucifix and also a reproduction of the famous little German Madonna of Altötting, gift of Pope Pius XII. Among the paintings, you should not miss that in the fourth chapel on the left, nearest the courtyard door, a 'Taking Down from the Cross' by Salviati.

Santa Maria della Pace

Santa Maria della Pace is to be visited early in the morning when it is open for service; at other times the caretaker who lives in the adjacent cloister will open the church. This is, as far as I know, the only church in Rome that asks an admission fee – asks, it isn't enforced. The church was built by Pope Sixtus IV in the late fifteenth century, in fulfilment of a vow to restore peace between nations. His architect was Baccio Pontelli. Pietro da Cortona restored it for Alexander VII in the seventeenth century. The delightful façade with its semi-circular porch is by Pietro da Cortona, and even if you are unable to visit the church you should at least note this, and also glance into the cloister designed by Bramante in 1504.

The plan of the church is unusual – an octagon, preceded by a narrow nave and followed by a diminutive sanctuary. Above the high altar is a venerated painting of Our Lady with her Divine Child formerly in the porch of St Andrew's of the Watercarriers. Tradition relates that a stone was thrown at this picture, and it bled, and it was the subsequent popularity of the Madonna that prompted Pope Sixtus to make it the focus of his Temple of Peace. Carlo Maderno designed this new altar to enshrine it in 1614. Above the chancel arch there is that phrase from the Christmas song of the angels *'et in terra pax'* – 'Peace on earth'.

There are several paintings that specially deserve your attention, but an effort is needed on your part if you are to see them to advantage. For instance, Baldassare Peruzzi's Presentation of Mary is, at least in some lights, best seen from the door by which you enter if you are coming from the cloister. There is another Madonna by the same artist in the first left-hand chapel of the nave, and in the chapel opposite there is a fresco by Raphael. The marble decoration of the second chapel on the right is by Michelangelo.

If, leaving the church, you turn right, you will find yourself in the Via dei Coronari. This means 'Street of the Rosarymakers' (crowns of beads), but today it is the centre of Roman antique dealing. Beware, however, if you think you are going to make bargains. Bear left, and the first piazza, opening on the right, is that of San Salvatore in Lauro – Our Saviour by the Laurels.

San Salvatore in Lauro

I think you should go to the far end of the piazza and look back at the church. The austere façade, dating only from 1862, accentuates the sculpture of the Madonna of Loreto riding through the sky on the Holy House of Nazareth, escorted by angels; within is a reproduction of the same venerated image – the statue of Loreto is one of the famous vested 'black' Madonnas – in a gloria of angels and clouds. The high altar itself dates only from 1792, but the Madonna claims to be the first reproduction of that at the Holy House. It was 'crowned' by the Vatican Chapter (which has the privilege of crowning statues of Our Lady) in 1644.

There was a church here with the dedication to our Saviour in the twelfth century, and the 'laurels' must refer to some nearby garden. The present church was completed in the eighteenth century; its predominant feature – groves of Corinthian columns – is due to the architects Mascherino and Sassi in 1727.

Notice in the fourth chapel on the right a Nativity by Pietro da Cortona. The left transept has a crucifix – the vested wooden type – which is a copy of one venerated at Sirolo. This is connected with the devotion here to the Holy House of Loreto. Sirolo is not far from Loreto, and they have in those parts a saying: 'Whoever goes to Loreto and not to Sirolo, has seen the Mother but not the Son'. The original is believed to be twelfth century. In contrast to the restraint which distinguishes this church, note two characteristically baroque monuments to cardinals on the walls of each transept.

There is much more to see. Entered either through the sacristy or direct from the street is a beautiful fifteenth-century cloister and, beyond it, another charming courtyard. These you could visit even if the church is closed. Further, if the custodian is about, you may ask to see the sacristy and refectory, and in the latter the tomb of Pope Eugenius IV – Pope of the Council of Florence. Sometimes cloister and refectory are used for art exhibitions – the monastery is no longer occupied by religious. Then you lose the opportunity to appreciate their monumental character, but can make the most of the exhibition. The cloister, arcaded on two levels, is often described as the finest renaissance cloister in Rome – you can at least compare it with that at Santa Maria della Pace. The courtyard beyond has a fountain and two beautifully sculptured doorways. Study the statues in detail. Look up over the doorway by which you entered for a sculpture of the liberation of St Peter from prison, a survivor from the earlier church.

In the refectory – from the days when this was a monastery of the Canons Regular of the Lateran – you should first note the fine fresco of 1550, by the Florentine painter Salviati, representing the Wedding Feast at Cana; this is a change from the Last Supper commonly chosen for refectories. There is a fine feeling of perspective about this painting. Notice the little dog in the foreground. Also attributed to Salviati, or at least to his school, are three paintings in the vault distinguished for profound symbolism. In the ovals are represented the Creation of Woman and Original Sin. They stand respectively for the fullness of God's creative work – the creation of Eve – and the entrance of evil into his scheme. In the rectangle is depicted the Temptation of Jesus, symbolic of the eternal conflict between good and evil. Personally I don't much admire the tomb of Eugenius IV by Isaias of Pisa, sculptured between 1450 and 1455, but this Pope should be interesting to the Rome pilgrim, for those great bronze doors of St Peter's were commissioned by him, and they record his Council of Florence that sought to achieve the task resumed so hopefully by recent popes – a reunion between the Churches of West and East.

Ponte Sant' Angelo

If, after leaving San Salvatore, you make your way to the Tiber, you will arrive near the Ponte Sant' Angelo, a bridge crossing to the Castle that was first built as a tomb for the Emperor Hadrian. The first bridge was built here by Hadrian himself to provide access to his memorial. It acquires character today from the statues of angels that flank it, by students of Bernini, each bearing an instrument of the Passion of Christ. If you know Latin, you will find it interesting to study the choice of texts carved to fit each instrument represented. The Pillar of the Scourging copies the relic preserved in the church of Santa Prassede. Originals of the angels of the Crown and Title are in Sant' Andrea delle Fratte, flanking the sanctuary. The angel of the cross is said to be by Bernini himself. Older than this choir of the Passion are the statues of Peter and Paul at the near end of the bridge.

If you turn your back to the bridge, you will soon find yourself in the Corso Vittorio Emmanuele, not far from the Piazza della Chiesa Nuova.

Piazza della Chiesa Nuova

The Chiesa Nuova, with its piazza, the Soup Tureen Fountain (La Terrina), the adjacent façade of the Aula Borrominiana, and the swaggering statue of the eighteenth-century composer of operatic libretti, Pietro Metastasio, is one of the best known features of Rome along the Corso Vittorio Emmanuele. The fountain dates from between 1580 and 1590 and was formerly in the Campo de' Fiori. The 'New Church' was built for that best loved of Roman saints, Pippo Buono, 'good Pip' – St Philip Neri, founder of the Oratory.

The 'Chiesa Nuova'

When he had already begun his work at San Girolamo della Carità, Philip was given a little church on this site originally dedicated to St Gregory the Great and believed to date from his time – the sixth century. By the twelfth it was known as Santa Maria in Vallicelli (the little valley) and a Madonna was venerated under that title. Romans still call it 'New Church', though it is four centuries old, but, as the inscription over the door tells you, it remains dedicated to Our Lady and St Gregory.

Designed in the form of a Latin cross (that is, with nave longer than choir and transepts), with a lofty dome over the crossing, its architects were Matteo de Città di Castello and Martino Lunghi the elder. It was built between 1575 and 1605.

I suggest you sit down, not far from the door, to capture the mood and observe some of the main features of this beautiful church. The vault of the nave is coffered, with baby angels skilfully squeezing themselves into the oddest positions. Its central painting, by Pietro da Cortona, is of a miracle reported during the building of the church. Philip told the builders that part of their scaffolding was endangering the little thirteenth-century Madonna – now above the high altar – and attributed his knowledge, which proved correct, to Our Lady herself. The inside of the dome and the apse are da Cortona's work too, the former representing the glory of the Trinity, the latter the glory of Mary. Above the altar, completed in 1608, the icon of Our Lady is enshrined in a canvas painted by Peter Paul Rubens, and his too are canvases either side the sanctuary. The figures in mail are soldier saints named Papias and Maurus; their relics lie beneath the high altar. Two male saints on the right were soldiers, too, Nereus and Achilleus, but Rubens unfortunately does not show them in mail, of which he made such a good job. The tabernacle of this altar is of quite unusual beauty but difficult to see well at a distance. By Ciro Ferri, it was added in 1681.

Now you should pace the side aisles, for the ten chapels flanking the nave are full of interest. The first on the right has excellent paintings of the Passion in the compartments of its apse. In the second is a copy of Caravaggio's Taking Down from the Cross; the original is in the Vatican.

In a chapel at the end of the left aisle the body of St Philip reposes below the altar: above it is a mosaic copy of a painting by Guido Reni. The wealth of inlaid marble and mother-of-pearl in both chapel and vestibule deserves attention.

You may ask in the sacristy to be shown into a room immediately behind this altar, and also into the saint's room and chapel upstairs. As is so often the case, this is almost entirely reconstruction, though filled with several pieces of furniture used by St Philip, as well as many relics and some very interesting paintings. The original rooms were seriously dam-aged by a fire caused by a stray rocket from a firework display at the Castel Sant' Angelo.

An interesting item exhibited here is a Nottingham alabaster of St John the Baptist – his head on a dish (not a halo) and the Lamb of God, given to St Philip from the loot of a captured Turkish galley. In the Middle Ages, Nottingham was famous for its alabaster sculpture.

You may glance into the courtyard of the adjacent residence, and even into the Library upstairs – this would be worth while if you are interested in old books and binding. On one of the landings is a vast sculpture reproducing the theme of Raphael's fresco of Leo I repelling Attila the Hun, in the Vatican.

Monte Giordano
Behind the Chiesa Nuova – take the turning to the left of the block – you could walk through the Piazza del Orologio to find before you, through a fine arch, the agreeable vista of water splashing among greenery. This is Monte Giordano. Don't hesitate to walk through and admire one of the most picturesque of Roman courtyards. 'Giordano' is simply the first name of one of the Orsini who held a fortress here in the Middle Ages.

Palazzo Massimo alle Colonne
You have now seen all of major interest in the district under discussion but I will mention one or two places in case you come across them in your travels. From the Chiesa Nuova walk down the Corso Vittorio Emmanuele – away from the river and St Peter's. As you approach Sant' Andrea delle Valle that is such a prominent landmark over the road, you will find on your left the slightly curved façade of the Palazzo Massimo alle Colonne, designed about 1526 by Baldassare Peruzzi. On 16th March 1583, St Philip Neri recalled from apparent death the fourteen-year-old son of the princely Massimi family. The youth had a long last conversation with St Philip, who had befriended him, prepared well for death, and died again in the saint's arms. On the anniversary the family, who still reside here, opens to the public several rooms and the private oratory. But at any time it is worth stepping into the beautiful little courtyards.

The Sapienza – Church of Sant' Ivo
Level with the church of St Andrew, turn left – after noting that charmingly proportioned fountain made by Maderno in 1614; it used to stand in the Piazza Scossa Cavalli on the way to St Peter's till the piazza gave place to the Via della Conciliazione. Along the Corso del Rinascimento a large building on the right is the Sapienza, once the seat of Rome's secular university which now has new buildings between Stazione Termini and San Lorenzo. Several great architects of the renaissance combined to design this building, but there is a special interest in the fantastic twisted spire of its church of Sant' Ivo, the Breton St Yves, patron of lawyers, for the Sapienza began in 1244 as a law school. Borromini is responsible for this architectural

oddity. You can see this spire by just entering the courtyard, but it often makes an intriguing feature when discovered from other angles.

Two 'rione' fountains

At the end of the Sapienza a few steps to the right, along the Via dei Straderari, will introduce you to another of the attractive little 'rione' or district fountains, each of which is meant to express a characteristic of its locality. Here the fountain is made up of books – for the university, stone balls – by way of allusion to the Medici coat of arms; the stag's skin refers you to the legend of St Eustace, whose church is nearby.

French Church of St Louis

At the end of the Via dei Straderari the French national church of San Luigi, St Louis, is a few steps to the left. This sixteenth/ seventeenth-century church is overcrowded with monuments in a style not always happy – the worst example, in the right aisle, is the war memorial. In the last chapel of the left aisle is something worth all else – Caravaggio's painting of the Call of St Matthew, the customs official. The other two paintings of St Matthew are by the same unmistakable artist. There is a pleasant little fifteenth-century sculpture of the Madonna at the entrance to this chapel.

The first chapel to the right is attractively frescoed by Domenichino with incidents from the life of St Cecilia.

Church of Sant' Agostino

Just after San Luigi a turning to the left – Via di Sant' Agostino – leads to the church of St Augustine; its façade – not, to be frank, very beautiful – is one of the earliest of the Roman renaissance, built of travertine from the ruins of the Colosseum. Inside you will see that it is a very *long* church, as if it clings to the spirit of gothic and, although lofty enough, has not yet discovered the unity and vertical movement which became the genius of renaissance and baroque. The finely balanced high altar is one of the more restrained works of Gian Lorenzo Bernini.

Inside the door is a large lamp-hung, heart-surrounded statue of Our Lady by Sansovino. It reminds me a little of Our Lady of Victories at Paris. There is another sculpture by Sansovino, of St Anne, in the second chapel on the left. The first chapel on the left has one of Caravaggio's fine paintings, a Madonna receiving the devotion of pilgrims.

The shrine of Augustine's mother, St Monica, who ought to

be patroness of all mothers with difficult sons, is in the chapel flanking the sanctuary to the left.

Portuguese Church of Sant' Antonio

Farther along the Via della Scrofa, just down a turning to the left, is the church of Sant' Antonio dei Portoghesi. Certainly one of Rome's lesser churches, it is so characteristically baroque – like that tiny Santa Maria in Trivio near the Trevi Fountain – that it ought not to be overlooked. The attractive gilt and stucco vault is marred by mediocre paintings, but at least walk up as far as the sanctuary to admire the well-balanced high altar, to look up into the dome, to note the urn of rare green marble from Egypt under the right transept altar, and to look back at the happy little rococo organ gallery over the entrance. Then you have seen all that matters, saving a glance into the first chapel on the left for its painting of Our Lady with SS. Sebastian and Antony the Abbot.

CHAPTER 17

The Pantheon, Minerva, Forum of Augustus – and thereabouts

San Giacomo – San Carlo al Corso – The Mausoleum of Augustus – Altar of Peace of Caesar Augustus – San Rocco – The Palazzo Borghese – San Lorenzo in Lucina – The Pantheon – The Maddalena – Santa Maria in Campo Marzio – The Minerva Obelisk – Santa Maria sopra Minerva – The Collegio Romano – Piè di Marmo – Il Facchino – Santa Maria in Via Lata – Palazzo Doria Pamphili – Piazza Colonna – San Bartolomeo dei Bergamaschi – Sant' Ignazio

This chapter describes a triangle with the Piazza del Popolo at its apex, the Via di Ripetta changing into the Via della Scrofa for its left side, the Corso for its right, and for base part of the Corso Vittorio Emmanuele, the Largo Argentina and the Via del Plebiscito.

San Giacomo degli Incurabili

The apex, to be precise, is the Church of Santa Maria dei Miracoli, but this is described in Chapter 19. Take the road between the two churches – the Corso – and you will soon come to San Giacomo degli Incurabili, St James of the Incurables, on the right. It is also known as San Giacomo in Augusta. The first title tells you it was annexed to a hospital, which still exists behind the church, and the second that you are near the Mausoleum of Caesar Augustus. This was the first church to be built in Rome on an elliptical, or oval, plan; its foundation stone was laid in 1592. The architects were eminent men, Volterra and Carlo Maderno, but it is a disappointing little building. Its faults are capped, literally, by a dreadful nineteenth-century fresco in the dome.

Still, walk patiently round the chapels and you may be interested. The central chapel on the right has a remarkable sculpture by Pierre Legros, representing St Francis of Paola, founder of the Order of Minims (see Chapter 22), praying to Our Lady for the sick. A fifteenth-century painting of the

Madonna has been inserted in the sculpture, and below are represented patients, and perspectives of the wards. The dome of the third chapel to the left is attractive – look up into it.

You could now look into the Church of Gesù e Maria across the Corso (see Chapter 18).

San Carlo al Corso

Following the Corso you reach San Carlo. There was formerly a church here dedicated to St Ambrose, fifth-century archbishop of Milan, and when his great sixteenth-century successor, St Charles Borromeo, was canonized in 1610 a new church was built dedicated to both saints. The architect was Onorio Longhi, but the lofty cupola is by Pietro da Cortona and, as is so often the case, the façade was not completed till much later, 1684.

San Carlo is a church of space and vistas. It is a good idea to walk up a side aisle glancing through the arches into the body of the church. Towards midday on a bright morning there are grand light effects. Notice that an ambulatory, or aisle, goes round the back of the high altar. If you follow it on the left side you will reach the chapel behind the high altar where the heart of St Charles is enshrined.

It is an experience to look up into the exceptionally lofty dome.

The painting over the high altar, by Carlo Maratti, about 1685, represents the glory of the titular saints Ambrose and Charles.

The Mausoleum of Augustus

Behind San Carlo is a piazza around the remains of the great mausoleum of Augustus. It was a similar type to that of Hadrian, now transformed into the Castel Sant' Angelo, but of course earlier, for Augustus built this in the year 27 B.C. and buried several of his family here. Not only the dignified and handsome Caesar Augustus (you can check that description for yourself from several statues and portrait busts in Rome) but Tiberius, Claudius, and Nerva were interred here. The rotunda was originally completed by a conical garden planted with trees and crowned by a bronze statue of the emperor. These circular mausolea, surmounted by earthen mounds, have their origin in the tumuli of prehistoric burial, such as we have in Britain, and which you will recognize readily in the great tombs of the Etruscan burial grounds north of Rome.

The Altar of Peace of Caesar Augustus

Between the Mausoleum and the Tiber a modern structure shelters the Ara Pacis Augustae, Altar of Augustan Peace, a reconstruction of fragments excavated very scientifically from under several buildings in 1903 and again between 1937 and 1939. It was originally consecrated in 9 B.C. for annual sacrifice to commemorate the stability Augustus had given to the Empire. Looking through the gate you may wonder if it is worth paying a fee to go in. The sculpture is interesting if you study it closely. Members of the imperial household, priests, and vestals are seen approaching processionally to assist at the sacrifice. The outer enclosure has a beautiful decoration of vine branches and acanthus which – perhaps along with other examples from antiquity – must be the inspiration behind the twelfth-century mosaic at San Clemente (see Chapter 8).

San Rocco

Facing the Tiber are two small churches. That nearer the Ara Pacis is San Rocco, St Roch. At a glance it seems to be just an overcrowded baroque church, but some of the paintings at least deserve attention – especially St Martin dividing his cloak and, in the second chapel on the left, a curious concave Nativity. Looking back towards the door you will see a fine carved wood organ case that I hope Grinling Gibbons would have appreci-

ated. At the end of the right aisle is a dark little shrine of Our Lady of Graces. The second of each month is dedicated to this devotion, which dates from 1645.

Across the road is San Girolamo degli Schiavoni – St Jerome of the Slavs (Jerome himself was a Dalmatian), built in the six-teenth century for refugees from Turkish domination. It is now the chapel of a Yugoslav College and seldom open to visitors.

The Palazzo Borghese

Face San Girolamo and bear to the right at an angle. Find your way to the Piazza Borghese. Here

15. *A stall in the Piazza Fontanella Borghese*

is the best open market in Rome, known to me, for old prints, books, and antiques. You should enter the courtyard of the splendid palace, completed by the Borghese Pope Paul V in the early seventeenth century; cross it to its enchanting little garden, at the right time of the year a feast of colour and water-music. The Palazzo itself is not visited.

San Lorenzo in Lucina

Cross the Largo della Fontanella Borghese and you will reach a piazza with the venerable façade of San Lorenzo in Lucina, yet another ancient Roman church dedicated to that third-century deacon martyr. According to tradition the grill on which he was roasted alive is preserved under the altar. Frankly, if you manage to appreciate the air of antiquity about the open narthex of this church – twelfth century, with older pagan columns re-used – you will not find much more to enjoy.

Historically the church is memorable as scene of the election to the papacy of St Damasus, great fourth-century restorer of the shrines of martyrs in the catacombs, and several times mentioned in this book on that account. As you see it today, the church is a dull seventeenth-century rebuilding. Over the high altar is a well-known seventeenth-century Crucifixion by Guido Reni.

The description of this section will continue as from the Pantheon – too well known a point of reference for me to complicate the issue by telling you how to get there from somewhere else.

The Pantheon

The Pantheon is far from being the most attractive of churches, but it has an interest that is unique – it is the only pagan temple of ancient Rome virtually intact and little altered, and now used as a church.

The name Pantheon, its ancient pagan title, is often translated 'to all the gods'. More probably it meant 'the all-holy'. As it stands the Pantheon dates from the second century A.D. when Hadrian rebuilt it, but he reproduced on the lintel above the great doors an inscription from the earliest Pantheon of 27 B.C.: *'Built by Marcus Agrippa when Consul for the third time'*. This you can read standing in the piazza.

After the conversion of Constantine in 312 pagan religions were not prohibited, and for some time the Pantheon continued to be used as a temple. In the fifth century it was closed, but not till 608 did the Emperor Phocas permit Pope Boniface IV to turn it into a church. The Column of Phocas in the Forum is said to have been erected partly as a mark of appreciation. The dedication in honour of Our Lady and All Martyrs is believed to be the origin of the feast of All Saints.

Before you enter, stand in that grove of immense columns, each a granite monolith. The doors before you are among the few ancient doors of bronze remaining in Rome, because the metal was so easy to melt down and use for something 'more contemporary'! In fact, some of the bronze that adorned this temple was used by Bernini for the twisted columns of his canopy over the high altar of St Peter's – and what was left over was sent to the Castel Sant' Angelo to make cannon.

Within the church you will be impressed most of all by the shape – a rotunda. Not only is the temple a perfect round, but if the circumference of the dome were continued it would form a ball just touching the pavement. The diameter of the dome is a few feet more than St Peter's, which probably makes it the biggest in the world *in this sense*, but of course St Peter's dome is loftier and has greater volume. There are no windows to the Pantheon except the opening in the centre of the dome, through which rain can enter to run away down the drain beneath.

I am afraid the atmosphere is more that of a show place than of a church, and once you have gained your general impression of this remarkable and unique relic of ancient Rome you have had the best of it. For once I propose to describe a church in a way I usually avoid, and to ask you to walk round, turning to the right within the door; I will mention each feature of interest in turn. Do not follow the walls too closely, or you will fail to see anything in the right proportion.

There are three chapels to each side. The first has a delicate little fresco of the Annunciation attributed to the early renaissance painter Melozzo da Forli (1438–98). The next contains the sarcophagus of King Victor Emmanuel II – the same king of united Italy after whom the great white monument that dominates the city is named. The last chapel on the right has a painting of the Umbrian school, fifteenth century, representing Our Lady between St John the Baptist and St Francis.

Opposite the entrance to the temple is the small sanctuary and choir. The wall of the apse enshrines a Madonna in Byzantine style, now assigned to the thirteenth century, though tradition would give it a much longer history.

The next chapel after the sanctuary has a good sixteenth-century crucifix in cedar wood, and just after it, before a statue of Our Lady, is the tomb of Raphael – whose famous Transfiguration you will see in the Vatican Art Gallery, or at least the mosaic copy of it in St Peter's. In 1833 the tomb was opened to make sure the great renaissance artist was really there. To his right is buried his fiancée, Maria Bibbiena, who died before they could marry. Raphael left an endowment to the Pantheon for Masses to be offered for the repose of his soul. The Madonna del Sasso – 'of the rock', so called because Mary's foot rests on a boulder – was commissioned by Raphael and executed by Lorenzetto.

Next is the monument to King Umberto I and his Queen, Margherita di Savoia. The pagan-type altar in porphyry, the slab of alabaster, and the enrichment in silver and bronze are more pleasing than the corresponding tomb of Victor Emmanuel.

The final chapel is known as 'St Joseph in the Holy Land, of the Virtuosi at the Pantheon' – an elaborate title. The explanation is that in the sixteenth century a canon of this church restored the chapel, packing the floor with earth from Palestine (as Helena had done at Santa Croce twelve centuries earlier). Then, to secure the maintenance of worship there, he founded a confraternity of artists, sculptors, musicians. The two architects Sangallo were members, and more recently Canova. Nearby are buried Baldassare Peruzzi, architect, the sculptor Flaminio Vacco, the violinist Arcangelo Corelli. Such are the 'Virtuosi at the Pantheon'.

The fountain in the piazza before the Pantheon was designed towards the end of the sixteenth century by Jacopo della Porta, but it was modified in 1711. The water it splashes is Acqua Vergine, the same as the Trevi.

The Maddalena

Turn your back on the Pantheon, take either turning leading forward out of the piazza, and a few steps will bring you to the Maddalena, church of St Mary Magdalen. This is the only church in Rome that can be said to be in the rococo style. If you have spent some days with this guide-book you will have an idea of the vitality and musical movement of baroque – take that to an extreme and you have rococo. As a developed style it is more common and perhaps more successful in German-speaking countries. Its slightly extravagant quality is obvious at once in the Maddalena from the plan. It is a cruciform church with a dome, but the nave is an added ellipse.

I suggest that you sit in the nave, not too far back, capturing the mood of this exciting little building. Then look up at the frescoes on the vault of the nave, in the dome, in the transepts, over the chancel, and in the apse. They are early eighteenth century, a little later than the church itself, built by C. Fontana and G. C. Quadrio between 1669 and 1698 – the façade is later. The subject over the nave is the raising of Lazarus at the prayer of his sister Mary, and in the apse it is the Preaching of Christ. This latter is by Aureliano Milani, rather 'romantic' in tone with its bare and stricken trees. Sculpture either side the altar, by P. Bracci, represents Mary arriving at the empty tomb, and encountering the risen Christ in the garden.

A chapel off the right transept has a crucifix said to have disengaged its arm to comfort St Camillus, founder of the Priests Ministers of the Sick who serve this church, in 1582. From the sacristy – left of the sanctuary – you may visit his room, and under the large altar to the right he is enshrined.

While you are still at the sanctuary end of the church, look back towards the door to appreciate a beautiful organ loft of 1735. Then, in the nave, note over the second altar on the left a painting of the Madonna holding the Divine Child simply radiating light. There is a tradition that the artist, Giordano, painted the canvas in one night. To the right is a fifteenth-century Madonna known as 'Health of the Sick'.

Santa Maria in Campo Marzio

Carry on to reach the Piazza di Campo Marzio. Among the tightly packed cars you will discover a pagan altar and, although the presence of a church in this piazza is not too obvious, a glance upwards will show you the apse of Santa Maria in Campo Marzio peering above the shops and traffic. A gate leads to a courtyard with a notice stating that here is the residence of the Catholic Syrian Patriarch's representative to the Holy See. At the far end of this courtyard, through a grille, is a beautiful glimpse of a mediaeval Rome.

The church is cruciform, a version of seventeenth-century baroque in more restrained mood. Walls left uncoloured allow the fine canvases behind the altars to be appreciated, instead of lost in the gloom of crowded side chapels. Above the high altar is an ancient venerated Madonna.

The Minerva Obelisk

To visit the Minerva, return to the Pantheon and pass to the left of that great temple. You will recognize the Piazza della Minerva less by the church, which has a very dull façade, than by the little elephant, attributed to Bernini, with an obelisk on its back. The obelisk was found in a nearby temple of Isis and Serapis – this was a quarter of ancient Rome much devoted to the cult of Eastern deities. The obelisk dates from the sixth century B.C. and was dedicated to the Pharaoh Ofra, mentioned in the Book of Jeremiah (44.30).

Santa Maria sopra Minerva

To Romans, the Minerva – Santa Maria sopra Minerva; that is, St Mary's built over a temple to Minerva – is important as the church where St Catherine of Siena, patroness of Italy, is buried. Books that concentrate on art will tell you that it is the only medieval gothic church in the city. Well, it will not strike you as very gothic, seen from the piazza, and even within it is so overladen with decoration of the renaissance and later that you have to look to observe its gothic structure.

I have known people to find this church disappointing. The interior is gloomy, and its twenty-three chapels contain so much that a catalogue would wear you out. Yet the Minerva is a church to visit, more than once, I think – a church to slip into for a prayer, and each time to check up on one or two of its treasures.

St Catherine is buried beneath the high altar, her sculptured effigy, attributed to Isaias of Pisa (1430), always visible. It is quite the custom for everyone to enter the sanctuary and mount the altar steps to pray at her shrine.

Catherine, who died at thirty-three, was a charming girl of Siena who became a tertiary of the Dominicans, led a heroic life of charitable service to others, bore the stigmata of Christ made invisible at her own prayer, and whose persuasions brought the popes back to Rome from Avignon. Through the sacristy is her room in which she died in 1380. It was reconstructed here from another site in Rome in 1630. I have witnessed a very beautiful ceremony on the feast of St Catherine, April 29th. Shortly before the time for Mass, vested clergy gather at the door of the church. So does an expectant crowd. At last runners arrive who have carried from Siena in relays a burning torch 'of faith and love'. It enters the church and the festal Mass begins.

In the right aisle note the seventh chapel along, larger than the preceding. It has a fine canvas by Federico Fiori (known as Baroccio) of the 'Institution of the Eucharist', painted in 1594. The Blessed Sacrament Confraternity established in this chapel was the first to be approved by the Holy See; one of its earliest members was St Ignatius of Loyola.

The chapel in the right transept has magnificent frescoes painted by Filippino Lippi between 1488 and 1493. At the back the subject is the Assumption and, below, the Annunciation with St Thomas Aquinas and Cardinal Carafa, who built the chapel; to the right the Victory of St Thomas over heresy and, above, the Crucifix speaking in praise of St Thomas.

Statues flank the entrance to the sanctuary at right and left. The one to the right, of St John the Baptist, was sculptured by a little-known artist in 1858, but it is very pleasing; the Christ to the left is by the best known of all artists, Michelangelo, but you may be mildly disappointed. The cross is disproportionate; the bronze loin cloth is an addition (part of this has been removed in recent years).

In the choir behind the altar, and not really visible, are the tombs of Leo X, who set Luther aflame, and Clement VII, who refused to nullify Henry VIII's marriage with Catherine of Aragon.

To the left of the choir is a passage leading to the street at the back of the church, and here, with a monument let in the floor, lies the Dominican artist Fra John of Fiesole, known to all the world as Fra Angelico. In fact he has been beatified – Beato Angelico. He died here in 1455.

The next chapel has, over the altar, a fine painting of St Mary Magdalen by Marcello Venusti, but far more important is the renaissance tomb in the wall to your left. A renaissance tomb it is, to a fifteenth-century Giovanni Arberini, but below the effigy is a fifth-century B.C. sculpture of Hercules struggling with a lion. Consider the posture of both man and beast and admit that here is a masterpiece – a little-known one too.

In the transept chapel on this side is a very slight sculpture of which I am rather fond. It is a Madonna with the Infant Jesus and two Saints John as children – John the Baptist and John the Evangelist. This is by a seventeenth-century sculptor, Franco Siciliano. Its pedestal, later and by another hand, has a very pretty Nativity.

The sixteenth-century cloister and some rooms opening off it can be seen, but they are not of great interest. Historically, it is worth knowing that this monastery was the scene of the trial of Galileo in 1633, when he was made to repudiate on his knees his teaching that the earth revolved round a static sun, instead of the contrary. There is a tradition that, as he rose to his feet he muttered to himself: '*E pur si muove*' – 'It does move though' … Had he really been overheard, these might have been famous last words.

I hope I have conveyed the impression that there is far more to be seen at the Minerva; my description is a mere selection.

The Collegio Romano and Piè di Marmo

You may leave the Minerva by a side door to the left of the

sanctuary. At the end of the alley, turn right into the Piazza del Collegio Romano, the great seminary founded after the Council of Trent under Jesuit direction. It has been succeeded by the Gregorian University. Popes and saints studied here, including St Aloysius Gonzaga, St Camillus de Lellis, St Leonard of Port Maurice – all heroes somewhere in these pages. With your back to the college, bear right a few steps to find the marble foot – Piè di Marmo – at a corner in the street of that name. Leonard van Matt's picture book of Rome has a splendid plate of a Roman cat curled up on this monumental relic of a great antique statue.

Il Facchino

Leave the Piazza del Collegio Romano by the Via Lata at the far end and note on your left, just before you reach the Corso, a sixteenth-century wall fountain known as Il Facchino – the Porter, a man carrying a little barrel. It is uncertain what he represents, perhaps a true street porter, or a water-vendor from the time when Romans drank Tiber water from cleaner upstream reaches. An eighteenth-century English traveller used some to brew tea 'and found it excellent'. After a brief stay in Rome you will decline to believe this.

Santa Maria in Via Lata

In the Corso, at the corner, is Santa Maria in Via Lata, adjacent to the great Doria Pamphili Palace. This church has been closed for some years. Don't confuse it with the nearby Santa Maria in Via. An important tradition attached to the crypt adjacent to this church, entered from the Corso, makes out that Peter and Paul lived here during their Roman apostolate, and that in particular Paul's two years of honourable arrest in a hired lodging were spent here. In this of course it challenges the rival tradition of San Paolo alla Regola (see Chapter 12). Legendary details claim more, and make this also the residence of Paul's secretary Luke and Peter's disciple Martial, who became first bishop of Limoges in France.

The church of St Mary itself has a hazy history till the present building replaced a predecessor in the seventeenth century. Pietro da Cortona's baroque façade was so much appreciated that Pope Alexander VII struck a medal to commemorate it, and indeed it is good, but it is difficult to notice the merits of anything in this busy narrow artery of modern Rome – called 'Corso' because horse races were held here well into the last century. The interior of Santa Maria is ornate and seems to be crowded. There is a choir of carved wooden stalls, an altar attributed to Bernini, columns encased in Sicilian jasper, and a richly coffered ceiling. Of the earlier church remain fragments of cosmatesque pavement. A medieval icon of Our Lady is enshrined above the high altar, and below it are relics of the third-century deacon martyr Agapitus.

The Doria Pamphili Palace

The Doria Pamphili Palace flanks the Corso next to Santa Maria, in the direction of the Victor Emmanuel Monument. You may at least glance into its courtyards, and at certain times – entering from the Piazza del Collegio Romano – visit some of the apartments with a good collection of furniture and paintings.

Turn in the other direction – away from the Victor Emmanuel Monument – and you promptly reach the Piazza Colonna – thick with parked cars and flanked by the endless stream of traffic in the Corso. It takes an effort to appreciate the great second-century column to the philosopher emperor Marcus Aurelius – surmounted since the sixteenth century by a statue of St Paul – the fountain designed for Gregory XIII by Jacopo della Porta, and the diminutive façade of San Bartolomeo dei Bergameschi.

Piazza Colonna

The column – hence the name of the piazza, 'Colonna' – is not easy to study, but standing near the fountain you can make out a military operation involving a pontoon bridge. It is also said to represent the rainfall obtained for the armies of the pagan Emperor by the Christian Twelfth Legion, which ensured his victory and also won some relief from persecution for his Christian subjects, and for themselves the title of the 'Thundering Legion'. I have not managed to identify this on the column. The water it plays is Acqua Vergine. In the nineteenth century lemonade vendors set up booths around it, selling drinks made with fountain water.

San Bartolomeo dei Bergameschi

The tiny eighteenth-century church of St Bartholomew, for the people of Bergamo, is also known as Santa Maria della Pietà. The altar enshrines a Madonna under that title. At the time of revising this text the church is closed for restoration, but I understand the people of Bergamo have set up a memorial here to their compatriot, Pope John XXIII. Notice across the piazza a pleasant blue and white terracotta wall shrine of Our Lady.

The turning after San Bartolomeo will lead to Sant' Ignazio, but on the way you pass through the Piazza di Pietra, with eleven great columns thought to be part of a second-century-A.D. Temple to Neptune. On the fourth column from the left, about fourteen feet up, is carved a crucifix.

Sant' Ignazio

Sant' Ignazio is Rome's second great Jesuit church in the centre of the city. This is because Ignatius himself had dedicated the church of his headquarters to the Holy Name – the Gesù. Pope Gregory XV, who canonized Ignatius, suggested a church in his honour. It was designed by a Jesuit priest, Fr Orazio Grassi, in the seventeenth century, and painted by a Jesuit brother, Andrea Pozzo, in the eighteenth.

Perhaps Pozzo's perspectives are the most intriguing feature of the church. He excelled in perspective devices, which you will easily notice in both the vault of the nave and in the dome. There is a special place marked in the nave from which you should view this perspective effect. The subject of the nave vault is the contribution of the early Jesuits to the glory of Christ's Church – Pozzo himself wrote an involved explanation of this. Tho' e in the apse represent the defence of Pamplona, where the soldier Ignatius was injured in the leg – an event which led to his conversion, and also the divine assurance which Ignatius received in the chapel at La Storta just outside Rome. Anyone with a devotion to the founder of the Society of Jesus may well care to make a pilgrimage there. A City bus service runs to La Storta from just across the Ponte Milvio. Other subjects in the paintings of the apse are connected with the lives of St Francis Xavier and St Francia Borgia.

In the third chapel on the right is buried St Robert Bellarmine, and in the right transept chapel St Aloysius Gonzaga – his altar designed by Brother Andrea Pozzo. Close by this altar a staircase leads up to the roof of the church and over the residence to the room of St Aloysius; it also communicates with other saints' rooms. Although I have found the staircase door open and the chapels disappointingly shut, it is worth the view over the rooftops of Rome, if you don't mind climbing twisting staircases.

CHAPTER 18

The Spanish Steps and thereabouts

*The Spanish Steps – La Barcaccia fountain – Keats' House
– Column of the Immaculate Conception – Santissima
Trinità dei Spagnuoli – Church of Gesù e Maria – Sant'
Atanasio – The Baboon fountain – Via Margutta
– Santissima Trinità dei Monti – The Pincian Hill
– The Villa Borghese*

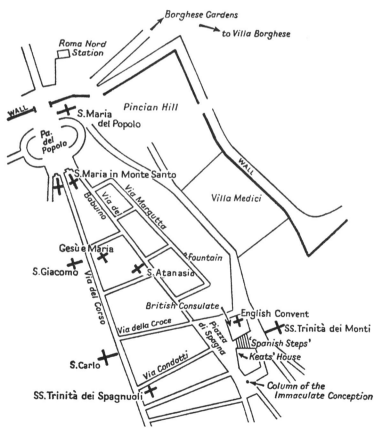

The Spanish Steps

If Mrs Beeton were to concoct a recipe for all that goes under this romantic name – the Spanish Steps – she would have to throw together some unlikely ingredients: steps of course (but built by a Frenchman), masses of flowers in season, twin towers of the Trinità dei Monti, a sunken boat fountain, throngs of tourists, a handful of artists, the Babington tea rooms for toast and nostalgia, a faint aroma of Keats and Shelley – garnish all over with layabouts.

To take the steps first – they are early eighteenth century, paid for by a Frenchman, designed by an Italian – Alessandro Specchi; they are called Spanish simply because of the proximity of the Spanish Embassy, though the quarter is cosmopolitan, artistic, and in no small degree English. The steps are certainly beautiful, but then steps are a speciality of Rome – beautiful not only to see but also to walk up and down. Both fountain below and church above are older than the steps, so that the genius of the architect has been in no small degree the skill with which he has 'blended his ingredients'.

For brief seasons the steps are massed with flower vendors' displays, but at all times it is the resort of what I have called layabouts – a slightly unfair translation of the more elegant Italian *'dolce far niente'*. Once upon a time the idleness of the loungers may have been sweet but it was far from pointless – they were waiting to be hired as artists' models. Dickens and other writers have bright passages in which they word-sketch the types who made a living on the steps by sheer 'being'. There were pipers with goatskin breeches – such as now you see in Rome only at Christmas – the patriarch who pretends to sleep but who is 'very attentive to the position of his legs', others who expect to be recognized straightway as members of the Trinity, the Holy Family, a band of brigands, or just the crowd. Some of these types were of Arab origin, from the mountain-top town of Saracinesco, where the men were noted for swarthy good looks and said to descend from African pirate bands who settled there.

La Barcaccia Fountain

The fountain, below street level, looks like a sunken barque. It plays two different kinds of water, one for the jet and the other for drinking. There are foot-shaped puddles where locals stand to draw water. The name of this fountain means 'the old boat'; it is said to commemorate a phenomenal Tiber flood that left a boat stranded here. There are other traditions. It was made in 1627 and opinions differ as to whether its sculptor was Gian Lorenzo Bernini or his father.

16. The Spanish Steps

Keats' House

To the left of the steps is the Babington tea room, which speaks for itself. Nearby is the British Legation – you may need its services. Just round the corner from there is an English convent of the Poor Servants of the Mother of God, with a church dedicated to St George and the Saints of England. To the right of the steps and overlooking them is Keats' House, where the poet lived and died. If you know little else of Keats, recognize in him the author of this well known line:

'A thing of beauty is a joy for ever.'

Many readers will know Dr Axel Munthe's *Story of San Michele* – he too lived and practised here. The Keats collection – exhibited in the rooms – was sent to the Abbey of Monte Cassino during the war and, when that was threatened, returned by the monks in the care of an unwitting German military escort.

The Column of the Immaculate Conception

To the right, as you face the steps, the narrow piazza extends to join the Piazza Mignanelli. At that end of the Piazza di Spagna is the original College of Propaganda Fide, the Church's missionary centre, which has new buildings on the Janiculum. There too is a column raised by Pius IX in honour of the Immaculate Conception. On the feast, 8th December, Rome's Fire Brigade crowns it with flowers. W. W. Story, in his *Roba di Roma*, describes the occasion when it was raised into position: 'Today, as I am writing, some hundreds of galley slaves in their striped brown uniforms are tugging at their winches and ropes to drag the column of the Immaculate Conception to its pedestal on the Piazza di Spagna.'

Santissima Trinità dei Spagnuoli

Opposite the Spanish Steps the Via Condotti leads to the Corso. A church on the left, at the Corso end, almost escapes notice – Santissima Trinità dei Spagnuoli – Holy Trinity of the Spaniards. This is one of Rome's several domed baroque churches on an elliptical plan. I find them all architecturally fascinating. Remember that the domes of the later part of St Peter's are elliptical. Certainly the finest of all these churches is Sant' Andrea al Quirinale, but there are surprising variations on this simple plan. Perhaps you are not quite sure what all this comment is about, but it will begin to register in the course of your visits.

Santissima Trinità was built for Spanish Trinitarian friars by a Portuguese architect, Manoel Rodriguez dos Santos, in the middle of the eighteenth century, a hundred years after Sant' Andrea. It lacks that vertical movement of Bernini's master-piece, leading the eye up to the entrance of light. The mood here is one of repose and quiet colour.

The Trinitarian Order was founded by two saints with for its object the redemption – that is, the *purchase back* – of slaves, of Christians taken captive by the Moors and carried off to African slavery. Of the side chapels around this church, the central one on each side has paintings of SS. John of Matha and Felix of Valois with black-and-white skinned slaves.

The Church of Gesù e Maria

You may turn right in the Corso and, when San Giacomo degli Incurabili is on your left, you will find opposite the Church of Gesù e Maria (it is sometimes easy to pass a church on your own side of the road without noticing it). Sit down to appreciate the paintings in the vault. The artist was Giaccinto Brandi. Notice the unusual division between the side chapels – a confessional surmounted by niches containing sculpture, all very well designed. The high altar too is a handsome composition – its painting of the Coronation of Our Lady also by Brandi. The last chapel on the left has a painting of a venerated Madonna of Divine Help. The architects of this church were Carlo Maderno and Girolamo Rainaldi. One of Rome's most popular cribs will be found here at Christmas.

The Greek Church of Sant' Atanasio

Back to the Piazza di Spagna. Leading off to the left is the Via del Babuino, 'Street of the Baboon', leading to the Piazza del Popolo. On the left are two churches. The first is Sant' Atanasio, church of the Greek Catholic community of Byzantine rite, and served by the adjacent Greek College. It is worth a visit at any time, but especially on Sunday to assist at the Byzantine liturgy – but check up on this beforehand. Church and college were founded by Gregory XIII. Beyond is the Anglican church – if you have any eye for architecture this will be self-evident.

The Baboon Fountain

This street is called 'of the Baboon' from the battered antique figure reclining above a fountain near the Greek church. This is popularly nicknamed 'the Baboon'. It was one of many statues in Rome to which were attached 'pasquinades', or lively little rhymes lampooning public figures and events – among them not least popes and their policies. This statue disappeared for about fifty years, when it was discovered in a palace courtyard and replaced.

Via Margutta

Parallel with the Via del Babuino (to the right as you face the Piazza del Popolo) is the Via Margutta, a street that might well escape you, for it leads from the Via del Babuino and back to it – the steep flank of the Pincian Hill prevents it going elsewhere. Here was the heart of the artist quarter. Today it lacks the alluring sordidness described by old writers, but it is worth a visit if you have leisure. Along it is one of the *rione* (district) fountains of Rome, adorned with sculptor's tools and artists' easels and brushes.

The presence of the artist community ensures a number of reasonable trattorias in an otherwise pricey neighbourhood. I have heard well of one in the Via dei Greci. Many of my Roman friends were fervent patrons of the German restaurant a few yards along on the left of the Via della Croce, leading off the Piazza di Spagna.

Santissima Trinità dei Monti

The towers at the top of the Spanish Steps belong to the church of Santissima Trinità dei Monti. By 1492 a chapel to the Trinity existed here on the slopes of the hill, where once were the gardens of the gourmet Lucullus. Hermits settled here; some of them were horribly tortured by soldiers during Charles V's sack of Rome, to make them reveal an imaginary cache of treasure. In the course of the sixteenth century, under the patronage of kings of France, the present church was built in a gothic style, though this is hardly perceptible, for the façade is classical and the interior was reconstructed by a French architect in the early nineteenth century. The church was built for the Order of Minims, but the French connection has been strengthened since the transfer, in 1821, to St Madeleine Sophie Barat, foundress of the well-known teaching Sisters of the Sacred Heart.

There is little to appreciate in the church (entrance usually by a door to the left, in the convent building) because the greater part is railed off for the community. Twisted columns in the sanctuary are thirteenth century, and may have been inspired by the original twisted columns around the tomb of Peter.

Old students of the Sacred Heart nuns may wish to venerate the painting of Our Lady known as Mater Admirabilis, preserved in the convent. It was painted in 1844 by an aspirant, but it was Pius IX who spontaneously gave it the title it has carried ever since. St Theresa of the Child Jesus came to pray before it that she would be permitted to enter Carmel at the age of fifteen.

The Pincian Hill

Turn left and you will make your way to the Pincian Hill, a pleasant public garden and panorama over Rome that is also approached from the Piazza del Popolo. This used to be a favoured resort of the aristocracy, and the tradition that it is here you must come for a view of Rome tends to overshadow the far better panorama of the city from the Janiculum, described in some detail in Chapter 26. The trouble with this view is that it does not really extend over ancient Rome at all. Still, the Pincian is indeed a pleasant place to relax and take the air, or on a Sunday evening in summer, after tea, listen to the band.

On your way from Santissima Trinità dei Monti you pass on your right the handsome sixteenth-century Villa Medici, now a French National Academy, and with a garden on the far side worth seeing.

Opposite the villa is a fountain which to my surprise plays Acqua Felice, the water brought to Rome in the sixteenth century by Pope Sixtus V, with its 'show' fountain (*mostra*) the Moses, near the Baths of Diocletian. The orb from which the jet springs is supposed to be a cannon ball, to be precise one fired, rather capriciously, by Queen Christina of Sweden as a salute to herself. The Medici Cardinal who built this fountain left Rome to marry and became Grand Duke of Tuscany – he was never a priest.

From the Pincian you may enter the Borghese Garden and, if you wish, visit the Borghese Galleries.

The Villa Borghese

The Villa Borghese was built, between 1613 and 1616, by the Dutch architect Jan Van Santen for Cardinal Scipione Borghese, nephew of Pope Paul V. The Cardinal intended the villa specially to house his already famous collection. It was 'modernized' in the mid-eighteenth century. Take care to appreciate the building as well as the collection it houses. The latter is not so extensive you cannot do it quite carefully in one visit. Since 1902 it belongs to the State.

The collection is fairly general – sculpture, mosaics, and paintings. In the Entrance Hall are some fine fourth-century mosaics of hunting scenes and gladiators contesting with wild beasts. They are incorporated in the pavement. The style is very simple and formalized – quite remote from that affected by sculpture of the same period. Particularly important here are some of Bernini's finest sculptures. In Room II is his 'David' – David slinging the stone at Goliath, executed when he was only twenty-one and said to be a self-portrait. In Room XV there are two self-portraits painted by Bernini. In Room VI is 'Aeneas and Anchises escaping from Troy', very close to a detail of Raphael's painting called 'The Fire in the Borgo' at the Vatican. Recent opinion tends to attribute this to Gian Lorenzo's father, Pietro Bernini. The subject occurs here again in a painting by Federico Barocci (1528–1612) in Room XV. In Room XIV you will find what is held to be the young Bernini's first work, at the age of about seventeen: the infant Jupiter (abandoned on Mount Ida) taking milk from the goat Amalthea. There are several works by Caravaggio, among them a John the Baptist and a David with the Head of Goliath, in Room XVI.

CHAPTER 19

The Piazza del Popolo and beyond

Santa Maria del Popolo – The Piazza del Popolo – Santa Maria in Montesanto – Santa Maria dei Miracoli – The Porta del Popolo – Sant' Eugenio – Villa Giulia – Ponte Milvio – Scots College

With one of Rome's best known piazzas as starting-point you will at least begin the day without getting lost. It might be an obvious course to describe the piazza first, but Santa Maria del Popolo is a church easily missed, so we shall begin there. The façade, and entrance, are to the right of the Gate.

Santa Maria del Popolo

This is one of Rome's earliest renaissance churches, crammed with beautiful things. Every chapel deserves pages of description so, more than in most places, I must strain out my enthusiasm and guide you to what matters most, or what can be more easily appreciated – not always the same.

History here is wrapped in legend. According to tradition Nero, after his flight from Rome and suicide, was buried on the slopes of the hill that overlooks this piazza, the Pincian. The proximity of his remains is said to have so pestered the inhabitants that Pope Paschal II, in the last year of the eleventh century, had them disinterred and thrown in the Tiber, and replaced their unhallowed memory by a shrine to Our Lady, called Our Lady of the People – Santa Maria del Popolo. In 1231 Gregory IX is recorded as having given the church its present venerated icon of Our Lady, a gift from the treasury of the Lateran.

Baccio Pontelli was architect of the present church, for Pope Sixtus IV, whose coat of arms, an oak tree, you will spot more than once on your way round. It was built between 1477 and 1479. Of this period you will more easily notice, outside, the façade and the dome, earliest Roman dome of the renaissance, and inside, the nave arches of travertine, Rome's most popular building stone.

The high altar enshrines the venerated icon from the Lateran, the Madonna del Popolo. The arch above it is enriched with

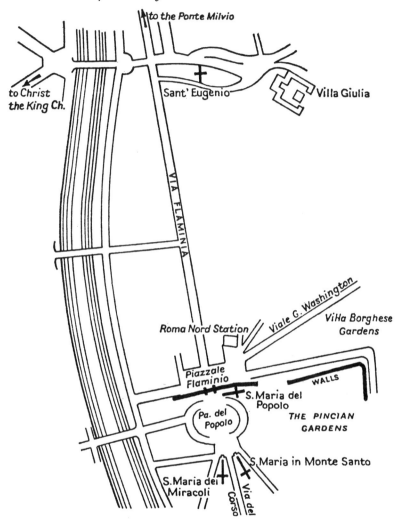

gilded stucco relief telling the legendary history of Pope Paschal founding the sanctuary in place of Nero's tomb.

There is a choir behind the altar where the friars of the Augustinian monastery used to say office when the community was larger than it is today – Luther among them, no doubt, on the occasion of his visit to Rome before his dispute with the Church. If there is a friar about he may take you through the sanctuary to see the painted vault by Pinturicchio, two beautiful renaissance tombs of cardinals by Sansovino, and – rare in Rome – stained glass of the life of Our Lord, on one side, and the life of Our Lady, on the other, by Guglielmo di Massilia (Marseilles) – a Frenchman, 1509.

To the left of the sanctuary there is a tiny chapel with two magnificent paintings which alone should lure anyone to Santa Maria del Popolo, Caravaggio's Conversion of St Paul and Execution of St Peter, of 1602. The conversion of St Paul – the fall from the horse, the animal's alarm, the blinding light from heaven – remains a popular subject with contemporary Italian artists. The chapel alongside this, to St Catherine of Alexandria, has rich and delicate stucco decoration; look up to see it!

In the left aisle (left as you face the altar) I draw attention especially to the square chapel, second from the door. It is a funeral chapel for the princely Chigi family, designed for them by Raphael about 1516, and his too are the mosaics in the vault of the Creator and signs of the Zodiac, as well as two of the four statues of prophets, Jonas and Elias. The Jonas pleases me especially as a worthy successor to the tradition of representing that subject, mentioned elsewhere in this book as one of the most popular in early Christian art. Habacuc and Daniel are by Bernini. Habacuc has a friendly lion licking his feet, and just outside the chapel there is a tomb to a Chigi princess (Maria Flaminia, died 1771) with a lovely lion, which you will not be surprised to hear was sculptured by Franzoni, who contributed nearly everything to the Vatican animal room. The painting of the Nativity is by Sebastiano del Piombo.

Just inside the door there is a really gruesome monument dating from 1672.

In the right aisle you will need to pause more than once. The first chapel was painted by Pinturicchio. His Nativity is exquisite – an adjective I don't usually care to use. Notice the ox and ass, shepherds and kings in miniature among the crags, and the angel flying busily overhead.

The next chapel was built for Cardinal Alderano Cybo between 1682 and 1687. Designed by Carlo Fontana, it is a study in the use of rich and sombre marbles – you may find it overpowering. In contrast, delicately coloured marbles have been used for the urn below the altar, containing the relics of the Virgin Martyr Faustina, from the catacombs.

The next chapel, St Augustine's, has more paintings by Pinturicchio, especially a Madonna enthroned and an Assumption.

In a small gallery under the direction of the Augustinians,

wedged between the church and the gate, there is nearly always an exhibition of work by younger Italian artists.

The Piazza del Popolo

Now for the piazza. Characteristically, it depends on obelisk and fountains for its effect, but in addition it has the Porta del Popolo, the church you have just visited, those apparently twin churches, Santa Maria dei Miracoli and Santa Maria in Montesanto, and the ever popular Pincian Hill. H. V. Morton, in his work on the Fountains of Rome, observes very well that it is 'the most splendid, but the least Roman' of piazzas. I am happy to quote someone else because I am afraid I have never cared too much for this end of the city. The piazza was brought to its present appearance by Valadier, architect to Popes Pius VI and VII – his name is French but he was born in Rome – who designed it early in the nineteenth century. It was meant to be the traveller's impressive entrance to the city, for in those days before the railway everyone who came from the north entered by the Via Flaminia and its Porta del Popolo.

Of course, churches, gate, and obelisk were already there. The obelisk was thirteen centuries old when Caesar Augustus brought it from Heliopolis in Egypt in a specially designed vessel and raised it in Rome some five years before the birth of Christ. Its hieroglyphs are prayers to the sun. Pope Sixtus V brought it here in 1589. Around it are four lions, similar to those at the foot of the Capitol but spouting water with far more conviction. Either side the piazza are water divinities; towards the river, Neptune with tritons; towards the hill, Mars with personifications of the Tiber and its tributary the Anio. Above the latter Valadier's waterfalls tumble from the flank of the Pincian.

You may wish to visit the two churches that separate three roads into Rome. That on the left is Santa Maria in Montesanto; on the right is Santa Maria dei Miracoli. Although attractive ornaments to the piazza, I think you will find your visit disappointing. Architecturally they are well known as a pair, for this reason: the dome of Santa Maria dei Miracoli is a circle, the other a sphere which, geometrically, could contain two interlacing circles. They were built in the second half of the seventeenth century – contemporary with Wren churches in the City of London.

Santa Maria in Montesanto

Santa Maria in Montesanto replaces a Carmelite church that stood hereabouts, belonging to friars of the province of

Montesanto in Sicily, hence its name. This explains too the icon of Our Lady over the high altar, sixteenth century, and from the former church. The dedication feast here is 11th July, Our Lady of Mount Carmel. The sanctuary has a sombre black and white dignity enhanced by its plain wooden stalls.

Santa Maria dei Miracoli

The title 'Our Lady of Miracles' of the other church refers to the reputation of its icon of Our Lady, over the high altar, acquired long before it found its home here. The first chapel to the right has an altar to Our Lady of Bétharram, a shrine a few miles from Lourdes, in France. Priests of the Sacred Heart, founded at that sanctuary, serve the church. The reproduction of Renoir's Madonna at Bétharram is quite unworthy of the original.

Although you may find your way up to the Pincian from the piazza, I have described it already in Chapter 18.

You may well not wish to go beyond the piazza, so I will explain that the road between the churches is the Corso, leading you to the Piazza Venezia, Forum and Palatine, and that on its right lies the quarter described in Chapter 17 and on its left that described in Chapter 18; to the left of Santa Maria in Montesanto is the Via Babuino, leading to the Piazza di Spagna and the Spanish Steps, and to the right the Via di Ripetta leading to the Tiber and the Pantheon. The bus terminus is through the gate, so is the entrance to the Borghese Gardens, and beyond the gate too you may find restaurants to suit an average pocket.

Porta del Popolo – the Flaminian Gate

Once through the Porta del Popolo you can look back at it. On this side it was designed by Vignola and built in 1564; the side facing the Piazza is a modification by Bernini, 1655. Notice, facing the Via Flaminia, statues of SS. Peter and Paul, one touching a book with his hand as if to draw attention to it, the other extending his hand towards what Cardinal Wiseman, in 'God bless our Pope', calls the 'frozen north'. It is a characteristic Roman joke about the Church that the former expresses where the laws of the Church are made, the latter where they are expected to be kept!

Across the Piazza Flaminia to the right is a railway station called Roma Nord. This is the terminus of an independently run line between Rome and Viterbo. It is useful for visiting hill towns north of Rome, especially Sant' Oreste, for the visit to Monte Soratte described in Chapter 31. To the right are the gates of the Borghese Gardens. They were designed by a Scot, More of Edinburgh, for Prince Marcantonio Borghese in the eight-eenth century.

At this point I shall add several places of interest down the Via Flaminia and beyond without implying that you should make a tour of them. They are simply for those who may have a special interest.

A few hundred yards along the Viale delle Belle Arti crosses the Via Flaminia. To the right is the interesting modern church of Sant' Eugenio and, beyond that again, the Villa Giulia with its Museum of Etruscan antiquities.

Sant' Eugenio

Sant' Eugenio was built by Pope Pius XII, in honour of his baptismal patron St Eugenius, a seventh-century pope, from gifts received on the occasion of the silver jubilee of his episcopate in 1942. There is a college annexed for young men studying for the priesthood at the Roman universities. The Pope consecrated the high altar in 1951.

Like some other 'modern' churches in Rome, it is really an attempt at updating baroque. The results do somehow express the Pope's personality and it has been nicknamed the 'Pius XII style'. I feel sure that a walk round Sant' Eugenio will convince you that if, in some respects, this style easily dates, it none the less produced work of quality. Particularly successful are the 'Triumph of the Cross' over the high altar, with a representation of the Pope himself, and figures symbolic of modern labour, the altar of Our Lady of Fatima with a fresco and glazed terracotta Annunciation, and a beautiful little baptistery opening off the cloister. The chapel of SS. Peter and Paul, to the right of the sanctuary, has a delightful fresco with a Roman working man walking home, with his child, along the Tiber bank.

The Villa Giulia

The Villa Giulia was the sixteenth-century palace of Pope Julius III, altogether too much of a pleasure lover in an age crying for reform. He was pope for only five years – during the reigns of our Edward VI and Mary Tudor – and this beautiful renaissance villa, designed largely by Vignola, is his monument. When he died 160 bargeloads of antique statues were transported down the Tiber to the Vatican. Today it is a State museum of antiquities of pre-Roman civilizations – notably Etruscan.

The Ponte Milvio

The Via Flaminia leads to the Ponte Milvio. You must have noticed how often the name of the Emperor Constantine recurs when telling the story of many Roman churches. He was the first Christian emperor, and his Edict of Milan in 313 brought peace and security to the Christian Church. Although the emperor put off baptism till old age, he built the first St Peter's, the first Lateran cathedral of Rome, and even raised equally wonderful churches over the Holy Places in Palestine. This advent of a new age was brought about, according to contemporary accounts, by a vision accorded to Constantine, on his way to Rome to overthrow his rival Maxentius, assuring him of victory in the Sign of the Cross. The victory took place here, and Maxentius is said to have been thrown into the Tiber from the Milvian Bridge, already over four hundred years old. The Battle of the Milvian Bridge is as much a key date to Christian and European history as 1066 is in the story of Britain.

The Ponte Milvio (sometimes called the Ponte Molle) has indeed been rebuilt – the gate dates from 1815 – but it is still substantially a two-thousand-year-old bridge. It has been amusing for residents in Rome to see the pompous new Flaminian Bridge nearby closed to traffic as unsafe while cars still use its venerable brother.

The Scots College

On the far side begins the Via Cassia. A bus along this road, to the suburb known (inaccurately) as Tomba di Nerone (Nero's Tomb), will take you to the New Scots College (1963) by Renato Costa, who also designed the Beda College opposite St Paul's. Here the architect has used a different colour scheme, red brick and dark red marble, in keeping with the local sandy landscape. The chapel merits a visit. On the right of the Via Flaminia before you cross the Tiber is the Olympic Village, built originally for the Olympic Games of 1960, and with some interesting sports stadia, and left along the Tiber bank on the far side is Mussolini's 'Foro Italico', handsomely designed sports stadia equipped with a great deal of statuary, fountains, and even an obelisk proper to that ultimate renaissance. The obelisk, in acknowledgement of the Duce's great contribution to Italian life (not forgetting his crimes), is still inscribed with his name, and capped with solid gold.

CHAPTER 20

A Walk from Santa Maria Maggiore to Santa Croce and the Lateran

*The Russian Church – Aqueducts – Holy Cross in Jerusalem
– Our Lady of Perpetual Succour – Santa Prassede (for the
Lateran and Scala Santa see Chapter 5)*

From St Mary Major's both Holy Cross – Santa Croce in Gerusalemme – and St John Lateran can be included in a round tour. As you stand in front of the façade two roads lead away. From a few steps along the road branching left – Via Carlo Alberto – Santa Croce can be glimpsed in the distance, and down the Via Merulana, straight ahead, lies St John Lateran.

The Russian Church

The walk to Santa Croce – about fifteen minutes – is interesting. A stone's throw from St Mary's, a church with a plain romanesque façade, approached by a double flight of steps, is Rome's Catholic Church of the Byzantine rite, serving the Institute for Oriental Studies, to the left, and the Russicum, or Russian College, to the right. Before the church was attached to these institutes it was known as St Antony's – after the Egyptian Antony, the first Abbot (d. 354) – and, as he is patron saint of animals, a Blessing of Beasts used to take place here annually about his feast (17th Jan.). This blessing now takes place outside Sant' Eusebio at the corner of the nearby Piazza Vittorio Emmanuele. The Russian Church, its present appearance mostly baroque eighteenth-century, is interesting to visit at any time for the sake of its beautiful iconostasis, or sanctuary screen, characteristic of the Byzantine liturgy, but visitors staying more than a week in Rome might well take advantage of this opportunity to assist at Sunday Mass here.

Aqueducts

After a few hundred yards the Piazza Vittorio Emmanuele II interrupts the road to Santa Croce. There is hardly anything beautiful in this quarter – late nineteenth-century development – but the piazza is the scene of a colourful and busy market, mostly foodstuffs. In the gardens is a ruin unique in Rome, the

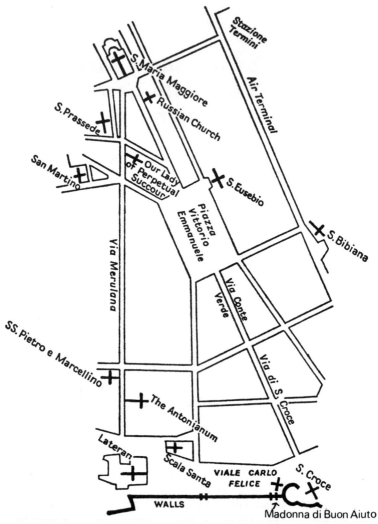

terminal fountain of one of the great aqueducts of antiquity. Its name is 'the Trophies of Marius', from two military trophies, or suits of armour sculptured in marble, which formerly adorned it, and which are now to be seen on the Capitol. On your road again, and to the left, there is a fine section of aqueduct, showing, above the arches, the water channel in good condition. This is a branch aqueduct constructed by Nero to carry water to the Palatine. Another turning to the left, just after this, gives a splendid side view of the Porta Maggiore, built in A.D. 52 as an ornamental arch carrying an aqueduct across a country road, but two centuries later incorporated in Rome's extended system of walls (the Aurelian walls).

Holy Cross in Jerusalem

From this point Santa Croce comes clearly into view. Its baroque eighteenth-century façade is topped by statues, like the Lateran and St Peter's. They have an elegance in keeping with the light and gracious lines that make Santa Croce remind you of churches in Austria and southern Germany. Baroque architecture is distinguished by the use of lines that could not be drawn with geometrical instruments – ellipses and twists and curves, the lines of a violin – and they are in evidence at Santa Croce. The façade, for instance, swells outwards, and indeed it closes an elliptical porch which you should appreciate by *looking in* before you step in.

The great interest here is the Passion Relics. The full name of the basilica is Holy Cross *in Jerusalem*, because when the Empress Helena returned from Palestine with the relics of the Passion she had discovered there – in the course of her son Constantine's reclaiming of the site of Calvary – she adapted several rooms of the Sessorian Palace as a church and packed the floor with soil from the Holy City which she had brought home as ballast in her ship. Santa Croce, therefore, however baroque and eighteenth-century its appearance today, is structurally a Roman building older than 325, the approximate date of its adaptation as a church. You may convince yourself of this by taking a walk round to the left of the basilica, where the walls of Roman brick are clearly to be seen, full of alarming cracks.

Since 1930 the relics have been transferred to a modern relic chapel, not without taste and certainly very convenient for public veneration. The entrance is near the end of the left aisle. You may go round the altar to examine the relics closely and on the way pick up one of the leaflets, available in several languages, which enable you to identify them.

The Passion Relics

The story of the finding of the Cross is fairly well documented in fourth-century writing. St Cyril of Jerusalem, who was a young man at the time, in his catechism classes a few decades later refers to particles of the true Cross already being scattered throughout Christendom. The two thorns strike one as surprisingly large and, oddly enough, the plant from which they come has not been identified. They do agree, however, with many other relics of holy thorns. The Crown for which the Sainte Chapelle at Paris was built comprises only a thornless base. The nail is of Roman type, and although one may correctly observe that more such nails are venerated here and there than were ever used at the crucifixion it is certain, historically, that many copies were cast by Popes containing filings from an original. The nail at Santa Croce is surely more likely to be authentic than doubtful copies preserved elsewhere.

The 'Title' is a most interesting relic. It came to light in 1492, built up in the wall of the basilica behind a mosaic that was under repair. The brick, inscribed TITULUS CRUCIS, which covered it, is preserved in the outer relic chapel. Prior to the discovery, there was no tradition of any such relic, neither here, nor, as far as I know, anywhere else. Yet at the end of the last century, at Arezzo in Northern Italy, a document was discovered, the travelogue of a fourth-century Spanish abbess on pilgrimage in the Holy Land, describing the veneration of such a relic in the courtyard on Calvary at Jerusalem.

17. *Part of the Title of the Cross, bearing the words 'Jesus of Nazareth King . . .' at Santa Croce*

An intriguing feature is that the words still legible on this fragment – *Jesus of Nazareth, King*, in Greek and Latin – are cut in the wood so as to read from right to left. This is correct for Hebrew – of which the barest trace remains, but very unexpected for these two languages. Both possible explanations appear to support the authenticity of the relic. One can well picture a Jew, acting under Roman orders and using the letters of a language he did not really know, setting them down one by one the way he wrote his own language. On the other hand, it is not unheard of for an occasional Greek or Latin inscription, on a tomb or a coin, to appear written 'back to front', for some unaccountable reason. But it is very improbable that a medieval forger would fake the Title in such a sophisticated way. In the outer chapel there is a reconstruction of the full Title indicating the portion preserved here. Another relic you will certainly notice is the great beam alleged to be part of the good thief's cross.

The apse of the basilica, behind the high altar, glows with delightful frescoes attributed to an Antoniazzo Romano about the year 1492. The Teaching Christ – subject of Rome's earliest Christian art – is depicted in gothic gentleness against a radiance of golden light, surrounded by a host of cherubim and a star-spangled sky. Below is the history of the Cross – reading from the left: Helena discovers the Cross; its identification by means of a miraculous cure; its Triumph and – after its capture by the Persians – its restoration to Jerusalem by the Emperor Heraclius. This latter part especially has some very pretty background scenes. Against the wall in the centre of the apse is an unusual tomb – of Cardinal Quiñones, 1536 – which includes a tabernacle for the Blessed Sacrament.

To the left of the sanctuary a ramp leads down to the chapel where the relics were preserved from St Helena's time down to 1930, its floor packed with Jerusalem soil. If you find the red electric light push you can floodlight the splendid fifteenth-century mosaics of the vault. They represent Christ teaching in the central roundel, the evangelists in four medallions, and the intervening space is occupied by charming scenes from the history of the Cross that will remind you of miniatures on a manuscript.

For the last four centuries Cistercians (but not Trappist Cistercians) have served this basilica. For a time Newman stayed in the adjacent monastery occupying a room with a view over the Alban Hills.

Bear left from Santa Croce to a gate in the Aurelian Wall and you will notice a chapel approached by steps, but closed. This is the 'Madonna di Buon Aiuto', Our Lady of Good Help, and there is a street procession with the venerated icon on the 8th of October.

From Santa Croce the tree-lined Viale Carlo Felice leads in a few minutes to the Lateran. You could go through the Gate by the Madonna of Good Help and walk as far as the next Gate. This would give you an experience of the Aurelian Wall (third century AD). Towards sundown the baroque statues topping the Lateran's façade can be most impressive. From many a Roman viewpoint they are a landmark on the skyline. The visit to this archbasilica is described in Chapter 5. Meanwhile, there are one or two places to note on our return to St Mary Major's along the Via Merulana.

The Antonianum

First, you pass on the right the great Franciscan University of the Friars Minor called the Antonianum, with a basilica dedicated in 1887 and a recently built aula with interesting sculptures of Franciscan saints. Then, on the left, below the modern street level, is the eighteenth-century church of San' Pietro e Marcellino, SS. Peter and Marcellinus, Roman martyrs, a box-like building with a curious dome, hardly worth visiting.

Our Lady of Perpetual Succour

As you approach St Mary Major's you will be quite unaware, as you pass rows of shops, that they are the ground-floor frontage of the General House of the Redemptorist Order – until you see a gothic church up a long flight of steps, with a mosaic of the well-known picture of Our Lady of Perpetual Succour over the door. As a matter of fact this church is not only gothic but English, and although it may not surprise you it did surprise Rome when it was built in 1858, by an English Architect, George Wigley, for a Scottish convert, Father Edward Douglas of the Queensbury family, and one critic wrote: 'It might easily be mistaken for a Protestant church'. It was restored for the centenary of the re-enthronement of the famous icon. This came from Crete at the very end of the fifteenth century and had formerly been in a church destroyed by one of Napoleon's generals; subsequently it was venerated in a private chapel. When the Redemptorists purchased property here for their Generalate in 1853 they resolved to restore the venerated picture to its former honours. Not only have they done this, but they have spread its devotion throughout the world. The icon is now enshrined above the high altar.

Santa Prassede

Over the road from Our Lady of Perpetual Succour turnings to the left of the Via Merulana will lead you to Santa Prassede, another ancient Roman church with columns taken from pagan temples, cosmatesque pavements, and ninth-century mosaics. Prassede (she has an English form 'Praxedes' but it is so unfamiliar that I shall use the Italian name) was sister to Pudentiana, traditionally daughters of the senator Pudens, host of St Peter at Rome. St Pudentiana's church, not far away, is described in Chapter 22. As in so many other cases there are excavations under this church of Roman houses where, in all probability, Christians assembled for worship before the first church was built here in the time of Pope Siricius – 384–399. As it stands today, Santa Prassede is a rebuilding begun by Pope Hadrian I and completed by Pope Paschal very early in the ninth century.

You may come upon Santa Prassede by its side entrance, within a stone's throw of St Mary Major's, but if you do it is better to follow the street round and enter by that venerable-looking portico in the Via San Martino ai Monti. A flight of steps leads you dramatically into the atrium, with ancient columns bedded in the walls.

Let us talk straightway of the mosaics in the apse and on the two arches that precede it, all the work of Pope Paschal, whose monogram you will easily find in the centre of the further arch. The picture in the apse very closely resembles that in St Cecilia's in Trastevere. Christ advances among the clouds of heaven, above his head the hand of the Father awards the crown of victory. Right and left are Peter and Paul with their arms affectionately round the shoulders of the sisters Prassede and Pudentiana. The saint to the right is probably the martyr Zeno, to the left is Pope Paschal with a model of his church. Notice in the palm tree beside the pope the phoenix bird, symbol of immortality because in the legends of antiquity it was believed to rise from its own ashes. The band of blue at the base of the mosaic, which is always symbolic of baptism as our entrance to the Church, is here conveniently inscribed JORDANES – the River Jordan in which Christ sanctified Baptism. Below is the Lamb of God, sign of Christ's sacrifice, with processions of sheep, who represent the apostles approaching him from either side. The Latin inscription records the dedication to Santa Prassede and the building by Pope Paschal.

I expect you will get rather tired if you try to study all the mosaics of this church, but if you are still keen you should look at the two great arches. That nearer the nave represents a walled city, the Heavenly Jerusalem, where Our Lord reigns among the blessed, its gates are guarded by angels, and saints approach from either side. The further arch – the one containing the apse – has over it the Lamb of God enthroned above the Book with Seven Seals (these are symbolic figures from St John's Vision in the Apocalypse), flanked by the candlesticks which stand for the Church of Christ, symbols of the Evangelists, and 'ancients' offering crowns of flowers.

Between the steps to the sanctuary, of rare Egyptian red marble, is a staircase descending to the 'confession' or crypt. In this narrow corridor are ancient sarcophagi enshrining the relics of SS. Prassede and Pudentiana – although they were not made for this purpose. One on the left has beautiful sculptures of the Good Shepherd, and also of Jonas reclining on the shore after his journey in the sea monster: in catacomb art this was a very common symbol of our life on earth – life in Christ represented by the fish, in the Church represented by baptismal water –, and of our arrival on the shores of eternal life where we find rest. At the end of this corridor an altar has been made up of beautiful cosmatesque work. As you turn left and leave the crypt by a staircase you may see overhead more fragments of early Christian tombs.

At this point the sacristy should be visited by anyone who wants to buy souvenirs. In a chapel on the right side of the nave are several vestments and articles of clothing of St Pius X.

To the right of the church is the chapel of St Zeno, a little gem of ninth-century mosaic, though you may recognize that the work in this church, which excels in interest, is inferior in technique to mosaics of the fourth to the sixth centuries. Pause first to study the entrance to this chapel. The columns flanking the door are of different marbles; to the left granite, to the right rare black porphyry. The lintel, a third-century fragment, is surmounted by a beautiful funeral urn set in a window, and around this are mosaics, the inner arch showing busts of Our Lady and saints, the outer Our Lord and apostles.

Pope Paschal built this little chapel in honour of his mother during her lifetime, and to enshrine relics of the martyrs Zeno and Valentine which he brought here from the catacombs. There is a portrait in mosaic of his mother, inscribed 'Theodora Episcopa', which means Mrs Bishop Theodora, just like Trollope's Mrs Proudie. The Valentine is the one whose feast in February is interesting to courting couples. The best feature of the mosaics in this chapel is over your heads, a medallion of Christ upheld by four beautifully drawn angels. This is reminiscent of the famous Ravenna mosaics. Notice that of the four columns supporting the vault, one has an upturned capital for its base.

In a niche behind the altar a charming mosaic of Our Lady with her Divine Child, between the sister saints of this church, is thirteenth century.

Opening from St Zeno's chapel is the sanctuary of the Pillar of the Scourging, brought from the Holy Land in 1223. The rare marble of this relic, and its elegant form, do not make its authenticity easy to credit, especially when you know there is a pillar of the scourging in the Church of the Holy Sepulchre at Jerusalem. However, it is a place where one may fittingly reverence the passion of Christ.

The second chapel from the door, on the left of the nave, is dedicated to St Charles Borromeo, a great bishop of the Counter-Reformation, and there you may venerate the table at which he sat and entertained the poor.

In a large chapel opening off the end of the right aisle is a beautiful cosmatesque tomb of a thirteenth-century archbishop of Troyes, and also fragments of sculpture that were once part of the ninth-century furnishing of this church.

CHAPTER 21

The Baths of Caracalla and thereabouts – The Via Appia

The Baths of Caracalla – San' Nereo e Achilleo – San Sisto
– San Cesareo – The Hypogeum of the Scipios –
Columbarium of the Freedmen of Livia – San Giovanni in
Oleo – St John before the Latin Gate – City Gates and Walls
– The Chapel of Domine Quo Vadis – The Appian Way –
Circus of Maxentius – Tomb of Caecilia Metella

The Baths of Caracalla are situated in a quarter of Rome that was always sparsely populated and remains secluded and quiet – except for the traffic crossing the Piazza Nuna Pompilio. Surrounded by an archaeological zone, municipal nurseries, sports grounds, and a few quiet residential roads, it makes a retreat for a breath of air and possibly a meal in one of the slightly pretentious restaurants you will find if you are observant.

The Baths of Caracalla
The huge bathing establishment comes into view soon after you leave Circo Massimo Underground station and follow the Via della Terme di Caracalla, a grand boulevard. It is said to be the largest mass of ruin in Rome after the Colosseum, and ruin is the word for it. Comparatively late, the Baths were begun in A.D. 212 by the Emperor Marcus Aurelius Antoninus, nicknamed Caracalla after the barbarian style of dress he affected. Like the Basilica of Maxentius in the Forum, a little later in date, they make the most of the Roman skill for building in brick and concrete and for vaulting with immense arches. 'Architecture' means 'to roof with an arch'. Formerly coated with marble and paved with mosaic – the latter survives only in fragments which are still colossal – the Baths have little beauty today beyond the sheer grandeur of ruin. Their treasures were plundered to adorn renaissance buildings or to stock museums. There was a time when, like the Colosseum, the Baths of Caracalla were noted for their wide variety of botanical specimens; today they are best known, I should think, for the opera performed here in the summer season. In Keats' House, by the way, there is a painting by Joseph Severn of the young Shelley composing his 'Prometheus Unbound', perched high up on the ruined walls.

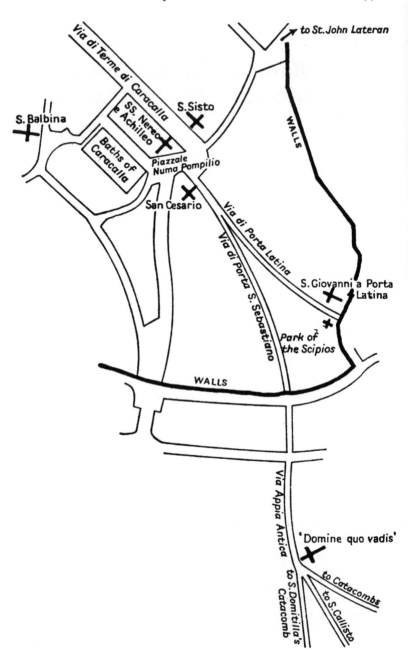

The best way to enjoy a visit – unless you are keen enough on archaeology to buy an official guide-book in English – is to wander at leisure, on the lookout for grand perspectives, striking fragments of mosaic, sculptured capitals caught in an unusual light. There is opportunity here for interesting photography. Sometimes it is possible to visit part of the extensive underground system contrived for the service of the bathrooms. It is said that the Baths of Caracalla could easily accommodate 1,600 bathers at a time.

Around the junction of roads at the Piazza Nuna Pompilio are three churches of varying interest. Between the Baths and the main road is San' Nereo e Achilleo, over the road San Sisto, beyond the piazza and a few yards down the right fork – Via di Porta San Sebastiano – is San Cesareo. The last is the most important, which I am anxious you should not miss, but if it should be closed try San' Nereo e Achilleo, which is similar. Ring the bell, and the custodian comes from his house at the back.

San' Nereo e Achilleo

The church of SS. Nereus and Achilleus is most ancient. It has an ancient name: *'Titulus Fasciolae'* – 'the title of the bandage'. This has been explained by a legend which is part of the *Domine, Quo Vadis* tradition. When Peter was fleeing from Rome – from martyrdom – a bandage fell from his leg at this place. Later an oratory marked the site. The present dedication is to two fourth-century soldier martyrs of the Catacomb of Domitilla, whose relics were removed from the underground basilica you can still visit at that catacomb and enshrined under the altar of this city church along with those of St Flavia Domitilla. There were two saints of that name, which they have given to the catacomb on their family property. This saint is said to have been the niece of the Emperor Vespasian, of the Flavian family.

As it stands at present, this church is a restoration by Cardinal Baronius in 1596, but he demonstrated the best antiquarian spirit of the renaissance by his zeal to preserve all that was best of this venerable building. So you can still admire the fine cosmatesque fittings of the sanctuary – beautifully inlaid marble and mosaic. They include an episcopal throne behind the altar of which the seat is more ancient, but Baronius made a mistake about that. Sixth-century Pope Gregory the Great, in his twenty-eighth homily, made it clear he was preaching before the shrine of the martyrs Nereus and Achilleus. Baronius, who had restored their relics here from the Senate House in the Forum, then a church of St Adrian, assumed that this was the place of the sermon, and he had its text inscribed on the back of the bishop's chair. When, however, the underground basilica was discovered in the catacomb of Domitilla in 1871 it was realized the sermon had in fact been preached there. This church dates, in all probability, from the time the relics were removed from the catacomb, the ninth century. Of this primitive building there is a mosaic in the apse representing the Transfiguration of Christ – a rare subject at that time.

San Sisto

San Sisto across the road is dedicated to Pope Sixtus II who was martyred in the Cemetery of Callixtus during a third-century persecution. To be blunt, this church is not much to look at, but it is important to anyone interested in St Dominic. He lived here when he arrived in Rome, till he was given Santa Sabina on the Aventine. Then, in 1218, he established Dominican nuns here. In the Chapter House, which you ask to see – it is a projecting wing of the convent and can be located from outside – he is said to have raised to life by his prayer Napoleone Orsini, a young nobleman killed by a fall from his horse. Paintings by a nineteenth-century friar represent this subject among others. If the church is closed, ask at the convent to be admitted.

San Cesareo

A few yards along the Via Porta di San Sebastiano is a church well restored, a sheer joy to visit. For cosmatesque work – that inlay of coloured marble and mosaic in sculptured white marble mentioned so often in this book – San Cesareo has few rivals. It is in fact thought to have been brought here in the sixteenth century by the architects restoring the transepts of St John Lateran.

The title San Cesareo in Palatio, St Caesarius in the Palace, does not mean there was a palace here. Caesarius was a deacon martyr of the second century. He suffered at Terracina and when, in the fourth century, the Emperor Valentinian I's daughter was healed at his shrine there, the relics were transferred to a church on the Palatine (*in Palatio*) as a mark of royal favour. Subsequently they were brought here and later removed again to Santa Croce.

Here is another modern instance of excavation having more to tell us than documents or even tradition. The earliest record of San Cesareo dates from 1192, but below the nave you can see a huge mosaic of what was probably a second- or a third-century bath house. There are also foundations of what may be the first church here, of the eighth century.

Serious rebuilding begun under Pope Clement VIII was completed in 1603. There has always been a problem to find anyone to care for churches in this sparsely populated quarter of Rome, and although restoration commenced in 1955 the church has been reopened for worship only since 1963. It is popular for weddings. If you find it closed, ring the bell at the door to the right.

The cosmatesque furniture here consists of pulpit, balustrades, a frontal to the altar, and an episcopal chair behind it. There are the most delightful little birds and beasts, sculptured in marble or depicted in mosaic, and some unusual colours for cosmatesque craftsmen, especially the pale blue.

Between the windows are paintings by Cavalier d'Arpino and Cesare Rosetti of the sufferings of Caesarius and of several martyrs named Hippolytus – as a compliment to Clement VIII whose baptismal name was Ippolito. The coffered ceiling has Clement's coat of arms for its motif, and St Caesarius in its centre panel. Over the latter is a canopy re-using ancient marble columns, and above the bishop's chair is a fifteenth-century fresco of the Madonna. The apse has a rarity in Rome, a sixteenth-century mosaic of God the Father, to designs by Cavalier d'Arpino. Notice too, outside the arch, his Annunciation.

The custodian will open for you a gate leading down to the mosaic floor of the bath house beneath the church, decorated in black and white with Neptune, sea maidens, and beasts, including a marine cow and a marine reindeer.

Next to San Cesareo is a charming medieval house where Cardinal Baronius lived when he was titular of the church. It is sometimes open to the public.

Now you have a choice of roads. The left fork, Via di Porta Latina, leads to the church of St John before the Latin Gate; the right fork takes you to the Porta San Sebastiano, formerly Porta Appia, beyond which the Appian Way leads to the Catacombs of St Callixtus and the Basilica of St Sebastian. You could take the right fork but, just before the Gate, cut through a park to visit St John's.

The Hypogeum of the Scipios

Both these roads are walled, fairly quiet, and pretty. Alongside them are vestiges of ancient tombs. This should puzzle you, if you have registered that under old Roman law all burials took place outside the walls. In this case the tombs got there first – the walls represent an extension of the city. One of these pagan cemeteries may be visited. The entrance is by the Park of the Scipios on the left, before you come to an arch over the road, with the gate just beyond it. That 'Arch of Drusus' carried a branch aqueduct to the Baths of Caracalla. Sometimes this little

18. St Sebastian's Gate on the Via Appia

cemetery is called a catacomb, and certainly its galleries are
similar. However, it is much smaller, and that makes the
difference. The pagans had small burial 'basements', for which
we use a word of Greek derivation – *hypogeum*; it just means
'underground'. The Christian catacomb is a development of this
system on an extensive plan. Generally speaking, catacombs are
nearly all Christian. Note that the family of the Scipios seem to
have buried their dead; perhaps they rejected cremation as a
new-fangled idea.

Columbarium of the Freedmen of Livia

The ticket you bought to the Hypogeum entitles you also to see
the Columbarium of the Freedmen of Livia. This is across the
park, and locked, so you must ask the custodian to accompany
you. Columbarium means a dovecote, because these mausolea
for cremated persons look like one; the alcoves take terracotta
urns containing the ashes of the dead. You will not be shown
all there is to see, but this columbarium for imperial employees
is interesting, and has attractive paintings.

San Giovanni in Oleo

Leave the park at this side and you will find yourself on the Via
Latina, close by a small round chapel known as San Giovanni

in Oleo – St John in Oil. It commemorates the unsuccessful attempt to martyr the aged evangelist by boiling him alive. This small circular building is by no means unusual; it was in early times a common shape for the shrines of martyrs. To find a pagan precedent, think of that little memorial to Romulus the son of Maxentius that you see in the Forum, and in which the Neapolitan Crib is now exhibited. True, this chapel as it now stands is renaissance, attributed by some to Bramante. It was built in 1500, and in 1698 Borromini modified it. The suggestion has been made that if it were properly examined and excavated it would prove to be on the site, at least, of a much earlier shrine to St John, or even over a pagan tomb. Although the legend of the boiling seems rather 'tall', it is a very ancient tradition in Rome. Should you really want to see inside, you must ask for the key at the Rosminian College over the road.

The Church of St John before the Latin Gate

Attached to the Rosminian House is the church of St John before the Latin Gate, now the Roman headquarters of the Institute of Charity, founded by Antonio Rosmini. Like so many other churches San Giovanni was once cluttered up with 'barockery'. It has been drastically purged and now wears an austerity appropriate to its certainly fifth-century origin. Some of the roof tiles have been found to carry makers' stamps dating from the end of the fifth century, which agrees with a tradition that the church was built by Pope Gelasius (492–496). It was restored about three centuries later and again in the twelfth century. The most remarkable discovery dates from that restoration. It is a series of paintings of great beauty – all previously hidden by plaster and a lower ceiling, and found at some risk by an enthusiastic young archaeologist. They represent the book of Genesis: humankind's creation and fall; and the New Testament: its redemption and renewal.

The Genesis story can be read between the windows, commencing on the right side of the church near the sanctuary, with the creation of the universe and of Adam and Eve. Over the entrance is the dispute between Cain and Abel. On the left wall are the stories of Noah, Isaac and Jacob. The Gospel story, from the Annunciation to the appearance of the risen Lord beside the Sea of Galilee, is painted in two tiers below the Old Testament series. The Crucifixion – right side near the door – takes up both tiers. May I repeat my advice to stand well over on the left to view paintings on the right, and *vice versa*?

In the sanctuary pavement, and also in the narthex, are interesting fragments of antique sculpture re-used.

19. Twelfth-century Creation of Man, St John before the Latin Gate

City Gates and Walls

I suggest you leave by the Porta Latina – and look back to appreciate this fine fifth-century gate, then skirt the walls to the right to rejoin the Via Appia at the Porta San Sebastiano – a gate in many respects still third century. The Aurelian Walls of Rome have fourteen gates and had 383 towers. In many places they have been repaired or reconstructed, and as you walk by them you will notice the coats of arms of popes who had the work carried out.

The first mile or two of the Via Appia are marred by ugly buildings and harassing traffic. Soon there is a junction; to the right leaves the Via Ardeatina (road to Ardea, ancient walled town near the coast). This is also the road to the Catacomb of Domitilla, the Ardeatine Caves, and the Shrine of Our Lady of Divino Amore. A gate at the very junction of the roads admits you to the Salesian property on which is the famous catacomb of Callixtus – and a number of other catacombs not open to the public. After proceeding some distance, turn round and enjoy one of the finest views of Rome's ancient walls and gates.

The Chapel of 'Domine Quo Vadis?'

On the left, just before the road junction, is the chapel of Domine Quo Vadis. One would have thought this name had become household since the film was made under that title, but

I find pilgrims and travellers who know nothing about it at all. The story goes that Peter, fleeing from Nero's persecution, encountered Our Lord here, approaching the city. Astonished, Peter cried, 'Lord, where are you going?' (*Domine, quo vadis?*). The Master, with the glance of reproach that once before had made Peter weep bitterly, answered: 'To Rome, to be crucified again.' Peter about-turned. Whether this tale be true or not, it does express Peter's personality as we meet it in the gospels. Don't be taken in by the marble impression of a foot, set among what appear to be original basalt paving stones of the Via Appia, just inside the chapel door. In the first place, this does not claim to be the original, which is preserved at St Sebastian's. Secondly, it is almost certainly a pagan offering after a safe journey – just like the Navicella. There is nothing against using a pagan object to adorn a Christian shrine – provided you are not deceived by it.

A few yards farther, at another turning, there is an abandoned chapel which represents a scruple of our Cardinal Pole, who in the sixteenth century thought the old Chapel of Domine Quo Vadis might have been sited at the wrong road junction.

The Appian Way

The Appian Way is almost undeservedly celebrated. So often is it crowded with traffic, its more attractive stretches are so far out (more than two miles beyond the walls), and the patches of original paving that appear in photographs are so pitifully slight that the traveller who hopes to see – and photograph – all at one glance is apt to be disappointed. I could explain how to follow the entire relic of the ancient road back to Rome from Frattochie (where it joins with the modern road), but I am sure few would follow my guidance and still less be grateful for it afterwards. The safest plan is to take a bus from the Colosseum, to the Tomb of Caecilia Metella. From there an hour's walk out, and back again, would show you the best and most characteristic stretch. There are some nice little trattorias too, where you could dine. If they prove expensive, these quiet surrounds are perhaps an occasion for a little extravagance.

The Circus of Maxentius

This Basilica of St Sebastian is described in Chapter 27; the catacombs beneath it in Chapter 29. Walking away from Rome you pass on the left the Circus of Maxentius, Constantine's rival. This gives you a good idea of how the Circo Massimo at Rome, of which hardly anything remains, appeared at its best, though it was much larger. The obelisk now over Bernini's fountain in the Piazza Navona came from here. Between the

Circus and the road is a vast open courtyard – imagine it colonnaded – around a farmhouse, and behind the house a large round structure that often has washing hanging out to dry on top; this is the base of a temple Maxentius raised to his 'divinized' son Romulus, in whose memory he also built the small round monument in the Forum, next to San' Cosma e Damiano.

The Tomb of Caecilia Metella

The road rises rapidly to the crest of the last flow of lava from the volcanic Alban Hills; on it is perched the swallow-tail battlemented tomb of Caecilia Metella, dating from Caesar's time. It was turned into a fortress by the Caetani family in the thirteenth century. Their courtyard straddles the road, with remains of their gothic castle chapel opposite the tomb. The Caetani added the battlements, and later others quarried away the marble from around the base of the great mausoleum – some of this is said to have gone to make the Trevi Fountain. High up on the tomb is a frieze of bulls' heads, which give it its popular name of Capo di Bove. It is possible to enter the mausoleum and also the adjacent courtyards, where you will find a good collection of sculpture from tombs on the Appian Way.

A little patient walking and the Way will begin to look 'just like the pictures' – the stone pines, fragmentary tombs, still eloquent sculptures, the very paving sometimes worn into ruts, away over the fields ruined villas, aqueducts, and on the horizon the Sabine and Alban Hills. Mussolini made this an 'archaeological zone', so that suburban development keeps its distance, but the wealthy manage to live here, some in villas lost among trees, a few in adapted tombs!

St Paul

This Appian Way dates from 312 B.C., and it is named after its author, Appius Claudius the Blind. It went all the way to the Bay of Naples, and was later extended to Brindisi. If you have a quiet moment while you walk along it, think of St Paul who came this way to Rome, trod where you tread, and saw much that you see now. His journey is recorded clearly in the twenty-eighth chapter of the Acts of the Apostles. We are surely in the steps of Peter too, though of this there is not the same documentary record.

CHAPTER 22

Churches within reach of the Via Cavour Underground Station

San Pietro in Vincoli – San Martino ai Monti – Santa Maria dei Monti – Sant' Agata dei Goti – San Lorenzo in Panisperna – Santa Pudentiana – San Francesco a Paola

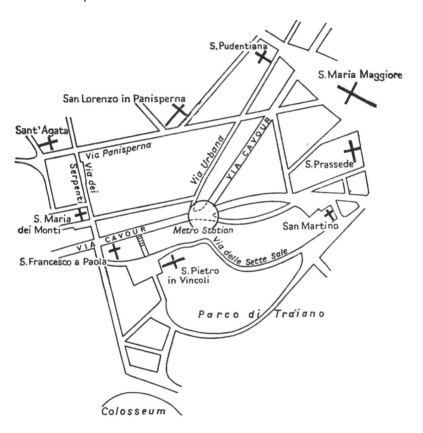

This is an unappealing, unromantic chapter title; I hope it doesn't put you off. I could have written 'The Slopes of the Quirinal and Esquiline Hills', but my object was to provide a useful landmark from which you will find your way, with help, through a real tangle of streets. The Via Cavour, a modern road running down the valley between the two hills from Stazione Termini to the Forum, is not what I should call a beaten tourist track, neither are the side streets, but I find them attractive and it is fun to get slightly lost now and then. Trattorias off the main road in this quarter are likely to provide a good buy.

Please be advised that one of the two entrances to the 'landmark' Metro Station is in a side street and you need to take the steps up to the main road before attempting to follow directions.

Turn down the Via Cavour towards the Forum, and soon on your left a steep flight of steps leads through a dark archway to San Pietro in Vincoli (St Peter in Chains).

San Pietro in Vincoli

Most people come here 'to see the Moses' – a famous sculpture by Michelangelo, but San Pietro would be worth your visit even without it. It was one of the early parish churches of Rome, called by the old name *'titulus Eudoxiae'*. The early parish churches were very often 'entitled' after the person who built them or in whose house they were set up. This Eudoxia was the wife of the Emperor Valentinian; she built a church here about 422 to receive a relic sent her from Jerusalem, the chain which had bound Peter there in prison (see the Acts of the Apostles, Chapters 5 and 12). According to tradition, the Romans already venerated the chain that had fettered Peter in the Mamertine prison under the Capitol, handed over by St Balbina, daughter of the gaoler. Legend completes the story by asserting that the two chains miraculously joined together.

The ancient church – you can see part of its floor – was virtually rebuilt at the end of the fifteenth century by Popes Sixtus IV and Julius II. It looks clean and beautiful and most dignified. Go down into the 'confession' before the altar to venerate the chains. The doors of the shrine are bronze renaissance work of 1477, by an artist known as Caradosso, representing the condemnation of Peter by Herod and his liberation by an angel. Their reproduction of ancient Roman interiors, perspective, and beautifully elegant figures are of a very high quality. If the chains are exposed, you may be unable to see the doors.

In the crypt behind is an ancient Roman sarcophagus said to contain the relics of the Holy Machabees, those seven young Jewish heroes who died rather than break the Law of Moses to please a tyrant.

To the right of the high altar is the Moses statute. It was made to be part of a monumental tomb which Julius II commissioned for himself and intended to be a major feature of the new St Peter's at the Vatican. The original ambitious designs were never fulfilled, and of the sculpture that figures in this composition only the Moses is entirely by Michelangelo. His figures of slaves intended for this tomb are in the Louvre at Paris. The Moses is powerful, that is its main virtue. The little goat-like horns are the result of a poor understanding of the text of Exodus – the 'horns' were meant to be a radiance or light that shone about his face when he came down from Mount Sinai. The flowing beard contains portraits of Michelangelo himself and Julius II, visible only in a favourable light. It is said that when it was set up here it caused a stir among the Jews of Rome, who came in great numbers to venerate it. This work was completed in 1545.

Through a door to the right of Moses is a little shop for souvenirs, and beyond that (ask before you go in) a sacristy with a superb painting by Domenichino of the Liberation of Peter. Its best detail is the soldier in black armour.

To the left of the nave there is a seventh-century byzantine mosaic of the martyr Sebastian. Late gothic and renaissance artists were fond of painting him as a nude young man at the moment of his attempted martyrdom by arrows. Here he is in byzantine costume and some critics describe him as old – I think he is just heavily bearded. The colours are beautiful.

If you ask at the Institute to the right of the church you may enter the fifteenth-century cloister. The Canons Regular of the Lateran, who serve San Pietro, are now limited to a small part of their original property.

San Martino ai Monti

The lane to the left of San Pietro in Vincoli leads to San Martino ai Monti, a church served by the Calced Carmelites. Here too is an ancient *'titulus'*, one of the early parish churches of Rome, named after its founder, *'Titulus Equitii'*, dating perhaps from the third century. That was before the conversion of the Empire and freedom for public worship. In those days the faithful worshipped in the house of a well-to-do Christian who reserved a room for this purpose. This is known as a 'house-church'. There were many such in Rome, but few can be identified with certainty; that is to say, the sites are known, often the house itself has been excavated below the floor of a later church, but it is almost impossible to identify the room actually used for the Christian assembly. Some authorities are confident this can be done at San Martino, and they identify as such the apartments you are shown leading off the crypt. Others maintain that these are a place of worship adapted in a Roman building at a later date.

The crypt itself is very beautiful, the work of a Roman architect of the seventeenth century, Pietro da Cortona. An inscription records the exceptional number of sainted popes and other saints re-buried here when barbarian raids on the Campagna necessitated their removal from the catacombs. The aisles of San Martino are famous for their landscape paintings by Gaspar Poussin, brother-in-law to the more famous Nicholas. I have read that these are the first landscapes to have been painted for a church – a kind of generalization I never believe in a hurry. All around this church, on the entablature above the columns, is a most unusual series of carvings symbolic of Old and New Testament history.

To return to our point of departure in the Via Cavour, a few steps farther on after the stairs to San Pietro in Vincoli a turning to the right leads in a matter of yards to Santa Maria de' Monti. This has very much the atmosphere of a parish church of a down-at-heel locality. which it is, but there are at least three treasures to make it visit-worthy.

Santa Maria de' Monti

First, over the high altar is a venerated medieval painting of Our Lady, patroness of this quarter of Rome. On 26th April, a copy is carried through the streets in a popular festa. Beneath a side altar is an effigy of one of the most unusual yet attractive of saints, Benedict Joseph Labre. This young Frenchman, after being turned away from Carthusian and Trappist monasteries, devoted his life to tramping the shrines of Europe, until he came to Rome in 1777. For six years he lived on the streets, often scavenging for food, sleeping in the vaults of the Colosseum, giving to others the occasional alms for which he never begged. This was his favourite church. He fell dying on the pavement just after he had come here for his evening prayers, and was carried into a nearby house – No. 2, Via dei Serpenti, where you may call to see the frightful rags he wore preserved as relics. Romans who, however shaky their religious practice, have an intuition for holiness, raised that cry for which, in my opinion, they are hungry today: '*Il santo e morto*' – the saint is dead.

His effigy is beautiful. In the Corsini Gallery there is a portrait of the saint by Cavalucci which suggests that this beauty is by no means just a pious attribute.

Thirdly, there is the interior of the dome. If you look up into it, given the right light, you will be taken aback at its splendour. This is the kind of surprise that awaits every patient explorer of Rome. Personally, I am confident that the more I see, the more I am missing unawares.

Sant' Agata dei Goti

You can reach Sant' Agata dei Goti by continuing along the Via dei Serpenti – by which you left the Via Cavour – as far as the Via Panisperna, then turning left. St Agatha's is at a right-hand corner. This church has a charm that I find quite fascinating, and if you do nothing here but rest and meditate you will take away the best it has to offer.

There are two entrances; one in the Via Mazzarino admits you to a lovely eighteenth-century courtyard festooned with creeper. From 1836 to 1926 the Irish College was here. The side entrance, in Via Panisperna, gives you a better idea of the antiquity of this church.

St Agatha's is called 'of the Goths' because, after the Gothic invasions from the north in the sixth century, Goths who remained in Rome retained it as a 'national church'. They were in fact heretics, Arians who held erroneous notions about Our Lord's divinity, so one might flippantly call this a very early instance of a dissenting chapel. The fabric of the nave and its beautiful columns of oriental granite date from this period.

The cosmatesque canopy over the high altar, and a section of cosmatesque pavement in the middle of the nave, are both of quite exceptional beauty. The pavement is a most unusual design for this type of work.

St Agatha's is noted for a devotion to a group of Greek martyrs whose relics were brought here from the catacombs, probably in the eighth century. They were a family of mother and father, two daughters and a son, all martyred in the third century. Some of their relics can be seen in a wall chest with gilded doors at the end of the right aisle. Their feast, on 2nd December, is usually celebrated with an evening liturgy in the Byzantine rite.

San Lorenzo in Panisperna

Far down the switchback Via Panisperna you can see St Mary Major's. Walking in that direction you will soon come level with the church of San Lorenzo in Panisperna. Climbing up to its tree-lined courtyard by a steep flight of steps seems to raise you in a moment above the noise and movement of the city – I have even heard birds singing here; you will soon appreciate how rare that is in Rome.

The church, in its present form, is a simple clear baroque building apparently designed to set off its wonderful frescoed wall behind the high altar – like a back-drop. It fails in its representation of St Lawrence, a feeble pietistic figure. All the rest: architecture, perspective, soldiers, horses, are impressive. It is said to be by a pupil of Michelangelo – the master would never have approved of that Lawrence.

Two saints buried here are Crispin and Crispinianus, brothers, traditionally early apostles of France, and patrons of cobblers. If you know your Shakespeare you may recall that Agincourt was fought on St Crispin's day (*Henry V*).

The church is now served by Franciscans, and there is a beautiful painting of St Francis in the first chapel on the left. Towards the end of her life St Bridget of Sweden – a queen – used to beg for the poor outside San Lorenzo, and was first buried here before her translation to Vadstena in Sweden. There is a modern statue to her in the courtyard, not particularly pleasing.

St Lawrence is not buried here, but at San Lorenzo fuori le Mura. This church is on the site of his martyrdom, and you may ask the sacristan to admit you to the chapel under the porch where an ancient oven is believed to be the one in which he was grilled alive.

If you now follow the Via Panisperna towards St Mary Major's, the Via Urbana on your left will take you to Santa Pudentiana, down in a hollow – the original ground level.

Santa Pudentiana

This is a church of *first* importance on two scores at least. One is that, according to venerable tradition, it is built over the house of Pudens the Senator, taken to be the same Roman Pudens mentioned in Paul's letter to Timothy, and believed to have been host at Rome to both Peter and Paul. Also, it contains the oldest apse mosaic in Rome, of about 390; one of great perfection and beauty.

If these traditions be exact, then soon after the executions of Peter and Paul we may suppose that a room in this house was adapted as a Christian place of assembly – a 'house church', and that subsequently, when peace came with the recognition of Christianity in the fourth century, a church, basically the present one, was adapted out of a part of Pudens' house – but as it had been rebuilt after the time of the apostles.

What you will notice immediately you enter is that recent restoration has stripped away much decoration which concealed the antiquity of Santa Pudentiana. Ancient columns have been revealed, and in the marble floor there are indications of the plan of the Roman buildings at a lower level.

The wonderful mosaic can be contemplated as I suppose its artists meant it to be, glowing in the half light, but as you will want to learn all you can about it you should put a coin in the little slot machine to the right of the sanctuary and it will light up for a few minutes. Sit down and take your time.

This apse is not fully rounded, and the lower part of the mosaic has been destroyed. A Christ of great dignity presides over his apostles seated around him in a beautiful courtyard. Although when this was made the emperors were already at Constantinople, this is a mosaic in Roman tradition, in fact it surpasses tradition with the grace and dignity of its figures. The open book Christ holds is inscribed '*Conservator Ecclesiae Pudentianae*' – Preserver of the Church of Pudentiana. The female figures behind the apostles may be SS. Pudentiana and Prassede, daughters of Pudens, but they may represent 'Church' and 'Synagogue' – that is, Gentile and Jewish elements in the Christian community. Note the background of buildings, maybe representing the churches built by Constantine over the holy places at Jerusalem. This would explain the great gemmed cross, because it was with such a monument that Constantine marked the site of Calvary. Note that only Christ wears a halo, evidence of the antiquity of this mosaic.

There is a passage behind the apse. On the left it leads to an altar with a statue by Jacopo della Porta of Christ delivering the keys of authority to St Peter. This altar contains part of a table alleged to have been in the house of Pudens and used by the Apostle for the Holy Sacrifice.

Opening to the left of the church is the Gaetani family chapel, rich with inlaid marble and a fine sculptured altarpiece of the Adoration of the Kings by Paolo Olivieri.

On the façade of the church are eighth-century sculptures representing the daughters of Pudens carrying vessels in which they gathered the blood of martyrs. St Prassede's church is at the far side of Santa Maria Maggiore.

Behind St Pudentiana's is a small chapel of Our Lady with medieval paintings. The sacristan will take you there through the church, or you may make your way round and look into it from the street.

There is an uncertain tradition that the captive British chieftain Caractacus and his family were lodged here, in the house of the Pudens family. They are said to have become Christians and to have undertaken missionary journeys to Britain.

San Francesco a Paola

If you have by now discovered an interest in baroque, I recommend you to return to the flight of steps from the Via Cavour to San Pietro in Vincoli, but instead of passing through the arch turn along the terrace overlooking the Via Cavour and its junction with the Via de' Serpenti. At the corner is the church of San Francesco a Paola, and the Generalate of the Order of Minims which he founded. It may be closed, but you should ask to be admitted at the door of the monastery. As a church it is like many of the seventeenth century, but its altarpiece captures the spirit of its time beyond all others. Our word 'tabernacle' for the shrine in which the Blessed Sacrament is reserved means a tent, and here a beautifully carved wooden tabernacle is set dramatically within the sculptured entrance of a great military pavilion, held back by angels. The inspiration is clearly that of the Old Testament mystery of God's presence among his people in the ark carried with them in their tent-temple; here is the 'tabernacle of the Lord of hosts'. This altar is attributed to Giovanni Antonio de Rossi.

There are interesting paintings, especially an icon of St Francis of Paola, copy of an alleged portrait, and in the sacristy a delightful series of the life and miracles of the saint by Agostino Masucci.

CHAPTER 23

In the Neighbourhood of Stazione Termini

*Santa Bibiana – The Tullian Wall – Baths of Diocletian –
The Museo Nazionale – Santa Maria degli Angeli – The
Naiads Fountain – The Moses Fountain – Santa Susanna
– Santa Maria della Vittoria – San Bernardo*

This chapter title may not sound attractive but it does make a
reliable point of reference.

Santa Bibiana

I should like to tell you how to visit the little church of Santa
Bibiana. The route is very simple, yet it is easy to be frustrated
and give up. Face the station, and then walk down its right side
– past the air terminal. The road seems to turn into a quaint little
'station' for trams – trams linked together like trains; you can
take one for a cross-country trip to Palestrina. Walk boldly
through this station, and a baroque church comes into view,
curiously offset by the modern style of the Stazione Termini
buildings which have literally made way for it. Santa Bibiana
was once in the fields, and it still has the air of a village church.
It is a rebuilding of the seventeenth century – none less than
Bernini designed the façade – but the 'mixed' antique columns
survive from the church consecrated in 467, and they are mixed
of course because they were taken at random from ruined
temples. The statue of the virgin martyr Bibiana behind the altar
is also Bernini's, but it hardly counts as one of his best works.
There are paintings of her life and martyrdom above the arcade.
As you kneel in this oddly remote little church you hear the
trams rattle by on one side and the trains on the other.

The Tullian Wall

Apart from Santa Bibiana all the interest lies straight ahead from
Stazione Termini. Even inside the station – down the steps to
the Metropolitana (Underground) for instance – you see fragments of Rome's first city wall, the so-called Tullian Wall, built
by King Servius Tullius in the fourth century B.C. There is more
of this on the right as you leave the station.

233

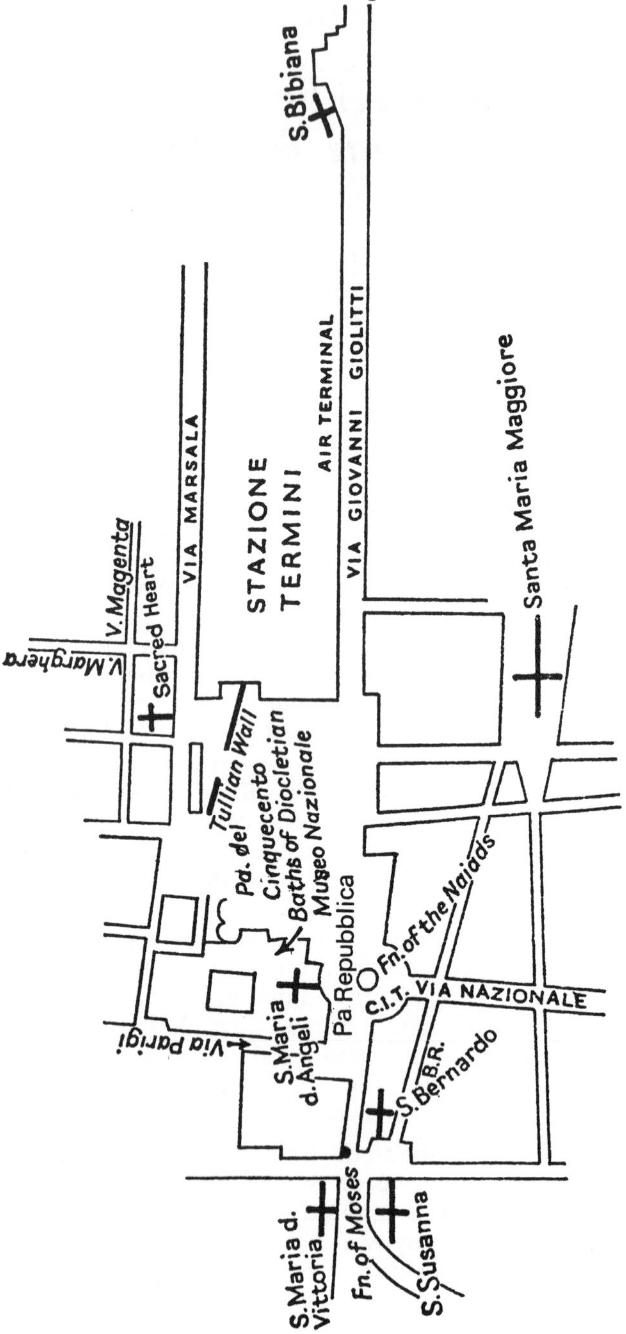
S.Bibiana
VIA MARSALA
STAZIONE TERMINI
AIR TERMINAL
VIA GIOVANNI GIOLITTI
Santa Maria Maggiore
V. Magenta
Sacred Heart
V. Marghera
Tullian Wall
Pd. del Cinquecento
Baths of Diocletian
Museo Nazionale
Pa Repubblica
Fn. of the Naiads
C.I.T.
VIA NAZIONALE
Via Parigi
S.Maria d. Angeli
B.R.
S.Bernardo
S.Maria d. Vittoria
Fn. of Moses
S.Susanna

The Baths of Diocletian

The newcomer to Rome can greet a ruin right away – the battered arches and vaults of the vast Baths of Diocletian straight across the Piazza del Cinquecento in front of the station. Few people have a realistic idea what a Roman bathing establishment really was, nor how vast one could be. These, for instance, covered an area of 32 acres. Firstly, there were of course baths – baths of hot, cold, or tepid water, swimming pools and honest-to-goodness bath tubs. Then the huge building was surrounded by shopping arcades, in its courts there were gardens, gymnasia and sports grounds, and in its halls rest rooms, libraries, art galleries, and shaded walks for recreation. You could almost live there.

The Baths of Diocletian were begun in 298 and completed in 306, the forced labour, according to tradition, of 10,204 Christian slaves who were subsequently executed and buried at Trefontane. What remains of this vast establishment is comprised in the Basilica of Santa Maria degli Angeli, the Museo Nazionale Romano, the Church of San Bernardo, and one or two other minor buildings. The rest disappeared; Pope Sixtus V is credited with having blown up 95,000 cubic metres of wall.

The Museo Nazionale

The entrance to the Museo Nazionale is very dull and offputting. I confess that I am personally allergic to museums – I like to find antiquities in the place they were made for – but I urge you not to miss this museum. Among other reasons, you pass through halls of Diocletian's Baths, through cloisters and gardens that are oases of peace at the hub of modern Rome, and the collection itself is of the highest distinction.

If you go straight forward from the ticket office you will come to an important collection of Christian sarcophagi (stone coffins), mostly of the fourth century. Usually, several subjects are woven into one composition of sculpture. I mention subjects that occur, so that you may attempt identification:

> Peter drawing water from a rock to baptize the house of Cornelius – alludes to Moses in the desert and symbolizes the admission of Gentiles to baptism; usually at the end of a sarcophagus.

> The raising of Lazarus – usually at one end of a sarcophagus.

> Miracle of the wine at Cana.

> The multiplication of loaves.

20. Roman faces (noseless) on a sarcophagus in the Baths of Diocletian (Museo Nazionale)

21. Family outing on a Roman sarcophagus in the baths of Diocletian (Museo Nazionale)

The woman with an issue of blood kneeling at Christ's feet. Arrest of St Peter.

Jesus cures the man born blind.

To continue, you return towards the ticket office and bear left. Notice, level with a great floor mosaic, a remarkable sarcophagus showing a cavalry encounter between Romans and barbarians. It deserves close study. The horses especially are finely sculptured.

After an open section a door leads to a bar on the left and to the right is an interesting exhibition of Roman terracotta, and the mummified body of an eight-year-old girl of the second century A.D. Please do not, at this point, decide you don't feel like refreshments and make your way back. The best part of the museum lies on the far side of the bar! You will find to the right a garden full of sculpture, and be surprised to learn that this was a hall equipped with public toilets. On the far side is preserved in position a large mosaic of Diocletian's Baths. If instead you turn left, a corridor – in which you should note on the walls two delightfully simple mosaics of leaves – leads to the Great Cloister of the Charterhouse. There are a hundred arches around its four sides. The size is surprising, but in a Charterhouse each monk had a complete little house with garden, chapel, and cloister of his own. This cloister is often attributed to Michelangelo, who certainly adapted the monks' church out of two bath halls. It was completed a year after his death, at the age of ninety, in 1564. In the centre of the garden is a fountain and a pool with the largest goldfish I have ever seen. Around it, nestling in the shrubbery, are huge antique heads of camel, horse, elephant, goat, and two oxen.

On your way back towards the bar the second door on the left of the corridor admits you to Room I of a series of halls of sculpture of the very highest quality. In Hall II there is a beautiful mosaic of marine monsters. Perhaps you will not realize it is under water until the attendant ruffles the surface.

There is a beautiful Discus Thrower, sold to Hitler in 1938, but retrieved after the war. A pagan altar from Ostia is one of the finest of its kind, sculptured with the legend of Romulus and Remus. This dates from A.D. 124. In the adjacent room is the handsome Sarcophagus of the Philosophers, a partial reconstruction from thirty-five fragments. Opposite this is another sarcophagus with pleasant pastoral scenes. Here again you will find Caesar Augustus, emperor at the time of Christ's birth, his expression as refined and gracious as ever.

At times different sections of this museum may be closed.

Santa Maria degli Angeli

The Basilica of St Mary of the Angels is an adaptation by Michelangelo of two bath halls; the cool bath – just inside the door; the cold bath – the transepts. The choir is largely an addition. Michelangelo made the transepts the main body of the church; its axis was swung round in 1749, and I think this spoiled the effect.

You may notice that you enter through a fragment of building, an apse of the hot bath. I am afraid the atmosphere of this church is, in my opinion, one of cold uninspiring space. It is said that Michelangelo, fearing damp, raised the floor level several feet, which ruined the former proportions. The transept altars with simulated architecture painted around them strike one as a poor sham, the vast paintings seem to lack colour, and the marble pavement looks drab.

Before you enter the main body of the church (that is, while you are still 'in the cool bath') notice a famous statue by Houdon, of 1766. It represents St Bruno, for this was a Carthusian church. It is now served by the Order of Minims. In the right transept is a remarkable novelty to find in a church – Rome's meridian line, latitude 15°, indicated in inlaid marble. At true noon the sun casts a shaft of light dead on this line – that is about 12.15 except when Italy is keeping artificial summer time, and then at 1.15 – and to facilitate this a part of the cornice on the right side of the end wall of this transept has been cut away. This dates from 1703.

Of the sixteen great columns, eight are those of the original baths hall, and eight imitations in stucco.

Some of the paintings here are original canvases from St Peter's, where they have been replaced by copies in mosaic. There is a venerated Madonna above the high altar.

The Naiads Fountain

Something had better be said about the Naiads Fountain at the top of the Via Nazionale and immediately opposite Santa Maria degli Angeli. Usually one accepts it as a lovely and refreshing sight, but on cleaning days the sculpture has very little to say for itself. Fr. Chandlery, in his *Pilgrim Walks in Rome* (1903), describes it as 'repulsive and scandalous in the extreme'. He wrote of the nymphs, which had just been added in 1901, for the rest of the fountain was set up by Pius IX, to celebrate the arrival in Rome of his new water supply, the Acqua Pia Marcia. The nymph with the sea horse represents Oceans, a swan is the sign of the Nymph of Lakes; a water snake is the symbol of Rivers, and a reptile that of Subterranean Waters. For the nymphs, a young lady from Anticoli Corrado in the Sabines was model, and for the sea god in the centre a young man from the same hill town.

The Charterhouse

Walking straight ahead, that is, leaving Santa Maria degli Angeli on your right, the turning on the right hand, Via Parigi, offers you a view of the Carthusian hermitages from the days when Santa Maria degli Angeli was a Charterhouse in the fields. They are now used as offices and store-rooms of the National

Museum, but I doubt that there is any other large city where you can have a bird's-eye view of a Carthusian hermit's cell.

Through an arcade on the left (instead of turning up the Via Parigi) is the British Railways Office in Rome. Back in the arcade of the Piazza della Repubblica was the main office of C.I.T., Italy's principal travel agents.

The Moses Fountain

Promptly you arrive at a piazza with three churches and a fountain. Even before you start looking at the fountain (through a maze of overhead tram cables) I warn you that to admire its statue of Moses is 'not done'. The sculptor, Prospero Antichi of Brescia, is supposed to have died of shame when it was raised into position and he became the laughing stock of Rome. It is said that Pope Sixtus V, who commissioned it for this terminal fountain of his new water supply, the Acqua Felice, forbade him to try to correct it. The mistake was due to his having attempted the sculpture without previously making a model and also without raising his block of travertine from the ground into a vertical position.

Moses is shown in the act of striking the rock that gave refreshing water to thirsty Israelites in the desert, and there are four appropriate Old Testament subjects by other sculptors, also four pleasant spouting lions added in the nineteenth century. Behind the fountain, not accessible to the public, is the original terminal station still fitted with its sixteenth-century equipment.

Of the two churches across the piazza, that on the left is St Susanna's, Rome's American church. It was rebuilt in 1595 as part of Pope Sixtus V's development of this quarter, and his sister Camilla contributed the chapel of St Lawrence.

Santa Susanna

Its interior – by Carlo Maderno – is a contrast to Santa Maria della Vittoria across the road. Here is a church more like a painted renaissance hall, full of light. The paintings include architectural motifs inspired by the twisted columns of Bernini's baldachino. The subjects allude to Susanna, virgin martyr, of whose home third-century remains in the crypt may be part, and to Susanna of the Old Testament. The Roman Susanna is believed to have been a niece of third-century Pope Caius. Her hand was demanded in marriage by Diocletian's adopted son Maximianus Galerus. She was martyred with her brother Gabinus. The Jewess Susanna was the victim of false charges of impurity by two evil old men, who were watching her when she went to bathe in her orchard. She was saved by the astuteness

of Daniel, who asked her accusers under which tree they had
seen her sin – one replied 'under a mastick' (whatever that may
be), the other 'under a holm'. Bearing these stories in mind you
will be able to interpret the paintings that cover the walls of this
church. Those of Susanna and the Elders in the nave are by
Baldassare Croce, those of the Christian Susanna in the apse by
Laureti and Cesare Nebbia. Note the beautiful coffered ceiling,
attributed to Baldassare Croce.

In the chapel to the left – that of St Lawrence – is the shrine
of an interesting Roman martyr, Genesius the Comedian,
patron of actors and, I suppose, of comedians too. Genesius was
a star of the fourth-century Roman stage who, to please the
persecuting emperor Diocletian, enacted a parody of the
Christian mysteries, in the course of which he was baptized.
During this sacrilege Genesius was in fact converted, and
accepted his baptism as true – theologians would not agree with
this, on the grounds that the person baptizing did not really
intend to do so. Summoned before Diocletian, Genesius told
him he had seen angels plunging into the baptismal water a
book in which his sins were written, and withdrawing it 'whiter
than snow'.

A small community of Cistercian nuns still occupies part of
the convent. Their choir is behind the altar. In the crypt you can
see the tombs of the community.

Also enshrined in this church, under the altar, is the martyred
Roman mother Felicity, with one of her seven martyr sons.
Their relics were brought here from the catacombs.

Mere half-sister to Santa Susanna is Santa Maria della Vittoria,
Our Lady of Victory, for you have only to step inside to realize
how much they differ. This is a church rich in baroque character,
sculpture, stucco, dark canvases, and a sort of gilded gloom.

Santa Maria della Vittoria

When the Discalced Carmelite Friars began building a church
here in 1608, it was at first named St Paul's. Then, at the Battle
of the White Mountain at Prague, imperial forces seemed to save
Bohemia for the Church. The Carmelite chaplain to the
victorious forces had worn round his neck a little picture of the
Nativity, which was carried in triumph to Prague and later
brought to Rome. A procession carried it from St Mary Major's
to the unfinished church of St Paul, which from that moment
carried its present title. In 1833 a fire destroyed the original
painting, and it was replaced by a copy which is enshrined
above the high altar.

You will be so busy waiting for crossing lights to turn green as you negotiate the busy piazza that only with difficulty are you likely to appreciate the external architecture of its churches. The architect of Santa Maria della Vittoria was Carlo Maderno, but the façade is by Giovanni Battista Soria. The interior is almost encrusted with ornament, culminating in the elaborate 'gloria' above the altar in which its little Madonna is set like a jewel. A glow of golden light from the cupola fills the church. Look up at the flurry of angels supporting cornice and vault, and then back towards the door to find two more holding aloft the beautiful choir gallery designed by Mattia de' Rossi, a collaborator of Bernini. The painting in the vault of the nave represents Mary among heavenly choirs and the fall of evil angels. The artist was Giovanni Domenico Cerrini, about 1675. His angels in the cupola are even more striking. The Entrance of the Image of the Madonna into Prague, in the apse above the high altar, was a contribution of the nineteenth-century restoration.

Many visitors come here just to see Bernini's dramatic sculpture of the Ectasy of St Teresa of Avila, Spanish sixteenth-century foundress of the Barefooted Carmelites (to which most Carmelite convents in Britain belong), a great mystic, and a thoroughly womanly writer – for evidence of this read her *Book of the Foundations*. This is one of the most celebrated baroque sculptures of Rome and perhaps Bernini's best-known work. Personally I am not willing to agree that it represents him at his best in the religious field. The angel, about to transfix the heart of the saint with a dart of divine love, represents a mystical experience reported in the saint's own writings. You may care to compare with this Bernini's treatment of a similar theme in the tomb of Blessed Ludovica Albertoni in the church of San Francesco a Ripa. The chapel belongs to the Cornaro family. The theatrical spirit in Bernini's sculpture appears in the way he has shown them conversing in 'boxes' either side of this chapel.

In a corresponding chapel across the nave is a sculpture which rather ambitiously pretends to balance Bernini's, an angel revealing Mary's virginal conception to St Joseph, by Domenico Guidi, a pupil of Alessandro Algardi. Far more successful are the panels representing adoration by the shepherds and the flight of the Holy Family into Egypt, by the French sculptor Monnot (1658–1733).

There are several very fine paintings in the church among which I particularly recommend a 'Trinity' by Guercino in the chapel just before St Teresa's.

Glance down the Via Venti Settembre as you leave the church

– the City Gate at the far end is the Porta Pia, named after Pius IV, under whom it was built in the mid-sixteenth century, to designs by Michelangelo. Pius was a Medici pope and his famous Florentine family were originally, as their name implies, surgeons, and surgeons in those days were barbers – there is supposed to be an allusion to this in the sculpture of the Porta Pia. The Gate is famous in modern history for the victorious entrance of Italian troops here in 1870.

San Bernardo

You should now cross the road twice, once back to Santa Susanna's, then forward towards the round church of San Bernardo. A pope's sister built part of Santa Susanna's, and a niece of Pope Julius III gave the Feuillants, a sixteenth-century Cistercian reform originating in France, this rotunda of Diocletian's baths – there was one at each corner of the vast structure – to adapt into an abbey church. Inside it may remind you slightly of the Pantheon. Its great dome is coffered with octagons. Around the walls are eight great statues of saints and two side altars of fine marble are dedicated to the Cistercian founders, St Bernard and St Robert of Molesmes. In my estimation the finest feature of this church is the painting of the founder of the Feuillant reform, the Venerable Jean de la Barrière, who died in Rome in 1600, by Andrea Sacchi. It is on the right side, by the entrance to the chapel of St Francis, an addition to the ancient rotunda.

CHAPTER 24

The Piazza Barberini and thereabouts

The Triton Fountain – The Bee Fountain – St Nicholas of Tolentino – Capuchin Church of the Immaculate Conception – The Palazzo Barberini Gallery – Quattro Fontane – Church of San Carlo – Palazzo del Drago – Sant' Andrea delle Fratte

The Piazza Barberini is the hub of modern tourist Rome – among its spokes the famous Via Veneto, where you find travel agents, the United States Embassy, night life, and the famous Capuchin charnel house. Architecturally, the piazza hardly exists – it is just a road junction swirling with traffic – a Piccadilly Circus lacking the power to evoke nostalgia.

There are two fountains in the piazza, the Triton, playing Sixtus V's Acqua Felice, and the Bee, spouting Pius IX's Acqua Pia Marcia for the thirsty. Romans are not ashamed to be seen drinking from public fountains in hot weather. Both fountains are by Bernini, architect to the Barberini Pope Urban VIII.

The Triton Fountain

The Triton, discoloured by three centuries of water from the Alban Hills, squats with his head thrown back, spouting his fountain into the air. Four dolphins support his scallop-shell throne. This fountain was made between 1642 and 1643. You will need to thread the traffic to study it closely. The figure of the Triton, by the way, is said to be copied from a smaller original in the older Eagle Fountain in the Vatican Gardens.

The Bee Fountain

The Bee Fountain at the foot of the Via Veneto is a direct compliment to Urban VIII's family name. You may have wondered why bees appear so frequently in the art of renaissance Rome – on the baldachino of St Peter's high altar, for instance. Bees were the heraldic emblem of the Barberini family – a very appropriate family emblem too, when you consider their industry and well organized domestic life. This Bee Fountain – the bees are at the base of a great shell – was Bernini's last work for Urban; the inscription gives you the date, 1644, last of a pontificate of twenty years.

St Nicholas of Tolentino

From close by the Bee Fountain Via Nicola da Tolentino leads uphill to the piazza and church of that name. Ornately designed by Giovanni Battista Baratta in the seventeenth century, since 1883 it has belonged to the Catholic Armenians. There is a college for students of the Armenian rite annexed.

The Armenian Church is one of those Eastern Churches of which the greater part has for many centuries been separated from the Holy See. Here at San Nicolo the 'Armenians' are of course those who have remained in Catholic Unity, and the priests ordained from the college may serve outside Armenia itself, most of them in the United States. The liturgy is celebrated in the Armenian language, following rites which originated in Antioch but have been influenced by both Byzantium (Constantinople) and Rome.

At first glance San Nicolo may show little signs of its use for an Eastern liturgy. Notice, however, the curtain waiting to be drawn across the sanctuary. This serves a purpose similar to that of the iconostasis in the Byzantine liturgy. The second chapel to the right is dedicated to St Gregory the Illuminator, fourth-century Apostle of the Armenians, and the altar in the left transept is dedicated to an Armenian martyr at Constantinople in 1707, the Blessed Der Gomidas. Suspended from the vault, a cardinal's hat will guide you to the nearby tomb of Antony Peter Hassan, Patriarch of Cilicia of the Armenians, who died in 1884.

The sculpture over the high altar is the work of Alessandro Algardi (1682–1769). The second chapel on the left, by Pietro da Cortona, has sculpture representing the apparition of the Madonna of Savona to Blessed Anthony Botta, and in the third chapel is a shrine of Our Lady of Good Counsel (see Chapter 20).

Among the paintings, one in the right transept of St John the Baptist, by Giovanni Battista Gaulli, is worth noting.

Cracks in the dome, right transept, and nave, are results of an early twentieth-century Roman earth tremor.

Capuchin Church of the Immaculate Conception

A few steps along the Via Veneto, on the right side, the simple façade of the Capuchin Franciscan church of the Immaculate Conception is approached by a double flight of steps. Part way up the right-hand flight is the entrance to the ossuary, one of Rome's best-known tourist attractions. The Capuchin friars – a sixteenth-century reform of the great Franciscan family – have ossuaries in many of their older friaries. Skeletons of the brethren are collected from the burial vaults after an appropriate delay and transferred to a bone cellar or 'ossuary'. The speciality here is their elaborate and rather ghoulish arrangement in patterns. I don't in the least mind admitting that I have never entered this pious exhibition; in fact I have deliberately avoided doing so – but there it is for those who enjoy such things.

The body of St Felix of Cantalice, a lay-brother who begged alms in Rome for forty years, and first canonized saint of the Capuchin reform, rests under a side altar in the second chapel on the left, and in the third on the right is enshrined Blessed Crispin of Viterbo. Their cells have been reconstructed in the sacristy entered from the end of the right aisle. Of many interesting paintings in this church you should make a point of seeing Hondhurst's 'Christ mocked by Jews' in the first chapel on the right.

Approached from the other side of the Via Veneto is Sant'
Isidoro, the Irish Franciscan church.

The Palazzo Barberini – National Art Collection

Back to the piazza. Across the far end runs a narrow street that
links the Spanish Steps with St Mary Major's, entering as Via
Sistina, leaving as Via Quattro Fontane. A short distance up the
latter is the Palazzo Barberini – another monument to Urban
VIII's passion for grandeur, although one must admit that he
was an industrious pope and even had scruples about expendi-
ture; among much else to his credit he founded the College of
Propaganda for missionary countries and also the Irish College
in Rome. His building was often at the cost of treasured ruins
of antiquity, and gave rise to the well-known quip: '*Quod non
fecerunt barbari, fecerunt Barberini*' – what the barbarians didn't do
the Barberini did! Today his palace houses the earlier section of
Rome's National Art Collection. Other paintings of the seventeenth and eighteenth centuries are exhibited at the Corsini
Palace in Trastevere.

Architects of the Palazzo Barberini were Carlo Maderno and
Bernini; it was further adorned by Borromini and Pietro da
Cortona – the last as both architect and artist. Others contri-
buted to its internal decoration.

In the first rooms through which you pass, remember to ask
an attendant to show you the chapel. Note, too, some delightful
small paintings, among them Giulio Romano's delicate
Madonna and Child. There are two by El Greco not to be
overlooked, an Adoration by Shepherds, and a Baptism of
Christ, in long frames to fit his elongated figures in silvery
tones. Scarsellino's paintings of events surrounding Christ's
Passion are little known, though very fine. Among portraits,
there is a Henry VIII by the younger Holbein, and Quentin
Matsy's beautiful portrait of Erasmus. By way of novelty, you
may enjoy Passarotti's Butcher's Shop and Fish Market. The
Great Salon has a ceiling frescoed by Pietro da Cortona. There
is an interesting portrait bust of St Philip Neri by Alessandro
Algardi.

Quattro Fontane

Continue up the hill and in a few steps you reach the famous
crossroads with fountains at each angle and the delightful little
church of San Carlo; this is known as Quattro Fontane – which
just means four fountains. Each follows the pagan convention
for a river divinity, a reclining figure emptying water from an
amphora – though in one case here it drips from a lion's mouth.

The water is Acqua Felice, named after Pope Sixtus V, whose Christian name was Felix, and his fountains date from 1588. Sixtus took up residence on the Quirinal – the Palace is away down on your right – and was responsible for the residential development of Rome in this direction. He used to love walking these streets to see how his town planning was getting on. The figures have identities; the males are the Tiber and its tributary the Anio, the females Strength, symbolized by a lion, and Loyalty, symbolized by a dog.

Church of San Carlo

You should stand back a little towards the Palazzo Barberini to obtain a good view of Borromini's charming little church of San Carlo alle Quattro Fontane. It was built in 1638, and is said to be to the plan and proportions of one of the great piers supporting the dome of St Peter's, and adjacent is a little cloister that also expresses Borromini's fondness for unusual shapes. It is the church of a Spanish Trinitarian monastery. This Order was founded by St John of Matha and St Felix of Valois for the rescue of Christians taken into slavery – there are always allusions to this mission in the art of Trinitarian churches. A chapel to the left of the sanctuary has a delightful ceiling and also – rather macabre – the mummified body of a Roman soldier martyr under the altar. The teeth seem to be in very good order. The church is dedicated to St Charles Borromeo.

San Carlo is rarely open, but you may ring the bell at the monastery door and ask the sacristan to admit you through the cloister. If he shows you the sacristy ask him to point out the tiny porcelain holy water stoup, a pretty cherub's head, said to be by Borromini.

Palazzo del Drago

At this point you could stroll along, past San Carlo, to take up Chapter 14 – the Quirinal. Opposite the side of San Carlo is the Palazzo del Drago, with the British Council Reading Room and Library upstairs – it might merit a visit just to acquaint you with the inside of a smaller Roman renaissance palace. Along here you will find moderately priced restaurants, some with English menus.

Sant' Andrea delle Fratte

One 'spoke' from the hub of the Piazza Barberini has remained unexplored. If you take the Via del Tritone and turn right along the Via Due Macelli you will soon notice on your left – but look up to observe it – Borromini's rather jolly jumbled brick cupola and belfry of Sant' Andrea delle Fratte – St Andrew of the Gardens. In the fifteenth century this was the Scots National Church in Rome – after the Reformation it eventually passed to the Order of Minims who still serve it.

Architecturally it is not distinguished, but it is certainly noted for its Madonna, no venerated statue of artistic beauty or naïve charm, but a chapel where a Jewish visitor from Alsace, Alphonse Ratisbonne, on the 20th January 1842, suddenly and unexpectedly received the favour of an apparition of Our Lady which effected his immediate conversion. He founded the Congregation of Our Lady of Sion to work for the restoration of God's Chosen People of the Old Testament to his Church of the New. The Sisters of Sion are well known in Jerusalem, where Monsieur Ratisbonne acquired the site of the Antonia fortress in which Pilate may have tried Christ.

In Monsieur Ratisbonne's own account, he explains that he was walking casually in the church of St Andrew while preparations were being made for a funeral. Suddenly all the light of the church seemed to concentrate into one chapel – that of St Michael as it then was – and in an intense radiance above the altar he saw Mary, who gestured gently to him to kneel. 'She did not speak', he wrote, 'but I understood everything.' The chapel of the apparition is to the left of the nave.

In the adjacent Accaromboni family chapel is some excellent carving of fruit in white marble against black, and also small modern monuments to sailors fallen in the last two wars. Paintings in the apse behind the high altar represent the martyrdom of St Andrew, and Christ multiplying loaves. Angels before the sanctuary carrying instruments of the Passion belong to that group by the school of Bernini that flank the parapets of Ponte Sant' Angelo.

If you follow the Via del Tritone, instead of turning off to visit Sant' Andrea, you will find on the right a shop stocking 'Ministry of Public Instruction' guide-books to monuments in the care of the State, all with English editions.

CHAPTER 25

Trastevere – 'Across the Tiber'

*San Crisogono – Sant' Agata – San Francesco a Ripa –
Santa Maria del Orto – Santa Caecilia – San Giovanni dei
Genovesi – San Benedetto a Piscinula – Ponte Sisto
Fountain – Santa Dorotea – Santa Maria della Scala – The
Corsini Gallery – Santa Maria in Trastevere – San
Cosimato – Villa Sciarra Park*

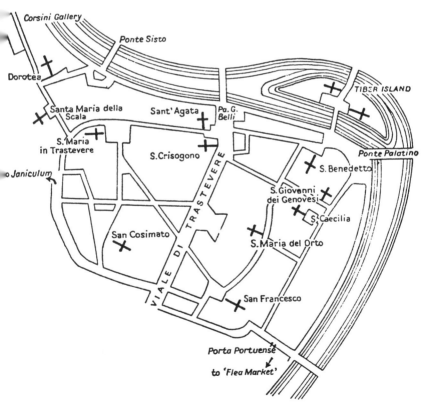

If you have never met 'Trastevere' before, it's just another word. If you know Rome it is a quarter all on its own, a town within the city. It means 'over the Tiber', and in ancient times it was the only part of Rome developed and walled to the west of the river (right bank). Hemmed in by hills – the Janiculum and Monteverde – old Trastevere is quite a narrow quarter. Although its streets and lanes may twist and confuse you, you can't go far wrong. The nineteenth-century Viale di Trastevere, which leads from the Ponte Garibaldi, cuts the quarter in two, and in fact enables the type of traveller who just can't get off a main road to pass through Trastevere seeing nothing of it.

If you have already noted the Tiber Island, the bridges thereabouts all lead into Trastevere. Augustus Hare, writing his delightful guide-book *Walks in Rome* less than a lifetime ago, describes the Trasteverini as hasty, passionate, and murderous (though he contrives to make this sound attractive), speaking their own dialect. If you wander in the back alleys long enough you may begin to feel the difference, but the only obvious expression I have noted is greater liberality in flinging garbage about.

San Crisogono

At the heart of the sector to the left of the Viale di Trastevere is the Basilica of Saint Cecilia, and at the heart of the sector to the right is Sant Maria in Trastevere. The first church you will notice on crossing the Ponte Garibaldi, near the upstream end of the Tiber Island, is San Crisogono (St Chrysogonus, whose name is in the Roman Canon of the Mass). It has a twelfth-century tower and a seventeenth-century façade, neither important. To describe the interior I will suppose you walk up the centre aisle of the nave to the altar, turn left to look into the sanctuary by its side entrance, then call in the sacristy to buy souvenirs and perhaps visit the excavations, and return up the left aisle venerating on your way the shrine of Saint Anna Maria Taigi. Notice the twenty-two ancient granite columns; two more supporting the chancel arch are porphyry. The floor is cosmatesque, but mostly hidden by benches. As you approach the sanctuary, however, you will notice some beautiful panels of mosaic inserted when Cardinal Scipio Borghese restored this church in the sixteen-twenties. The coffered ceiling, handsomely proportioned and coloured in gold and blue, has a fine central painting of the Glory of Saint Chrysogonus by 'il Guercino' – Gian Francesco Barbieri. There is some doubt as to whether this is a copy, and the original has been taken to London, or *vice versa*. The high altar itself dates from 1127; its baldachino is by Bernini, 1627. If you pass to the left of the sanctuary you can look into the choir and admire the beautiful nineteenth-century woodwork of its stalls and screens.

From the sacristy it is possible to descend a twisting iron staircase to excavations of the primitive Roman house – first and third centuries – and the early basilica, probably fourth century, that succeeded it. It lies to the left of the church above. That you will note easily, for the rest the place is not really maintained for visitors and is difficult to understand. You will be able to follow the wall of the great apse; the masonry in the middle is that of the confession or shrine of the martyr. There are a number of eighth-century paintings. In one corner is what appears to be a large font, but this identification is not certain.

As you leave the sacristy note a charming fragment of cosmatesque work in the wall.

The first chapel in this left aisle is the shrine of Saint Anna Maria Taigi, wife and mother of Trastevere who died in 1837. Her body under the altar is in the habit of a tertiary of the Trinitarians. In the adjacent monastery there is a room filled with her relics, a remarkable collection of 'old lady's things'.

Church of St Agatha

Across the Piazza Sonnino from San Crisogono is a church of St Agatha, of no special interest except for its 'Madonna del Carmine' – of Mount Carmel – carried through the streets annually in a popular festa on and about 16th July.

'Casa di Dante'

The medieval house which will have caught your eye when you crossed into Trastevere was a residence of the Anguillara family. It is known misleadingly as the Casa di Dante (house of Dante), not because the poet lived there but because it now houses a library of his works.

The sector of Trastevere left of the Viale should be visited for St Cecilia's, a place to note for the beauty of both church and atrium (courtyard). Then, to suit your interest and leisure, there is San Francesco a Ripa, St Francis at the Riverside, with a room where St Francis lodged, Santa Maria del Orto where sacred concerts are held, the fine cloister of San Giovanni dei Genovesi, and the tiny church of San Benedetto a Piscinula. The neighbourhood is interesting and you will find reasonably priced trattorias, not to mention one of Rome's most famous restaurants, opposite St Cecilia's, 'Da Meo Pataca'. At the end of this quarter, beyond Ponte Sublicio and the Porta Portuense (the

Gate of the road to Porto) are the streets where the Sunday Flea
Market is held.

I used to lose my way looking for St Cecilia's. Here I propose
a walk beginning with St Francis's, so if you want to go to St
Cecilia's straightway you must look for the yellow sign more or
less opposite San Crisogono and probably ask as well. Otherwise follow the Viale di Trastevere a few hundred yards till you
see San Francesco at the end of the Via di San Francesco a Ripa,
on your left. These streets are the scene of a popular festa
around St Francis's day, 4th October.

San Francesco a Ripa

The church itself need not detain you long; interest here lies in
devotion rather than in art. First impression is of a baroque
interior festooned with chandeliers. In the early thirteenth
century the Benedictine monks of SS. Cosmas and Damian in
Trastevere had a chapel of St Blaise here with a hospice for
travellers. They put up St Francis when he came to Rome, and
after his death the Pope instructed the abbot to hand over the
property to the Franciscans. At present the State has appropri-
ated most of the friary and there is only a small community here
to serve the church.

To find the cell of St Francis, pass through the church to the
sacristy (left corner) and there ask – it is known as the 'Stanza
di San Francesco'. If there is no one there, ask any friar in the
church. Sometimes, I must admit, no one can find the key. With
luck, you are taken upstairs to the small room carefully
preserved on every occasion of rebuilding. The baroque altarpiece of 1698 is a fantastic piece of mechanism by Franciscan
brothers. Its parts revolve to reveal, I am told, over a thousand
relics. Its most important feature is a portrait of St Francis
attributed to Margheritone d'Arezzo, and said to have been
painted for the lady Jacopa de' Settesoli who always befriended
St Francis when he came to Rome, and whose remains now rest
opposite his in the crypt at Assisi.

The room above St Francis's is also shown on request. It
contains relics of St Charles of Sezze, a Franciscan brother
mystic. Sezze is south of Rome in the Lepini hills. Here I was
once shown his mystically wounded heart – the wound was real
enough. His heart was visibly pierced by a shaft of light during
ecstatic prayer. It was stolen some years ago and never
recovered. The body of the saint rests under the altar of the third
chapel on the left of the church.

In the last chapel on the left – first as you leave the sacristy – is a remarkable piece of sculpture by Gian Lorenzo Bernini, the recumbent figure of Blessed Ludovica Albertone, a contemporary of Michelangelo, who became a tertiary in her widowhood and was buried here beside her husband in 1533. The friar who wrote her history described her married life in these gracious words: 'Her light ever shone clearly in her husband's eyes, and the sound of his lute ever filled her soul with melody'.

22. *Blessed Ludovica Albertone, by Gian Lorenzo Bernini, in the Church of San Francesco a Ripa*

I hope I am not alone in preferring this sculpture to Bernini's other recumbent figure, St Teresa's ecstasy in Santa Maria della Vittoria.

Santa Maria del Orto

From San Francesco the Via Altieri leads straight to Santa Maria del Orto (Our Lady of the Garden) on the left, so plain and tatty from outside, and so often locked, that you will wonder why I mention it. Should you find it open you will agree that it has attractions of its own, a lightness of touch and a fullness of colour, for it is full of frescoed space. The architect was Giulio Romano, about 1530, and it is not surprising to learn that he did not design the façade. This was the church of various Trastevere trade corporations – you might learn something of them by studying the tombstones. Gardeners were prominent, and the church originated from a Madonna over a garden gate. Another reason why I mention it is that, if you keep your eye on the

notices billed so plentifully outside Roman churches, you will
find sacred concerts are held here, usually in the late evening.

St Cecilia's

So, turning right down the road opposite the church and then
left, you will arrive at St Cecilia's. Four features here are most
important, and the others are just important. First, the courtyard preceding the church is a place of beauty. It is best when
the sun is out and the roses or lilies are in bloom. The *cantharus*
or water vessel in the centre is ancient, and in this lovely setting
enables you to appreciate how the atrium was a place for
cleansing both mind and body, in these days humbly replaced
by porch and holy water stoup.

Once in the church your eye will be carried straight to the
high altar, raised above the 'confession' of St Cecilia, and to the
great eighth-century mosaic in the apse beyond. These are the
three other 'most important' features. As you approach closer
you will, I feel sure, be captivated by Stefano Maderno's famous
sculpture of St Cecilia martyred.

23. Stefano Maderno's St Cecilia, as he saw her in 1599

The tradition concerning Cecilia is that she was martyred in
the bathroom of her own home – here where this church now
stands – first by being locked in and left with the hot air on and
then, when she was found still alive, hacked at by the
executioner with his sword. Her body was removed to the
catacomb of Callixtus and buried – it seems, exactly as found in
death – by her fellow Christians. Five hundred years later Pope
Paschal I was busy retrieving the bodies of saints from the
catacombs, which were then being abandoned. He enshrined
them under the altars of Roman churches. Cecilia's, however,
he could not find. According to archives which still survive (the
Latin record is inscribed in stone on the wall at the end of the

left aisle) he fell asleep during office at St Peter's and dreamed that a renewed attempt would be rewarded with success. In fact he found the body intact and incorrupt, brought it into Rome, and buried it in the new church he had built here – porch and apse are both his – over her home in Trastevere.

Cardinal Sfondrato in 1599 re-opened the tomb and found her still incorrupt. He commissioned Maderno to reproduce in marble what providence had preserved, and the inscription on the floor, difficult to read, is the sculptor's:

Behold the body of the most holy virgin Cecilia, whom I myself saw lying incorrupt in the tomb. I have in this marble expressed for you the same saint in the very same posture.

More than once in this church I have been asked how St Cecilia came to be patroness of music. This seems to be the explanation. Cecilia was compelled to marry, although in her heart she had resolved to remain a virgin consecrated to Christ. Her husband Valerian was not only converted to this way of thinking but also to the faith, and was martyred and is enshrined with her here. During the wedding, according to an ancient *Life* of St Cecilia: 'while the organ played she sang *in her heart* to the Lord....' This sentence was later used as an antiphon for the office of St Cecilia's Day, the words 'in her heart' being omitted. This gave rise to the notion that Cecilia had in fact sung to organ music.

The altar canopy is one of several in Rome by the great thirteenth-century architect Arnolfo di Cambio, in the gothic style. Beside it is a cosmatesque candlestick.

You should do your best to appreciate the mosaic. It was put up by Pope Paschal I in the very early ninth century and closely resembles that at Santa Prassede due to the same pope. Product of the revival of mosaic at Rome following the expulsion of artists from Constantinople, the figures are stiff, perhaps even stilted, compared with those at St Pudentiana and SS. Cosmas and Damian. But they have their charm. The central figure is Christ standing among the clouds of heaven, his garments Roman, with the *lati clavi*, the 'broad bands' of rank. His left hand holds the scroll of doctrine and his right is raised in blessing. Above his head the Father's hand holds a crown of victory. Peter and Paul flank him; Peter as ever with woolly hair and Paul with the high forehead. The other two at Christ's left (your right) are Valerian, Cecilia's husband, and St Agatha; to Christ's right: Cecilia herself and Pope Paschal. You can tell Paschal by the square halo, which indicates that the person represented was alive when the mosaic was made. Notice that Cecilia has amiably placed her arm round the Pope's shoulder. The date tree to the left has on its branch the phoenix, bird of immortality. The other elements of this mosaic are common to many others and are described more than once in this book.

To the right of the church is a Blessed Sacrament chapel with medieval frescoes, and nearer the door a corridor leads off to a chapel over what is traditionally venerated as the *calidarium* or hot bath where Cecilia was suffocated. There is more here than you think. Note the cosmatesque floor and altar. Look up into the miniature painted dome overhead. In the corridor are delightful landscapes by the Flemish artist Paul Brill (1554–1626) and a fine statue of St Sebastian.

Two early renaissance tombs by the door are by Paolo Romano, on the left, and Mino da Fiesole. The former is the tomb of an English Cardinal Easton.

If one of the clergy who serve this church is about – it is not a parish church – you may ask to be shown the excavations, for a small fee. They include a crypt arranged by Cardinal Rampolla, 1899 to 1901, to receive the sarcophagi that contain the relics of Cecilia, her husband Valerian, and other martyrs. The excavations are those of second- and third-century houses, and we may be fairly sure that a place of Christian worship has existed here from the fourth century.

The nave of the church, beautifully clear and clean and tranquil, is the result of Cardinal Sfondrato's late sixteenth-century reconstruction.

White-habited Benedictine nuns of St Cecilia occupy the adjacent convent. The lambs blessed at St Agnes's Basilica are sent here to be kept by the nuns till their wool is wanted for the pallium that lies close to St Peter's tomb, until it is sent to a newly appointed archbishop. In their choir, which is over the narthex of the church, beautiful paintings of angels by the thirteenth-century Roman artist Pietro Cavallini are preserved and sometimes a party of visitors will be shown round. Even if you are not interested in the work of Cavallini, it is an intriguing experience to be allowed into the nuns' strict enclosure.

The Cloister of the Genoese Church

In the streets between here and the Tiber there are picturesque medieval houses, some recently restored. To the left of St Cecilia's, San Giovanni dei Genovesi (St John's of the Genoese) has a handsome renaissance courtyard that you can visit even if the church is closed. The custodian objected to it being called a cloister because, as he pointed out, the house was originally a residence for the Genoese and not a monastery.

San Benedetto a Piscinula

If you slip through the streets opposite St Cecilia's you will come, in the piazza by the bridge that leads to the Tiber island, to the tiny church of San Benedetto a Piscinula – the name refers to some Roman baths that once existed nearby. In spite of its lack of size it has many of the interesting features that characterize an ancient Roman church – in fact more than some. Here we shall mention only that it is, by tradition, on the site of the house where the young Benedict lodged, at the end of the fifth century, before he fled from his Roman studies to seek the solitary life at Subiaco, and draw your attention to a thirteenth-century painting of the saint behind the altar and, opening off a chapel to the left as you enter, what is known as his room – more probably all that survives of the house where he lodged, if the tradition be a sound one. The bell tower is said to be the smallest in Rome (I wonder if it really beats the ruined one at the foot of the Ara Coeli steps) and its bell the oldest, dated 1069.

The Fountain of Ponte Sisto

To visit the other half of this quarter, on the far side of the Viale di Trastevere, I suggest crossing by the Ponte Sisto – second bridge towards St Peter's after the Tiber Island. As you reach the far bank – crossing the road with care at this one-way Lungotevere (the Tiber embankments are so called) you will find a little piazza with the Fountain of Ponte Sisto – better by night than by day. This fountain was built in 1613 by Giovanni Fontana (appropriately named!) to deliver Acqua Paola, which comes from north of Rome, to the other side of the Tiber. Its original position was near the Farnese Palace. When the Tiber was embanked in the eighteen-seventies the fountain was destroyed, but twenty years later, as the result of public agitation, its broken pieces were recovered by means of clever detective work – a lion's head was in the Tiber, and some parts had even been buried. The resurrected monument now stands on the wrong side of the Tiber.

Santa Dorotea

Bear to the right of the fountain, and after a few steps you will see the delicate baroque façade of Santa Dorotea. It is not really important, but the virgin martyr Dorothy is buried here, and I mention it in case this should be your name, or a friend's. The Acts of her martyrdom tell a charming story. Dorothy told her persecutors that she would soon stand in the garden of her divine Spouse amid fruits of paradise and roses unfading. She was mockingly asked to send back a gift of such unusual

produce – and did, by an angelic child messenger, so that the
pagan who had laughed at the poetry of her faith was himself
converted and died a martyr. Her bones clothed in wax, the
fourteen-year-old Dorothy rests in a glass coffin beneath the
high altar.

The sacristy of this church has been called, maybe with some
exaggeration, the 'birthplace of the Counter-Reformation',
because of the establishment there by St Cajetan, in 1517, of one
of the most powerful influences of Catholic renewal, the
Oratory of Divine Love. There is a painting of Our Lady
venerated under this title over the high altar in the church.

Santa Maria della Scala

A little farther and when you see to your right the old Porta
Settimiana, of 1498 with picturesque swallow-tail battlements,
turn left as far as the Piazza Santa Maria della Scala, with the
Discalced Carmelite church of that name. Madonna della Scala
means Our Lady of the Staircase. Its venerated Madonna has a
history characteristic of many now surrounded by the most
lavish settings in chapels or churches built specially for them.
They began as paintings on a street wall, over a gate, or, as in
this case, on the landing of a staircase in a private house. The
tradition of this Trastevere shrine is that a poor mother with a
deformed child came every day to pray before it. Finally,
overcome by her grief, she cried out, 'Mother of God, if you
were to ask me for any favour in my power, I would give it you
at once'. The child was cured, and popular enthusiasm led to
the building of this church. That was towards the end of the
sixteenth century.

This church is a Latin cross in shape – unlike so many of its
period that are crosses with equal arms. The vaults of nave and
choir and left transept, and the dome too, are decorated with
painting that feebly represents moulding – the right transept, in
striking contrast, has beautifully rich stucco relief. This is to
honour the altar of St Teresa – the great St Teresa of Avila – the
relic of whose foot is kept here. The altar opposite St Teresa's
enshrines the Madonna from the staircase. The chapel next to
that, opening on to the nave, has a rather impressive sculpture
of St John of the Cross in the style of Bernini. Like some other
Roman churches, Santa Maria della Scala is festooned with
chandeliers. I counted forty-three.

The Corsini Gallery

Perhaps on another occasion you will return to the Porta
Settimiana and pass through it into the Via della Lungara. A

short distance along on the left is the Palazzo Corsini, given its present form by Ferdinando Fuga, who also designed the façade and baldachino at St Mary Major's. I thought the gallery here one of the most agreeable I had ever visited. It may be because it is rarely overcrowded – this part of Rome is off the beaten track; there is an air of serenity, and the views from the windows over the slopes of the Janiculum are lovely. Maybe too a certain thoughtfulness in arrangement has had something to do with it. There are paintings of renaissance Rome that may interest you, a good Flemish section, a roomful of Canaletto's views of Venice. By Caravaggio – whose paintings are so easy for anyone to enjoy – there is a 'Narcissus looking at his reflection', and there are several paintings in the style of Caravaggio, notably a Christ driving traders from the Temple, and a Last Supper, by Valentin. There is also Cavalucci's portrait of Benedict Joseph Labre, the tramp saint of the Colosseum.

From Santa Maria della Scala it is a few steps to the Piazza and Basilica of Santa Maria in Trastevere. I always feel that the mood of both piazza and church is that of main square and cathedral of an ancient city, a city of Trastavere that can almost afford to disregard a certain other place over the water.

Santa Maria in Trastevere

St Mary's has a tradition, not to be despised, that seems to exceed the bounds of possibility. It claims not only to be the oldest dedication to Our Lady of any church in Rome, but also that its foundation precedes the 'Peace of the Church' of 313 – that when Christians elsewhere were worshipping in rooms in private houses, the Trasteverini had a church of their own. The tradition is that there was a legal dispute with tavern keepers in the third century over the occupation of a veterans' hospice – a sort of primitive Chelsea Hospital – and that the Emperor Alexander Severus decided in favour of the Christian community, with the prudent judgment, 'I prefer that it should belong to those who honour God, whatever be their form of worship'.

A still older tradition attempts to link the choice of this site with the existence of a natural oil spring here, said to have sprung forth about the time of the Nativity, and to have been cherished by Christians as symbolic of our Redemption. I mention this because the observant may notice inscribed in more than one place: '*Fons olei*' – oil spring; this is the explanation.

The church as you see it dates from a rebuilding by Pope Innocent II about 1139, with later additions down to some crude restoration work in the last century. The general air of this venerable church is that history has fused in it – it is as timeless as anywhere in Rome. The impression it makes on me is always profound and lasting.

Even the narthex (broad porch) is thick with history – on its walls are catacomb inscriptions of the third and fourth centuries, fragments of ninth-century sculpture, medieval paintings. In the nave you must pause awhile – not, I think, to take in details, for the beautiful apse mosaics will hold your attention for some time and exclude anything else. They are not all of one date – the half dome itself is of the twelfth-century rebuilding, the mosaics of the Life of Our Lady below are attributed to Pietro Cavallini, about 1290. The whole resembles St Mary Major's very closely, but notice that here Christ retains the central position. I think this is a superior composition.

Mary is clothed in rich Eastern garments, and her Son's arm embraces her. Of the figures flanking them – to the extreme left is Pope Innocent II the builder, holding a model of the Church, St Lawrence the Deacon and Pope St Callixtus, martyred nearby and buried beneath the altar. To the right are Peter and Popes Saint Cornelius, Julius, and Calepodius – the last-named also buried beneath the altar. At the bottom of the beautiful fan pattern over the head of Christ is the hand of the Father awarding the crown of victory and, on either side, pretty floral designs flanking the Lamb of God. The pattern of fruit and flowers under the arch is of exceptional beauty.

Famous are the mosaics by Pietro Cavallini of the Life of Our Lady. Put yourself in a position to see them properly and if necessary ask the sacristan to switch the light on. It is hard to praise them enough. The first, to the left, is the birth of Our Lady; the reclining figure is St Ann. Notice how, after her delivery, she is being tempted with a little light refreshment. The other subjects – Annunciation, Nativity, Epiphany, Presentation in the Temple, and Falling Asleep of Mary are in the same charming style and repay study. In the last subject, the little figure in Our Lord's arms represents the soul of Mary. At the back of the apse is an ancient bishop's chair, and outside the apse are very large mosaics of the prophets Jeremiah and Isaiah.

The canopy over the altar is a contribution of the nineteenth-century restorers.

To what else should your attention be drawn? You are used to these rows of ancient columns – as usual, they are by no means all the same – to cosmatesque floors, and to coffered ceilings. The ceiling over the nave here has a rather eccentric pattern; its central panel is a painting of the Assumption by Domenichino.

If you ascend the steps at the end of the right aisle you will notice some black marble weights; probably you have noticed them in other churches and maybe heard pious legends to explain them. They are ancient standard Roman weights – originally kept in temples and eventually passed on to churches. Their part in the life of ancient Rome was similar to that of our own 'standard measurements' fixed into the wall of Trafalgar Square, below the National Gallery.

Look up at the door at the end of this aisle and you will see the Royal Arms of England, for the chapel beyond was restored by the Cardinal Duke of York, bishop of Frascati, and to Stuart royalists uncrowned King Henry IX of England – brother to bonny Prince Charlie. The Chapel contains a Madonna originally venerated in a Trastevere street.

On the far side of the sanctuary there is a similar chapel, where a picture, at least eighth century, is venerated as Our Lady of Clemency. There are some noted frescoes here of the Council of Trent, painted in the seventeenth century by Pasquale Cati.

From this chapel return down the left aisle. Below the steps a door leads into a room with fragments of sculpture and mosaic fixed to the walls, including an antique mosaic of ducks eating snails. The next chapel is an eccentric bit of architecture by Gherardi, another of whose novelties you saw in San Carlo ai Catinari.

As you are about to leave the church, notice a delightful renaissance holy oil aumbry, signed by 'Mino' – doubtless the famous Mino da Fiesole.

From the piazza you should look back at St Mary's to see other mosaics on its façade, probably twelfth century. Ten ladies flanking the Madonna are virgins – eight of them with lamps burning and wearing crowns; the two with veils and unlit lamps are widows. Near the top of the bell tower is a mosaic Madonna.

Piazza di Santa Maria in Trastevere

I like to imagine the visitor taking a little refreshment outside a café in the square, enjoying the to and fro of Trastevere life and the splashing of the fountain. The palace to the left (as you look at the church) used to be a residence of the Benedictines of St Paul's in the days when malaria drove them into Rome for the summer months. They were here when the basilica took fire in 1823. Later the English Benedictine Cardinal Gasquet lived here when he worked on the Vulgate. In the revolution of 1849 this piazza was the scene of most brutal murders of eight priests. The beautiful fountain is the work of Carlo Fontana (seventeenth century).

San Callisto

If, with your back to the basilica, you turn right out of the piazza, you will see a little church, now closed, of St Callixtus, whose relics are under the altar of Santa Maria in Trastevere, and after whom is named the most famous of all catacombs – he was in charge of it as a deacon. The well in which he was drowned is preserved in the church.

Close by is the narrow Via della Cisterna with, on its right, the 'rione' fountain of Trastevere. Each *rione*, or district, of Rome was provided in 1927 with a small drinking fountain which in some way expressed the interest of that particular neighbourhood. Trastevere, a favourite eating and drinking resort for Romans, is represented by a barrel, a vat, and two wine measures.

San Cosimato

A glance at the plan at the beginning of this chapter will enable you to make your way to the Piazza di San Cosimato, Trastevere's market place and often very untidy during the day. There is a church of San Cosimato here. You will spot its ancient porch easily enough, but have difficulty to find an obvious way in. The next gate admits to an almshouse. If you make a polite request at the porter's lodge he will probably allow you through. There are two cloisters, one romanesque, the further one renaissance; both beautiful. They have the interest of being alive – the old folk sit out here to pass the time of day. If you give them a smile and a kind word in passing they will be only too pleased and you will no longer feel an intruder.

You may have to ask to find your way into the church. It dates from 1475 and its façade is a surprising mixture of gothic and renaissance. It has good carved wooden doors with a Franciscan interest – for Poor Clares used to be here. Make your way to a chapel to the left of the sanctuary to see a very good renaissance altar with the relics of martyrs.

Villa Sciarra Park

By turning right at the huge Ministry of Public Instruction on the Viale di Trastevere you can make your way uphill to the Villa Sciarra Park. Here are fifteen acres of terraced grounds, with shady walks and some white peacocks – pleasant if you are staying on this side of Rome but not, I think, to be hunted out specially.

CHAPTER 26

The Janiculum

San Pietro in Montorio – The Fountain of Acqua Paola –
The Panorama from the Janiculum – The Garibaldi
Monuments – Tasso and St Philip Neri – Sant' Onofrio.

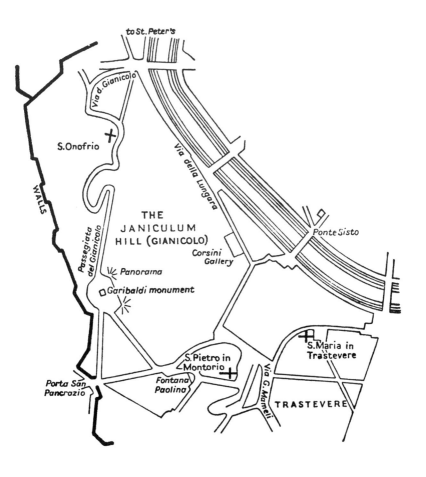

The Janiculum (Gianicolo) is a long hill of golden sand beside the Tiber, between Trastevere and St Peter's. Outside the original walls, it does not count as one of Rome's seven hills. There is no finer viewpoint over the city; in many ways and at almost any time it makes a delightful walk that you can fit into morning, afternoon, or evening. You may of course begin at either end, but I shall follow a preference I have somehow acquired and guide you from Trastevere.

San Pietro in Montorio

Not far down the Viale di Trastevere is the Ministry of Public Instruction (*Ministero della Pubblica Istruzione*). Instead of passing it, turn right and follow the tree-lined road as it bears right. When the Via Manili begins to hairpin up the hill, steps just before a fountain are a useful short cut. Or you may turn the first bend and take a lane of steps with a Way of the Cross in ceramic, erected in 1957, leading you straight to the piazza before San Pietro in Montorio – St Peter's on the Golden Hill – where you can make a restful pause while enjoying the first of the Janiculum's several panoramas.

There seems to have been a secluded little monastery hereabouts during the Middle Ages. The present church, externally austere and simple, was built at the expense of kings of France and Spain towards the end of the fifteenth century. Internally it is not so much the architecture of the church as the artistic contents of its chapels that will engage you – and really they are superb. Perhaps I should renew old advice – to appreciate the chapels on the right, view them from the left of the church, and *vice versa*, even then you may need to go round again to examine detail.

The first chapel to the right has a striking painting of the Scourging of Christ by Sebastiano del Piombo. It is not surprising to learn that this artist was first a musician, for he gives a movement of music, almost of dance, to his figures, even with this subject. He also creates interesting architectural depth with a minimum of perspective. The figure of St Francis to the right is very expressive.

Next is a fresco called the Madonna of the Letter by Pomarancio – from mid-sixteenth century till Pope Clement XI brought it indoors in 1714 it was an open-air shrine in a Trastevere street. Be sure you are standing well back to see, over the arches of these chapels, excellent paintings by an unknown sixteenth-century artist of Virtues and Sybils – Sybils were pagan prophetesses brought into Christian art because they were credited with having foretold our redemption.

The first chapel on the left of the nave has a beautiful painting of the Stigmata of St Francis by Giovanni de Vecchi – the saint himself strangely mystical – even with a touch of the style of El Greco. Next, the Raymondi Chapel is to designs by Bernini – the dramatic use of light is characteristically his, but the sculpture of St Francis in Ecstasy, which happens to be by Baratta, would be worthy of the master. Look up at the vault. Note also, around this chapel, a delicate frieze of roses and birds in relief. The tomb to the left, of Francesco de' Raymondi (died 1638), shows the deceased blandly reading his book and marking a page with his finger while the resurrection of the dead goes on just below.

In the next chapel is a pleasant St Anne attributed to sixteenth-century Antoniazzo Romano – his children are always charming.

There follows the large chapel of the Pietà with fine paintings of the Passion of Christ by Theodore van Baburen and David de Haen. By the first is the Taking down from the Cross above the altar. To appreciate everything you need to move around a bit to find points of vantage. You should not miss those high up in lunettes, Christ Mocked, and The Prayer in the Garden.

Before the sanctuary gates are large apsidal chapels to right and left. On the balustrades before the left-hand chapel are interesting arms; they appear to be a hedgehog gazing at the sun, or *vice versa*! The chapel to the right has a painting by Giorgio Vasari (1552) of the Conversion of St Paul, but he avoids the dramatic fall from horseback on the road to Damascus, and shows us instead a youthful but blinded Paul led to the house of Ananias. As this episode is recorded in 'A Street called Straight' the freedom with which the artist sets the scene before a spacious semicircular colonnade is amusing.

Raphael's Transfiguration, now in the Vatican Gallery, with its mosaic reproduction in St Peter's, was formerly above the high altar here. Now there is a copy of Guido Reni's Crucifixion of St Peter (Peter was crucified upside down).

Bramante's Tempietto

You have not seen everything. Many come here to disregard the church and admire only Bramante's Tempietto in the courtyard of the Franciscan monastery. You may approach it either by leaving the church through a door on the right side, or through an arch to the right of the façade. This has always been regarded as a masterpiece of the renaissance, for its grace and harmony of proportion. There are two chapels, one above the other. In the lower you look down at a patch of the Janiculum's golden sand, erroneously venerated as an alternative site for the martyrdom of St Peter. Peter was martyred between the two 'goals' (*meta*) of Nero's stadium at the Vatican, but in the Middle Ages the word *meta*, used to designate these posts in ancient Acts of the martyrdom, were taken to stand for two well-known pyramidal tombs, one at St Peter's, the other beside the Gate to the Ostian Way – the latter still stands. This site was picked midway between them. This useless essay in pious archaeology has at any rate given us the Tempietto, completed in 1502. In the upper chapel there is a charming little relief in fifteenth-century style of the martyrdom of St Peter, and Bernini has most beautifully decorated the dome of the crypt in stucco, representing the life of St Peter – his Call, events on the Sea of Galilee, Liberation from Prison, etc.

The Fountain of Acqua Paola

Irish Earls of Tyrone and Tyrconnell, who fled to Rome at the end of Elizabeth's reign, are buried in the sanctuary. Make your way uphill to the most grandiose of Roman fountains, the *mostra*, or display, of Paul V's Acqua Paola, brought to Rome from Lakes Bracciano and Martignano over the restored arches of Trajan. These generous cascades first splashed into their pool in 1612; the fountain was designed by Flaminio Ponzio and Giovanni Fontana. A branch of this aqueduct supplies the fountains in St Peter's Square.

You pass through the gates of the Janiculum gardens, and to your left another drive sweeps in from the Porta San Pancrazio. In the triangle of grass between the two you will usually find miniature donkeys who draw carriages in which children take rides in stately imitation of grown-ups down below in the city. This is the road you should take if later you wish to visit the Basilica of San Pancrazio described – briefly – in Chapter 27.

This hill, and its hinterland, was the scene of fighting in Garibaldi's defence of Rome against the French in 1848. His short-lived republic was only the pattern of the unified Italian Nation realized in 1870, but the hero was, of course, far from forgotten, and busts of his distinguished followers have been planted all along the walks – quite entertaining to study if the views fail to enthrall you.

The Janiculum Panorama

At the great Garibaldi monument, which no one could miss, the view from the esplanade will be something like this, if you take your position more or less at the centre:

Background, left to right:	Monte Soratte (on a very clear day); Sabine Hills, Prenestine Hills, Alban Hills.
The City, left to centre:	Note first the huge white building of the Law Courts – just below it you will make out the Castel Sant' Angelo, and the slender dome of San Giovanni dei Fiorentini. Then you may recognize the Chiesa Nuova, with beyond the lofty cupola of Sant' Agnese, overlooking the Piazza Navona. More or less centre in the field is the very flat dome of the Pantheon.
Centre to right:	Towards you is the Palazzo Farnese – three dark arches, and beyond it Sant' Andrea delle Valle. The stumpy dome is the Gesù, and a prominent one San Carlo ai Catinari. You should certainly recognize the Victor Emmanuel Monument – to the left of it is the leaning Torre delle Milizie, and to the right the Capitol, best identified if you know its belfry. Behind these in the distance Santa Maria Maggiore can be recognized by twin domes and a bell tower. The trees away to the right mark the wooded heights of the Palatine. On the skyline beyond, a row of statues will identify the façade of St John Lateran.

At certain times of year this panorama, viewed a little before sundown, takes on wonderful tones of ochre and russet.

The Garibaldi Monuments

The monument behind you, in the centre of this hill-top piazza, is to Giuseppe Garibaldi, gentle swashbuckling freebooter and hero of Italy's struggle for national consciousness, unity, and freedom in the mid-nineteenth century. A little farther down the hill you will find his wife Anita waiting for you, bestride a prancing mustang, with one hand holding her baby and the other brandishing a pistol – a really fiery bit of sculpture. Giuseppe's courtship of this little Amazon must have been the briefest in history. Garibaldi related that, as he approached the shores of Brazil 'wanting someone to love him, and that immediately', he spotted the pretty Anita, stepped ashore, went up to her and said, 'Maiden, thou shalt be mine', and the deal was clinched. The bronze sculpture on the pedestal is worth crossing the road to see properly.

Be careful not to let the hairpin bends of the Passegiata del Gianicolo waste your time. If you keep to the city side there are short cuts that will bring you out on the road again by Sant' Onofrio. It is worth crossing to the far side of the road for occasional views of St Peter's and the Vatican City with its Leonine (ninth century) walls and a glimpse of the tower that Pope John adapted as a summer house.

Memories of Tasso and St Philip Neri

On your way down one of these short cuts you will find yourself by a hoary old oak, carefully preserved, and just below it a very classic example of a Roman sarcophagus used as a fountain. Here was once a pretty corner of the hermitage garden of Sant' Onofrio, in the days before the Janiculum became a public parade. The Italian poet Tasso used to sit here, and it was also a favourite resort of St Philip Neri with his troops of youngsters, taking the air on Roman Sundays.

To reach Sant' Onofrio's you have only to climb a few steps. Sit in the shade beside the splashing fountain, and you are in a world apart. It was a world apart when Blessed Niccolo da Forca Palena went there in 1439 to live in seclusion, a hermit with one of the finest views in the world. Just before he died he left the site to an order called, after St Jerome (in Latin, *Hieronymus*), Hieronymites. Throughout a century the church and monastery assumed their present appearance. They retain their rustic character. The church has become the property of the Knights of the Holy Sepulchre and is served by the American Franciscan Friars of the Atonement.

Above the high altar, in the ribbed apse, gleam paintings attributed to Baldassare Peruzzi – a Coronation of Our Lady backed by a gilded Mystic Rose. This is flanked by the Nativity to the left, and to the right the Flight into Egypt; the latter especially pleasing. Above the tomb to the right of the sanctuary is a still more charming Madonna, showing Jesus a book, of about 1480.

Torquato Tasso, contemporary with Shakespeare, ended his days in this monastery. Just inside the door to the left there is a modest memorial close to the place of his burial, placed here in 1601, but in the vestibule of the chapel beyond is a completely disproportionate nineteenth-century monument to the poet – if you saw this at Stratford you would certainly take him for Shakespeare.

To the right of the church is a chapel to the Madonna of Loreto with a painting of Mary riding on the Holy House by Agostino Carracci with the unusual detail that the Divine Child is busy emptying a pot of water. In the dark chapel nearer the door wait a moment till you can see better, then glance up at a charming Annunciation painted on the vault by Antoniazzo Romano.

There is a cloister here that will delight you – don't hesitate to walk into it. Dating from the fifteenth century, it has been painted by Cavalier d'Arpino and others with the life of Sant' Onofrio, a fourth-century Egyptian hermit usually distinguished in art by his long hair. The interest of these paintings lies less in their skill, in fact they are rather naïve, than in some charming landscape backgrounds.

Immediately opposite is the Salita di Sant' Onofrio by which you can return to the Tiberside – this is the road built by the hermits to provide access to their solitude. A few paces along the Salita steps lead down to the embankment, where, turning left, you will find reasonably priced trattorias if you need a meal – but you could also go off to eat in more familiar territory near the Vatican, or cross the Tiber to the Corso Vittorio Emmanuele.

CHAPTER 27

Basilicas outside the Walls (excluding St Paul's)

San Lorenzo – Sant' Agnese – San Sebastiano – San Pancrazio

San Lorenzo fuori le Mura (St Lawrence outside the Walls)

It can certainly be said of San Lorenzo that it is unlike any other church in Rome. The simplest reason to offer for this is that it is in fact two churches made into one. It takes some time to grasp how this was done and, till you succeed, your visit can be perplexing. That applies anyway to the architecture; as a pilgrim, it is easy to enter and pray at the tomb of St Lawrence, deacon and martyr. San Lorenzo is at the gates of the Campo Verano, Rome's great and beautiful cemetery, and funeral services in the basilica are very frequent.

The two churches that now make up San Lorenzo were built in connection with an extensive system of catacombs here. The further of the two churches was first built in the fourth century over the tomb of Lawrence – but as his grave was in a catacomb gallery it was necessary to cut away the hillside and isolate the shrine, in order to construct the basilica around it. This church was reconstructed by Pope Pelagius II towards the end of the sixth century, and his basilica remains to this day – it is the church *beyond* the altar. In the early thirteenth century Pope Honorius III built a nave in front of this old basilica, transforming the latter into choir and sanctuary of a new church, fully twice as large as the old. As these two churches were built 'head on', the tomb of St Lawrence, which had been at the altar end of the old basilica, is in the centre of the new one.

If this sounds confusing, some of it will be quite obvious as soon as you enter. For the moment, approach the basilica and admire its fine narthex. This is the work of the same Vassalletti family of craftsmen who made the beautiful cloisters of St Paul's and the Lateran; indeed you will easily recognize as theirs the band of cosmatesque work, inlaid marble and mosaic, above the colonnade of ancient columns. A photograph of San Lorenzo after the allied air raid on Rome, which had the railway goods yard as its objective, shows this façade as completely wrecked – yet every particle has been restored with wonderful skill to its former place. Still more amazing is the reconstruction of the thirteenth-century frescoes inside the narthex; they represent the life and martyrdom of the deacons Stephen and Lawrence, and a campaign of the Emperor Henry II against the Slavs. There are interesting sarcophagi – antique stone coffins – in this narthex; you should not miss the large one to the left, with sculpture in low relief of winged children gathering the grape harvest. It dates from the fifth century and is thought to have been used as the tomb of Pope Damasus II.

Once you have entered, the interior is so impressive that it is as well to pause awhile taking it in. The lack of alignment will enable you to appreciate at once that it consists of two churches joined together. The part where you are standing is thirteenth century, beyond the 'kink' is sixth century. Under your feet stretches a very fine cosmatesque floor – the usual geometrical patterns of inlaid marble, large roundels of dark green serpentine and rich purple porphyry offset by arabesques and tiny patterns of the same colours against a background of grey and buff.

Before moving down the nave, notice just inside the door another ancient sarcophagus. It was placed under a baldachino like the canopy of an altar, in cosmatesque style, when it was re-used as the tomb of a Cardinal William Fieschi, who died in 1256. Already a thousand years old, it was hardly the most appropriate memorial, for the sculpture represents a pagan marriage festival. The wedding sacrifice is in the centre, symbolic figures stand to the left, and the groom and bride, with their witnesses, to the right.

Towards the altar is a fine cosmatesque choir enclosure, with its lofty pulpit for singing the Gospel and a handsome paschal candlestick. The Ionic capital of the column immediately behind this pulpit is interesting. If you climb the pulpit – but you should ask permission for that – or even from the floor if you are sharp eyed, you will make out, carved into the roundels of the capital, a frog and a lizard. A possible explanation is that these columns come from the Portico of Octavia, for the Roman historian Pliny relates that its architects were two Spartan slaves whose names meant, respectively, frog and lizard, and that they carved these little reptiles into their work by way of signature.

Below the altar, and entered from the nave, is the 'confession', or crypt where Lawrence is enshrined along with the first deacon Stephen, of whose martyrdom by stoning you read in the Acts of the Apostles. His body is said to have been taken from Jerusalem to Constantinople, and then brought here by Pope Pelagius when he built this basilica. The tradition concerning Lawrence is that, as deacon under Pope Sixtus II during a persecution by Valerian in 258, he was asked to surrender the 'treasure' it was his duty to distribute to the poor. Lawrence took to the Prefect a long train of sick and poor people –these, he said, were the riches of the Church. He was roasted alive where the Church of San Lorenzo in Panisperna now stands, and was buried here in the catacomb.

To see the high altar to advantage, as well as to admire the sixth-century basilica of Pope Pelagius, you must ascend the steps to the side of the confession. The canopy over the high altar has an inscription giving its date (1148), the abbot of the adjacent monastery under whom it was erected, and the names of its craftsmen – John, Peter, Angelo, and Sasso.

The raised floor where you are standing was of course inserted in the thirteenth century, so that you are more than midway up the columns of the sixth-century nave. It has the advantage that you can study them easily. Notice a feature common to many Roman churches, but particularly dramatic here, that the architrave – that is, the flat sculptured stone across the top of the columns – is made up of many fragments. They were all taken from Roman buildings. There is something artless in the haphazard way they are stuck together. All the capitals are Corinthian, that is, decorated with the acanthus leaf, but the two nearest the altar are unusual; they are sculptured with suits of Roman armour.

At the far end of this choir is a bishop's throne and a screen, both in cosmatesque style, dating from 1254.

You will notice that there is a gallery over the aisles of this earlier part of San Lorenzo, and the explanation often given is that it was reserved for the use of women, following an Eastern custom. That may be true, but I think the reason for its existence here (and also at Sant' Agnese) is simply that, since the church was originally built against the side of a hill, it was convenient to have an entrance at 'first floor' level.

From the choir, look back towards the nave, and you will see on the principal arch of this sixth-century church the mosaic set up there by its builder, Pope Pelagius II, in which he appears himself – the figure to the left without a halo, holding a model of the church. The other figures, from left to right, are Lawrence, Peter, Paul, Stephen and Hippolytus, a Roman martyr. The figure of Christ, seated on an orb of blue that represents the firmament – not the world – is very gracious. To left and right are Jerusalem and Bethlehem with their names written on their gates.

There are three other things to see before you leave San

Lorenzo. Beneath the choir is the original floor level of the early basilica, and at its far end a porch adapted as a chapel to receive the remains of Pope Pius IX, who died in 1871. He had planned to be buried at St Mary Major's, but in the end preferred to come here to 'be buried among the poor'. Down here you will find yourself behind the confession that you entered from the nave. It is backed by a large upright stone that has been described before now as 'stained with the martyr's blood'. Perhaps it did indeed receive his remains when he was first laid to rest in the catacomb.

In the left aisle of the nave is the entrance to two catacombs, known by the names of Cyriaca and Hippolytus. Although there are paintings of some interest in them, they are no longer very extensive, and the Franciscans who serve San Lorenzo seldom open them to visitors – this in spite of the fact that some guide-books and even official hand-outs list them as some open to the public.

On the opposite side of the church is the sacristy, with a small shop for postcards and guide-books. Beyond it you may visit a beatiful eleventh century romanesque cloister, simple but full of charm. Around the walls is a complete museum of fragments of inscription and sculpture from the catacombs – and part of one of the bombs that fell on the basilica.

Sant' Agnese fuori le Mura (St Agnes outside the Walls)

If you have your own transport there is an almost direct route from San Lorenzo to Sant' Agnese, via the Piazza Bologna. This chapter is not, however, describing a round tour. I expect most pilgrims will reach Sant' Agnese by taking a bus from outside Stazione Termini. The church is on an important road – the Via Nomentana.

There are several reasons why you should not omit Sant' Agnese. Many will want to make a pilgrimage to the shrine of the child-martyr Agnes – for whom read up the account of a visit to the church of Sant' Agnese in Agone in the Piazza Navona. There is too a catacomb, well worth visiting, for it is in good condition, with many of its tombs still sealed with their closing slabs, but with no paintings at all. Finally the basilica and mausoleum of Costanza, taken together, are among the most important monuments of early Christian art and architecture in Rome.

If you read the chapter on the catacombs you will learn how the tombs of martyrs were isolated, the rock around them cut

away, and a church so built that the relics of the martyr were
below the altar. When the catacomb gallery in which the martyr
was interred was just inside the flank of a hill, it sometimes
happened that the church so built was partly subterranean, *in*
the hill, and partly on the surface. This was the case here, as
indeed at San Lorenzo as well. Walk round the back of the
basilica and you will see its apse is well below street level. You
don't need to do that, for when you have crossed the courtyard
of the abbey of Canons Regular of the Lateran who serve this
church you will descend long flights of steps before you enter
the church. You are going down the hill to catacomb level! On
the walls of this long 'porch' are set up many interesting
inscriptions and sculptures from the catacomb, including part
of Agnes' early shrine carved with her figure, arms extended in
prayer. There is also a tablet inscribed with one of the poems
Pope Damasus had set up before the martyr's shrines in the
fourth century.

In the basilica, notice its ancient columns, taken from
buildings that were in ruins when this was new, and also the
galleries either side. The entrances to these galleries were at
ground level on the flank of the hill. For the same reason, there
are similar galleries at San Lorenzo. Although the mosaics of the
apse have been restored, they date from 635–638. Above Agnes
is the hand of the Father awarding the martyr's crown of
victory, and around are rather crudely drawn clouds – you can
see how they were *meant* to be rendered in the mosaic of Santi
Cosma e Damiano. Below are two zones of starry sky, the stars
like enlarged snowflakes. The three figures represent Agnes, in
stiff gemmed Byzantine garments, to her left Pope Honorius
who built the church as it stands – he holds a model of it; to her
right Pope Symmachus who probably built the original church
here in the fifth century.

The baldachino over the altar dates from 1614, and the statue
of the saint too is seventeenth century. Notice the beautiful
antique candlestick used for the paschal candle. The white
marble around the apse, with vertical stripes of porphyry, is
original, in spite of its modern appearance. This is, incidentally,
in a simplified form, the motif of the memorial over the tomb of
Peter built by Constantine, recently discovered and described in
the section on the Vatican Scavi. Note too the beautiful coffered
ceiling.

Even if you are not visiting the catacomb you should ask to
be admitted to the tomb of the saint, where her bones have been
discovered, along with those of her milk-sister Emerentiana, in
a handsome silver sixteenth-century coffer. A 'milk-sister' is the

daughter of one's nurse. Emerentiana was martyred by stoning while she prayed at the tomb of Agnes.

It seems that even prior to the building of a church over the catacomb tomb of Agnes, Constantine had raised nearby a great cemeterial basilica. You can see its remains in the garden – though you may have to nose around to find them. They are more impressive seen from neighbouring streets. The best theory is that this vast structure was not a church in the ordinary sense, but a great covered cemetery for Christians who wished to be buried near St Agnes. A gaping ruin, one part survives in almost perfect condition. This is the mausoleum of Constantine's daughter Costanza – in English, probably Constance. It is a circular tomb, like so many others of the period – Hadrian's, and that of Caesar Augustus. There is a very similar tomb of her mother Helena too, ruinous, in an outlying suburb. The central rotunda is surrounded by a circular aisle, vaulted with the most beautiful fourth-century mosaics, and separated from the main apartment by an elegant colonnade. In an apse in this colonnade once stood the porphyry sarcophagus of Costanza herself. It is now in the Vatican Museum and its place here is taken by a replica. What you must not miss, however, are those mosaics. Walk round half the aisle craning your neck to appreciate them – the other half is almost identical. The theme is not Christian – there are flowers, birds, *amorini* (little winged babies that in Christian art usually become cherubs) and in two compartments delightful little vintage scenes: dancing in the wine press, and the wagons coming to Rome with the grape harvest. In apsidal recesses are mosaics of about a century later, and quite inferior in quality, representing the Lord giving the Gospel, and giving the Keys.

There was a time when those vintage scenes were taken for real bacchanalia – festivities in honour of the rowdy god of wine. A society of bohemian types used to celebrate orgies in local taverns, which wound up with irreverent ritual around the sarcophagus of Costanza. The mausoleum is now a church, used mostly for weddings.

Should you be in Rome in January, you should certainly come here on the 21st, the feast of St Agnes, for the blessing of the lambs which are afterwards cared for by the Benedictine nuns of St Cecilia's in Trastevere, and from whose wool is woven the pallium, a woollen badge of pastoral office that the Pope sends to newly appointed archbishops, after it has rested above the Tomb of St Peter. How full of beautiful symbolism is this delightful custom, and how linked with the earliest symbolism of authority in the Church – Christ's loving care for lost sheep. For this function it is wise to apply for a reserved place.

San Sebastiano fuori le Mura (St Sebastian's outside the Walls)

St Sebastian's ranks with St Peter's, San Clemente, and Santi Giovanni e Paolo among the most important early Christian excavations of Rome. There is a catacomb with a basilica over it, remains of interesting pagan mausolea and a Roman house and, most important of all, a rather mysterious site known as the '*Memoria Apostolorum*' where, it seems, at least part of the relics of Peter and Paul (maybe their heads) were concealed during a third-century persecution.

To attempt a sequence – first there was a hollow, a miniature valley, leading off the Via Appia; on its flanks were constructed handsome pagan mausolea with entrances against the side of the valley and, inside, steps leading down to subterranean burial chambers. Here, at least by the third century, the Christian community developed an extensive catacomb known as 'the Cemetery in the Hollow Place' – '*ad Catacumbas*'; you notice at once that all the Christian underground cemeteries eventually took a common name from this one. In the fourth century a great basilica was constructed over the site, possibly by Constantine. This is in part the present church. It certainly does not appear fourth century as you approach it from the Via Appia – in fact the façade is eighteenth century and the interior is largely a reconstruction to the designs of the seventeenth-century architect Flaminio Ponzio. The church of the fourth century covered a number of earlier structures – all we have mentioned and in addition a Roman villa at the back. The catacomb here, by the way, was never lost. Now if you go round the back of the church, by following the turning off the Via Appia – Via delle Sette Chiese, the road of the Seven Churches – you will easily recognize walls of the primitive structure, and you could ask the friars to admit you to a part of the aisle of the original basilica in a fine state of preservation.

Notice the handsome wooden ceiling (18th cent.), and turn to the place of greatest interest in the church, the chapel on the left with the shrine of the soldier-martyr Sebastian, whom they attempted to martyr by arrows directed at non-fatal parts of his body, so that he would die slowly from loss of blood. The opportunity of representing an agonizing nude figure of a saint made him a popular subject with late medieval and renaissance artists. Here is a characteristically baroque recumbent figure by Giorgetti, a pupil of Bernini, said to be after the master's model. In the relic chapel opposite is preserved the original 'footprint' from 'Domine Quo Vadis'. Walk up the nave to find the chapel on the right, built in the eighteenth century to the designs of Carlo Fontana.

To the left of the façade is the entrance to the catacombs, where Franciscan friars sell souvenirs and, with a team of lay guides, show you round a limited zone of the catacomb. The tour includes a visit to the 'Memoria Apostolorum'. At a glance it will mean little to you, but you will be shown a reconstruction and – once you have grasped that what is today underground was formerly open air – may be able to picture it to yourself as a small sunny, vine-festooned, open-air trattoria, beside the Appian Way with a grand view towards the hills. A trattoria in fact it was not, but it was the place where visitors to the cemetery found amenities to take refreshment before returning to the city. They regarded this as a kind of sacramental act of communion with the dead whom they venerated. Now in this case, apparently during a persecution of Valerian in 257, their visits were made in honour of Peter and Paul, whose relics in whole or in part are thought to have been brought here from their monuments on the Vatican Hill and beside the Via Ostiense for greater security. On the plaster wall third-century pilgrims have scratched their records. You will hardly be able to make them out, except a few, but many have been deciphered, and the apostles' names occur many times: 'I have taken refreshment for Peter and Paul', 'Peter and Paul pray for Victor'.

You may ask to see the aisle of the Constantinian basilica, where there is an interesting collection of inscriptions, sculpture, and other fragments from the catacomb and a reconstruction of the basilica in its original form to explain this complex site. There is also a mysterious 'well' for which fanciful explanations have been given, but it is now believed to be the shrine of a fifth-century martyr bishop named Quirinus.

From St Sebastian's there is an old lane called the Via delle Sette Chiese that leads to St Paul's outside the Walls via the Catacombs of Callixtus, Domitilla, and Comodilla (these last closed). You will not find seven churches along it, as its name suggests, but in the days when pilgrims went on foot to the four major basilicas and three others besides – St Agnes', St Sebastian's, and St Lawrence's – this was their short-cut through the country from St Paul's. It is still in part rural, but too thick with traffic for safe walking.

San Pancrazio (St Pancras)

Of the church of St Pancras – also outside the walls – little need be said. The arrangement is similar to those already described: catacombs, and a basilica over the site of the martyr's tomb. In this case however the catacombs, although listed as 'open on application', have been closed for some time, and are not in any case of great interest, and the fifth-century basilica has been twice rebuilt, in the seventeenth and nineteenth centuries, losing most of its interest in the transformation. It is served by the Discalced Carmelites, who run a parish and have built a modern study house on the property.

If you have your own reasons for making a pilgrimage to St Pancras, it is within walking distance of the summit of the Janiculum, at the further end from St Peter's. Leaving the Garibaldi monument, the right fork leads to Porta St Pancrazio, a gate rebuilt after the republican defence of Rome in 1849 – an occasion when the suggestion is supposed to have been made to line the walls with nuns, trusting French gallantry to prefer defeat rather than sacrilege and dishonour. The roads outside the walls here, either to right or left, make a pleasant walk. Bear ahead, branching left at the entrance to the Doria Pamphili park, and the church soon appears on your right.

Pancras was a boy martyr of fourteen, who suffered probably in the fourth-century persecution of Diocletian. Devotion to him reached Britain at a very early date, for outside the walls of Canterbury there is an ancient church dedicated to him, probably built during the Roman occupation, and old St Pancras church behind the London station of that name is traditionally at least as old as the mission of St Augustine.

When I was a student at the Beda College the Doria Pamphili Park was the private property of that princely family. There was an open invitation to us to use the park as an amenity. It was agreeable to watch a Sunday game of cricket with the dome of St Peter's in the background. The lovely park and gardens are now open to the public.

CHAPTER 28

From St Paul's to Trefontane

Our Lady of Revelation – Trefontane Abbey – Church of Saints Vincent and Anastasius – Church of the Three Fountains – Santa Maria Scala Coeli – Our Lady of the Apostles – Pontifical Beda College – E.U.R. Garden City

Trefontane, or 'Three Fountains', is a Trappist Abbey at the site of St Paul's martyrdom, a little over a mile beyond the Basilica of St Paul's outside the Walls. The simplest way there is to take the local bus which leaves from a terminus outside the north transept of St Paul's, where the Basilica faces a park. It is also possible to take the Metro (Underground) to Laurentina and walk back to Trefontane.

If you come from Rome via the Porta San Paolo you are following the steps of St Paul on his way to martyrdom. The gate was not there in his time, but the apostle would have seen the pyramid-tomb to Caius Cestius as he passed by.

Our Lady of Revelation
Should you take the bus to Trefontane, when you are set down you will find, right by the bus stop, the entrance to the shrine of Our Lady of Revelation. The shrine itself is a small artificial cave in the hillside that has been developed into chapel, promenades, etc. Our Lady is said to have appeared here on the 12th April 1947 to a Roman tramcar employee, Bruno Cornacchiola, and his three children. At that time Bruno was an active anti-Catholic propagandist. 'Virgin of Revelation' is the title the *'bella Signora'*, as his children called her, gave herself.

A tunnel has been excavated in the rock behind the shrine. At each end is a tablet beginning with a verse from the *Magnificat*: 'From henceforth all generations shall call me blessed'. There follow brief quotations about Mary from saints and writers down the centuries. The tunnel itself is full of votive tablets. The Conventual Friars Minor (Franciscans) have a small monastery and seem to be exercising a sort of watching brief. A visit to this popular little sanctuary can be a very moving experience. You may ask the friars for brochures in English.

279

Trefontane Abbey

Across the road is the entrance to the Trappist monastery. A statue of St Benedict a little way down the drive will draw your attention to a fact few people realize – that Trappists are a reform of the Cistercians and that all Cistercians are Benedictines; the purpose of St Bernard's reform was to follow the Rule of St Benedict – as he saw it – more strictly. As you pass through the gatehouse, notice a section of the old Roman road by which Paul was led here to his execution in the year 67. Painted on the walls of the gatehouse are frescoes representing the property of the monastery in the Middle Ages – you will make out hill towns and a harbour.

Church of SS. Vincent and Anastasius

There are three churches here. The largest is the Abbey Church of SS. Vincent and Anastasius. Although there is ample evidence of churches and shrines here from earliest times, the present magnificently austere romanesque building is generally accepted as the rebuilding of Pope Innocent II in the very early twelfth century, just before St Bernard himself arrived and installed his Cistercians. Men may ask to be shown the monastery, of which the cloister has been quoted by good authorities as the earliest of all cloisters – in part sixth century. The surrounds of the monastery are pleasantly rustic, with farm buildings, plantations of trees, fountains, flowers, and cats.

Church of the Three Fountains

An avenue to the right of the abbey leads to the Church of the Three Fountains, the traditional site of Paul's martyrdom by beheading. A popular legend makes out that the saint's head bounced three times and at each place a fountain of water sprang up, and in fact the fountains (sealed now because the water was polluted) exist in the church, dating from 1599. There is some history behind this story however. The old name for Trefontane was *Ad Aquas Salvias*, and there was a Roman military post here. A Greek life of St Paul states that he was executed beside three springs and near a stone-pine tree. In other words, the springs were there first. During excavations in 1875, behind the church, fossilized stone-pine cones were found. I think there is good reason to respect the traditions of Trefontane. Note the fine mosaic floors brought to this church from the ruins of Ostia. The column in the corner is said to be one on which Paul was beheaded – more likely a relic of some earlier building.

Santa Maria Scala Coeli

The other sixteenth-century church here, approached by a flight of steps (that appear to have architect's building information scratched on them) is known as Santa Maria Scala Coeli – Our Lady Ladder of Heaven. The crypt is part of the much earlier church which St Bernard visited, and where he is said to have had a vision of souls entering heaven through his prayers – hence the name. Find the light on the way down the steps. The structure is taken to be part of the garrison building where Paul possibly spent some time before his execution. There is a tradition that more than ten thousand Christian slaves who had been made to build the Baths of Diocletian are buried here. They are venerated as St Zeno and Companions. The probability is that there are extensive catacombs in the hillside, not yet investigated. Note that St Zeno's relics were removed by Pope Adrian II to a new shrine at Santa Prassede, in the ninth century.

There is a shop in the gatehouse, which sells chocolate, liqueurs, and other confections made by Cistercian monks and nuns.

Our Lady of the Apostles

If you are returning via St Paul's I should like to mention the splendid modern Church of Our Lady of the Apostles not far from the Metropolitana (Underground) Station of Basilica San Paolo. Turn right when leaving the station; you will soon see it on the hill – and at midday you will hear its carillon playing melodies. Built against a hillside, there are really two distinct churches, one above the other, entered from different levels. The upper church serves a Congregation of Sisters, the lower a Congregation of Priests. If you ask permission to enter the lower church, which is private, it is possible to ascend a staircase to the upper church. Both are interesting and rank high among examples of modern church architecture in Rome.

The Pontifical Beda College

Between St Paul's and the Tiber is the Pontifical Beda College, a seminary for English-speaking late vocations originally founded near St Peter's over a hundred years ago to provide a shorter training course for convert clergymen. Eventually it moved to cramped accommodation near the Piazza Barberini, and only in 1960 came to the present site (Vatican territory) and new buildings designed by Renato Costa, who still more recently has built a new Scots College on the Via Cassia. The chapel is dominated by an impressive crucifix by Monteleone.

A feature of unusual interest is the series of half-abstract stained-glass windows on the theme of creation praising God, and the priesthood mediating the things of God to men. Modern Beda students are not necessarily converts, but men who are able to realize their vocations only after having followed some other walk of life.

E.U.R. Garden City

On high ground to the west of Trefontane you could visit the modern garden suburb of E.U.R. If you are keen on modern architecture or town planning a half day there would be well spent. To reach E.U.R. direçt from Rome take the Metropolitana (Underground), or a bus from Trastevere. Begun by Mussolini just before World War II as an Exhibition Centre – Rome Universal Exhibition gives it the initials – it subsequently developed as a government and business centre; there are also sports dromes and facilities, ornamental gardens, delightful residential quarters and the new generalates or study houses of a number of religious institutes. For centre-piece there is a handsome ornamental water surrounded by cherry trees given by Japan. Some of the earlier buildings that superficially look modern in style are in fact the *dernier cri* of a classical renaissance – but some of the best efforts in modern building are well represented at E.U.R. There is (over near Trefontane) a Museum of Roman Civilization with plaster casts of Roman monuments, useful for study if not for appreciation, and also – far more interesting – models of Roman theatres, circuses, aqueducts, road construction, etc. Many visitors go there just to see the large scale model of Rome about the third century.

The principal church – SS. Peter and Paul, with the great dome – is disappointing. A church worth a visit is that of the new General House of the Marist Brothers. This is on private property, but you could ring at the lodge and ask to be admitted. Standing with your back to Rome, the Marist Church is over the lake to your extreme left, on high ground.

CHAPTER 29

The Catacombs

History – Catacombs of Callixtus, Domitilla, St Sebastian – The 'Memoria Apostolorum' – Catacombs of Priscilla, St Agnes, St Pancras and St Lawrence

The catacombs of Rome carry a mysterious allure just in their name. Too few people properly appreciate their significance, even after a visit, and some of the excitement about them is due merely to the fact that they are underground.

History

Now what they are not is – hiding places. In many a book, or even a sermon, you will hear of the 'Church of the Catacombs', as if the Christians lived underground for centuries, to emerge into forgotten daylight when Constantine brought peace to the Church in 313.

Catacombs are quite simply Christian burial grounds of the first four centuries, and as such they were registered with the State and perfectly well known to the Roman authorities. A catacomb might be confiscated in time of persecution, but even then Roman respect for the dead was too great to allow damage to be done.

Catacombs have interest and attraction, and what is more immense artistic and theological importance, because the slabs closing the tombs carry inscriptions and sculpture, and walls and vault were enriched with paintings. From these we learn a great deal of the thought and faith and piety of the first Christians; they are just as important as the famous 'writings of the early Fathers'; in fact they tell us more about our religion as it was really lived by ordinary people.

After the peace of the Church the practice of burying underground declined, but the tombs of martyrs were isolated by excavating away the rock around them, and the chapel, or church, so fashioned was enriched with marble, mosaic, and paintings, and hung around with many lamps.

If the martyr's tomb were at a deep level, such a church would be completely underground (fig. a); if it were some distance into

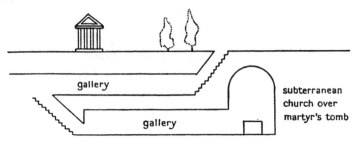

fig. a

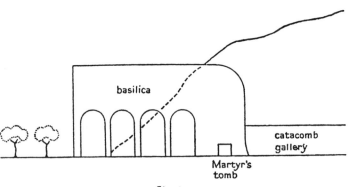

fig. b

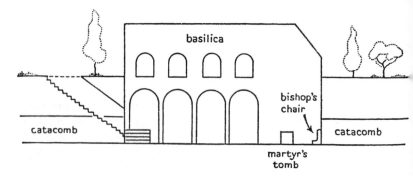

fig. c

a hillside the façade of the church might emerge into the open air (fig. b); and if the tomb were on the uppermost gallery of the system, then possibly the upper part of the church would emerge above ground (fig. c).

During barbarian attacks from the fifth to the ninth centuries the catacombs were sacked and damaged. In quiet times popes restored the martyrs' tombs, but eventually they had all the relics of confessors for the faith brought into Rome and placed under the altars of the churches – this is the origin of sealing the relics of saints, and especially of martyrs, in altar stones, or of interring them beneath the altar.

Catacombs were almost exclusively Christian. When they originated, in the first century, the pagan practice was mostly cremation. All tombs were outside the city walls, lining the country roads. More important families owned mausolea, usually two storeys high, and freed slaves were often entitled to burial on the ground floor, or in a basement which, if the family owned much property round the tomb, could be extended underground as far as its boundaries. This was particularly easy as the local rock – tufa – is the result of a soft but firm deposit of volcanic ash from the Alban Hills. Such small private excavations are called *hypogea* – which is simply Greek for 'underground'. A catacomb is a much larger version of the same thing, liable to total ten miles in length, but as a close network on several levels over a modest area.

Of Rome's seventy-odd catacombs about ten are Jewish or belong to some little-known sect.

Throughout the Middle Ages these Christian catacombs were lost and forgotten – save one – the catacomb under the basilica of St Sebastian. Scholars knew about them, however, from the records of early pilgrims to the shrines of martyrs, and in the late sixteenth century Antonio Bosio found his way into many – leaving his name on the walls in candle-smoke. The cemetery below St Sebastian's was called '*ad catacumbas*', meaning 'in the hollow', because the galleries were excavated from the wall of a slight valley. As others were discovered they were popularly given the name that really belonged to St Sebastian's 'catacomb' only.

In the nineteenth century a young archaeologist, John Baptist de Rossi, noticed on the step of a stone staircase in a gardener's cottage along the Via Appia this fragment of an inscription: . . . NELIUS MART. He knew that in the lost cemetery of Callixtus a Pope Cornelius was buried. Eventually he found his way below ground and located the other half of the inscription, with the letters COR . . . Soon he was able to lead Pope Pius IX to the tomb chapel of second-century popes in the recovered Catacomb of St Callixtus – Pius fell on his knees and wept.

Under the Lateran Treaty between the Italian State and the Holy See all catacombs become Vatican territory – even those discovered subsequently. Because they are known to attain a length of up to ten miles a possible total of six hundred miles has been estimated – but I consider this to be an exaggeration, as many are quite short. The Pontifical Commission for Sacred Archaeology sees to their maintenance and further excavation, but those only are regularly open to visitors where a religious community is established at the surface to supervise the guiding and services in the chapels of the catacomb.

In any case the visitor will only be guided along a carefully selected section, usually illuminated by electricity. Groups specially interested may, in the off-season, apply for an extended tour. At the height of the season visits can be a little disappointing – if you are tagging along at the end of a queue unable to hear the guide. I very strongly recommend anyone who wishes to savour the atmosphere – the spiritual and religious atmosphere – of the catacombs to arrange to assist there at Mass.

Catacombs, generally speaking, are open from 8.30 to 12 and about 3 to 5.

24. Mass in the Catacombs

Catacombs of Callixtus, Domitilla, and St Sebastian

Of the three catacombs most commonly and easily visited, two are on the Via Appia – Callixtus and St Sebastian's, and the Catacomb of Domitilla is within walking distance. A bus stop from which you could approach the catacombs on foot, a short distance along the old pilgrims' road, the Via delle Sette Chiese (Road of the Seven Churches), is 'Piazza dei Navigatori' in the Viale Christoforo Colombo. If you took transport to the Chapel of 'Domine quo vadis' on the Via Appia you could enter the Salesian property by the gate opposite the chapel and have a pleasant walk to the Catacomb of Callixtus.

Catacomb of Callixtus

How this catacomb was discovered has been told in the general history of catacombs above. Almost at the foot of the entrance staircase are the chapels of the Popes and of St Cecilia. Nine third-century popes were interred in the first chapel; in the place of honour – behind the present altar – was interred Pope Sixtus II, who was followed here and executed in the course of a third-century persecution. The great slab with, incised upon it, verse about the martyrs by fourth-century Pope Damasus, is a good example of reconstruction. Fragments of it were found lying about. The missing text was made up from manuscript records of Pope Damasus's compositions. You may recognize these 'Damasan inscriptions' elsewhere by their unusually fine lettering.

Nearby for about five centuries lay buried the body of the virgin martyr Cecilia, patroness of musicians. In 821 Pope Pascal I, busy collecting the remains of martyrs for Roman basilicas, was unable to trace her relics. On the walls of St Cecilia's in Trastevere is the record of a dream he had – during matins – at St Peter's, as a result of which he returned to the catacomb and found her body, perfectly intact and interred just as she died, where you now see a reproduction of Stefano Maderno's famous statue. The original is in Trastevere, and according to the sculptor's assertion on oath, that is how he saw her body when Cardinal Sfondrato exhumed it in 1599.

The principal other interest in these galleries is second-century paintings representing baptism, the Eucharistic Meal (i.e. the Mass), and the Consecration.

Two little chapels on the surface are third-century mausolea – one is full of fragments of sculpture from damaged sarcophagi (stone coffins) found here. One of these would appear to have been the gardener's house in which de Rossi made the momentous discovery described earlier in this chapter.

Buying souvenirs

The best souvenirs of your catacomb visit are reproductions cast in a plastic material made of marble dust, of the statue of St Cecilia or of the Good Shepherd – the earliest statue of Christ, though it is not known now where it was originally found. Another good buy are reproductions in terracotta or metal of catacomb lamps. There are also rosaries with catacomb earth sealed into a medal or crucifix.

Catacomb of Domitilla

Should you use the bus service to the Piazza dei Navigatori the Catacomb of Domitilla soon appears on your right as you follow the Via delle Sette Chiese. If you leave St Callixtus's from the gate giving on to the Via Ardeatina you are only a few minutes from the Catacomb of Domitilla, so-called after either of two early martyrs of that name. Most distinctive of this catacomb is the vast underground basilica built about 390 around the tombs of two soldier martyrs, Nereus and Achilleus. The basilica was discovered and reconstructed in 1871. Note columns formerly part of the canopy over the altar, on one of which is carved the martyrdom of Achilleus – unique. There are many paintings in this vast catacomb – you are generally shown a fourth-century one of a Roman Lady named Veneranda being introduced into paradise by her patroness, St Petronilla – a document in the history of the veneration of saints, and also a beautiful painting of Christ seated with his apostles, about the same date. What you are less likely to see is the finest mosaic in all the catacombs, Christ between Peter and Paul, with other details, notable for a most ingenious and seemingly very modern use of colour. This was only recently discovered. German Brothers of Mercy maintain this catacomb, and if you assist at Mass it is possible to arrange a light breakfast in their beautiful garden or, in winter for small groups, indoors.

Nearby are the Ardeatine Caves, where over three hundred victims of a reprisal during the occupation of Rome are buried at the place of their execution. The scene on Sundays, when relatives visit the tomb, is very touching.

Catacomb of St Sebastian

Back to the Appian Way. Next after the Salesian property of St Callixtus is the Basilica and Catacomb of St Sebastian, served by Franciscan Friars Minor. You will see a large notice 'Memoria Apostolorum', to be awkwardly translated for the sake of clarity – 'Place where the apostles are commemorated'. As a catacomb it is rather dull – the part the public are usually shown anyway.

But remember that this is the cemetery originally called 'catacomb', one never lost, and accordingly it was known and very much loved by St Philip Neri, sixteenth-century founder of the Oratory, who used to spend nights in vigil in one of the chapels. A tablet put up by the London Oratory commemorates this.

The 'Memoria Apostolorum'

The 'Memoria Apostolorum' is the important thing here. It is, however, very much an archaeological site – the visitor has difficulty in conjuring up, from fragmentary remains, what the place really was.

You are shown a site, underground – it was originally in the open air. There is a wall covered with barely decipherable scratches. Many of these are prayers to the Apostles Peter and Paul, dating from the third century, or statements that a 'refreshment' (*refrigerium*) had been held in their honour. What does all this mean, and what is it doing here?

To understand the explanation you must appreciate that when the ancient Romans, Christian or pagan, visited their dead, they came a long way from the city. Accordingly they brought provisions with them, and burial places were often fitted up with special rooms where they could take a meal together. From being a mere matter of convenience, this was raised to the dignity of a religious rite in honour of the dead, who were thought of as present – a sort of act of spiritual communion with the departed. It seems that Christians did this too when visiting the tombs of martyrs. The problem is, why did they do it here when Peter and Paul are clearly buried beside the Via Cornelia (Vatican Hill) and the Via Ostia, and not on this Via Appia? To find the answer has been a thorny problem, but the solution offered here is one which has gained fairly general acceptance.

Peter's and Paul's relics, or at least part of them, must have been brought here, as to a place of relatively greater safety, in a period of persecution. There are in fact third-century documents which tell us that the feast (that is, the anniversary of martyrdom) of Peter and Paul was commemorated here as well as at the actual sites of their tombs. The suggestion, which fits well evidence there is no time to give here, is that a temporary transfer did occur during a persecution by the Emperor Valerian in 257.

Such then is the famous 'Memoria Apostolorum'. Nearby you will be shown three mausolea which, when they were built in the early third century, were also in the open air. There is no reason to suppose they were Christian. They are very attractive, with beautifully preserved moulded ceilings, and were pretty well unrivalled in Rome till the famous excavations were made under St Peter's.

The basilica of St Sebastian is described in Chapter 27.

Catacombs of Priscilla and St Agnes

These two catacombs are on the other side of Rome in built-up areas, and consequently make less attractive excursions. Priscilla's is important, however, for its paintings, so it should be visited by anyone intrigued by catacombs or by early Christian art. The catacomb of St Agnes will appeal to anyone with a devotion to that saint, or an interest in Church history, and should certainly complete a visit to the basilica above and its neighbouring mausoleum of Costanza.

Catacomb of Priscilla

The Catacomb of Priscilla is entered from a Benedictine Convent on the other side of the road – the Via Salaria – to the catacomb, which lies under the Villa Ada park. There are more paintings in the limited zone accessible to visitors than elsewhere. The subjects are unusual too. They include two representations of Our Lady, one of the Magi, the Veiling of a Nun (third or fourth century), and the Eucharistic Meal. One of the Madonnas is presented as the earliest painting of Mary in Rome, perhaps mid-second century.

Catacomb of St Agnes

The Catacomb of St Agnes, on the other hand, has no paintings, but many of the tombs are still sealed, a fairly unusual feature, and there are interesting inscriptions. This catacomb is less likely to be crowded, but to offset this advantage there is no multilingual corps of guides. The basilica of St Agnes is described in Chapter 27.

Catacombs of St Lawrence and St Pancras

These Catacombs are sometimes listed as open to visitors. Only after several attempts did I manage to see the Catacomb of St Pancras, entered from the church of that name – see Chapter 27. It was of no great interest. Although I never found the friars at San Lorenzo (Chapter 27 also) willing to show their catacomb, it is always worth a try.

CHAPTER 30

The Lenten Station Churches

The Station churches are those appointed one to each day in Lent for special morning and evening services, so this Chapter will interest you mostly if you are in Rome for Lent. Many Easter pilgrims, however, arrive a little before the feast and could well visit a Station church or two.

The Stations originated as an expression of 'community' in the early Church, the Roman people gathering around their bishop (the Pope) when he came to each day's Station to celebrate Mass. If you have an old daily Missal you may find that it prints at the head of each Lenten Mass the Roman Station Church – this of course only applies since the missal used at Rome was adopted throughout the Latin Church.

The Station services comprise a Mass and a Procession singing the Litanies of the Saints, followed by veneration of relics. To be sure of the times you need to look at a notice posted on or near the door of the preceding day's Station church. Stations are liable to be changed if restoration work is in progress at the proper Station church. Besides the functions, the Station churches expose all their treasures, in some cases without closing for the siesta, and catacombs, crypts, saints' rooms, etc., that may usually be closed, are kept open for pilgrims. Stations vary in quality – some drag, doors open late, and the Romans, having got wise to this, arrive in poor numbers; other Stations are very popular and are attended by large and devout crowds. Two of my favourite Stations are those at SS. Cosmas and Damian and at San Pietro in Vincoli.

Ash Wednesday: Santa Sabina on the Aventine
(Also Sant' Alessio and Santa Maria in Cosmedin, both near Santa Sabina)

Thursday: San Giorgio in Velabro
(Also Gesù e Maria in the Corso)

Friday: San' Giovanni e Paolo on the Coelian – five minutes from the Colosseum
(Also San Gregorio al Coelio, nearby)

Saturday: Sant' Agostino

First Sunday in Lent: St John Lateran

Monday:	San Pietro in Vincoli, near Via Cavour Metro Station
Tuesday:	Sant' Anastasia – at the foot of the Palatine
Wednesday:	St Mary Major's
Thursday:	San Lorenzo in Panisperna
Friday:	Santissimi Dodici Apostoli, near the Piazza Venezia
Saturday:	St Peter's

Second Sunday in Lent: Santa Maria in Domnica, on the Coelian (Also San Gregorio al Celio and Santa Maria Maggiore)

Monday:	San Clemente, near the Colosseum
Tuesday:	The Station should be Santa Balbina, but recently it has been transferred each year to other churches.
Wednesday:	Santa Caecilia in Trastevere
Thursday	Santa Maria in Trastevere
Friday:	San Vitale, in the Via Nazionale
Saturday:	San' Marcellino e Pietro, in the Via Merulana

Third Sunday in Lent: San Lorenzo fuori le Mura

Monday:	San Marco, opposite the steps to Ara Coeli and the Campidoglio
Tuesday:	Santa Pudenziana, near St Mary Major's (Also Sant'Agata dei Goti, not far from Via Cavour Metro Station)
Wednesday:	San Sisto Vecchio, near the Baths of Caracalla (Also San' Nereo e Achilleo, almost opposite San Sisto, and Santa Maria in Vallicella – the Chiesa Nuova – in the Corso Vittorio Emmanuele and San Girolamo della Carità, near the Piazza Farnese)
Thursday:	San' Cosma e Damiano, by the Forum
Friday:	San Lorenzo in Lucina, off the Corso
Saturday:	Santa Susanna, not far from the Naiads Fountain (Also Santa Maria degli Angeli – opposite the Naiads Fountain)

Fourth Sunday in Lent: Holy Cross in Jerusalem

Monday:	Santi Quattro Coronati, nor far from the Colosseum

Tuesday:	San Lorenzo in Damaso, off the Corso Vittorio Emmanuele (Also Sant'Andrea delle Valle, on the same Corso)
Wednesday:	St Paul's outside the Walls
Thursday:	San Martino ai Monti, through the Colle Oppio Park from the Colosseum (Also San Silvestro in Capite, the English Church)
Friday:	Sant' Eusebio, not far from Stazione Termini (Also Santa Bibiana, alongside Stazione Termini)
Saturday:	San Nicolo in Carcere, near the Tiber Island
Fifth Sunday in Lent: St Peter's	
Monday:	San Crisogono, in Trastevere
Tuesday:	The Station should be in Santa Maria in Via Lata, but for some years it has been transferred elsewhere.
Wednesday:	San Marcello in the Corso
Thursday:	Sant' Apollinare, near the Piazza Navona. (Also Santa Maria Nuova, by the Colosseum)
Friday:	The Station should be in San Stefano Rotondo, on the Coelian, but for some years it has been transferred elsewhere.
Saturday:	San Giovanni a Porta Latina (Also San Cesareo near the Baths of Caracalla, and Sant' Agnese on the Via Nomentana)
Palm Sunday:	St John Lateran.
Monday of Holy Week: Santa Prassede, near St Mary Major's	
Tuesday:	Santa Prisca, on the Aventine (Also Santa Maria in Campitelli, near the Theatre of Marcellus, San Saba on the Aventine, and Santa Maria del Popolo, in the Piazza del Popolo)
Wednesday:	St Mary Major's
Holy Thursday:	St John Lateran
Good Friday:	Holy Cross in Jerusalem
Holy Saturday:	St John Lateran
Easter Sunday:	St Mary Major's

CHAPTER 31

Journeys from Rome

*The Alban Hills – Divino Amore, a shrine of Our Lady –
The Excavations at Ostia – The Madonna of the Crags at
Castel Sant' Elia – Monte Soratte – Anzio and Nettuno;
Pilgrimage to St Maria Goretti and Our Lady of Graces –
The Franciscan Shrines around Rieti – Subiaco, the Shrine
of St Benedict, and Tivoli – Genazzano and its Shrine of
Our Lady of Good Counsel – Orvieto, a Pilgrimage for
Corpus Domini – Assisi, the Shrine of St Francis*

THE ALBAN HILLS

They rise south of Rome, encircling two beautiful lakes – Albano
and Nemi – which were once volcanic craters. Nestling among
them are the towns – it's completely misleading of English
guide-books to call them villages – known as the 'Castelli
Romani'. Three are bishops' sees: Frascati, Albano, and Velletri.
Coach tours to the *castelli* may allow you glimpses of both lakes,
of the towns of Albano, Arriccia, Castel Gandolfo with the Pope's
country villa, Genzano famous for its Corpus Christi flower
carpets, Frascati noted for its wine, and for palatial villas of the
Roman nobility, and perhaps also the Greek Abbey of Grottaferrata.

If you are not taking an organized coach trip but have your
own transport, read this chapter, have a map at your elbow,
and take your choice. Should you depend on public transport
you must be more selective, although the services are fast and
frequent. This is what you could reasonably attempt:

1. Metro and bus to Castel Gandolfo, stroll round part of Lake
   Albano, lunch at a country trattoria; bus to Rocca di Papa,
   climb Monte Cavo and have tea at the restaurant on the
   summit.

2. Metro and bus to Genzano and walk round Lake Nemi
   (either direction). You could lunch at Nemi and return by
   bus from there or from Genzano, or take a bus from
   Genzano in the afternoon to Velletri, returning thence
   direct to Rome.

3. Metro and bus to Frascati, stroll out to the Franciscan

Friary, or further to the Camaldolese hermitage; take an afternoon bus to Grottaferrata and return thence direct to Rome.

On a half-day you could attempt part of those programmes. A map is helpful if you are travelling from one place to another, and good maps are hard to come by in Rome, so I suggest you keep an open mind and cheerfully accept any variations you have to make in your route.

Bus services now depart from Anagnina, on the Metropolitana (Underground) Line B.

Most pilgrims feel they must see Castel Gandolfo, so well known as the pope's summer residence. Pope John never favoured the villa. This charming little town gives you the best view over Lake Albano, so you need not imagine a visit is necessary to the town of Albano in order to see the lake; it is in fact over the crest of the hill. Albano has the usual features of interest – Roman theatre and churches, but none the less does not rate high among the *castelli* and I am not recommending it.

Castel Gandolfo

At Castel Gandolfo the bus will deposit you outside the town gate. Through it is the façade of the palace, the town piazza with a fountain, and a handsome church by Bernini. There are souvenir shops and cafés, restaurants and wine cellars. Castel Gandolfo, though obviously geared to tourist traffic, remains agreeably unspoilt. There is really little to do, because the palace is not normally open to visitors – except of course that audiences may be arranged when the Holy Father is in residence. Here is a place best enjoyed by doing nothing gracefully. To the left, as you stand with your back to the palace, there are terraces with grand views over the lake, some 430 feet below. Papal residence here dates only from the seventeenth century.

Lake Albano

Lake Albano, like that of Nemi, is a volcanic crater, fed by subterranean springs. The level of the lake has been controlled for over two thousand years by an 'emissarium' or outlet tunnel excavated through the hillside that empties water onto the plain below Albano. It should be possible to walk through the tunnel, made by Roman engineers some three centuries before Christ. If you are interested in seeing just the entrance to this amazing relic of antiquity, leave the town through the gate and bear right down the hillside. Follow the lakeside road to the right and the emissarium may be found some distance before the end of the road, signposted but not very clearly. The attendant who

25. View over Lake Albano from Monte Cavo

operates it will admit you if he is about. Down at the lakeside too are facilities for boating and water sports.

It is possible to walk round the lake by footpath as far as the English College Villa, which you see straight across the lake from Castel Gandolfo. However, if ·losing your way would worry you, don't attempt this. The route is straight through the town, passing a number of quiet boarding houses and the Propaganda College country villa – where Stations of the Cross flank the road. At the T junction, with a Franciscan monastery beyond, turn left, and take the footpath leading off to the left after a few yards. From Castel Gandolfo to the Villa is about an hour and a half's walk. The only control of the path that I can suggest is that it keeps a fairly level altitude above the lake, and for some distance after leaving the road you should notice to the right slight remains of an ancient aqueduct gallery. Where you gain the main road after the English Villa, cross it to catch a bus direct to Rome, or take a bus in the other direction to Rocca di Papa for a more frequent return service.

You can also reach the Villa more easily by following the lake in the other direction. That way you pass the Centre of the Movement for a Better World (*Migliore Mundo*), an apostolate led by the Jesuit preacher Father Lombardi with conspicuous success in some parts of Latin America. The Centre was a gift from Italian Catholic Action to Pius XII – and from him to the Movement. If you are interested, you will be welcome.

English College Villa

It is possible to stay at the English College Villa – 'Pallazuola' – during the holidays. The church is that of a thirteenth-century Cistercian monastery, and there are cloisters and a delightful terraced garden. Further down the steep flank of the hill are remains of an ancient hermitage dedicated to St Michael.

Superstitious beliefs hang about Lakes Albano and Nemi. Some years ago the headless body of a girl was found in the woods that clothe the walls of the crater that is now Lake Albano. The following morning the surface of the lake was thick with a red weed risen from the bottom that gave it the semblance of a sea of blood. So I am told.

Monte Cavo

To reach the summit of Monte Cavo – about 3,000 feet above sea level – you should either take a bus to Rocca di Papa and follow a direct path, or you may find someone to show you an alternative route from near the English College Villa. Tracks converge near the summit and you follow the remarkably preserved Roman road made for processions from the Temple of Diana by Lake Nemi to the Temple of Jove on the summit. The slopes are pleasantly wooded and the views delightful. The restaurant that replaces the shrine to Jove was formerly a Passionist Monastery built by the Stuart pretender Henry IX of England, otherwise Cardinal Henry Duke of York. The climb makes a bracing walk on a chill day in spring or autumn, and when you are ensconced by the open log fire with a pot of tea and a lavish helping of *dolce* (cake), you can look up and realize that you are taking afternoon tea in church. On the way up to the summit, by the way, you may pass a wayside shrine with a painting of the Face of Christ so cunningly done that the eyes, as you contemplate it, appear to open and close. The walk up Monte Cavo is not beyond any reasonably active person taking time.

The Madonna del Tufo

A short walk from Rocca di Papa, beside the road towards Lake Albano and the English College Villa at Pallazuola, there is a shrine to Our Lady under the title of Madonna del Tufo – 'tufo' being the rock of Monte Cavo in the sanctuary, from which a prayer to the Mother of God is said to have protected travellers. The church is neither modern, nor old, nor interesting.

Frascati

The visit to Frascati is to be recommended, but bear in mind that it is away from the lakes.

I am inclined to compare Frascati with Richmond. Its lofty position, views, parks, palaces, and general air of well-being all contribute to this – it only lacks the river. Characteristic are the beautiful villas of the Roman aristocracy, but they are not generally accessible to the public. Then of course it is the centre of the vineyards that produce the best-known table wine of Rome – you ask for 'Frascati' when you don't want to pay too much and can't think of anything else. The cellars (*cantine* – in the singular *cantina*) seem to sell wine all the day round, either in underground vaults or at terrace tables. This is the popular attraction of Frascati, both for local Italians and even for sophisticated tourists. Then if you are very English (or even Scots) with an angle on history you will want to visit the cathedral of that last of the Stuarts, Henry Cardinal Duke of York, sometimes called Henry IX. You could undertake a walk (uphill) through beautiful woodland, calling at the Franciscan Friary, and ending up either at the ancient site of Tusculum – old Frascati – or at the Camaldolese hermitage-monastery. There is your choice of interest if you propose to spend a day at Frascati.

There are six villas, in renaissance and baroque styles, with beautiful parks. It is possible to visit some by application at the estate offices here or in Rome, but most visitors are content with the glimpses they have of them in their walks or rides through this lovely wooded countryside. From the main terrace at Frascati you can look out to the sea, to Rome, to distant ranges of mountains; behind you the stately Villa Aldobrandini, built in the reign of our Queen Elizabeth I, nestles among trees, its characteristic feature that daringly 'broken' pediment. Some of the carriage drivers waiting for custom by the terrace seem to have permits to enter the grounds and will offer to take you to see the waterfalls, and further up in the hills to Tusculum – make sure you fix the fee. Frascati horses wear feather head-dresses like red Indians.

The Cathedral is a little to the left of the terrace as you face the Villa Aldobrandini. Close by the main doors you will see the British royal arms and a memorial to Prince Charles Edward (Karolus Odoardus is what you read) and Henry Duke of York, bishop of Frascati. It records that Bonnie Prince Charlie was buried here, and so he was, till he was transferred to the crypt of St Peter's where he lies with the Old Pretender (James III) and the Cardinal Duke (Henry IX). Not far distant is the Church of the Gesù (Holy Name of Jesus) by the architect Pietro da Cortona, rich with painting.

Either side of the Cathedral are narrow formal gardens running uphill. Follow the one to the right and it will take you along a pretty lane to the gate of the Aldobrandini Villa. Continue uphill – by the track, not by the tarmacked road – and a cordonata, a stepped lane, leads off on the left to the Capuchin Franciscan monastery, founded in 1611. If you ring the bell a friar will show you, on request, a museum of Ethiopian interest, and the rooms occupied by Cardinal Massaia, a Franciscan missionary in Ethiopia, who died in 1889. On one of the documents exhibited you will find Mussolini's signature.

The friary church has a painting of the Holy Family attributed to Giulio Romano, pupil of Raphael – notice, once you have found a good position, the attractive architectural background of a curved colonnade. Across the nave is St Francis receiving the stigmata in a landscape setting characteristic of the Flemish Paul Brill. Beside this picture is the tomb of Cardinal Massaia with a remarkable statue of him, seated, that revolves – you can move it with your hand. Watch the Cardinal's eyes. I know of no other monumental revolving tomb!

Tusculum and Camaldoli

Uphill again, by the main road this time, Tusculum may be reached. It is an ancient city of which the Romans slew or mutilated all the inhabitants in the eleventh century. For an alternative, you may visit Camaldoli, a hermitage monastery. Both are signposted and not far distant. There is not much at Tuscolo of a monumental nature, but take care to go up as far as the cross if you wish to see everything. On a fine day the views are wonderful, and it is a pleasant site for a picnic. The hermitage monastery is occupied by the Camaldolese Order which is similar to the Carthusians; that is to say, each monk has his own little house, but certain services are attended in common.

You could take a bus from Frascati to Grottaferrata – a few minutes ride – or travel there direct from Rome. This is a pleasant little town well worth visiting for its Greek Catholic Abbey.

The survival of a monastery of Byzantine rite in communion with the Holy See, with nearly a thousand years of unbroken history, is splendid witness to Catholic unity. It bears witness also to the fact, which ought to be considered more carefully, that Catholics using the Greek language and the Byzantine liturgy existed in Italy before the schism between the Pope and the Patriarch of Constantinople – a division traced to misunder-standings of 1058, but which in our time both Pope and Patriarch have solemnly repudiated.

The Greek Abbey of Grottaferrata

In Sicily and the south of Italy there are populations of Greek origin which have never lost their ancient rite – the same as that used by the Greek Orthodox Church. In the eleventh century they were subject to persecution by Saracen invaders, and a band of refugee monks under the abbot St Nilus travelled north in 1004. It is important to point out that a number of Eastern communities had by this time established themselves in Rome as a consequence of persecution at home. The ailing abbot settled in the Alban Hills, where he was given the site of a Roman villa near which there stood, perhaps already used as a Christian chapel, an ancient tomb with barred windows – the *grotta ferrata* (cave with iron bars) that became the first chapel of the monastery and is incorporated in the present stately church. Abbot Nilus died within the year.

The Abbey of Grottaferrata was completed by its founder's favourite disciple and second successor, St Bartholomew. Much of the fabric of the church is his, and some of the detail. Of course, it would be foolish to pretend that these Italo-Greek monks have never been subjected to Latin influence; it is indeed remarkable that they have survived at all as a community with their own rites and traditions. The abbey church today is an interesting blend of Byzantine and Latin in art, but every effort has been made, especially in recent years, to preserve the purity of the liturgy.

You approach the abbey along the main street of Grottaferrata – and should you manage to do this on the feast of the Annunciation, 25th March, you will thread your way through the busy market that celebrates the annual festa. At first sight, the monastery could be taken for a castle. Those massive artillery fortifications were provided to protect the community by Cardinal Giuliano della Rovere between 1483 and 1491, probably to designs by the architect Baccio Pontelli.

As you enter the narthex (porch), stand back to appreciate the wonderful door; part of the eleventh-century church, it is called *Porta Speciosa*, the Beautiful Door. The sculpture of jambs and lintel is a pattern of beasts and foliage and acanthus leaves, with an inscription in Greek reminding you to leave earthly thoughts behind. Of the same date is the door of cedar wood and the mosaic above that represents Christ between Mary and St John the Baptist – in the East especially John the Baptist is regarded as the link between monasticism of the Old Testament and that of the New. The kneeling figure probably represents Abbot St Bartholomew.

The interior of the church is very much altered by baroque additions – a Farnese cardinal added the ceiling, a Barberini the sculptures above the iconostasis (a sanctuary screen characteristic of the Byzantine liturgy). These angels venerating the thirteenth-century icon of Our Lady of Grottaferrata – it may be older – are by Bernini. They are represented in attitudes of prayer appropriate to East and West: folded and joined hands. Some of the later ornamentation has been removed in the interests of restoring the Greek character of the church, especially since 1910.

If you see a monk, you might ask him to open the doors of the iconostasis and show you the hanging dove in which the Blessed Sacrament is reserved under the species of bread and wine – an Eastern tradition that was common in the West as well down to the Reformation.

Above the chancel arch is a mosaic of special interest. It represents apostles seated either side an empty throne. You will notice they hold scrolls, except for the evangelists Mark and John (second to the left of the throne, and third to the right) who are distinguished by their bound Gospel books. From the starry firmament overhead rays of light touch the head of each apostle to indicate the inspiration of the Holy Ghost, and the empty throne reminds them of the promise of Christ to return at the end of time. This mosaic is assigned to about the end of the thirteenth century.

A chapel entered from the right of the nave received its present decoration in 1610, the gift of Cardinal Farnese. Its frescoes by Domenichino represent a miracle of St Nilus – the cure of a possessed girl by means of oil burning before an icon of the Madonna; the building of the church by Abbot Bartholomew, and the meeting of the Emperor Otto III with St Nilus – in these last two the detail is worth special attention.

On the right side of the church, near the door, is the primitive 'iron-barred cave' given to Abbot Nilus, from which Grottaferrata takes its name. It has been beautifully furnished in a style appropriate to the Byzantine rite. Finally, on no account miss the baptismal font, almost a mystery for its expert employment of early Christian themes. The 'man fishing' can be found in the

catacombs – in that of St Callixtus, for instance – and also in the
third-century mosaic discovered under St Peter's. It represents
Christ with obvious allusion to baptismal water. While the date
of the font remains uncertain, it has been suggested that it is
older than the abbey itself.

You may ask to see the remains of a Roman villa and also, at
certain times, an interesting museum. There is a souvenir shop
where I hope you will at least buy a memento of your pilgrimage
to Our Lady of Grottaferrata – there are reproductions of the
icon. Slides of the Greek liturgy celebrated at the abbey can also
be brought here. At Epiphany there is a solemn function in
honour of Christ's baptism celebrated at the fountain in the
courtyard.

There is also a catacomb at Grottaferrata, known as 'Ad
Decimum'. Discovered early this century, it is not generally
open to the public, but an annual function is arranged here by
the Greek community and the *Collegium Cultorum Martyrum*
(College for the Veneration of the Martyrs), which has an office
at Via Napoleone III, near St Mary Major's in Rome.

Lake Nemi

South of Lake Albano lies Lake Nemi, another crater of the same
extinct volcanic system. As soon as its steep walls slope to the
shore they are industriously terraced as flower gardens and
strawberry beds – the best time to visit Nemi is the spring.

Genzano, the west wall of the crater, is easily reached by
coaches that continue either to Nemi or Velletri, and from there
pleasant walks may be taken round the lake to Nemi town. The
easier route is to climb streets to the Palazzo at Genzano and
then take a lane to the left. This is suitable for cars but not
coaches. Walkers can take a choice of footpaths. For leisurely
progress, allow and hour and a half to Nemi on foot.

Genzano by the way – and no more will be said about it – is
noted for carpeting a whole street with flowers for Corpus
Christi (which Italians know as 'Corpus Domini'), and also for
restaurants where you are served game. Remember that if you
should choose to come here for Corpus Christi you would have
to forgo Orvieto.

In ancient times Diana, goddess of the chase, was worshipped
on the shores of Nemi. Signposts still direct you to the ruins of
her temple, but you won't find them – farmers have dug them
over. A priestly road led from her shrine to the top of Monte
Cavo. You can trace it in places through the woods, and as you
approach the summit it remains in almost perfect condition.

There is a bloodthirsty history of a priest-king of Nemi,
custodian of Diana's temple. To acquire this rank you had to be

a runaway slave and murder the priest already in office. You were then secure from the claims of your former master but, of course, exposed to the intimate attentions of any would-be successor, some other runaway slave who shared your ambitions. Read about this in Fraser's *Golden Bough*.

Sunken in the lake for centuries were two Roman galleys of extraordinarily luxurious appointments, enriched with work in marble, mosaic, and bronze. Attempts were made to retrieve them from 1496 on; success came only in 1928 when the lake was drained of 40,000,000 cubic metres of water. These masterpieces of antiquity were destroyed by wanton vandalism of the occupying power during the last war.

Nemi itself is a charming little town clustered round its massive fifteenth-century fortress-palace, with highly photogenic twisting streets seldom explored by visitors. There are two churches. The smaller, on the piazza near the bus terminus, belongs to the Mercedarian friars (who look like Dominicans) and over its altar is preserved a venerated crucifix carved by a Franciscan brother in 1669. Normally veiled, it is exposed on Sundays and Fridays while the church is open.

Above Nemi is the modern house of the Divine Word Fathers, where missionaries come for refresher courses. Designed by the Swiss architect Galizia, it is a fascinating instance of adaptation to a narrow site. The church has a sweeping concave roof which nowhere rests on the walls, but only on the concrete frame. Unusual stained-glass effects are achieved by overlaying several thicknesses. The dignity of the immense sheer wall behind the altar can only be appreciated in the course of a solemn liturgy. This Divine Word house is not of course open to visitors, but anyone seriously interested should ask at least to see the church.

Below the castle rock at Nemi is an interesting hermitage chapel dedicated to St Michael with altar and baldachino supported by antique columns that may have come from the ruins of Diana's Temple. The direct path from the village is hazardous, and to find the easier route it would be as well to hire the services of a village lad who knows the cave (I used to think this kind of advice occurred only in nineteenth-century guide-books). As it makes a good picnicking ground even if you miss the hermitage I shall attempt to describe the route. Pass through the palace archway, down the terrace overlooking the lake and through the further gate, where you may encounter the municipal garbage tip. Immediately a good cobbled path descends to the left. Take this as far as a red waterworks building, which you leave to your right, following a neat terrace several hundred yards long. At the end a track goes down, but

you look for one going up, which brings you within minutes –
as you round the bluff – to the locality of the cave. The cave is
at the foot of the undercliff, above a group of mimosa trees, if
you know how to recognize them.

On the tip of the castle rock, signposted from the piazza and
approached through Nemi's narrowest streets, is a terrace
restaurant which is the ideal place to eat at Nemi, the Trattoria
'Sirena del Lago'. It makes the day.

Velletri

I think Velletri deserves a mention, although it is the Cinderella
of the Alban Hills, remote from both wooded heights and lakes.
Although you go down to Velletri, it is none the less a hill town,
resting on a terrace which overlooks a plain to the distant Lepini
Hills. The cathedral has great charm, and its romanesque crypt
has been recently excavated and restored.

DIVINO AMORE – A ROMAN SHRINE OF OUR LADY

I should not like to bring anyone out to Divino Amore in the
expectation that he is going to see anything really remarkable.
It is just a characteristic small shrine to Our Lady of Divine Love,
full of ex-votos from the grateful, but with no vision as its origin
and no wide reputation for the miraculous. But it certainly is
the best loved country shrine of the Romans – it was to this
Madonna they turned in their dark hour of need during the last
war.

Apart from the chapel on the hill, the establishments of the
religious communities that have been founded here and named
after it, and a few modest eating places, Castel di Leva is hardly
a place. The shrine does justify a bus service, which runs from
the Lateran, following one route, and also from the Porta San
Paolo – the stop is outside the gate, at the beginning of the Via
Ostiense; a timetable is billed up and the buses are marked
'Divino Amore'. If you are anxious to make a real pilgrimage,
assemble on a Saturday night (summer months only), at
midnight, by the obelisk of Axum, an Ethiopian trophy from
Mussolini's war in Abyssinia, near the Circo Massimo Metropolitana (Underground) Station and just outside the Food and
Agriculture Office (FAO to Italians). Each week a group marches
by night to reach the shrine in time for early Mass – men only,
I think!

Pass through the courtyard and enter the eighteenth-century
chapel; the venerated painting is above the altar. To the right of
the courtyard steps lead down to the more recently constructed
crypt. An electric light switch in the apse will show up quite
pleasant modern mosaics. Flanking Christ to the left is a pilgrim,

beset by dogs, appealing to a Madonna painted over a castle gate. This incident in 1740 was the origin of a devotion to a medieval fresco of Mary with her Divine Child painted on the gatehouse of Castel di Leva – the gate, from which the painting has been removed and brought up to a chapel built to receive it, still exists and can be seen by taking steps that lead down behind the church. A picture to the right of the figure of Christ represents Pius XII who turned to the Madonna of Divino Amore when Rome was threatened with destruction in the course of the war. There is, by the way, a great fresco of his prayer in the parish church of Garbatella, not far from St Paul's outside the Walls.

It would not be wise to count on getting a satisfactory full meal at Divino Amore, but those with a car could continue their outing to the coast at Ostia, or to Anzio and Nettuno, or inland to Castel Gandolfo and the Alban Hills.

THE EXCAVATIONS AT OSTIA

If you are keen on ruins – and would like to see some even better than the Forum, if not up to the level of those at Pompeii or Herculaneum – you should spend half a day at Ostia 'Scavi' (excavations). At the same time you will be making a pilgrimage to the memory of St Augustine and his mother St Monica. Trains run to 'Ostia Scavi' from the Underground platforms at Stazione Termini and from the Station at Porta San Paolo. From other Metropolitana (Line B) stations you can take any train, changing at Magliana. Trains are fairly frequent. It may be prudent, however, to ascertain that the excavations are in fact open; they have been known to close for weeks at a time. Visits in winter are less interesting, as the mosaics are covered with sand to protect them from frost. In late summer the perfume of herbs among the ruins is enchanting. The ruins are a most pleasant place for a picnic, but there are trattorias between the station and the scavi if you wish to eat out.

Ostia was the port of Rome from about 300 B.C. to about 300 A.D., after which it fell into disuse. It is situated beside the Tiber and was originally on the coast. The sea receded – and the actual port had to follow it. The great harbours of Claudius and Trajan have not been properly excavated; their remains lie on private property between Ostia Scavi and the new Fiumicino airport. Ostia in its heyday was Rome's entrepôt and the seat of Rome's food supply. The most important and characteristic of its buildings are the great granaries for the storing of grain. Ostia means 'gate' – gate to Rome, but as the sea receded and commerce gathered around the docks a new centre arose named Porto (port), to which Constantine transferred the municipal rights of Ostia in 314. Today Porto too has disappeared, and if Ostia really has a successor today it is the pleasant little harbour of Fiumicino.

When you enter the excavations at the ticket office, bear in mind that you are not yet among the ruins of the city. A city of the dead precedes the city of the living. The ancient paving stones under your feet are the old road from Rome, the Via Ostiense, leading to the Porta Romana – the Rome Gate of Ostia. The ruins either side are those of tombs and mausolea. Soon you reach vestiges of the walls and gate, which you can easily miss if you are not observant. Interesting sites, however, can be identified by framed drawings of reconstructions hanging nearby. These not only enable you to picture things as they were, but also to understand what may remain of them. You will know you have entered the city when you find more regular remains beside the road, and on the right an interesting mosaic or two.

You will soon notice to your right a more substantial ruin with steps up to a first floor. From the platform you have excellent views over the Baths of Neptune, with great black and white mosaics of sea animals and mythical figures. On a fine day there

26. *Mosaic from the Baths of Neptune at Ostia*

is a pleasant outlook towards the coast and the Alban Hills. A little further up the road and you find on your right the theatre, a massive first-century structure in part preserved and in part well restored – it is still sometimes used for drama. There is a refreshment bar here and other amenities. Notice, between the theatre and the road, remains of an early Christian shrine to martyrs of Ostia executed at this spot.

Behind the theatre is the Square of the Corporations, a vast piazza surrounded by a colonnaded walk onto which opened the offices of the merchants of the Mediterranean world. Mosaic pavements in front of each office carried – and in most cases still do carry – subjects indicating their place of origin. They are mostly made up of lighthouses, ships, fishes, and animals, or produce. In the middle of the piazza is a temple to Ceres, goddess of crops – appropriate to this centre of trade.

From this point on it is no longer practical to attempt description of a route through the ruins of Ostia. You may read what follows, and then, wandering at leisure, try to recognize what is described, or identify other buildings of the same type, or if you are really keen you should equip yourself with the English edition of the official guide. But even that needs study prior to your visit. I shall mention one or more examples of each major type of building to be found here.

Most of the inhabitants of Ostia lived in apartments, as Romans still do. Their maximum height was four storeys. The ground floor opening onto the street was shops, with a mezzanine floor above, where the shopkeeper had a loft to which he climbed by a wooden staircase. The courtyards often have small shrines to gods and in several cases, in the block itself, there is a Mithraic temple. A good instance of all this is the Casa di Diana, off a turning on the right some distance after you leave the theatre. Off the Via della Foce, however, there are three blocks which, unless you study a reconstruction, appear to be one. This consists of the Insula (word used at Ostia to designate an apartment block) di Serapide, named after a shrine to Egyptian Serapis in the courtyard, the Baths of the Seven Sages with excellent mosaics and paintings, and the Insula degli Aurighi, named after very competent paintings of charioteers on the ground floor.

Near the Casa di Diana and in the same street a building with an interesting overhanging upper storey, the Thermopolium, is a food shop or small restaurant. There are paintings of dishes of food over the counter. Apart from this the best shops known to me at Ostia are a couple of fishmongers with nice clean marble slabs to cut up fish and mosaic floors representing the trade.

27. *An apartment house intact to the first floor in the Street of the Charioteers,*
Ostia

There are a number of houses of the villa type, homes of the
well-to-do, such as you may recall from first chapters of a Latin
primer. One of the best is the Domus di Amore e Psyche. The
Domus dei Pesci (house of the fishes) has a charming mosaic of
fish and a cup which has led to the suggestion that it is
Christian. The house of the Dioscuri, if you can find it, has
perhaps the best mosaics. The name 'domus' at Ostia is given
to these houses of the villa type.

For social life I suggest you look at the School of Trajan,
premises of a rich commercial association. There are vestiges of
a fine concave pillared façade, a spacious courtyard with
fountains, shrines to the gods, offices, and banqueting halls.

The Capitol of Ostia, principal city temple, is something you
won't mistake. Robbed of its marble and pillared glory, it looks

today like a scarred old Norman keep. It is worth climbing the steps to look down on the Forum and across the ruins of the city generally.

Not far from the School of Trajan is the Christian basilica. It was adapted from a bath house in the fourth century, Ostia's period of decline. The identification as a church is made with every confidence from the inscription on a lintel at the end of the left aisle: IN CHRISTO GEON FISON TIGRIS EUFRATA CHRIST-IANORUM SUMITE FONTES, not an easy text, but the third to sixth words are the names of the rivers of paradise, clearly taken as symbolic of baptism – Gihon, Phison, Tigris and Euphrates. Perhaps the adaptation from a bath house led to a baptistery in an unusual position.

Here, you can be almost certain, Augustine came to Mass with his mother Monica, when they were waiting for a ship to take them home to Africa. Monica caught the fever from which she died, to the intense grief of Augustine that he admits so touchingly and eloquently in his *Confessions* – a book worth bringing to Rome with you so that you can read the appropriate chapters here at Ostia. Perhaps it was in an apartment block you have visited that Augustine stood with his mother at an open window, looking across to the Tiber, and talking of the things of God. Perhaps it was in the Bath of the Seven Sages that Augustine took the hot bath that released his tears.

On the Tiber side of the ruins, behind the Capitol, is an excellent museum that should only be omitted if you are really short of time.

Monica was buried at Ostia, presumably in a Christian cemetery, and Augustine asked a friend to write an epitaph which has come down to us in Christian literature. Some years ago, excavating near the little renaissance church of St Aurea in the village, a fragment of an inscription was found – a part of Monica's epitaph. The church of St Aurea was obviously founded in the Christian cemetery. You will find that fragment on the wall of a chapel to the right. The relics of St Monica have long since been transferred to Sant' Agostino at Rome.

St Aurea's church is in the little walled village that was medieval Ostia, a few yards from the papal artillery fort, built by the popes in the late fifteenth century to defend the river. As a result of heavy flooding in the sixteenth century the Tiber moved some distance away and rendered the castle useless. This Castle of Ostia may be visited.

Finally, if you have your own transport, it is possible to take the road to Fiumicino; leave your vehicle – unless it is just a car – at the signpost on the right to Isola Sacra, and walk a few hundred yards to the excavated remains of the first-to-third-century cemetery of Porto. It gives you a clear idea what the burial ground under St Peter's was like before Constantine filled it in to construct his basilica. Towards the end of the enclosure a mausoleum on the left, with steps to the upper floor, has a charming mosaic and sculptured sarcophagi. Some mausolea have terracotta mouldings over the doors representing the trade or profession of the deceased – for instance, on the extreme left near the entrance is a doctor performing an operation. The excellent preservation of this site is due to its having been covered by windswept sand.

THE MADONNA OF THE CRAGS AT CASTEL SANT' ELIA

The 'Madonna ad Rupes', in a ravine near Nepi, about an hour and a half north of Rome by bus, is certainly off the tourist map. Frankly, there is not so much to see, but given a fine day you will find this devotional little shrine a relief from the crowded stir of Roman life and its immediate setting a panorama of haunting beauty.

The bus service – from Castro Pretorio – is limited, so it should be enquired about in advance. Some buses go only as far as Nepi, but you can walk the extra mile and a half to the shrine. Others set you down at the gates of the Franciscan Friary. At the end of the drive a door admits you to a staircase cut in the soft volcanic rock by which you descend 144 steps to a terrace overlooking a lovely ravine. To the right you can see the churches of Nepi crowning the crags on which the town is built, and to the left Monte Soratte, crowned by an ancient basilica of St Sylvester and a shrine of Our Lady, rises in solitary dignity from the plain.

Opening off the terrace is a shrine chapel of Our Lady cut in the rock. It was given its present form towards the end of the eighteenth century by Brother Joseph Rodio, a Franciscan tertiary hermit, who was advised to establish himself here by St Benedict Joseph Labre, the pilgrim tramp of the Colosseum. At that time there was no monastery at the top of the cliff, the staircase did not exist, and the cave-chapel of Our Lady, and a few other caverns around it, were abandoned relics of a monastery established in the fifth century in the ravine below. It was Brother Joseph's idea to enlarge the shrine and provide easier access by cutting the stairs – all the work of his own hands. German Franciscans now occupy the monastery and serve the shrine. Adjacent to the chapel is a shop where you may buy souvenirs, and also a small museum of very early vestments, some twelfth century.

You may ask to return to the top of the cliff by terraced paths that will lead you out through the monastery gardens and vineyards, or you may borrow two keys, one to the 'saints' road', a perfectly safe cliff track that takes you down to the tenth-century basilica, abbey church of the former monastery, full of beautiful frescoes. This is no longer regularly used for worship, though I have heard Mass sung here, and oddly enough it was in English, for it was the first Mass of a newly ordained American.

If you have time to spare it is worth calling to see the beautifully restored Romanesque crypt of Nepi Cathedral, and in the Campo Santo (cemetery), just outside the town, there is a small catacomb – a feature very rare away from Rome.

I know of no adequate restaurant at Castel St Elia and doubt whether you would find much at Nepi either, so this trip recommends itself to those who can enjoy a picnic. There is a terrace just below the entrance to the sanctuary with special accommodation for this purpose. On the other hand, if you have your own car you could return via Civita Castellana and Monte Soratte, described next – both places have better facilities for eating out.

MONTE SORATTE

Monte Soratte is one of the most distinctive mountains I have ever seen. Perhaps in terms of mere altitude (just over 2,000 feet) it isn't a mountain, but I think its appearance warrants that description. Approaching from Rome by train or road the view is admittedly mediocre – it should be seen from the Sabines, at for instance Montopoli, or from Castel St Elia. Its outline is a little reminiscent of the spine of a cow having a siesta, and there is in fact a good ridge walk along that spine.

Trains to Sant' Oreste leave from a terminus called Roma Nord outside the Porta del Popolo. The station is about three miles from the town of that name, which is part way up the mountain. Some trains are met by a bus, and others replaced by a bus all the way from Rome. If you come by your own transport, follow the Via Flaminia as far as Sant' Oreste station and then turn off right. On the way – a distance of about thirty miles – you could visit several interesting hill towns. Look out, too, for traces of the ancient Via Flaminia beside the modern road.

Sant' Oreste town is not important. From the terrace a track leads up to the Shrine of Our Lady of Graces – not too stiff a climb of a little over half an hour. This chapel was built in 1506 but its Madonna, a fresco, is older, brought here from a neighbouring hermitage oratory in 1721. Franciscans, Cistercians, Lateran Canons, Trinitarians, Theatines and Sons of Divine Providence have all had their turn at caring for the

28. *One of the many medieval votive paintings on the abandoned basilica at Castel Sant' Elia*

shrine. Perhaps they gave it up because it is apt to be snowbound for weeks in winter. At one time it was offered to the Quarr Benedictines.

You may have borrowed from the priests at Sant' Oreste keys not only to the shrine but also the venerable church on the summit, some few hundred yards further. You would probably not recognize that crude mass of masonry as a church, but the interior is impressive, with interesting medieval frescoes and sculpture of the ninth century or earlier. In the crypt is the cave where St Sylvester lived in the fourth century, till he was summoned to Rome as pope. The abbey of monks that once lived here moved downhill to Our Lady of Graces. Mass is still offered at St Sylvester's on the saint's feast, 31st December.

Beyond the church you may succeed in locating a track that follows the ridge, and makes a very pleasant walk with splendid views. The building in the distance is described on maps as a bandits' lookout.

In spring and autumn (in summer the paths are inclined to be overgrown) you can ask at Sant' Oreste to be shown the way downhill to the hermitage of St Romana. She was a lady hermit who used to climb the mountain daily to consult Sylvester, who got tired of this. One winter he forbade her to come back 'until the roses bloom again'. Next day he saw her plodding as usual up the track and prepared to administer stiff words of correction. The fact was, however (so the old tale relates), that Romana had woken up to find her hermitage garden under a thick mantle of snow, in the midst of which had miraculously blossomed one bush of fresh and fragrant roses. If you can find the hermitage, it is most interesting, with an ancient baldachino where an altar once stood and several paintings, including a charming Madonna, probably of the fifteenth century – over the inner door. The last hermit died in 1866 and is said to have been buried here.

There are potholes nearby.

ANZIO AND NETTUNO – A DAY AT THE COAST – PILGRIMAGE TO ST MARIA GORETTI AND OUR LADY OF GRACES

Anzio and Nettuno lie side by side on the coast some forty miles south of Rome. Anzio is modern, with shipping, hotels, and bathing; Nettuno is old-world and boasts two celebrated shrines in one church. There is a train service from Stazione Termini. If you have a car I suggest you take the Via Cristoforo Colombo to Castel Fusano and then follow the sea road.

Anzio achieved fame in the last war as an Allied bridgehead in Italy, but the United States Forces Cemetery is nearer Nettuno. Between the two towns, on the shore, is a fifteenth-century papal artillery fortress. Beyond you will notice – if you are walking along the sands – how Nettuno is still hugged by its medieval fortifications. By a third attempt I dare say you would guess that the name means 'Neptune', the old sea god. From Anzio, by the way, there are occasional sailings to the tiny island of Ponza.

On the further outskirts of Nettuno, by the sea, is the Sanctuary of Our Lady of Graces, where you will also find the shrine of St Maria Goretti. The church, served by the Passionist Fathers, is a rebuilding of an old shrine of Our Lady begun under St Pius X in 1912, and completed as a result of devotion to the child martyr of Nettuno, Maria Goretti.

This little peasant girl lived about six miles from Nettuno; you may visit the house at Le Ferriere. Still not yet twelve years old she resisted an assault by Alessandro Serenelli at the cost of her life, dying next day in the Orsenigo Hospital between Nettuno and Anzio. In 1950 Maria was canonized to promote esteem for purity among young people in the modern world. Her body rests under the altar of a new chapel to the right of the church, and in the sacristies there is an interesting and agreeably simple series of pictures illustrating her life and martyrdom. Her feast is celebrated at Nettuno on 6th July.

The reputation of this modern Agnes or Dorothy ought not to be allowed to obscure the Madonna of Graces, whose beautiful medieval statue is enshrined above the high altar. This is said to have been brought to Italy for safety from an English shrine at the Reformation – just as Our Lady of Aberdeen was taken to Brussels and has been venerated there ever since. This Madonna was on her way to Naples when storms forced the ship to take shelter here at Nettuno, a circumstance accepted as providential. On the Saturday before the first Sunday of May Our Lady is carried to the town church of San Giovanni to return in festal procession the next day.

THE FRANCISCAN SHRINES AROUND RIETI

It has been my experience that once you can persuade the pilgrim away from the beaten tourist track he really begins to enjoy himself. So I wish to press the claims of the 'Holy Valley of Rieti'. This quiet little town, about two hours bus ride north of Rome (bus departures from Via Palestra, near Termini Station), lies in a beautiful alluvial plain surrounded by mountains, among them the snow-capped Terminillo refreshing you with cool breezes. St Francis must have loved this place, and in return it cherishes his memory dearly. Every little hill is crowned with its Franciscan monastery. Four are woven intimately into the story of St Francis. At Greccio he set up his first Christmas crib, at Fonte Colombo he wrote the Rule, at La Foresta he sang his Canticle of the Sun, and from Poggio Bustone he sent out his first band of apostles.

The problem may be – what can be done in a day? If you have your own car or coach you could do all four, but it may be wiser to choose two or three. Otherwise you would need two nights based at Rieti. Still, a visit to Greccio at least, or to either Fonte Colombo or La Foresta, can easily be managed in a day. Local buses from Rieti run to Greccio and Fonte Colombo, and La Foresta is less than three miles uphill from the station and bus terminus.

The monasteries I am about to describe have all been restored, each retains the character of a small and simple friary, and there is much left to see just as it was in the time of the Poor Man of Assisi. Remember always to ask for a friar to guide you, or you may miss the things that matter most.

Some fifteen kilometres from Rieti, perched against the side of a wooded cliff, remains that cave-chapel at Greccio where Francis made the First Crib that Christendom had known for centuries. It was Christmas 1223. You will see besides the primitive dormitory and refectory, not to mention souvenirs of later Franciscan saints. There is a contemporary painting of Francis and fourteenth-century frescoes of the Nativity. Nearby a Franciscan Secular Institute runs a retreat house.

Much closer to Rieti, among wooded heights, is Fonte Colombo, known as the Franciscan Sinai, because it was here Francis wrote the Rule, living in a crevice between rocks. You may sit there and capture the unchanged mood of his retreat. In the fifteenth-century church is a beautiful sculpture of Christ approving his work: 'Nothing written in the Rule is yours; everything it contains is mine'. Friar John of Pisa made this in 1615, using wood of the tree beside which Christ appeared.

La Foresta looks like a picturesque cloistered farmhouse. Here Francis lay sick by the little Church of St Fabian, half blinded by his eye affliction and unable even to sleep. When visitors nearly stripped his host's vineyard, Francis promised that the remainder of the grapes would produce as much wine as ever, and so they did. Here too he composed his Canticle of the Sun.

Poggio Bustone is another characteristic friary suspended like a bird's nest under overhanging rocks.

SUBIACO, THE SHRINE OF ST BENEDICT, AND TIVOLI

Subiaco, about forty miles east of Rome and high up in the Simbruini mountains, is the place where St Benedict began his monastic life early in the sixth century: the cradle of monasticism – at least, as we know it in the West. Tivoli, on the same road but much nearer Rome, is a hill town with the famous renaissance water gardens of the Villa d'Este, and, in the plain below, ruins of the summer villa of the Emperor Hadrian. They would deservedly be the objects of two separate visits, but it is possible to see the Sacro Speco at Subiaco in the morning and Tivoli in the afternoon. At Easter and in mid-summer it is just as well to see the Villa d'Este gardens in the evening when they are floodlit.

Buses run frequently to Subiaco from the bus terminus at Castro Pretorio, a few minutes walk from Termini Station; the run takes nearly two hours. There is an occasional service from the town to the monastery, otherwise you hire a taxi or walk – half an hour uphill to the Abbey of Santa Scholastica, and for the Sacro Speco (Holy Cave of St Benedict, which is what you have really come to see) a further twenty minutes. If on foot you should look out for short-cuts on the left – after the bridge across the ravine – rather than follow the twisting car road.

St Benedict, at about eighteen years of age, ran away from studies in Rome to seek a life of solitude and prayer in these hills. In the lofty cliffs overlooking a great artificial lake – one of Rome's ancient reservoirs – he found this cave. Later he was persuaded to accept the leadership of disciples for whom he founded twelve small monasteries along this valley. Although there are fragmentary remains of most of them only one survives as a monastery, the Abbey of Santa Scholastica, dedicated to Benedict's sister. Since the eighth century, however, a small monastery, or rather a retreat for hermits, has been constructed against the cliff face, resting on enormous buttresses rising from the valley. This is called the monastery of St Benedict or the Sacro Speco. Apart from the significance as a site which few can rival for its influence on European, indeed on world culture, it is picturesque in the extreme and its chapels, staircases and galleries have been covered with frescoes by Byzantine, Roman, Sienese, and Umbrian artists over a thousand years.

It would be impossible to describe all these paintings here. A twelfth-century series by a Roman artist with the unmusical name of Conxolus is worth noting because it depicts the history of Benedict at Subiaco. Two or more by a fifteenth-century painter of the Umbrian school complete the series with incidents from Benedict's later days at Monte Cassino.

One of these you can see from inside the cave itself. You will need to locate the light switch, then stand with your back to the rock and look above the door. The subject is the young Benedict living at this very spot, while his friend the monk Romanus lowers to him from the cliff top a basket of food with a little bell attached. In the lower main church paintings of the same series represent Benedict with his young disciples Maurus and Placid. Placid goes down to the lake to draw water and falls in. Obedient to Benedict, Maurus runs to his rescue, not realizing till afterwards that he walked on the water. In another a Goth servant of the monastery (the Goths were invading barbarians at this time) loses his billhook in the lake; Benedict holds the haft underwater and the hook swims back to rejoin it. In some of these paintings, as indeed in early art at almost any time or place, you must appreciate that several parts of the same story, even several actions of the same person, are all woven into one picture.

In the upper main chapel, to the right of its beautiful cosmatesque altar, are the Umbrian paintings. The most interesting one represents St Scholastica at her last meeting with her brother Benedict. They used to have a meal together, once a year, somewhere near Cassino. On this occasion Scholastica begged her brother to spend the whole night with her in holy conversation. He refused, so she wept and prayed, and heaven sent such a deluge that Benedict understood that sometimes God prefers love and compassion to the mere keeping of regulations.

All the other paintings of the Sacro Speco are interesting. In one chapel there is a portrait of St Francis, most probably painted when he came here to assist as deacon at the consecration of an altar. The Lady Chapel has a delightful Nativity – note the shepherds especially. In the main chapel the Passion of Christ, on a vast scale, repays study – if you have time; it is a loss just to pass through. Of striking gentleness is the entrance of Christ into Jerusalem on Palm Sunday. There are said to be over forty horses in the Passion pictures. To see everything you must ask a monk to unlock gates and put lights on.

There is a little courtyard where the brethren keep ravens in memory of those fed by the saint. Ask for the shop to be opened if you wish to buy souvenirs. It is also worth knowing that there are toilets here for the use of visitors. Finally, the terrace outside the Sacro Speco has a drinking-water fountain and is a good place for a picnic lunch.

I may seem to dismiss the Abbey of Santa Scholastica with scant treatment, but this is only because, if you have to make a choice, you should devote your time to the Sacro Speco. Santa Scholastica has developed on the site of one of St Benedict's twelve little monasteries. On your way to the Sacro Speco you will have passed above its picturesque huddle of roofs tiled in all those lovely tones of Italian terracotta. Inside there are two cloisters, one of them early cosmatesque but without the inlaid mosaic and coloured marble that usually characterizes this work. The tower was built in 1052. It was the first bell tower near Rome in this style of northern origin; later nearly all Roman churches were equipped with them, as you can check for yourself – Santa Maria in Cosmedin and the nearby St George in Velabro are obvious instances. The church, in its present form eighteenth century, is by an Italian architect, Quarenghi, who subsequently worked in Russia for Catherine the Great. Remains of a very early chapel, probably just a little after St Benedict, have been discovered under the floor of the church.

On the upstream side of the bridge across the Anio are remains of Nero's Villa, originally built across a dam and for some yards up the banks of the reservoir on either side – U shaped. You will notice further remains across the far side. This fragment, close to the mule track up to St. Scholastica's, is believed to be St Benedict's first monastery after he left the Sacro Speco – very few visitors are aware of this or take any notice of this true cradle of Benedictine monasticism.

The mountains near Subiaco are skiing centres for much of the year.

Tivoli deserves more attention than it usually receives. Here is an opportunity to linger in, to get the feel of, a typical Italian hill town. Yet most tourists rush in and out of the gardens and apart from that never get beyond the terrace and the bus stop.

The Villa d'Este gardens do indeed merit a visit. From the terrace, where all the buses stop, anyone will direct you to the attractive little piazza full of souvenir stalls, especially brassware and ceramics, the latter a cheaper buy. The Villa d'Este is adjacent to St Mary's, an old Benedictine Abbey which, in 1550, passed into the hands of Cardinal Ippolito d'Este, who transformed it into a palace and laid out the fantastic water gardens. These gardens are not very extensive, but their position, terraced on the hillside, is magnificent, with views across the Campagna to Rome and over the rooftops of old Tivoli to the Sabine Hills. The site is particularly suited for ambitious fountains, owing to the considerable height of the water supply above the gardens. This provides high pressure for lofty jets.

It is quite easy to walk round and be fairly sure you have seen everything. 'Rometta' – little Rome – is supposed to be reminiscent of antique Rome; about all you can really distinguish is the little barque with obelisk for mast that represents the Tiber Island as it used to be, embanked in the form of a galley. The Avenue of a Hundred Fountains speaks for itself. The finest vista leads your eye up to the 'Hydraulic Organ' designed by Bernini. Note that it is possible to walk behind the fall of water of the great Fontana Ovata, if that amuses you.

Leading off the little piazza of Santa Maria Maggiore are streets that will take you down into the old town, built on a spur dominating the deep ravine in which the Anio flows once it has tumbled over cliffs from its higher level. Wander through the narrow streets and collect impressions of how Italians live – in hot weather almost entirely out of doors. The Cathedral has, in a dark chapel on the right side (put the light on), a most beautiful twelfth-century sculpture in wood of the Taking Down from the Cross. There are elements of byzantine, romanesque, and gothic in this tender composition – for the byzantine, note the hands. On the other side of the nave is preserved an ancient icon of Christ (eleventh century), shown only on rare occasions. Once a year it is carried in procession through the streets.

Not far from the Cathedral is a beautifully restored romanes-que church, San Pietro della Carità. You will have noticed its splendid apse from the gardens. Its note is simplicity, its date twelfth century. In the crypt are relics of the early martyrs of Tivoli. There are other interesting churches in the town, but I think this will be enough for most visitors.

In the upper part of Tivoli are two pagan temples of the first century B.C., one supposed to be dedicated to the Tiburtine Sybil, the other to Vesta. They are perched overlooking the ravine, and before this part of the town was developed they were favourite subjects with 'romantic' artists. The gardens here, called Villa Gregoriana, are also worth visiting, though some of their alleged beauty spots are disfigured with garbage. The Anio tumbles down its great cascades in these gardens, but they are best seen from the far side of the ravine. If you are taking a picnic it is an idea to stroll out there, and perhaps lunch by the shrine of Our Lady of Quintiliolo (on the site of Quintilian's villa).

Hadrian's Villa is approached from the road back to Rome – but if you go there direct from Rome there is no need to come as far as Tivoli. This was a palace built by the Emperor Hadrian (who gave his name to that Wall between the British and the Picts) for a retirement of cultured leisure. He planned to reproduce famous monuments he had seen on his Eastern travels. This makes it sound like an eighteenth-century 'folly' – there was a touch of that about it. The Villa was completed in A.D. 134.

Renaissance popes excavated among the ruins of Hadrian's Villa so that many of its treasures are now to be seen in the Vatican. Others are in collections throughout Europe, including the British Museum.

Principal monuments to see are the Greek Theatre (small, like a court theatre), Thermae or Baths, the 'Canopus' – reproduction of an Egyptian shrine, the inaccurately named but impressive Maritime Theatre, and the Palace proper. Other ruins are unidentified or have quite lost trace of their original appearance. The place is beautifully planted with cypresses some two centuries old.

There is a Ministry of Public Instruction guide-book in English which covers both Hadrian's Villa and the Villa d'Este.

GENAZZANO AND ITS SHRINE OF OUR LADY OF GOOD COUNSEL

To begin with, don't confuse Genazzano with Genzano. The latter is in the Alban Hills, south of Rome; our destination is in the Simbruini Hills, west of Rome. If you are travelling by car, you could combine the trip with one to Subiaco, for the shrine of St Benedict or to Palestrina, a hill town with remains of a famous Roman Temple with a magnificent mosaic symbolic of the River Nile. Otherwise you travel by bus from the Castro Pretorio, not far from Termini Station. It is possible to remain in the bus as far as San Vito Romano, a hill town about five miles beyond Genazzano, and walk back along a road with wonderful panoramic views.

Genazzano is an old hill town with delightfully picturesque streets and a shrine known throughout the world. The journey will give you the benefit of a breath of mountain air, but you need either to take a picnic or to be content with pretty rough local hostelries. Avoid coming here on major feasts.

Buses never enter the streets. You encircle the town and are set down outside the walls of the great Colonna Palace. A short walk downhill – past the house where Martin V was born, pope whose bronze effigy you see in the confession of the Lateran – brings you to the 'Santuario', the shrine of Our Lady of Good Counsel. The painting is venerated in a chapel, out of alignment with the rest of the church, at the end of the left aisle.

Among miraculous madonnas, Our Lady of Good Counsel is one of great sweetness. It is painted on plaster, mildly Byzantine in style, light and fresh in colour. The canopy over the shrine is renaissance work of about 1500, hard to appreciate in its cramped position. Notice, above the picture, sculpture in metal representing its miraculous transport as a flight escorted by angels. Now look down to the nineteenth-century painting over the entrance depicting the same tradition even more dramatically. The Augustinians were building a new church here, dedicated to Our Lady of Good Counsel, in 1467, when the painting is alleged to have appeared miraculously on its walls or, to gild the story, flew there from Albania, across the Adriatic. Two Albanian pilgrims – picture on the left – turn up and give evidence to this effect. I think many traditions of this sort – Loreto is another – must be related to the fifteenth-century Turkish threat to, and eventual invasion of the Near East, when individuals and communities took refuge in Italy, bringing religious treasures with them. On the other hand, the miraculous element is often supported by meticulous legal depositions, as in this case of Genazzano.

The church itself is a rebuilding between 1621 and 1628 of the fifteenth-century church. A slight change of position accounts for the shrine being out of alignment with everything else. Much of the decoration, the gilding of the vault for instance, is nineteenth century. Characteristically baroque altar rails in the style of Bernini come from a Roman church; they were given by Irish Augustinians in 1954. Beneath the high altar is the tomb of Blessed Stefano Bellesini, Augustinian parish priest of Genazzano, who gave his life ministering to plague victims in 1840. A record of this is the beautiful painting over the sacristy door.

At the end of the right aisle is a painting of the Crucifixion, damaged in several places, and, in a case nearby, of a twisted sword. The damage was inflicted by an enraged soldier in the fifteenth century and, according to contemporary accounts, the sword resisted every attempt to straighten it on the anvil.

To appreciate old Genazzano you should leave the main streets and explore narrow lanes against the steep sides of the hill. It is all very photogenic, if you can get the sun to co-operate. For a walk, or a picnic place, enter the Palace courtyard and you will find a bridge to a pleasant informal park around the ruins of a medieval aqueduct, with lovely views over the hills. A little farther on, at the end of this park, is San Pio, summer villa of the Irish Augustinians in Rome.

ORVIETO – A PILGRIMAGE FOR CORPUS DOMINI

A visit can be made to Orvieto quite comfortably from Rome in about an hour and a half from Stazione Termini. A funicular takes you up to the town.

The Corpus Christi (Corpus Domini to Italians) Procession at Orvieto ranks high among the devout, dramatic, and colourful traditions of Catholic Europe. The object of special devotion is the Santo Corporale, a bloodstained altar-cloth sometimes named after Bolsena where a miracle is said to have occurred in 1263.

According to the tradition, one Peter of Prague, a Bohemian priest anxious about the truth of the doctrine of Christ's presence in the Blessed Sacrament, was on his way to Rome as a pilgrim when, while he celebrated Mass in the crypt of the church of St Cristina at Bolsena, some miles west of Orvieto, blood flowed from the host onto the corporal. Pope Urban IV, residing at Orvieto, had the corporal brought there and in 1290 the foundation stone of the present superb cathedral was laid. The annual Corpus Christi Procession is a pageant, but a very dignified and devout one, in which the Corporal, carried with the Blessed Sacrament, is escorted by civic dignitaries in medieval costume and historical tableaux through the wards of the city, where the streets are strewn with sweet scented flowers, windows hung with rich material and – nowadays – music and singing very competently broadcast all the way. There is nothing riotous nor merely 'folklorique' about the Orvieto Procession. Hitherto it has begun at ten o'clock and lasted till twelve. Other local events, such as trade and craft exhibitions, are usually arranged to take place over the feast.

The *'vino liquoroso'* of Orvieto is excellent and inexpensive, but some say it does not travel well, so it would be advisable to ask before buying a bottle to bring back home.

Orvieto Cathedral is among the grandest in Italy. It was begun twenty-seven years after the arrival of the Corporal and brought to completion during the fourteenth and fifteenth centuries – a handsome monument to the Italian gothic style, of which you will have seen all too little at Rome. It is built in horizontal bands of white Carrara marble and dull greenish basalt. Well over twenty architects are known to have presided over its composition, but its authors, so to speak, who were also responsible for the famous series of sculptures of Old and New Testament history on the façade, were Lorenzo Maitani from Siena, and his son Vitale. The completion of the façade, with its beautiful rose window, was by Orcagna. The external mosaics have been so often restored as to leave little of the original – to find a fragment of that you have to visit the Victoria and Albert Museum at South Kensington.

The most impressive feature of the interior is its general impression, which owes so much to the massive columns and the striking contrast of horizontal patterns with a vertical movement. In the choir is a handsome window of fourteenth-century stained-glass and frescoes of the birth of Mary and the childhood of Jesus by Ugolino di Prete Ilario with, in the vault, the Trinity among angels and teachers. Some of this work is by Pinturicchio.

The Lady Chapel to the right of the nave, at the sanctuary end, is frescoed by Fra Angelico and Luca Signorelli; Michelangelo is said to have come here to study the latter's work before beginning on his 'Judgment' for the Sistine Chapel. Flanking the sanctuary are beautiful sculptured altars in renaissance style, representing the Visitation and the Visit of the Magi, by Simone Mosca, and to the left of the sanctuary you will notice a Pietà by Ippolito Scalza, of 1579.

At the end of the left aisle is the chapel of the Holy Corporal, frescoed by Ugolino di Prete Ilario, with Old Testament types and subsequent miracles of the Eucharist and, above all, the reliquary of the Corporal. Except at Easter and Corpus Christi and a few rare occasions this reliquary is closed, but this enables you to see its rich fourteenth-century enamels.

The town is charming, with many shops selling local products, especially domestic pottery, which is a good buy. A curiosity is the deep well excavated in the sixteenth century by the architect Sangallo, and known as the Pozzo di San Patrizio – St Patrick's Well.

ASSISI – THE SHRINE OF ST FRANCIS

A journey to Assisi from Rome is quite a hard day's work, but so many organized pilgrimages include it in their itinerary that something must be said. I have led several parties from Rome, and we have never managed to work in more than Mass and a quick visit to Our Lady of the Angels with its chapel of the Porziuncula, another to the Basilica of St Francis where the saint is buried, and a call on our way out at Santa Chiara. This means that San Damiano and the Hermitage of the Carceri had to be omitted. I have heard of people making the day trip by train, changing at Perugia, and hiring a taxi to rush round the shrines. That is 'doing' Assisi, but I doubt whether it is a worth-while pilgrimage or intelligent sightseeing.

Just in case Assisi is little more than a name, let me explain that St Francis, most lovable character of medieval history, established his poor and simple brotherhood around a chapel known as 'the little plot' – Porziuncula, in the plain below Assisi, which itself is a typical Italian hill town. This friary of St Francis was more a village than a monastery as you would imagine one now, and even when more impressive buildings replaced it the primitive chapel, the cell of Francis, and some other cells belonging to his early followers were carefully preserved. It was here that Francis died in 1226, at the age of forty-five. The Basilica of St Francis on the edge of the town consists of two vast churches one above the other, masterpieces of medieval Italian gothic architecture and frescoed art. In a nineteenth-century crypt excavated below them is the tomb of St Francis, discovered in 1818, and in the sacristy is a collection of intimate relics – but remember, this basilica never existed at all in St Francis's lifetime, and it was opposed to his ideals that Franciscans should have such great churches. Santa Chiara (St Clare's) is a convent with the shrine and relics of St Clare, first nun of St Francis's Order of Poor Ladies, today known after her as Poor Clares, and here is enshrined the famous crucifix from the chapel of St Damiano that spoke to Francis and set him on his vocation.

If you come from Rome by coach it is convenient to visit the Basilica of St Mary of the Angels first. This is a sixteenth-century church of no great merit, and that in a way is just as well, for it leaves the glory to the humble little chapel of the Porziuncula, a chapel that in its general appearance remains as Francis knew it – the basilica is little more than a setting for this treasure of the Franciscan Order. You may be able to assist at Mass there, but if not you should try to find time for a few moments of recollection in the spirit of Francis, and to appreciate the beautiful fourteenth-century frescoes of Ilario da Viterbo. Beyond the Porziuncula chapel, to the right of the high altar, is a chapel incorporating remains of Francis's cell, with a famous della Robbia statue of Francis, the face said to be modelled from the saint's death mask. Talking of della Robbia – this is the name of a fifteenth-century family specializing in glazed terracotta, mostly in blue and white – one of their lovliest compositions is an altarpiece in a chapel to the left of the left transept of the basilica.

To visit the shop, and remains of the early monastery – which you will not, however, find quite as Francis left it – take the door in the right transept marked 'ROSETO' – this refers to the rose bushes in which Francis threw himself in the course of a temptation, and which since grow thornless. In the little cloister notice the statue of Francis with a pair of white doves nesting in his arms – real doves. There is too on the wall a ceramic street name from Jerusalem, where Franciscans are custodians of the Holy Places. The shop is exciting, with an admirable display of souvenirs at good prices – suggested 'buys' are reproductions in wood or ceramic of the 'Crucifix of San Damiano', St Francis's 'Canticle of the Creatures' (ask for the language of your choice) or copies of the beautiful Annunciation in the Porziuncula chapel. You may also obtain from the friars on request leaves from the rose bushes.

Of the great Basilica of San Francesco, begun in 1228, the most beautiful part, in my estimation, is the frescoed lower church. From here you descend to the crypt with an aisle around the tomb of Francis. A coffer on the steps down to the crypt contains the remains of Jacopone da Settesoli, the devoted lady whose friendship Francis accepted so simply that she was allowed to enter the enclosure at the Porziuncula, where all other women were prohibited, to visit the dying saint. Francis solved the problem by calling her 'Brother Jacopone'! Opening from the lower church to the left is the relic chamber where you may see garments and handwriting of the saint, and the mittens which covered his wounded hands – Francis bore the stigmata, or mysteriously imprinted wounds of Christ. The upper church has some fine cosmatesque work – the altar, for instance – and celebrated paintings including the life of Francis by Giotto and Cimabue. There is another pilgrims' shop adjacent to the basilica.

Santa Chiara, at the far end of the town, is visited for the shrine of the saint in the crypt – the body is called incorrupt but it has a blackened mummified appearance – and a chapel opening off the right side of the nave where a veiled Poor Clare waits behind a grille to explain to you another collection of relics of Francis and Clare. In this chapel is the crucifix formerly in the chapel of San Damiano, below the town, where it called to Francis to repair the church – first understood by the saint literally but later historically by a reform of simplicity and true poverty in an age of luxury and pride. A walk round Santa Chiara will reveal other treasures of art discreetly illuminated.

If you have time to visit San Damiano, down lanes beyond Santa Chiara, and the Hermitage of the Carceri, they will take you back to the spirit of early Franciscan life. San Damiano was the first home of St Clare and her nuns. Today it is a friary, but remains little altered.

The Cathedral of San Rufino contains the font, from an earlier church, in which St Francis was baptized. Of many other churches the Benedictine Abbey of San Pietro is rewarding.

CHAPTER 32

Help with the Menu

One of the traveller's worst dilemmas is being presented with a menu in an unknown language. Many Roman restaurants furnish an English version, but – especially if you try to cut costs – you will be embarrassed time and again. The following cannot undertake to resolve all problems, but it gives a fairly good coverage of the average Italian menu. I am indebted for it to the Brothers Polese of the Piazza Sforza Cesarini.

Hors d'Oeuvres:

Antipasto misto – mixed hors d'oeuvres; usually a copious dish of cold meats or fish, etc., a meal in itself.

Other 'antipasti' may include 'proscuitto' – ham; 'salame' – sliced sausage, usually served with olives and butter.

Soups and Pastas (pasta: a foodstuff made from flour, like spaghetti and macaroni, often replaces soup or hors d'oeuvres):

Zuppa di verdura – vegetable soup (usually served in very generous helpings).

Minestrone di riso – also called minestrone in English of course – a thinner vegetable soup with rice.

Minestrone di pasta – minestrone with one of the numerous flour-made compositions called 'pasta', such as spaghetti.

Stracciatella alla Romana – soup with beaten egg.

Consommé tortellini – clear meat soup with pasta stuffed with meat.

Brodo – broth, a good clear meat soup. They are inclined to 'put things in it' – I used to insist on 'brodo chiaro' – a clear broth.

Risotto – savoury rice dish.

Ravioli – pasta with meat stuffing.

Spaghetti al pomadoro – Spaghetti with tomato sauce.

Fettucine alle bolognese – noodles with meat sauce.

Spaghetti alle vongole – spaghetti with clams.

Cannelloni – stuffed noodles.

Meat Dishes:

Bistecca di lombo ai ferri – grilled sirloin steak ('ai ferri' = grilled).

Pollo   bollito – boiled chicken.
       arrosto – roast chicken.

Cotoletto di vitello – veal cutlet.

Scaloppine al Marsala – veal cooked with marsala wine.

Bistecca – beefsteak.

Spezzato di vitello – stewed veal.

Trippa alla Romana – Tripe, served in the Roman manner.

Fegato – calf's liver.

Ossobuco – veal knuckle.

Cervella – brains.

Fish:

Calamaretti fritti – fried squid.

Gamberetti fritti – fried shrimps.

Soglioglo – sole.

Cozze – mussels.

Scampi – prawns.

    (In season there are good dishes of mixed sea food – so copious you hardly need accompanying vegetables.)

Egg Dishes (the word 'uova', for 'egg', remains 'uova' in the plural):

Uova strapazzate – scrambled eggs.

Uova al piatto – fried eggs.

Omelette con verdura – omelette with herbs.

Omelette con funghi – omelette with mushrooms.

Omelette con formaggio – cheese omelette.

Contorni – Vegetables:

Patate fritte – fried potatoes.

Patate al burro – creamed potatoes.

Spinaci in padella – spinach.

Fagiolini – beans (haricots).

Piselli – peas.

Insalata verde – green salad.

Insalata mista – mixed salad.

Cheese:

The types don't lend easily to translation – the word is 'formaggio'.

Bel Paese is a popular brand of cream cheese; Gorgonzola is usually better than it is in England; Groviera means 'Gruyère'; Provolone is a dry Italian cheese, either 'piccante' – sharp, or 'dolce' – a milder taste.

Frutta:

Mele – apples; Pere – pears; Arance – oranges; Ciligie – cherries;
   Fragole – strawberries; Banane – bananas; all those words
   are in the plural; to insist on one, change the last letter to
   'a': – but 'arancia'.

It may be simpler to ask for 'Frutta assortita di stagione' – a
dish of seasonal fruit.

Dolce – Sweet (limited choice from cakes, flans, ice-creams;
   puddings in our sense are rare)

Zuppa inglese – a very rich trifle, although the expression seems
   to mean 'English soup'.

Torta – tart or cake or flan.

Pasticceria assortita – assorted cakes.

Caffé – coffee

For everyday purposes, the wine served will usually be local
and inexpensive. If in doubt, insist on 'vino locale sciolto'.

'Asti Spumante' is similar to champagne, but far cheaper.

A Note on eating Pizza

A pizza is a square piece of pastry decked with a savoury grill.
Generally speaking, it is served only in the evening – say from
5 p.m. to midnight. If a restaurant is called a 'pizzeria' it
certainly serves pizza, either at table only, or also to take away
in the hand. There are bars that serve pizza to take away. Some
bars serve small pizzas that can be hotted up in a moment and
eaten with a beverage – these are often served all day. Pizza at
table can be the main dish of a more elaborate meal.

Once you have acquired a taste for pizza and know where to
buy one that suits your palate, you will be able to cut your cost
of living to a very moderate figure.

Beware of the pricing of pizzas in some bars and restaurants
– they may be priced by the etto. An etto is about two ounces,
so that you could ask for 'due etti' if you want a fairly substantial
helping – but that would be twice the price on the ticket.

Here are some varieties of Pizza:

> Pizza marinara – sea food.
> Pizza napoletana – sea food.
> Pizza con funghi – mushrooms.
> Pizza con cipolle – onions.
> Pizza con salsiccie – sliced sausage.
> Pizza capricciosa – mixed grill; recommended.
> ...and variations on these themes.

Index

This index is necessarily selective. It was found impossible to mention all architects and artists; those listed were considered special in the context. Saints, apart from titulars of churches, are also chosen because of their interest to the Roman scene. With few exceptions the names of churches are in Italian because that is how you need to ask for them or find them on a map. The chapters dealing with outside Rome are indexed in less detail.

Burns & Oates publish books of general Christian interest including lives of the saints, prayer, spirituality and mysticism, church history, doctrine and life, theology, philosophy, Bible reading.

A free catalogue will be sent on request:

BURNS & OATES, Dept A,
Wellwood, North Farm Road, Tunbridge Wells, Kent TN2 3DR
Tel: (01892) 510850   Fax: (01892) 515903
E-mail: Searchpress@searchpress.com